THE POEM: An Anthology

THE POEM: An Anthology

SECOND EDITION

Edited by

Stanley B. Greenfield
and
A. Kingsley Weatherhead

Both of the University of Oregon

PRENTICE-HALL, INC.
Englewood Cliffs, N. J. 07632

Printed in the United States of America

ISBN: 0-13-684431-6

Library of Congress Catalog Card Number: 73-179749

10 9 8 7 6 5 4 3 2

PRENTICE-HALL INTERNATIONAL, INC., *London*
PRENTICE-HALL OF AUSTRALIA, PTY. LTD., *Sydney*
PRENTICE-HALL OF CANADA, LTD., *Toronto*
PRENTICE-HALL OF INDIA PRIVATE LIMITED, *New Delhi*
PRENTICE-HALL OF JAPAN, INC., *Tokyo*
PRENTICE-HALL OF SOUTHEAST ASIA PTE. LTD., *Singapore*
WHITEHALL BOOKS LIMITED, WELLINGTON, *New Zealand*

ACKNOWLEDGMENTS

The Wanderer Reprinted from POEMS FROM THE OLD ENGLISH translated by Burton Raffel by permission of University of Nebraska Press. Copyright © 1960, 1964, by the University of Nebraska Press.

The Friar's Tale from: CHAUCER'S MAJOR POETRY edited by Albert C. Baugh. Copyright © 1963, by Meredith Publishing Company. Reprinted by permission of Appleton-Century-Crofts.

After great pain, a formal feeling comes Copyright, 1914, 1942, by Martha Dickinson Bianchi. From THE COMPLETE POEMS OF EMILY DICKINSON edited by Thomas H. Johnson, by permission of Little, Brown and Co.

I heard a Fly buzz when I died, It was not Death, for I stood up, Because I could not stop for Death, A narrow Fellow in the Grass, Further in Summer than the Birds, Go not too near a House of Rose Reprinted by permission of the publishers and the Trustees of Amherst College from Thomas H. Johnson, Editor, THE POEMS OF EMILY DICKINSON, Cambridge, Mass.: The Belknap Press of Harvard University Press, Copyright, 1951, 1955, by The President and Fellows of Harvard College.

Hap, The Darkling Thrush, Channel Firing, The Convergence of the Twain, "Ah, Are You Digging on My Grave?", The Oxen, Afterwards, In Time of "The Breaking of Nations" reprinted from COLLECTED POEMS OF THOMAS HARDY by permission of the Hardy Estate, Macmillan & Co., Ltd., London and The Macmillan Company of Canada Limited. Reprinted with permission of The Macmillan Company from COLLECTED POEMS by Thomas Hardy. Copyright 1925 by The Macmillan Company.

Neutral Tones, New Year's Eve From COLLECTED POEMS OF THOMAS HARDY by permission of the Hardy Estate; Macmillan Ltd., London, and The Macmillan Company of Canada Limited. From THE COLLECTED POEMS OF THOMAS HARDY by Thomas Hardy. Reprinted by permission of The Macmillan Company, 1952, 1960, 1962, and 1965.

The Windhover, Pied Beauty, Spelt from Sibyl's Leaves From *Poems of Gerard Manley Hopkins*, Third Edition, edited by W. H. Gardner. Copyright 1948 by Oxford University Press, Inc. Reprinted by permission.

1887, Loveliest of trees, The Carpenter's Son, 'Terence, this is stupid stuff' From "A Shropshire Lad" —Authorised Edition—from THE COLLECTED POEMS OF A. E. HOUSMAN. Copyright 1939, 1940, © 1959 by Holt, Rinehart and Winston, Inc. Copyright © 1967 by Robert E. Symons. Reprinted by permission of Holt, Rinehart and Winston, Inc. Reprinted by permission of The Society of Authors as the literary representative of the Estate of the late A. E. Housman, and Messrs. Jonathan Cape Ltd., publishers of A. E. Housman's *Collected Poems*.

ACKNOWLEDGMENTS

v

Eight o'clock, Epitaph on an Army of Mercenaries From THE COLLECTED POEMS OF A. E. HOUSMAN. Copyright 1922 by Holt, Rinehart and Winston, Inc. Copyright 1950 by Barclays Bank Ltd. Reprinted by permission of Holt, Rinehart and Winston, Inc. Reprinted by permission of The Society of Authors as the literary representative of the Estate of the late A. E. Housman, and Messrs. Jonathan Cape Ltd., publishers of A. E. Housman's *Collected Poems.*

The Rose of the World Reprinted with permission of The Macmillan Company from COLLECTED POEMS by William Butler Yeats. Copyright 1906 by The Macmillan Company, renewed 1934 by William Butler Yeats. From "COLLECTED POEMS OF W. B. YEATS" by Permission of Mr. M. B. Yeats and the Macmillan Co. of Canada Ltd.

The Magi Reprinted with permission of The Macmillan Company from COLLECTED POEMS by William Butler Yeats. Copyright 1916 by The Macmillan Company, renewed 1944 by Bertha Georgie Yeats. From "COLLECTED POEMS OF W. B. YEATS" by Permission of Mr. M. B. Yeats and the Macmillan Co. of Canada Ltd.

Easter 1916, The Second Coming, The Leaders of the Crowd Reprinted with permission of The Macmillan Company from COLLECTED POEMS by William Butler Yeats. Copyright 1924 by The Macmillan Company, renewed 1952 by Bertha Georgie Yeats. From "COLLECTED POEMS OF W. B. YEATS" by Permission of Mr. M. B. Yeats and the Macmillan Co. of Canada Ltd.

Leda and the Swan, Sailing to Byzantium, Among School Children Reprinted with permission of The Macmillan Company from COLLECTED POEMS by William Butler Yeats. Copyright 1928 by The Macmillan Company, renewed 1956 by Bertha Georgie Yeats. From "COLLECTED POEMS OF W. B. YEATS" by Permission of Mr. M. B. Yeats and the Macmillan Co. of Canada Ltd.

After Long Silence Reprinted with permission of The Macmillan Company from COLLECTED POEMS by William Butler Yeats. Copyright 1933 by The Macmillan Company, renewed 1961 by Bertha Georgie Yeats. From "COLLECTED POEMS OF W. B. YEATS" by Permission of Mr. M. B. Yeats and the Macmillan Co. of Canada Ltd.

Richard Cory, For a Dead Lady, Reuben Bright The following poems by Edwin Arlington Robinson are reprinted by permission of Charles Scribner's Sons: "Richard Cory" and "Reuben Bright" from THE CHILDREN OF THE NIGHT (1897) and "For a Dead Lady" from THE TOWN DOWN THE RIVER (Copyright 1910 Charles Scribner's Sons; renewal copyright 1938 Ruth Nivison).

Mr. Flood's Party Reprinted with permission of The Macmillan Company from COLLECTED POEMS by Edwin Arlington Robinson. Copyright 1921 by Edwin Arlington Robinson, renewed 1949 by Ruth Nivison.

Mending Wall, After Apple-Picking, Stopping by Woods on a Snowy Evening, Once by the Pacific, Desert Places, Design, Come In From COMPLETE POEMS OF ROBERT FROST. Copyright 1923, 1928, 1930, 1939 by Holt, Rinehart and Winston, Inc. Copyright 1936, 1942, 1951, © 1956, 1958 by Robert Frost. Copyright © 1964, 1967 by Lesley Frost Ballantine. Reprinted by permission of Holt, Rinehart and Winston, Inc.

Peter Quince at the Clavier, Sunday Morning, Anecdote of the Jar, Bantams in Pine-Woods, The Emperor of Ice-Cream Copyright 1923 and renewed 1951 by Wallace Stevens. Reprinted from THE COLLECTED POEMS OF WALLACE STEVENS by permission of Alfred A. Knopf, Inc.

Arrival, The Red Wheelbarrow, Poem (As the Cat . . .) From THE COLLECTED EARLIER POEMS of William Carlos Williams. Copyright 1938, 1951 by William Carlos Williams. Reprinted by permission of New Directions Publishing Corporation.

The Dance William Carlos Williams, THE COLLECTED LATER POEMS. Copyright 1944 by William Carlos Williams. Reprinted by permission of New Directions Publishing Corporation.

To a Dog Injured William Carlos Williams, PICTURES FROM BRUEGHEL AND OTHER POEMS. Copyright 1954 by William Carlos Williams. Reprinted by permission of New Directions Publishing Corporation.

Snake From THE COMPLETE POEMS OF D. H. LAWRENCE, Volume I, edited by Vivian de Sola Pinto & F. Warren Roberts. Copyright 1923, renewed 1951 by Frieda Lawrence. Reprinted by permission of The Viking Press, Inc.

Corot, Piano From THE COMPLETE POEMS OF D. H. LAWRENCE, Volume I, edited by Vivian de Sola Pinto & F. Warren Roberts. Copyright 1920 by B. W. Huebsch, Inc., renewed 1948 by Frieda Lawrence. Reprinted by permission of The Viking Press, Inc.

A Virginal, In a Station of the Metro, Portrait d'une Femme, The Return From Ezra Pound, PERSONAE. Copyright 1926, 1954 by Ezra Pound. Reprinted by permission of New Directions Publishing Corporation.

Hurt Hawks Copyright 1928 and renewed 1956 by Robinson Jeffers. Reprinted from SELECTED POETRY OF ROBINSON JEFFERS by permission of Random House, Inc.

Poetry Reprinted with permission of The Macmillan Company from COLLECTED POEMS by Marianne Moore. Copyright 1935 by The Macmillan Company, renewed 1963 by Marianne Moore and T. S. Eliot.

In Distrust of Merits Reprinted with permission of The Macmillan Company from COLLECTED POEMS by Marianne Moore. Copyright 1944 by Marianne Moore.

Saint Nicholas, From O TO BE A DRAGON by Marianne Moore. Copyright © 1958 by Marianne Moore. Originally appeared in The New Yorker. Reprinted by permission of The Viking Press, Inc.

The Love Song of J. Alfred Prufrock, Sweeney Among the Nightingales, Journey of the Magi From COLLECTED POEMS 1909–1962 by T. S. Eliot, copyright, 1936, by Harcourt, Brace & World, Inc.; copyright, © 1963, 1964, by T. S. Eliot. Reprinted by permission of the publisher. From COLLECTED POEMS 1909–1962 by T. S. Eliot. Reprinted by permission of Faber and Faber Ltd.

Winter Remembered, Bells for John Whiteside's Daughter Copyright 1924 by Alfred A. Knopf, Inc. and renewed 1952 by John Crowe Ransom. Reprinted from SELECTED POEMS, Revised Edition, by John Crowe Ransom, by permission of the publisher.

Winter Remembered, Bells for John Whiteside's Daughter Copyright 1924 by Alfred A. Knopf, Inc. and renewed 1952 by John Crowe Ransom. Reprinted from SELECTED POEMS, Revised Edition, by John Crowe Ransom, by permission of the publisher.

Piazza Piece Copyright 1927 by Alfred A. Knopf, Inc. and renewed 1955 by John Crowe Ransom. Reprinted from SELECTED POEMS, 3rd ed., revised, by John Crowe Ransom, by permission of the publisher.

Ars Poetica, You, Andrew Marvell From COLLECTED POEMS by Archibald MacLeish. Reprinted by permission of Houghton Mifflin Company.

Anthem for Doomed Youth, Dulce et Decorum Est, Strange Meeting Wilfred Owen, COLLECTED POEMS. Copyright Chatto & Windus, Ltd., 1946, © 1963. Reprinted by permission of New Directions Publishing Corporation. From THE COLLECTED POEMS OF WILFRED OWEN. Reprinted by permission of Mr. Harold Owen and Chatto and Windus Ltd.

in Just— Copyright, 1923, 1951, by E. E. Cummings. Reprinted from his volume POEMS 1923–1954 by permission of Harcourt, Brace & World, Inc.

a man who had fallen among thieves Copyright, 1926, by Horace Liveright; copyright, 1954, by E. E. Cummings. Reprinted from POEMS 1923–1954 by E. E. Cummings by permission of Harcourt, Brace & World, Inc.

r-p-o-p-h-e-s-s-a-g-r Copyright, 1935, by E. E. Cummings; copyright, 1963, by Marion Morehouse Cummings. Reprinted from POEMS 1923–1954 by E. E. Cummings by permission of Harcourt, Brace & World, Inc.

pity this busy monster, manunkind Copyright, 1944, by E. E. Cummings. Reprinted from his volume POEMS 1923–1954 by permission of Harcourt, Brace & World, Inc.

"anyone lived in a pretty how town": Copyright, 1940, by E. E. Cummings. Reprinted from his volume POEMS 1923–1954 by permission of Harcourt Brace Jovanovich, Inc.

"i sing of Olaf": Copyright, 1931, 1959, by E. E. Cummings. Reprinted from his volume POEMS 1923–1954 by permission of Harcourt Brace Jovanovich, Inc.

"Ode to the Confederate Dead" (Copyright 1932 Charles Scribner's Sons; renewal copyright © 1960 Allen Tate) from POEMS by Allen Tate and "The Subway" (Copyright 1937 Charles Scribner's Sons; renewal copyright © 1965 Allen Tate) from SELECTED POEMS by Allen Tate are reprinted by permission of Charles Scribner's Sons.

Jazzonia From THE WEARY BLUES, by Langston Hughes. Copyright 1926 by Alfred A. Knopf, Inc. and renewed 1954 by Langston Hughes. Reprinted by permission of the publisher.

"Heritage," "Yet Do I Marvel" Copyright, 1925 by Harper & Row, Publishers, Inc., renewed, 1953 by Ida M. Cullen. Reprinted by permission of Harper & Row, Publishers. From ON THESE I STAND by Countee Cullen.

The Bear on the Delhi Road, Irapuato From ICE, COD, BELL OR STONE by Earle Birney, reprinted by permission of The Canadian Publishers, McClelland and Stewart Limited, Toronto, Canada.

New Hampshire, February From *Collected Poems 1930–1960* by Richard Eberhart. © 1960 by Richard Eberhart. Reprinted by permission of Oxford University Press, Inc. From COLLECTED POEMS by Richard Eberhart. Reprinted by permission of the author and Chatto and Windus Ltd.

Am I My Neighbor's Keeper? From *The Quarry* by Richard Eberhart. Copyright © 1964 by Richard Eberhart. Reprinted by permission of Oxford University Press, Inc. From THE QUARRY by Richard Eberhart. Reprinted by permission of the author and Chatto and Windus Ltd.

Nearing Again the Legendary Isle, Rest From Loving, Florence: Works of Art, When They Have Lost Copyright 1954 by C. Day Lewis, reprinted by permission of the Harold Matson Company, Inc. From COLLECTED POEMS 1954 by C. Day Lewis. Reprinted by permission of Jonathan Cape Ltd. and The Hogarth Press.

Father and Son, End of Summer From SELECTED POEMS 1928–1958 by Stanley Kunitz. Copyright ©, 1929, 1930, 1944, 1951, 1953, 1954, 1956, 1957, 1958, by Stanley Kunitz. Reprinted by permission of Atlantic-Little, Brown and Company.

Lullaby, One Evening, Musée des Beaux Arts Copyright 1940 by W. H. Auden. Reprinted from SELECTED POETRY OF W. H. AUDEN by permission of Random House, Inc. From COLLECTED SHORTER POEMS 1927–1957 by W. H. Auden. Reprinted by permission of Faber and Faber Ltd.

Hammerfest © Copyright 1962 by W. H. Auden. Reprinted from ABOUT THE HOUSE, by W. H. Auden, by permission of Random House, Inc.

Bagpipe Music, The Sunlight on the Garden, Cushenden From *The Collected Poems of Louis MacNeice*, edited by E. R. Dodds. Copyright © The Estate of Louis MacNeice 1966. Reprinted by per-

Christ Climbed Down, I have not lain with beauty Lawrence Ferlinghetti, A CONEY ISLAND OF THE MIND. Copyright © 1958 by Lawrence Ferlinghetti. Reprinted by permission of New Directions Publishing Corporation.

Grasse: The Olive Trees Copyright, 1948, by Richard Wilbur. Reprinted from his volume CEREMONY AND OTHER POEMS by permission of Harcourt, Brace & World, Inc.

Year's End Copyright, 1949, by Richard Wilbur. Reprinted from his volume CEREMONY AND OTHER POEMS by permission of Harcourt, Brace & World, Inc.

Love Calls Us to the Things of this World From THINGS OF THIS WORLD, © 1956, by Richard Wilbur. Reprinted by permission of Harcourt, Brace & World, Inc.

The Whitsun Weddings, First Sight From THE WHITSUN WEDDINGS, by Philip Larkin. Copyright © 1964 by Philip Larkin. Reprinted by permission of Random House, Inc. and Faber and Faber Ltd.

In the Mountain Tent "In the Mountain Tent," copyright 1961 by James Dickey. From POEMS 1957–1967 by James Dickey. Originally appeared in THE NEW YORKER. Reprinted by permission of Wesleyan University Press.

Buckdancer's Choice "Buckdancer's Choice," copyright 1965 by James Dickey. From POEMS 1957–1967 by James Dickey. Originally appeared in THE NEW YORKER. Reprinted by permission of Wesleyan University Press.

Five Poems from Mexico From Denise Levertov, THE JACOB'S LADDER. Copyright © 1960 by Denise Levertov Goodman. Reprinted by permission of New Directions Publishing Corporation.

To the Western World Copyright © 1957 by Louis Simpson. Reprinted from A DREAM OF GOVERNORS, by Louis Simpson, by permission of Wesleyan University Press.

Walt Whitman at Bear Mountain Copyright © 1960 by Louis Simpson. Reprinted from AT THE END OF THE OPEN ROAD, by Louis Simpson, by permission of Wesleyan University Press.

From THE LIGHT AROUND THE BODY by Robert Bly: "Counting Small-Boned Bodies," "Driving through Minnesota during the Hanoi Bombings." Copyright © 1967 by Robert Bly. Reprinted by permission of Harper & Row, Publishers, Inc.

A Supermarket in California Copyright © 1956, 1959 by Allen Ginsberg. Reprinted by permission of CITY LIGHTS BOOKS.

To Aunt Rose Copyright © 1961 by Allen Ginsberg. Reprinted by permission of CITY LIGHTS BOOKS.

First Party at Ken Kesey's with Hell's Angels Copyright © 1968 by Allen Ginsberg. Reprinted by permission of CITY LIGHTS BOOKS.

From AFTER EXPERIENCE by W. D. Snodgrass: "Manet: 'The Execution of the Emperor Maximilian,' " Copyright © 1963 by W. D. Snodgrass. "An Archaic Torso of Apollo" by Rainer Maria Rilke, translated by W. D. Snodgrass, Copyright © 1968 by W. D. Snodgrass.

April Inventory Copyright © 1957 by W. D. Snodgrass. Reprinted from HEART'S NEEDLE, by W. D. Snodgrass, by permission of Alfred A. Knopf, Inc.

Lemuel's Blessing From THE MOVING TARGET by W. S. Merwin. Copyright © 1962 by W. S. Merwin. Reprinted by permission of Atheneum Publishers. Appeared originally in *The New Yorker.*

The Asians Dying, Fly From THE LICE by W. S. Merwin. Copyright © 1966, 1967 by W. S. Merwin. Reprinted by permission of Atheneum Publishers. "The Asians Dying" appeared originally in *The New Yorker.* "Fly" appeared originally in *The Atlantic Monthly.*

Young From ALL MY PRETTY ONES. Copyright © 1961, 1962 by Anne Sexton. Reprinted by permission of the publisher, Houghton Mifflin Company.

On the Move, To Yvor Winters 1955 Reprinted by permission of Faber and Faber Ltd. from *The Sense of Movement.*

"The Jaguar" from THE HAWK IN THE RAIN by Ted Hughes. Copyright © 1957 by Ted Hughes. Reprinted by permission of Harper & Row, Publishers, Inc.

Riprap Reprinted by permission of Origin Press.

Blue Moles © Copyright 1962 by Sylvia Plath. Reprinted from THE COLOSSUS AND OTHER POEMS, by Sylvia Plath, by permission of Alfred A. Knopf, Inc. Reprinted by permission of Mrs. Olwyn Hughes.

Elm "Elm" from ARIEL by Sylvia Plath. Copyright © 1963 by Ted Hughes. Originally appeared in *The New Yorker,* and reprinted by permission of Harper & Row, Publishers. Reprinted by permission of Mrs. Olwyn Hughes.

"Daddy" from ARIEL by Sylvia Plath. Copyright © 1963 by Ted Hughes. Reprinted by permission of Harper & Row, Publishers, Inc. © Ted Hughes 1965. From ARIEL published by Harper & Row, New York, and Faber and Faber, London.

Preface to a Twenty Volume Suicide Note, Notes For a Speech Copyright © 1961 by LeRoi Jones. Reprinted by permission of CORINTH BOOKS.

In the Interest of Black Salvation From *Black Pride.* Copyright © Don L. Lee, 1968. Reprinted by permission of Broadside Press.

But He Was Cool or: he even stopped for green lights   From *Don't Cry, Scream.* Copyright © Don L. Lee, 1969. Reprinted by permission of Broadside Press.

From F. W. Bateson, *English Poetry* (London, 1950), pp. 143-144. Reprinted by permission of Barnes & Noble, Inc. and Longmans, Green & Co. Limited.

From S. F. Johnson, "Wyatt's 'They Flee From Me,'" *Explicator*, Vol. XI (Apr., 1953), item 39. Reprinted by permission of *Explicator* and the author.

E. E. Duncan-Jones, "Wyatt's 'They Flee From Me,'" *Explicator*, Vol. XII (Nov., 1953), item 9. Reprinted by permission of *Explicator* and the author.

Frederick M. Combellack, "Wyatt's 'They Flee From Me,'" *Explicator*, Vol. XVII (Feb., 1959), item 36. Reprinted by permission of *Explicator* and the author.

From Arnold Stein, "Wyatt's 'They Flee From Me,'" *Sewanee Review*, Vol. LXVII (1959), pp. 30-33. Reprinted by permission of *Sewanee Review*.

From Albert S. Gerard, "Wyatt's 'They Fle From Me,'" *Essays in Criticism*, Vol. XI (1961), pp. 359-360. Reprinted by permission of *Essays in Criticism*.

From THE WELL WROUGHT URN, copyright, 1947, by Cleanth Brooks. Reprinted by permission of Harcourt, Brace & World, Inc.

From Allen Tate, *The Man of Letters in the Modern World* (Meridian Books, 1958), pp. 204´06 Reprinted by permission of The Swallow Press, Inc.

From Robert M. Adams, "*Trompe-l'oeil* in Shakespeare and Keats," *Sewanee Review*, Vol. LXI (1953), pp. 252-253. Reprinted by permission of *Sewanee Review*.

From Earl Wasserman, *The Finer Tone* (1953), pp. 58-61. Reprinted by permission of Johns Hopkins Press.

From Alvin Whitley, "The Message of the Grecian Urn," *Keats-Shelley Memorial Bulletin*, V (1953), pp. 1-3. By permission of the Keats-Shelley Memorial Association and the author.

From Howard Baker, "Wallace Stevens and Other Poets," *Southern Review*, Vol. I, No. 2 (Autumn, 1935), p. 376. Reprinted by permission of *Southern Review*.

From Yvor Winters, *On Modern Poets*, (Meridian Books, 1959, c 1957), pp. 15-16. Reprinted by permission of The Swallow Press, Inc.

J. P. Kirby, "Stevens' 'Anecdote of the Jar,'" *Explicator*, Vol. III (Nov., 1944), item 16. Reprinted by permission of *Explicator* and the author.

From Charles C. Walcutt, "Interpreting the Symbol," *College English*, Vol. XIV (May, 1953), pp. 447-449. Reprinted with the permission of the National Council of Teachers of English and Charles C. Walcutt.

For our children—

Sayre and Tamma;

Lyn, Leslie, and Andrea.

In making the selection of poems in this book we have kept in mind primarily their usefulness in the teaching of poetry: certain poems are included simply because acquaintance with them is a *sine qua non* of a knowledge of English poetry, and thus they are a part of the teaching of poetry; most, however, have been chosen because they lend themselves to the demonstration of one or another characteristic feature of poetry—its techniques and its themes. Most of the poems are well-known and many have long been accepted as masterpieces; but since lesser poems are often as instructive as more important ones, we have not excluded a few whose merit is neither accepted nor certain.

We have included poems from the earliest times down to the present day and arranged them in chronological order, so that, even though the book is designed primarily for a course introducing poetry rather than one in literary history, some sense of the latter may be derived from it and also a sense of the evolution of poetic genres and the handling of themes—how a sonnet, for example, changes between Wyatt and Wordsworth, an elegy between "Lycidas" and Arnold, or a love poem between Burns and Auden. (An alternate table of contents in Appendix II gives a selective grouping of poems by genres and subjects.) Except for sonnets taken from their sequences, we have included no extracts from long poems. There is a kind of distortion involved in representing Pope's "The Rape of the Lock," for instance, by the scene at the dressing table or the card game, or Spenser's "Epithalamion" by the passage derived from the *Song of Songs;* and this we have sought to avoid. Although our policy has precluded us from drawing attention to certain major poems, one cannot *teach* a long poem by the examination of a short extract from it. In several cases we have included a fairly large sampling of the poet's work so that the student may derive some sense of a characteristic style.

The texts of older poems have been Americanized in spelling and modified in punctuation and the use of capitals in order to make them conform to a usage more familiar to students. In certain words, however, where a change would radically alter pronunciation or conceal a nuance, an older spelling has been retained. A *grave* accent indicates that a vowel or syllable which would normally be inaudible or unstressed is to be sounded or stressed.

We have supplied notes throughout where they are required to clarify lines that are syntactically difficult and to give meanings of words; we have not glossed *every* word that a freshman or sophomore may not have in his day-to-day vocabulary, assuming that he will use his college dictionary while reading. For the most part, the notes do no more than give a first-level meaning for a line or a word; we have tried to avoid offering interpretations or indicating symbolic meaning, ambiguity, or other richnesses, except in a few cases where, without a minimal interpretation, no meaning at all would be forthcoming.

The book is introduced by an essay demonstrating how the various elements of poetry work together to produce the unique experience that constitutes a poem. It demonstrates also the use of a critical vocabulary, major terms of which are supplied by a glossary that follows.

In Appendix I we have collected some short pieces of criticism and some excerpts from longer critical works, which focus on a particular problem in each of three poems, in order to demonstrate how various intelligent and plausible critical readings may be at odds with one another in interpretation. In Wyatt's "They Flee from Me," the question as to who or what is designated by *they* has been extensively argued, and some parts of that argument, which is based on various readings by scholars and critics, are represented. Similarly, the announcement that "Beauty is truth," at the end of Keats's "Ode on a Grecian Urn," gives rise to the problem of how such a bald philosophical remark may be integrated with the poem. In the third group of critical pieces, the symbolic value of Wallace Stevens's jar, in "Anecdote of the Jar," is variously discussed.

We are grateful to Sharon DeLano and Shari Meats for clerical assistance and to Joan Yeatman and John Scally for assistance in the early stages.

S.B.G.

A.K.W.

CONTENTS

THOMAS CAMPION (1567–1620)

JOHN DONNE (c. 1572–1631)

BEN JONSON (1572–1637)

RICHARD LOVELACE (1618–1658)

ANDREW MARVELL (1621–1678)

HENRY VAUGHAN (1622–1695)

JOHN DRYDEN (1631–1700)

ALEXANDER POPE (1688–1744)

THOMAS GRAY (1716–1771)

WILLIAM COLLINS (1721–1759)

WILLIAM BLAKE (1757–1827)

ROBERT BURNS (1759–1796)

WILLIAM WORDSWORTH (1770–1850)

SAMUEL TAYLOR COLERIDGE (1772–1834)

WALTER SAVAGE LANDOR (1775–1864)

GEORGE GORDON, LORD BYRON (1788–1824)

PERCY BYSSHE SHELLEY (1792–1822)

JOHN KEATS (1795–1821)

RALPH WALDO EMERSON (1803–1882)

ALFRED, LORD TENNYSON (1809–1892)

EMILY DICKINSON (1830–1886)

ALGERNON CHARLES SWINBURNE (1837–1909)

THOMAS HARDY (1840–1928)

GERALD MANLEY HOPKINS (1844–1889)

A. E. HOUSMAN (1859–1936)

WILLIAM BUTLER YEATS (1865–1939)

EDWIN ARLINGTON ROBINSON (1869–1935)

ROBERT FROST (1874–1963)

WALLACE STEVENS (1879–1955)

WILLIAM CARLOS WILLIAMS (1883–1963)

D. H. LAWRENCE (1885–1930)

EZRA POUND (1885–   )

ROBINSON JEFFERS (1887–1962)

MARIANNE MOORE (1887–   )

T. S. ELIOT *(1888–1965)*

JOHN CROWE RANSOM *(1888–   )*

ARCHIBALD MacLEISH *(1892–   )*

WILFRED OWEN *(1893–1918)*

E. E. CUMMINGS *(1894–1962)*

ALLEN TATE *(1899–   )*

DYLAN THOMAS (1914–1953)

RANDALL JARRELL (1914–1965)

WILLIAM STAFFORD (1914–   )

ROBERT LOWELL (1917–   )

LAWRENCE FERLINGHETTI (1919–   )

RICHARD WILBUR (1921–   )

W. D. SNODGRASS (1926–   )

W. S. MERWIN (1927–   )

ANNE SEXTON (1928–   )

THOM GUNN (1929–   )

TED HUGHES (1930–   )

GARY SNYDER (1930–   )

SYLVIA PLATH (1932–1963)

LeROI JONES (1934–   )

DON L. LEE (1942–   )

THE POEM: An Anthology

INTRODUCTORY ESSAY:

The Experience of a Poem

Coming upon a poem for the first time is much like meeting someone new one's immediate response may be favorable, indifferent, or even downright hostile. Further acquaintance with the new person may alter one's reaction. But for such intensification or modification of feeling to occur, one must submit to a sympathetic knowledge of that person's being. So a poem may be enjoyed on first sight for its brilliant imagery, perhaps, or its satisfying sound relationships, the appeal of wit or an intellectual concept pointed with subtlety, or for all these together. For example, at first sight Keats was transported, he declares, by Chapman's poetic translation of Homer. If life and literature teach us anything, however, it is that our responses depend on the breadth and depth of our own vision, and a poem cannot bring more joy or enlightenment or enrichment than the reader can perceive. Since a poem is a concentrated and often complex expression, it requires reading and rereading: a puzzling out of word meanings, of word relationships, of various sound and sense patterns; sometimes an understanding of poetic tradition and **convention**; sometimes an awareness of historical or biographical matters, or of an age's or an individual's taste and ideas about the involvement of man with man, man with nature, man with the universe. Then, at length, the poem begins to play its comprehensive human role, expanding the consciousness of the reader, becoming part of the means by which he looks at the world, becoming his. Yet even then he will not feel its full impact: not till he can talk about the poem, can explain its operation to others, has he truly mastered it. And to do so, to interpret or to explicate it, demands a special vocabulary.[1]

An adequate discussion of the elements of a poem would require a volume in itself. Since there are many such volumes nowadays, this introductory essay will attempt merely to offer the reader a few examples of how he may enter into the poetic experience. Our limited purpose will best be served, we feel, by looking in some detail at three "love poems" from different centuries and by calling attention to the features they share with all poetry. Inasmuch as these poems all express grief at the absence or departure of the loved one, the reader will be able to compare and contrast the differences in effects and the linguistic means the poets used to achieve those effects.

Let us turn our attention first to the anonymous sixteenth-century **lyric** "Western Wind":

[1] See the Glossary beginning on page 551. All **boldface** words are defined there, as well as many others.

Western wind, when wilt thou blow,
The small rain down can rain?
Christ, that my love were in my arms,
And I in my bed again!

That the emotional force of this lyric cry has not been lost in the twentieth cen-
tury is witnessed by the inclusion of this poem in almost every anthology of
English poetry. It is not just the recurrent experience of love-loneliness, the
poem's subject, that causes us to respond, but its patterning of language and
verse. A more detailed understanding of the cooperation of elements in this
deceptively simple poem is instructive: it makes us aware of certain inherent
ambiguities, alternative meanings, that a superficial reading might miss.

Consider first the sense of the poem: the **dramatic** situation and the rele-
vance or irrelevance of asking certain questions. For though it is very important
to ask questions of a poem in order to make it yield up its meaning, it is most
important to ask the *right* questions. In this poem the situation of the speaker,
the **persona,** seems clear: he (or she?—is there any evidence in the poem, or
is our decision about the sex of the speaker personal?) is separated from his
beloved and longs for the sexual intimacy that the separation denies him. Should
we ask *why* the lovers are parted? In this poem, no! One could posit many
causes, but the lyric is obviously not interested in economic or psychological
or political matters—they lie outside its scope. It is the *fact* of separation, its
emotional impact on the speaker (and thus on the reader), that is the poem's
concern. (In some poems, like the **dramatic monologues** of Browning, the
poet *is* asking us to understand the psychology and character of the persona.
In "Soliloquy of the Spanish Cloister," for example, we are meant to question
the reliability of the speaker's picture of Brother Lawrence: the centrality of
the poem's experience lies in our recognition of his motivation and nature.)
But what, precisely, has the state of the weather, suggested in the first two lines
of "Western Wind," to do with the speaker's condition? For this poem this *is*
a relevant question, for it raises a point about the poem's **structure,** the unity
of its distinct parts or divisions; it points to an issue raised by the poem itself,
not to something extraneous to it. The answer to the question may not be so
simple as it seems, and it involves another question: What is the relationship
of the second line to the first? What has the wind, more precisely the *western*
wind, to do with the rain, the *small* rain? Here we enter upon matters of **dic-
tion** and the **connotation** of words, upon matters of **syntax, context,** and
poetic tradition.

The word *small* has some nine or ten definitions in the dictionary. One must
choose what best fits the immediate context. Surely it is not the size of the rain-
drops the poet wishes to emphasize, but the gentleness of the rain. And it is this
quality of gentleness that informs the nature of the love feeling expressed in
the last two lines. The love is not a wild, passionate animal sexuality—though

its sexuality is undeniably emphasized by the concrete word *bed*—but something with a softness and a refinement. But this is not all, for the *western wind* contributes to the meaning. The western wind is that same Zephirus that Geoffrey Chaucer, some two centuries earlier, invoked in the famous opening lines of *The Canterbury Tales:*

Whan that Aprille with his shourès sootè	showers; sweet
The droghte of March hath percèd to the rootè,	drought; pierced; sap-duct
And bathèd every veyne in swich licour	such; moisture
Of which vertu engendred is the flour;	power; created; flower
Whan Zephirus eek with his sweetè breeth	also
Inspirèd hath in every holt and heeth	quickened; field; heath
The tendre croppes . . .	

The western wind is the partner of the April showers in revitalizing the vegetation; it is the soft warm wind that heralds the springtime (unlike its blustery brother the east wind, as anyone who has spent some time in England will testify)—and in the springtime, as we know, a young man's fancy . . . The wind and the rain of the poem can thus be seen to suggest the quickening of life in the world of growing things; and the cry of the last two lines is a human parallel to the longed-for resurgence of "living" in the natural world. The speaker, uttering his lament from the "drought" of his heart in the drought of winter, is invoking the western wind *so that* the gentle rain may come and fructify the earth. (Many editions supply an initial *That* in the second line to fill the syntactic ellipsis, but there is no sanction for it in the manuscript, and it destroys the rhythm as well as eliminates a certain sharpness of feeling.[2]

We may also ask whether the lover is *invoking* Christ in the third line, as he does the Western Wind in the first, for the return of his beloved. This would seem blasphemous; and though there is a loose syntactic parallelism here with the first two lines, there is a shift from the direct invocation and question of those lines to an ejaculation and indirect wish (signaled by *that* and the subjunctive verb form *were*). Christ is an exclamation, serving to release the speaker's pent-up tensions: it establishes a dignified tone consonant with the refinement connoted by *small*. One should consider the difference in tone if the persona had exclaimed *Gee!* The importance of the denotation and connotation of words, and their tonal effect on meaning, may be seen to good advantage by comparing revisions a poet makes with his original version. For example, Robert Frost, in "Stopping by Woods on a Snowy Evening," originally had written *the steaming horses* in line 5 instead of *my little horse,* and in line 7 *a forest and a lake* instead of *the woods and frozen lake.* Both changes contribute to the

---

[2] One recent critic claims that *can* in line 2 means "did" and that the speaker is therefore not asking *for* rain but for a wind to blow the rain away. Such a reading would require a different interpretation of the whole poem, but it does not seem probable to us.

sense of awe, to the sense of the insignificance of man and animal with respect to the vastness of nature, that is part of the total impact of the poem.

An important point about patterning in poetry emerges from the preceding discussion. Although the parts of a poetic structure are held together by certain parallels in thought and construction, by word repetition, etc., such parallels and repetition are never exact. Even in the noticeable recurrence of the word *rain* in line 2 of "Western Wind," which creates the idea of a repeated or continual falling, the syntax changes it from noun to verb, from the thing to the action. A good poem is dynamic: it moves, it progresses in the development of its language and thought, and this movement is part of its meaning and of the feeling it gives us. We can see this even more clearly if we consider the sense of space suggested throughout "Western Wind." The appeal to the wind creates an atmosphere of spaciousness with its suggestion of the sweep of the wind as it blows from western regions; the rain closes the poem in somewhat, cutting off the wider vistas in an anticipation of the interior setting of the last two lines, when the poem comes to rest within the narrow confines of the bed. This is quite an achievement in the space of four lines. It is part of the meaning of the poem, though we may only become aware of it when alerted.

Understanding the structure, the relation of the parts of a poem to each other and to the whole, is one of the most important aspects of reading poetry. Its counterpart in human intercourse is our coming to understand the relationship between a person's behavior and his utterances, or between successive actions that may at first puzzle us because they seem discontinuous with each other or with the general impression we have formed of the person. Usually the structural units of a poem are clearly indicated, as in "Western Wind," by the difference in subject matter, or by narrative progression as in Emily Dickinson's "I heard a Fly buzz" or Blake's "A Poison Tree," or by logical divisions of thought as in the premises and conclusion of Marvell's "To His Coy Mistress." A subtler structural unity may lie in the relationship between different images in a poem, like those in the three quatrains of Shakespeare's Sonnet 73, where the similarity and difference between the end of a year, the end of a day, and the end of a fire are the essence of the poem's unity and progressive intensification of feeling. Occasionally the relationship of a key phrase or section of a poem to the whole is most puzzling: the essays in Appendix I on "Beauty is truth, truth beauty" of Keats's "Ode on a Grecian Urn" illustrate some attempts to resolve this kind of difficulty.

We can see something further of various structural ties in the next poem we shall discuss, Wordsworth's "She dwelt among the untrodden ways," a poem that fruitfully lends itself to an examination of some additional aspects of poetry:

> She dwelt among the untrodden ways
>   Beside the springs of Dove,
> A maid whom there were none to praise
>   And very few to love:

A violet by a mossy stone
Half-hidden from the eye!
—Fair as a star, when only one
Is shining in the sky.

She lived unknown, and few could know
When Lucy ceased to be;
But she is in her grave, and, oh,
The difference to me!

More of a "story" emerges from this poem than from "Western Wind"—and more of the nature of the beloved. The first stanza tells us of the rural remoteness in which the *maid* (what are this word's connotations?) *dwelt*. Notice the past tense, which at first reading merely suggests that she used to live there but does not tell us why she no longer does. The second stanza—to which we shall return—offers us a couple of comparisons that suggest certain qualities of the maid. The first line of the third stanza repeats the sense of the first line of the first; but the second word, *lived*, subtly brings out a meaning in the *dwelt*, which it has replaced, and draws our attention, with a sense of shock, to the full significance of the word *dwelt* and its past tense. The power of *dwelt*, when that full significance is revealed, is due to **understatement**; it anticipates and is related to the understatement in the final line, which declares as a climax the meaning of Lucy's death to the speaker. In this poem, too, we can readily see the circularity yet progression in the structure. But we wish to focus more particularly on the second quatrain, which introduces an element of **imagery** not present in "Western Wind." And we may also notice how carefully this stanza integrates the total poetic structure.

One of the chief means of poetic statement is **metaphor**, a term sometimes broadly used to cover the more narrowly viewed *metaphor*—an *implied* comparison between two dissimilar-seeming things—and **simile**—an *explicit* comparison, often specifying the quality or qualities the two things have in common, and employing the words *like* or *as* (sometimes *than*). Both of these **figures of speech** are employed here: the metaphor of the violet and the simile of the star. What qualities of Lucy are suggested by the violet image? We think perhaps of a "shrinking violet" and make the association of shyness, an association that the second line of the stanza reinforces. (We must be careful in making such associations, however; sometimes poets deliberately defy connotations in their imagery; we must beware of cliché-thinking, of stereotypes, in reading a poem.) But violets are also pretty in a soft, gentle way; they imply delicacy, fragility; they suggest a warm color. Violets are among the first flowers of spring and, as such, a reference to them has **overtones** of young love. How many of these connotations apply in this particular context? Does the placing of the violet by a "*mossy* stone" support or deny any of them?

The tenor of the star simile is quite clear: Lucy is "*fair* as a star"—and that fairness is emphasized by the uniqueness accorded the star in the evening sky. Obviously, the simile in a way reinforces the metaphor's potential meaning of "beautiful" and also of a hidden quality in that beauty which must be searched for: it is as difficult to spot the first star of evening as it is to find a half-hidden violet. And these similarities in the suggestiveness of the two images unify the stanza. But there are important differences, too, and these serve to unify the whole poem and help to move the "action" from the living Lucy to the dead one. For the violet, as we have just seen, is "alive," suggests color and warmth, youth and love—it is also something we can touch—whereas a star, however fair, is "dead," its shining quality has a hardness, and it is distant and "cold," untouchable. The star appears in the evening, at the end of day; the violet appears at the beginning of earth's reawakening from its winter slumber. But paradoxically, the violet does have an implication of early death: early come, early go; and delicacy does not endure. (*Moss,* too, yoked with the flower here, is not only soft and green; it also has overtones of death, being associated with tombstones and graves.) Thus the violet metaphor continues in the living vein of stanza 1, but submerged in it are the implications of the death to be revealed; and these implications are more strongly felt in the star simile, which thus prepares us emotionally, though subtly, for the bald announcement of the last stanza. And the value suggested by both images prepares us for the final exclamation of loss, with its understated intimation of the greatness of that loss.

It should be appreciated that metaphor is not always so obviously presented as it is in the violet image of Wordsworth's poem. Comparison is often only hinted at, in what may be called a submerged metaphor. For example, in Karl Shapiro's "Auto Wreck," various words describing the ambulance in the first stanza have metaphoric overtones: *floating down; wings; dips down; brakes speed; rocking, slightly rocking.* Do these add up to anything? They seem to suggest a comparison of the ambulance to a scavenging bird, perhaps a vulture, a comparison that seems appropriate for the context, and tonally additive, though students have sometimes disagreed with this interpretation. That such disagreement about metaphorical implications *can* arise, even among presumably knowledgeable critics, is illustrated in the essays on Wyatt's "They Flee From Me" in Appendix I.

To return to Wordsworth's poem, we shall not say much more except to call attention to the deceptive simplicity of various kinds that cloaks the depth of its emotion. The diction is simple: most of the words are monosyllabic and none, except for *untrodden* in the first line and *difference* in the last, has more than two syllables. (Does this lend effectiveness to the shock value of the last line?) The rhythm is uncomplicated and the rhyme words are about as commonplace as can be: *ways/praise; Dove* (the name of a river)*/love; stone/one; eye/sky; know/oh; be/me.* And, as we indicated above, the statements of the poem are low-keyed, underplayed. It is this contrast between the strictly controlled surface elements of the poem and the intensity of its inner emotion that provides a quality we may call **tension,** that makes the poem ever fresh and keeps it from falling into **sentimentality.** And we might note also, since it is written in the **ballad stanza form,** that the very same kind of tension exists in **ballads,** where a violence of action and of feeling is expressed in regular and repeated simplicity of external form.

More complex in almost every respect—structure, imagery, tone, rhythm, sound patterns—is the modern poet John Crowe Ransom's "Winter Remembered":

> Two evils, monstrous either one apart,
> Possessed me, and were long and loath at going:
> A cry of Absence, Absence, in the heart,
> And in the wood the furious winter blowing.
>
> Think not, when fire was bright upon my bricks,
> And past the tight boards hardly a wind could enter,
> I glowed like them, the simple burning sticks,
> Far from my cause, my proper heat and center.
>
> Better to walk forth in the frozen air
> And wash my wound in the snows; that would be healing;
> Because my heart would throb less painful there,
> Being caked with cold, and past the smart of feeling.
>
> And where I walked, the murderous winter blast
> Would have this body bowed, these eyeballs streaming,
> And though I think this heart's blood froze not fast
> It ran too small to spare one drop for dreaming.
>
> Dear love, these fingers that had known your touch,
> And tied our separate forces first together,
> Were ten poor idiot fingers not worth much,
> Ten frozen parsnips hanging in the weather.

As in both "Western Wind" and "She dwelt among the untrodden ways," the emotions of the persona are linked with nature, but here the phenomenon of winter extends itself into a **symbol.** First, however, the winter is a physical phenomenon in its own right, one of the two slightly **personified** evils that "possessed" the speaker. The more important of the two, the sense of loss at the separation from the beloved, is further emphasized by the contrast of the second stanza: although his room was snug against the external cold, with a bright fire in the hearth, the speaker felt no internal warmth, removed as he was from the beloved who fed the "fire" of his heart. In the third stanza he describes how he thought it would be better to anesthetize his feelings by taking his heart's wound—the internal evil—out into the numbing of the "frozen air" and into the painfully antiseptic "snows"—the external evil. The fourth stanza relates the apparent success of this therapy, describing the effect upon the body and the heart: while the "heart's blood" did not actually freeze, it "ran too small" to permit the speaker to dream, to continue to nourish memories of the beloved or hopes that she might return. But love, for Ransom, as for the seventeenth-century poets before him and for many a modern poet since, is not merely an abstract relationship conducted by an almost abstract *heart*; the exorcism, the eradication of the memory, calls for not only a cessation of dreaming but for some mortification of the flesh. Thus in the last stanza the poet records the freezing of his fingers, which had been the initial agents of his relationship with the woman. And the descent here from the "poetic" discussion of "heart" to the more concrete image of the members of the flesh brings a concentration of emotion and pathos to the last stanza, a pathos intensified by the apostrophe "Dear love."

Are we to assume from this that the therapy calculated to assuage the pangs of absence has not worked? Or are we to think of the persona as address-ing the woman long after an absence, which proved temporary, was over? In either case, as the poem develops and the literal winter is employed to deal with the winter in the heart, the two monstrous evils of the initial stanza are fused into one. The title of the poem, it becomes clear, refers to more than a simple, particular wintertime recalled: it is, in fact, not *a* winter, but *winter* remem-bered. That is to say, winter earns a symbolic value as the poem proceeds; it becomes a symbol for absence, for the cold of separation.

Poetic symbols, it should be noted, may be more difficult to pin down in meaning than Ransom's "winter." Blake's "sick rose," for example, demands by its imagery some sort of symbolic interpretation, but whether we have here in the flower and the worm that attacks and kills it woman destroyed by man, beauty by lust, idealism by selfishness, natural good by technological evil—or what might be called a multivalent or many-valued symbol—is hard to say. For some critical disagreement over the symbolism of the jar in Wallace Stevens's "Anecdote of the Jar," the reader should consult Appendix I.

But we should make a few further remarks about "Winter Remembered." The diction and imagery of the poem emphasize the grotesqueness of the situation as the speaker felt it, e. g., "these eyeballs [not *eyes*] streaming," line 14; and the parsnips metaphor, with its suggestion of dirty whiteness, of vegetable rather than animal life. The vital relationship of the speaker to his beloved is elementally captured in the almost **metaphysical** image of stanza 2: she is his "proper heat and center." These are some of the poetic elements that contribute to the power of Ransom's poem. But there is something here not present in the other two poems we have considered, which lends depth to this poem. That is its allusiveness. For there are several allusions to Shakespeare's works in the poem that serve to enhance or enrich its meaning: in the first stanza, an echo from the dirge in *Cymbeline*: "Fear no more the heat o' the sun/Nor the furious winter's rages"; in the third and fourth stanzas, a suggestion of King Lear's exposure to the howling storm and his "Blow, winds, and crack your cheeks"; and in the last stanza, an echo of Macbeth's "Life is a tale told by an idiot. . . ." That these provide overtones of meaning relevant to the emotions of Ransom's poem should be readily apparent. (Many modern poets are fond of this kind of allusiveness; T. S. Eliot is a good example.)

In our discussion of the three poems, we have been talking mainly about the "sense" in our experience of the poem. Sound and rhythmic patterns, however, are also important to the total effect and meaning. A significant sound element in many poems (though used less frequently in much modern poetry) is rhyme. For example, in "Western Wind" the rhyme of the second and fourth lines, *rain/again*, provides a **formal** tie for the natural and human segments of the poem. And we have already noted the contribution of the monosyllabic rhymes in Wordsworth's poem to the feeling of simple, heartfelt emotion that is central to that poem's experience. In "Western Wind" we also become aware of the **alliteration** of the /w/'s in the first half of the first line, of the /au, o/ similarity (**near-assonance**) in the last two words of that line, and of the **consonance** of the nasal sounds /m, n/ in the second. It is not just that these sounds delight our ears: by their "openness" or capability of continuance, they provide part of the feeling of spaciousness initiated by the concept of the wind itself, which we remarked on earlier. This effect may be contrasted with that which the explosive or stopped sounds of /b/ and /d/ provide in *bed*, a reinforcement of the sense of narrow compass that the denotation of the word itself supplies. In "Winter Remembered" we might note how the /o/ and /aw/ sounds of the second line suggest the lingering of the two monstrous evils —a feeling that is augmented by the **feminine ending** of *going* (and by the use of **feminine rhyme** in the second and fourth line of every stanza). It should be remembered, however, that sounds have no "meaning" in and of themselves, but that context can make them meaningful, though not every context does so: consider, for example, the /w/ sound in "He wangled a winch from a waspy wench."

Mention of feminine ending brings us to the subject of **meter**. Meter and rhythm are complex, and whole books as well as hundreds of essays have been devoted to them. The beginner in the study of poetry may well be forgiven if he recoils from the technical vocabulary in which discussions of rhythm and meter are couched. Nevertheless, he should know *something* about them, and we will touch here on their most essential features.

What is the dominant metrical pattern that emerges when we read "Western Wind" aloud? It is traditionally called **iambic**, an alternation of relatively unstressed (see **stress**) syllables with stressed ones, as in the second line: |The small| rain down | can rain|. The idea of *relative* stress is important, for the first *rain* obviously bears greater stress than *the* or *can;* but in its **foot** (feet being shown by the single bar) it clearly has less stress than *down*. Since there are three feet in this line, we call the meter iambic **trimeter**. A significant variation from the iambic rhythm is in the anapestic foot in the middle of the last line: |ĭn mȳ bēd|, which in context suggests a hurry-up effect appropriate to desire. We may also notice how an inversion of the iamb at the opening of the third line produces **a trochee** (|Chrīst, || thăt) which, coupled with the **caesura** or pause (marked ||) in the middle of the foot gives rhythmic explosiveness to the expletive *Christ.* The first line also has an explosiveness in its rhythmic underlining of the invocation to the western wind, but it is not of the same sort, and not as strong in its effect—fittingly enough: here is a headless line, with the unstressed first syllable omitted (though supplied in many editions by the word O). It may be **scanned** as follows: | (˘) Wēst|ĕrn wīnd, || whĕn wīlt| thŏu blōw||, though different readers may dispose the **accent** differently in the third foot of this iambic **tetrameter** line, making *when wilt* either a trochee or a *spondee* : |—˘| or |——|.

The effects of different rhythms and meters on our emotional pulses are interesting to contemplate, but we will just mention here the difference between the strong "riding" feeling Byron achieves with his anapests in "The Destruction of Sennacherib" ("The Assyrian came down like the wolf on the fold") and the colloquial speech feeling Browning achieves, even with the use of rhymed **couplets**, in "My Last Duchess":

> That's my last Duchess painted on the wall,
> Looking as if she were alive. I call
> That piece a wonder, now: Fra Pandolf's hands
> Worked busily a day, and there she stands.

Browning's effect is achieved by the carefully varied caesuras, the run-on or **enjambed** lines, and the several variations on the basic iambic foot. It might be fitting to conclude this discussion of the effects of rhythm and meter, and their relationship to other elements in a poem, by suggesting that all these elements are like the parts of the tree and the dancer and the dance in Yeats's "Among School Children":

> O chestnut-tree, great-rooted blossomer,
> Are you the leaf, the blossom or the bole?
> O body swayed to music, O brightening glance,
> How can we know the dancer from the dance?

The student we have most in mind in writing this introduction and assembling this anthology will study the foregoing exercises in criticism. He will make use of the approaches they suggest and exemplify, and of the terminology here and in the glossary, in studying and discussing other poems. He will recognize something of the complexity that exists even in a short poem. He will recognize also that a good poem is not to be approached with naked intuition alone, nor with a battery of stock or outworn responses. There is, of course, room for wide disagreement about a poem and for latitude in its interpretation; the collection of essays in Appendix I illustrates something of this, as we have observed earlier. The student may then well ask whether *his* reading of a poem is not as good as that of his instructor or of a published critic. Sometimes indeed it is—as good or even better. But he must realize that the scholarly explications in the appendix, even though they may differ, have grown out of training not only in poetics but in broad areas of human concern. And this training, coupled with familiarity with the larger part of the poet's total output, has been brought to bear on every detail of the poem before any one part of it is conclusively interpreted. In other words, the experience of a poem calls for experience.

THE WANDERER

This lonely traveller longs for grace,
For the mercy of God; grief hangs on
His heart and follows the frost-cold foam
He cuts in the sea, sailing endlessly,
Aimlessly, in exile. Fate has opened
A single port: memory. He sees
His kinsmen slaughtered again, and cries:

    "I've drunk too many lonely dawns,
Grey with mourning. Once there were men
To whom my heart could hurry, hot
With open longing. They're long since dead.
My heart has closed on itself, quietly
Learning that silence is noble and sorrow
Nothing that speech can cure. Sadness
Has never driven sadness off;
Fate blows hardest on a bleeding heart.
So those who thirst for glory smother
Secret weakness and longing, neither
Weep nor sigh nor listen to the sickness
In their souls. So I, lost and homeless,
Forced to flee the darkness that fell
On the earth and my lord.

                Leaving everything,
Weary with winter I wandered out
On the frozen waves, hoping to find
A place, a people, a lord to replace
My lost ones. No one knew me, now,
No one offered comfort, allowed
Me feasting or joy. How cruel a journey
I've travelled, sharing my bread with sorrow
Alone, an exile in every land,
Could only be told by telling my footsteps.
For who can hear: "friendless and poor,"

Note. This Old English poem is translated here by Burton Raffel.

13

And know what I've known since the long cheerful
   nights
When, young and yearning, with my lord I yet feasted
Most welcome of all. That warmth is dead.
He only knows who needs his lord
As I do, eager for long-missing aid;
He only knows who never sleeps
40   Without the deepest dreams of longing.
Sometimes it seems I see my lord,
Kiss and embrace him, bend my hands
And head to his knee, kneeling as though
He still sat enthroned, ruling his thanes.
And I open my eyes, embracing the air,
And see the brown sea-billows heave,
See the sea-birds bathe, spreading
Their white-feathered wings, watch the frost
And the hail and the snow. And heavy in heart
50   I long for my lord, alone and unloved.
Sometimes it seems I see my kin
And greet them gladly, give them welcome,
The best of friends. They fade away,
Swimming soundlessly out of sight,
Leaving nothing.
                 How loathsome become
The frozen waves to a weary heart.
      In this brief world I cannot wonder
That my mind is set on melancholy,
60   Because I never forget the fate
Of men, robbed of their riches, suddenly
Looted by death—the doom of earth,
Sent to us all by every rising
Sun. Wisdom is slow, and comes
But late. He who has it is patient;
He cannot be hasty to hate or speak,
He must be bold and yet not blind,
Nor ever too craven, complacent, or covetous,
Nor ready to gloat before he wins glory.
70   The man's a fool who flings his boasts
Hotly to the heavens, heeding his spleen
And not the better boldness of knowledge.

---

44. thanes: freemen who served as bodyguard to a lord or king. **71. heeding his spleen:** giving vent to his anger.

What knowing man knows not the ghostly,
Waste-like end of worldly wealth:
See, already the wreckage is there,
The wind-swept walls stand far and wide,
The storm-beaten blocks besmeared with frost,
The mead-halls crumbled, the monarchs thrown down
And stripped of their pleasures. The proudest of
    warriors
Now lie by the wall: some of them war   80
Destroyed; some the monstrous sea-bird
Bore over the ocean, to some the old wolf
Dealt out death; and for some dejected
Followers fashioned an earth-cave coffin.
Thus the Maker of men lays waste
This earth, crushing our callow mirth.
And the work of old giants stands withered and still."

He who these ruins rightly sees,
And deeply considers this dark twisted life,
Who sagely remembers the endless slaughters   90
Of a bloody past, is bound to proclaim:
     "Where is the war-steed? Where is the warrior?
         Where is his war-lord?
Where now the feasting-places? Where now the mead-
    hall pleasures?
Alas, bright cup! Alas, brave knight!
Alas, you glorious princes! All gone,
Lost in the night, as you never had lived.
And all that survives you a serpentine wall,
Wondrously high, worked in strange ways.
Mighty spears have slain these men,
Greedy weapons have framed their fate.   100
     These rocky slopes are beaten by storms,
This earth pinned down by driving snow,
By the horror of winter, smothering warmth
In the shadows of night. And the north angrily
Hurls its hailstorms at our helpless heads.
Everything earthly is evilly born,
Firmly clutched by a fickle Fate.
Fortune vanishes, friendship vanishes,
Man is fleeting, woman is fleeting,

73. **ghostly:** non-material. 78. **mead-halls:** the gathering places of the lords and their thanes (**mead:** beer made from honey).

110   And all this earth rolls into emptiness."

So says the sage in his heart, sitting alone with
    His thought.
It's good to guard your faith, nor let your grief come
    forth
Until it cannot call for help, nor help but heed
The path you've placed before it. It's good to find your
    grace
In God, the heavenly rock where rests our every hope.

ANONYMOUS (early 13th century)

SUMER IS ICUMEN IN

Sumer is icumen in,
Loudè sing cuccu!
Groweth sed and bloweth med
And springth the wudè nu.
Sing cuccu!

Ewè bleteth after lomb,
Loweth after calvè cu;
Bullock sterteth, buckè verteth,
Murie sing cuccu!
10   Cuccu, cuccu,
Wel singest thu, cuccu;
Ne swik thu naver nu.

Sing cuccu nu! Sing cuccu!
Sing cuccu! Sing cuccu nu!

Spring has come in; sing loud, cuckoo; seed grows and meadow blossoms and the woods leaf-out anew. Sing, cuckoo! The ewe bleats for the lamb; the cow moos after the calf; the bullock leaps, the buck farts; sing merrily, cuckoo. Cuckoo, cuckoo, well do you sing cuckoo; never stop now. Sing cuckoo, etc.

ANONYMOUS (later 13th century)

UBI SUNT QUI ANTE NOS FUERUNT

Where beth they beforen us weren,
Houndès ladden and havekès beren,
And hadden feld and wode?
The richè levedies in hoere bour,
That wereden gold in hoere tressour,
With hoere brightè rode?

Eten and drounken and maden hem glad;
Hoere lif was all with gamen ilad:
Men kneleden hem beforen.
They beren hem well swithè heye,   10
And, in a twinkling of an eye,
Hoere soulès weren forloren.

Where is that lawing and that song,
That trailing and that proudè yong,
Tho havekès and tho houndes?
All that joye is went away,
That wele is comen to weylaway,
To manye hardè stoundes.

Hoere paradis hy nomen here,
And now they lien in helle y-fere: 20
The fuir it brennès evere;
Long is 'ay!' and long is 'ho!'
Long is 'wy!' and long is 'wo!'
Thennès ne cometh they nevere.

Where are they, who were before us, led hounds and bore hawks and had fields and woods? The rich ladies in their bowers, who wore gold in their tresses, with their bright faces? (They) ate and drank and made themselves glad; their life was all spent in gaiety: men kneeled before them. They bore themselves very loftily, and in the twinkling of an eye their souls were lost. Where is that laughing and that song, that trailing (of robes) and that proud going (i.e., gait), those hawks and those hounds? All that joy is gone away, that well-being has come to woe, to many hard times. Their paradise they took here, and now they lie in hell together; the fire it burns ever; long is (their)

Dreye here, man, thenne, if thou wilt,
A luitel pine that me thee bit,
Withdraw thine eyses ofte.
They thy pinè be ounrede,
And thou thenkè on thy mede,
30   It shall thee thinken softe.

If that Fend, that foulè thing,
Thru wickè roun, thru fals egging,
Nethere thee haveth icast,
Up and be god champioun!
Stond! ne fall namore adoun
For a luitel blast.

Thou tak the rodè to thy staf,
And thenk on Him that thereonne yaf
His lif that wes so lef!
40   He it yaf for thee: thou yelde it Him,
Ayein His fo that staf thou nim
And wrek Him of thef!

Of righte bileve thou nim that sheld
The wiles that thou best in that feld,
Thine hond to strengthen fonde.
And kep thy fo with stavès ord,
And do that traitre seyen that word,
Biget that murie londe!

Thereinne is day withouten night,
50   Withouten endè strengthe and might
And wreche of everich fo,
Mid God Himselven echè lif,
And pes and rest withoutè strif,
Welè withouten wo.

"Ah!" and long is (their) "Oh!" Long is (their) "Alas!" and long is (their) "Woe is me!" Thence will they come never.

Endure here, man, then, if you will, a little suffering that anyone bids you; withdraw your comforts often. Though your pain be severe, if you think about your deserts, it shall seem soft to you. If the Fiend (Devil), that evil thing, through wicked advice, through false egging-on, downward has cast you, (rise) up and be a good champion! Stand! don't fall down anymore on account of a little blast (of wind). Take the cross as thy staff and think about Him that thereon gave His life that was so dear. He gave it for you; repay it to Him: take that staff against His foe and avenge Him on that thief. Take the shield of right belief, while you are in the field to try to strengthen

Maiden, moder, Hevenè Quene,
Thou might and const and owest to bene
Oure sheld ayein the Fende.
Help us sunnè for to flen,
That we moten thy Sone y-seen
In joye withouten ende.   60

Amen.

ANONYMOUS (early 15th century)

I SING OF A MAIDEN

I sing of a maiden
That is makèles;
King of all kinges
To her sone she ches.

He cam al so stille
Ther his moder was,
As dew in Aprille
That falleth on the grass.

He cam al so stille
To his moderès bour,   10
As dew in Aprille
That falleth on the flour.

He cam al so stille
Ther his moder lay,
As dew in Aprille
That falleth on the spray.

your hand, and hold your foe with a staff's point and make that traitor say the word
(of surrender); achieve that happy land. Therein is day without night and strength and
might without end and vengeance on every foe, with God Himself eternal life and peace
and rest without strife, well-being without woe. Maiden, mother, Heaven's Queen,
you have the power and are able and ought to be our shield against the Fiend. Help us
to flee from sin so that we may see thy Son in joy without end. Amen.

2. **makèles:** matchless (i.e., without equal and without mate). 4. **ches:** chose.
5. **al so:** as. 6. **Ther:** where; **moder:** mother. 10. **bour:** chamber. 12. **flour:** flower.
16. **spray:** small branch

Moder and maiden
Was never non but she;
Wel may swich a lady
20   Goddès moder be.

ANONYMOUS (early 16th century)

WESTERN WIND, WHEN WILT THOU BLOW

Western wind, when wilt thou blow,
The small rain down can rain?
Christ, that my love were in my arms,
And I in my bed again!

BALLADS

ANONYMOUS (date uncertain)

SIR PATRICK SPENS

The king sits in Dumferling town,
    Drinking the blude-reid wine:
"O whar will I get a guid sailòr
    To sail this ship of mine?"

Up and spake an eldern knicht,
    Sat at the king's richt knee:
"Sir Patrick Spens is the best sailòr
    That sails upon the sea."

The king has written a braid letter,
10   And signed it wi' his hand,
And sent it to Sir Patrick Spens,
    Was walking on the sand.

19. swich: such.

2. blude-reid: blood red. 3. whar: where; guid: good. 5. eldern: elderly. 9. braid
letter: an open letter.

The first line that Sir Patrick read,
  A loud lauch lauched he;
The next line that Sir Patrick read,
  The tear blinded his ee.

"O wha is this has done this deed,
  This ill deed done to me,
To send me out this time o' the year,
  To sail upon the sea?   20

"Make haste, make haste, my merry men all,
  Our guid ship sails the morn."
"O say na sae, my master dear,
  For I fear a deadly storm.

"Late, late yestreen I saw the new moon
  Wi' the auld moon in her arm,
And I fear, I fear, my dear mastèr,
  That we will come to harm."

O our Scots nobles were richt laith:
  To weet their cork-heeled shoon;   30
But lang owre a' the play were played,
  Their hats they swam aboon.

O lang, lang, may their ladies sit
  Wi' their fans into their hand,
Or e'er they see Sir Patrick Spens
  Come sailing to the land.

O lang, lang, may the ladies stand
  Wi' their gold kems in their hair,
Waiting for their ain dear lords,
  For they'll see thame na mair.   40

Half o'er, half o'er to Aberdour
  It's fifty fadom deep,
And there lies guid Sir Patrick Spens,
  Wi' the Scots lords at his feet.

14. lauch: laugh. 16. ee: eye. 23. na sae: not so. 25. yestreen: yesterday evening. 26. auld: old. 29. laith unwilling. 30. weet wet; shoon shoes. 31. owre: before; a': all. 32. aboon: above. 38. kems: combs. 39. ain: own. 40. thame na mair: them no more. 41. Half o'er: halfway across. 42 fadom: fathom.

Anonymous (date uncertain)

THE WIFE OF USHER'S WELL

There lived a wife at Usher's Well,
    And a wealthy wife was she;
She had three stout and stalwart sons,
    And sent them o'er the sea.

They hadna' been a week from her,
    A week but barely ane,
When word came to the carlin wife
    That her three sons were gane.

They hadna' been a week from her,
    A week but barely three,
Whan word came to the carlin wife
    That her sons she'd never see.

"I wish the wind may never cease,
    Nor fashes in the flood,
Till my three sons come hame to me,
    In earthly flesh and blood."

It fell about the Martinmas,
    When nights are lang and mirk,
The carlin wife's three sons came hame,
    And their hats were o' the birk.

It neither grew in syke nor ditch,
    Nor yet in ony sheugh;
But at the gates o' Paradise,
    That birk grew fair eneugh.

10

20

6. **ane:** one. 7. **carlin:** old woman. 8. **gane:** gone. 14. **fashes:** troubles. 15. **hame:** home. 17. **Martinmas:** Feast of St. Martin, November 11. 18. **mirk:** dark. 20. **birk:** birch (suggesting, by its unseasonableness, that they have returned from the dead; cf. the explicit statement of the lines following). 21. **syke:** field. 22. **ony:** any; **sheugh:** trench.

"Blow up the fire, my maidens,
    Bring water from the well;
For a' my house shall feast this night,
    Since my three sons are well."

And she has made to them a bed,
    She's made it large and wide,   30
And she's ta'en her mantle her about,
    Sat down at the bed-side.

Up then crew the red, red cock,
    And up and crew the gray;
The eldest to the youngest said,
    "'Tis time we were away."

The cock he hadna' crawed but once,
    And clapped his wings at a',
When the youngest to the eldest said,
    "Brother, we must awa'.   40

"The cock doth craw, the day doth daw,
    The channerin' worm doth chide;
Gin we be missed out o' our place,
    A sair pain we maun bide.

"Fare ye weel, my mother dear!
    Fareweel to barn and byre!
And fare ye weel, the bonny lass
    That kindles my mother's fire!"

ANONYMOUS (date uncertain)

THOMAS THE RHYMER

True Thomas lay on Huntly bank;
    A ferly he spied wi' his ee:
And there he saw a lady bright
    Come riding down by the Eildon Tree.

27. a': all. 31. ta'en: taken. 36. Cockcrow was the time for spirits to return to
their graves. 40. awa': away. 41. daw: dawn. 42. channerin': complaining. 43. Gin: if.
44. sair: sorry; maun bide: must endure. 45. weel: well. 46. byre: cowshed.

Title. Thomas was a 13th-century Scots minstrel. 2. ferly: marvel; ee: eye.

Her skirt was o' the grass-green silk,
    Her mantle o' the velvet fine;
At ilka tett of her horse's mane
    Hung fifty silver bells and nine.

True Thomas he pulled off his cap
10   And louted low down to his knee:
"All hail, thou mighty Queen of Heaven!
    For thy peer on earth I never did see."

"O no, O no, Thomas," she said,
    "That name does not belong to me;
I am but the Queen of fair Elfland,
    That am hither come to visit thee.

"Harp and carp, Thomas," she said,
    "Harp and carp along wi' me;
And if ye dare to kiss my lips,
20   Sure of your body I will be."

"Betide me weal, betide me woe,
    That weird shall never daunton me."
Syne he has kissed her rosy lips,
    All underneath the Eildon Tree.

"Now ye maun go wi' me," she said,
    "True Thomas, ye maun go wi' me;
And ye maun serve me seven years
    Through weal or woe, as may chance to be."

She mounted on her milk-white steed;
30   She's ta'en True Thomas up behind;
And ay whene'er her bridle rung,
    The steed flew swifter than the wind.

O they rade on, and farther on—
    The steed gaed swifter than the wind—
Until they reached a desert wide,
    And living land was left behind.

7. **ilka tett:** each tuft. 10. **louted:** bowed. 17. **Harp and carp:** play and speak.
21. **Betide me weal . . . woe:** come fair or foul. 22. **weird:** fate; **daunton:** frighten.
23. **Syne:** afterwards. 25. **maun:** must. 34. **gaed:** went.

"Light down, light down now, True Thomàs,
    And lean your head upon my knee;
Abide and rest a little space,
    And I will show you ferlies three.   40

"O see ye not yon narrow road,
    So thick beset with thorns and briars?
That is the path of righteousness,
    Though after it but few enquires.

"And see ye not that braid, braid road
    That lies across that lily leven?
That is the path of wickedness,
    Though some call it the road to Heaven.

"And see not ye that bonny road
    That winds about the ferny brae?   50
That is the road to fair Elfland,
    Where thou and I this night maun gae.

"But Thomas, ye maun hold your tongue,
    Whatever ye may hear or see;
For if you speak word in Elfinland,
    Ye'll ne'er get back to your ain countrie."

O they rade on, and farther on,
    And they waded through rivers aboon the knee,
And they saw neither sun nor moon,
    But they heard the roaring of the sea.   60

It was mirk, mirk night, and there was nae sternlight,
    And they waded through red blude to the knee,
For a' the blude that's shed on earth
    Rins through the springs o' that countrie.

Syne they came on to a garden green,
    And she pulled an apple frae a tree:
"Take this for thy wages, True Thomàs,
    It will give thee tongue that never can lie."

    37. Light: alight. **45. braid:** broad. **46. lily leven:** lovely open ground. **50. brae:** hillside. **56. ain:** own. **58. aboon:** above. **61. mirk:** dark; **nae sternlight:** no starlight. **62. blude:** blood. **63. a':** all. **64. Rins:** runs. **66. frae:** from.

"My tongue is mine ain," True Thomas said;
70   'A gudely gift ye wad gie to me!
I neither dought to buy nor sell
              At fair or tryst where I may be.

"I dought neither speak to prince nor peer,
              Nor ask of grace frae fair ladie."
"Now hold thy peace," the lady said,
              "For as I say, so must it be."

He has gotten a coat of the even cloth,
              And a pair of shoes of velvet green;
And till seven years were gane and past,
80   True Thomas on earth was never seen.

ANONYMOUS (date uncertain)

THE THREE RAVENS

There were three ravens sat on a tree,
    Down a down, hay down, hay down,
There were three ravens sat on a tree,
    With a down.
There were three ravens sat on a tree,
They were as black as they might be,
    With a down, derry, derry, derry, down, down.

The one of them said to his mate,
"Where shall we our breakfast take?"

10   "Down in yonder greenè field,
There lies a knight slain under his shield.

"His hounds they lie down at his feet,
So well they can their master keep.

---

70. gudely: goodly; **wad:** would; **gie:** give. **71. neither dought:** would not be able.
72. tryst: market place. **77. even:** smooth. **79. gane:** gone.

2, 4, 7. These lines constitute a refrain, which is to be repeated in the following
stanzas in the same positions.

"His hawks they fly so eagerly,
There's no fowl dare him to come nigh."

Down there comes a fallow doe,
As great with young as she might go.

She lift up his bloody head,
And kissed his wounds that were so red.

She got him up upon her back   20
And carried him to earthen lake.

She buried him before the prime,
She was dead herself ere even-song time.

God send every gentleman
Such hawks, such hounds, and such a leman.

ANONYMOUS (date uncertain)

THE TWA CORBIES

As I was walking all alane,
I heard twa corbies making a mane;
The tane unto the t' other say,
"Where sall we gang and dine today?"

"In behind yon auld fail dyke,
I wot there lies a new-slain knight;
And naebody kens that he lies there
But his hawk, his hound, and lady fair.

"His hound is to the hunting gane,
His hawk to fetch the wild-fowl hame,   10
His lady's ta'en another mate,
So we may make our dinner sweet.

15. fowl: bird. 21. earthen lake: pit. 22. prime: six a.m. 23. even-song time: dusk.
25. leman: beloved.

Title. twa corbies: two ravens (or crows). 1. alane: alone. 2. mane: moan.
3. The tane: the one. 4. sall: shall; gang: go. 5. auld: old; fail dyke: turf wall. 6. wot:
know. 7. kens: knows. 9. gane: gone. 10. hame: home. 11. ta'en: taken.

"Ye'll sit on his white hause-bane,
And I'll pick out his bonny blue een;
Wi' ae lock o' his golden hair,
We'll theek our nest when it grows bare.

"Mony a one for him makes mane,
But nane sall ken where he is gane;
O'er his white banes when they are bare,
20   The wind sall blaw for evermair."

ANONYMOUS (date uncertain)

THE DEMON LOVER

"O where have you been, my long, long love,
    This long seven years and mair?"
"O I'm come to seek my former vows
    Ye granted me before."

"O hold your tongue of your former vows,
    For they will breed sad strife;
O hold your tongue of your former vows,
    For I am become a wife."

He turned him right and round about,
10   And the tear blinded his ee:
"I wad never have trodden on Irish ground,
    If it had not been for thee.

"I might have had a king's daughtèr,
    Far, far beyond the sea;
I might have had a king's daughtèr,
    Had it not been for love o' thee."

"If ye might have had a king's daughtèr,
    Yer sel' ye had to blame;
Ye might have taken the king's daughtèr,
20   For ye kend that I was nane.

13. **hause-bane:** neck bone. 14. **een:** eyes. 15. **ae:** one. 16. **theek:** thatch.

1. **long love:** lover of long ago. 2. **mair:** more. 10. **ee:** eye. 11. **wad:** would.
20. **kend:** knew; **nane:** none.

"If I was to leave my husband dear,
    And my two babes also,
O what have you to take me to,
    If with you I should go?"

"I have seven ships upon the sea—
    The eighth brought me to land—
With four-and-twenty bold mariners,
    And music on every hand."

She has taken up her two little babes,
    Kissed them baith cheek and chin: 30
"O fair ye weel, my ain two babes,
    For I'll never see you again."

She set her foot upon the ship,
    No mariners could she behold;
But the sails were o' the taffetie,
    And the masts o' the beaten gold.

She had not sailed a league, a league,
    A league but barely three,
When dismal grew his countenance,
    And drumlie grew his ee.   40

They had not sailed a league, a league,
    A league but barely three,
Until she espied his cloven foot,
    And she wept right bitterly.

"O hold your tongue of your weeping," says he,
    "Of your weeping now let me be;
I will show you how the lilies grow
    On the banks of Italy."

"O what hills are yon, yon pleasant hills,
    That the sun shines sweetly on?"   50
"O yon are the hills of heaven," he said,
    "Where you will never win."

30. baith: both. 31. fair ye weel: farewell; ain: own. 35. taffetie: taffeta, a silk cloth. 40. drumlie: perturbed.

" O whaten a mountain is yon," she said,
    "All so dreary wi' frost and snow?"
"O yon is the mountain of hell," he cried,
    "Where you and I will go."

He strack the tap-mast wi' his hand,
    The fore-mast wi' his knee,
And he brake that gallant ship in twain,
60   And sank her in the sea.

ANONYMOUS (date uncertain)

THE CHERRY-TREE CAROL

Joseph was an old man,
    And an old man was he,
When he wedded Mary
    In the land of Galilee.

Joseph and Mary walked
    Through an orchard good,
Where was cherries and berries,
    So red as any blood.

Joseph and Mary walked
10   Through an orchard green,
Where was berries and cherries,
    As thick as might be seen.

O then bespoke Mary,
    So meek and so mild:
"Pluck me one cherry, Joseph,
    For I am with child."

53. **whaten:** what sort of.

O then bespoke Joseph,
    With words most unkind:
"Let him pluck thee a cherry
    That brought thee with child!"   20

O then bespoke the babe,
    Within his mother's womb:
"Bow down, then, the tallest tree,
    For my mother to have some."

Then bowed down the highest tree
    Unto his mother's hand;
Then she cried, "See, Joseph,
    I have cherries at command!"

O then bespoke Joseph:
    "I have done Mary wrong;   30
But cheer up, my dearest,
    And be not cast down."

Then Mary plucked a cherry,
    As red as the blood;
Then Mary went home,
    With her heavy load.

Then Mary took her babe,
    And sat him on her knee,
Saying, "My dear son, tell me
    What this world will be."   40

"O I shall be as dead, mother,
    As the stones in the wall;
O the stones in the streets, mother,
    Shall mourn for me all.

"Upon Easter-day, mother,
    My uprising shall be;
O the sun and the moon, mother,
    Shall both rise with me."

GEOFFREY CHAUCER (1343?–1400)

THE FRIAR'S TALE

Whilom ther was dwellynge in my contree
An erchedekene, a man of heigh degree,
That boldely dide execucioun
In punysshynge of fornicacioun,
Of wicchecraft, and eek of bawderye,
Of diffamacioun, and avowtrye,
Of chirche reves, and of testamentz,
Of contractes and of lakke of sacramentz,
Of usure, and of symonye also.
10 But certes, lecchours dide he grettest wo;
They sholde syngen if that they were hent;
And smale tytheres weren foule yshent,
If any persoun wolde upon hem pleyne.
Ther myghte asterte hym no pecunyal peyne.
For smale tithes and for smal offrynge
He made the peple pitously to synge.
For er the bisshop caughte hem with his hook,
They weren in the erchedeknes book.
Thanne hadde he, thurgh his jurisdiccioun,
20 Power to doon on hem correccioun.
He hadde a somonour redy to his hond;
A slyer boye nas noon in Engelond;
For subtilly he hadde his espiaille,
That taughte hym wel wher that hym myghte availle.
He koude spare of lecchours oon or two,
To techen hym to foure and twenty mo.

Note. *The Canterbury Tales* is a group of narrative poems within the dramatic frame-
work of a springtime pilgrimage to Canterbury. Among the pilgrims are a friar and a
summoner: the former a member of one of the begging religious orders, the latter a petty
officer of the religious diocese who "summoned" people to the church court for ecclesiasti-
cal offenses. Friars and summoners were traditionally at odds with each other, and

THE FRIAR'S TALE

Once there was dwelling in my district
an archdeacon, a man of high rank,
who boldly executed his duty
in the punishing of fornication,
of witchcraft, and of pimping too,
of slander and adultery,
of church robberies and breaches of wills
and of contracts, and neglect of sacraments,
(punishing) also usury and simony.
But indeed, he caused the greatest grief to lechers;   10
They sure had to sing (a sad song) if they were caught!
And people overdue in their church taxes were cruelly punished
if any parson wanted to complain about them.
No monetary penalty could escape him (the archdeacon).
For too-small tithes and church offerings,
he made the people sing piteously.
For before the bishop caught them with his hook,
they were (recorded) in the archdeacon's book.
He had, within his jurisdiction,
the power to execute punishment upon them.   20
He had a summoner ready to hand;
there was no slicker rascal in England;
for he craftily maintained a body of spies
that informed him as to what might advantage him.
He could spare one or two lechers (as stool pigeons)
to lead him to twenty-four more.

Chaucer's pair take turns telling stories at each other's expense. *The Friar's Tale* launches
this dramatic exchange.

17. **hook:** the bishop's staff has a hook on the end, like a shepherd's crook.

For thogh this Somonour wood were as an hare,
To telle his harlotrye I wol nat spare;
For we been out of his correccioun.
30   They han of us no jurisdiccioun,
Ne nevere shullen, terme of alle hir lyves.—
     "Peter! so been the wommen of the styves,"
Quod the Somonour, "yput out of my cure!"
     "Pees! with myschance and with mysaventure!"
Thus seyde oure Hoost, "and lat hym telle his tale.
Now telleth forth, thogh that the Somonour gale;
Ne spareth nat, myn owene maister deere."—
     This false theef, this somonour, quod the Frere,
Hadde alwey bawdes redy to his hond,
40   As any hauk to lure in Engelond,
That tolde hym al the secree that they knewe;
For hire acqueyntance was nat come of newe.
They weren his approwours prively.
He took hymself a greet profit therby;
His maister knew nat alwey what he wan.
Withouten mandement a lewed man
He koude somne, on peyne of Cristes curs,
And they were glade for to fille his purs,
And make hym grete feestes atte nale.
50   And right as Judas hadde purses smale,
And was a theef, right swich a theef was he;
His maister hadde but half his duetee.
He was, if I shal yeven hym his laude,
A theef, and eek a somnour, and a baude.
He hadde eek wenches at his retenue,
That, wheither that sir Robert or sir Huwe,
Or Jakke, or Rauf, or whoso that it were
That lay by hem, they tolde it in his ere.
Thus was the wenche and he of oon assent;
60   And he wolde fecche a feyned mandement,
And somne hem to chapitre bothe two,
And pile the man, and lete the wenche go.
Thanne wolde he seye, "Freend, I shal for thy sake
Do striken hire out of oure lettres blake;
Thee thar namoore as in this cas travaille.
I am thy freend, ther I thee may availle."
Certeyn he knew of briberyes mo

27. this Somonour: the summoner who is a pilgrim in the dramatic framework of
the *Tales* and who breaks in on this tale at line 32. 35. oure Hoost: the landlord of
the Tabard Inn, where the pilgrims of the *Tales* had assembled. He had proposed a story-

For even if this Summoner (here) gets as mad as a hare,
I won't hesitate to tell of his deviltry;
for we're beyond his authority to punish.
They (summoners) have no jurisdiction over us,   30
nor ever shall while they live.——
    "By St. Peter! so are the women in the brothels,"
quoth the Summoner, "beyond my province!"
    "Peace! —or may you have bad luck and misfortune!"
said our Host, "and let him tell his story.
Now tell on, however much the Summoner may protest;
spare nothing, my own dear master."——
    This false thief, this summoner, quoth the Friar,
always had pimps ready at hand,
(who came to his call) as any hawk in England (came) to the lure,   40
who told him all the secrets that they knew;
for their acquaintance (with him) was not of recent vintage.
They were his agents, secretly.
He made for himself great profit thereby;
his master (the archdeacon) did not always know what he had gained.
Without a legal writ, he knew how to summon
an ignorant man, on threat of excommunication;
and they were happy to fill his purse
and provide him great dinners at the ale-house.
And just as Judas was treasurer of (the Apostles') small funds   50
and was a thief, just such a thief was he;
his master got only half his due amount.
He was, if I am to give him his due praise,
a thief, and also a summoner, and also a pimp.
He had wenches in his employment too,
who, whether Sir Robert, Sir Hugh,
Jack, Ralph, or whoever it might be
who slept with them, they whispered it (who it was) in his ear.
The wench and he were thus in cahoots;
and he would get a forged legal writ   60
and summon them both to court,
and fleece the man and let the woman go.
Then he would say (to the man), "Friend, for your sake
I will have her (name) stricken out of our records;
You needn't trouble yourself any further in the matter.
I'm your friend, wherever I can help you."
Sure, he knew more about extortions

telling game to pass the time *en route* to Canterbury, and had accompanied the pilgrims
to judge the stories. **37. myn . . . deere:** a polite form of address.

Than possible is to telle in yeres two.
For in this world nys dogge for the bowe
That kan an hurt deer from an hool y-knowe
Bet than this somnour knew a sly lecchour,
Or an avowtier, or a paramour.
And for that was the fruyt of all his rente,
Therfore on it he sette al his entente.
      And so bifel that ones on a day
This somnour, evere waityng on his pray,
Rood for to somne an old wydwe, a ribibe,
Feynynge a cause, for he wolde brybe.
And happed that he saugh bifore hym ryde
A gay yeman, under a forest syde.
A bowe he bar, and arwes brighte and kene;
He hadde upon a courtepy of grene,
An hat upon his heed with frenges blake.
      "Sire," quod this somnour, "hayl, and wel atake!"
"Welcome," quod he, "and every good felawe!
Wher rydestow, under this grene-wode shawe?"
Seyde this yeman, "wiltow fer to day?"
      This somnour hym answerde and seyde, "Nay;
Heere faste by," quod he, "is myn entente
To ryden, for to reysen up a rente
That longeth to my lordes duetee."
      "Artow thanne a bailly?" "Ye," quod he.
He dorste nat, for verray filthe and shame
Seye that he was a somonour, for the name.
      "Depardieux," quod this yeman, "deere broother,
Thou art a bailly, and I am another.
I am unknowen as in this contree;
Of thyn aqueyntance I wolde praye thee,
And eek of bretherhede, if that yow leste.
I have gold and silver in my cheste;
If that thee happe to comen in oure shire,
Al shal be thyn, right as thou wolt desire."
      "Grantmercy," quod this somonour, "by my feith!"
Everych in ootheres hand his trouthe leith,
For to be sworne bretheren til they deye.
In daliance they ryden forth and pleye.
      This somonour, which that was as ful of jangles,
As ful of venym been thise waryangles,
And evere enqueryng upon every thyng,

70

80

90

100

80. yeman: a small landowner. 92. bailly: estate manager.

than could be told in two years.
For there is no hunting hound in this world
that knows how to tell a wounded deer from a sound one   70
better than this summoner could sniff out a sly lecher
or an adulterer or a loose woman.
And because this (practice) was the major source of his income,
he devoted all his efforts to it.
   It so happened that one day
this summoner, always alert for a victim,
rode to summon an old widow, an old hag,
pretending he had a reason, because he wanted to practice a bit of extortion.
And it happened that he saw riding before him
a carefree yeoman, at the edge of the forest.   80
He carried a bow and bright, sharp arrows;
he wore a short green coat,
and on his head a hat with black fringes.
   "Sir," said this summoner, "Hail, and well-met!"
"Welcome," quoth he, "and every good fellow!
Where do you ride, in this forest grove?"
said this yeoman, "Will you (go) far today?"
   The summoner answered him and said, "No;
Close by here," quoth he, "it is my intention
to ride, to collect a rent   90
that is owed to my lord."
   "Are you then a bailiff?" "Yes," quoth he.
He dared not, for the deep filth and shame (of it),
say that he was a summoner, on account of the (implications of the) name.
   "By God," said this yeoman, "dear brother,
you are a bailiff and I am one too.
I am not known in this district;
I'd like to get to know you better,
and become a brother to you, if you so wish.
I have gold and silver in my chest;   100
if you should happen to come to our county,
all will be yours, just as you desire."
   "Many thanks," said this summoner, "by my faith!"
Each lays his hand in the other's,
to be sworn brothers till they should die.
They ride forth making pleasant and sociable conversation.
   This summoner, who was as full of idle chatter
as butcher-birds are full of spite
and was constantly asking questions about everything,

110   "Brother," quod he, "where is now youre dwellyng
Another day if that I sholde yow seche?"
This yeman hym answerde in softe speche,
    "Brother," quod he, "fer in the north contree,
Where-as I hope som tyme I shal thee see.
Er we departe, I shal thee so wel wisse
That of myn hous ne shaltow nevere mysse."
    "Now, brother," quod this somonour, "I yow preye,
Teche me, whil that we ryden by the weye,
Syn that ye been a baillif as am I,
120   Som subtiltee, and tel me feithfully
In myn office how that I may moost wynne;
And spareth nat for conscience ne synne,
But as my brother tel me, how do ye."
    "Now, by my trouthe, brother deere," seyde he,
"As I shal tellen thee a feithful tale,
My wages been ful streite and ful smale.
My lord is hard to me and daungerous,
And myn office is ful laborous,
And therfore by extorcions I lyve.
130   For sothe, I take al that men wol me yive.
Algate, by sleyghte or by violence,
Fro yeer to yeer I wynne al my dispence.
I kan no bettre telle, feithfully."
    "Now certes," quod this somonour, "so fare I.
I spare nat to taken, God it woot,
But if it be to hevy or to hoot.
What I may gete in conseil prively,
No maner conscience of that have I.
Nere myn extorcioun, I myghte nat lyven,
140   Ne of swiche japes wol I nat be shryven.
Stomak ne conscience ne knowe I noon;
I shrewe thise shrifte-fadres everychoon.
Wel be we met, by God and by Seint Jame!
But, leeve brother, tel me thanne thy name,"
Quod this somonour. In this meene while
This yeman gan a litel for to symle.
    "Brother," quod he, "wiltow that I thee telle?
I am a feend; my dwellyng is in helle,
And heere I ryde about my purchasyng,
150   To wite where men wol yeve me any thyng.

113. **north contree**: traditionally associated with hell and devils.

said, "Brother, where is your home   110
in case I should be looking for you some other day?"
The yeoman answered him courteously,
   "Brother," said he, "far in the north country,
where I hope I'll see you some time.
Before we part, I'll give you such good directions
that you won't be able to miss my house."
   "Now, brother," said this summoner, "I beg you
teach me, as we ride along the way,
since you're a bailiff as I am,
some trick, and tell me truly   120
how I may gain most in my job;
and don't stint out of conscience or (sense of) sin,
but tell me as a brother, how you do it."
   "Now, by my troth, dear brother," said he,
I'll tell you a true story:
my income is very limited and small.
My master is hard on me and demanding,
and my job is very laborious,
and therefore I make my living by extortions.
Truly, I take all that men will give me.   130
Always, by trickery or by force
from year to year I get what I spend.
I don't know how to put it any better, truly."
   "Now really," quoth this summoner, "so do I.
I stint not, God knows, in taking anything
unless it's too heavy or too hot.
Whatever I can get by secret dealings,
I have no conscience about.
If it were not for my extortion, I could not live,
and I won't repent of such tricks.   40
I have neither a (weak) stomach nor a conscience;
I curse all these father-confessors.
We're well met, by God and St. James!
But, dear brother, tell me your name,"
quoth this summoner. Meanwhile
this yeoman smiled a little.
   "Brother," he said, "do you want me to tell you?
I am a devil; my dwelling is in hell,
and here am I riding on business,
to find out whether men will give me anything.   150

My purchas is th' effect of al my rente.
Looke how thou rydest for the same entente
To wynne good, thou rekkest nevere how,
Right so fare I, for ryde wolde I now
Unto the worldes ende for a preye."
        "A!" quod this somonour, *"benedicite!* what sey ye?
I wende ye were a yeman trewely.
Ye han a mannes shap as wel as I;
Han ye a figure thanne determinat
160 In helle, ther ye been in youre estat?"
        "Nay, certeinly," quod he, "ther have we noon;
But whan us liketh, we kan take us oon,
Or elles make yow seme we been shape
Somtyme lyk a man, or lyk an ape,
Or lyk an angel kan I ryde or go.
It is no wonder thyng thogh it be so;
A lowsy jogelour kan deceyve thee,
And pardee, yet kan I moore craft than he."
        "Why," quod this somonour, "ryde ye thanne or goon
170 In sondry shap, and nat alwey in oon?"
        "For we," quod he, "wol us swiche formes make
As moost able is oure preyes for to take."
        "What maketh yow to han al this labour?"
        "Ful many a cause, levee sire somonour,"
Seyde this feend, "but alle thyng hath tyme.
The day is short, and it is passed pryme,
And yet ne wan I nothyng in this day.
I wol entende to wynnyng, if I may,
And nat entende oure wittes to declare.
180 For, brother myn, thy wit is al to bare
To understonde, althogh I tolde hem thee.
But, for thou axest why labouren we—
For somtyme we been Goddes instrumentz,
And meenes to doon his comandementz,
Whan that hym list, upon his creatures,
In divers art and in diverse figures.
Withouten hym we have no myght, certayn,
If that hym list to stonden ther-agayn.
And somtyme, at oure prayere, han we leve
190 Oonly the body and nat the soule greve;
Witnesse on Job, whom that we diden wo.
And somtyme han we myght of bothe two,
This is to seyn, of soule and body eke.

My business profits are the whole of my income.
See, the way you are riding for the same purpose
to make profit, you care not how,—
just so do I, for now I would ride
to the end of the world for a victim."
　　"What!" said the summoner, "bless me, what are you saying?
I thought you were really a yeoman.
You have a man's form, just like me;
have you a definite shape, then,
in hell, where you are in your natural condition?"   160
　　"Certainly not," said he, "we have none there;
but when it pleases us we can take one for ourselves,
or else make it appear to you that we are shaped
sometimes like a man, or like an ape;
or I can ride or walk like an angel.
It's no miracle that this is the case:
a lousy juggler can deceive you,
and, by God, I have more skill than he."
　　"Why," said the summoner, "do you then ride or walk
in various shapes, and not always in one?"   170
　　"Because," he said, "we assume such forms
as best enable us to catch our prey."
　　"Why do you take all this trouble?"
　　"For many reasons, dear Sir Summoner,"
said this devil, "but there is a time for all things.
The day is short, and it is past nine o'clock,
and as yet I haven't made any profit today.
I will devote myself to profit, if I can,
and don't intend to reveal our (the devils') ploys.
For, my brother, your intelligence is all too mean   180
to understand, even though I told them to you.
But, since you ask why we work (so hard)—
sometimes we are God's agents
and the means for carrying out His commands,
when it pleases Him, upon His creatures,
by various devices and in various shapes.
Without Him we have no power, to be sure,
if it pleases Him to oppose us.
And sometimes, at our request, we have permission
to afflict only the body and not the soul;   190
take Job, for example, to whom we brought grief.
And sometimes we have power over both,
this is to say, soul and body.

And somtyme be we suffred for to seke
Upon a man, and doon his soule unreste,
And nat his body, and al is for the beste.
Whan he withstandeth oure temptacioun,
It is a cause of his savacioun,
Al be it that it was nat oure entente
200   He sholde be sauf, but that we wolde hym hente.
And somtyme be we servant unto man,
As to the erchebisshop Seint Dunstan,
And to the apostles servant eek was I."
    "Yet tel me," quod the somonour, "feithfully,
Make ye yow newe bodies thus alway
Of elementz?" The feend answerde, "Nay.
Somtyme we feyne, and somtyme we aryse
With dede bodyes, in ful sondry wyse,
And speke as renably and faire and wel
210   As to the Phitonissa dide Samuel.
(And yet wol som men seye it was nat he;
I do no fors of youre dyvynytee.)
But o thyng warne I thee, I wol nat jape,—
Thou wolt algates wite how we been shape;
Thou shalt herafterwardes, my brother deere,
Come there thee nedeth nat of me to leere,
For thou shalt, by thyn owene experience,
Konne in a chayer rede of this sentence
Bet than Virgile, while he was on lyve,
220   Or Dant also. Now lat us ryde blyve,
For I wole holde compaignye with thee
Til it be so that thou forsake me."
    "Nay," quod this somonour, "that shal nat bityde!
I am a yeman, knowen is ful wyde;
My trouthe wol I holde, as in this cas.
For though thou were the devel Sathanas,
My trouthe wol I holde to my brother,
As I am sworn, and ech of us til oother,
For to be trewe brother in this cas;

---

202. **Seint Dunstan:** 10th-century Archbishop of Canterbury, who according to legend made the devil serve him. 210. Phitonissa: pythoness, witch. Here the Witch of Endor, who, at Saul's request, invoked Samuel, who foretold Saul's defeat at the hands of the Philistines (I Samuel xxviii. 7-19). 211. There is some dispute about whether

And sometimes we are permitted to seek
out a man and cause his soul unrest,
and not his body, and everything is for the best:
when he withstands our temptation,
it brings about his salvation,
although it was not our intention
that he should be saved, but that we should get hold of him.   200
And sometimes we are servants to a man,
as to the Archbishop St. Dunstan;
and to the Apostles, I was also a servant."
   "Yet tell me," said the summoner, "truly,
do you make new bodies for yourselves always
out of the elements?" The devil answered, "No.
Sometimes we assume a disguise, and sometimes we arise
in dead bodies, in various ways,
and speak as reasonably and properly and well
as Samuel did to the Witch (of Endor).   210
(And yet some men will say it was not he [Samuel];
but I'm not interested in your theology.)
But I'll warn you of one thing, (and here) I'm not kidding—
you will at any rate know how we are shaped;
you will hereafter, my dear brother,
go where you won't need to learn from me;
for you will, by your own experience,
know better how to lecture on this subject
than Virgil, when he was alive,
or Dante either. Now let us ride quickly,   220
for I wish to keep company with you
until it happen that you forsake me."
   "No," said the summoner, "that will never happen!
I am a yeoman—everybody knows that;
I'll keep my agreement in this matter.
For even if you were the devil Satan (himself),
I would keep my pledge to my brother,
as I have sworn, and each of us (has sworn) to the other,
to be a true brother in this business;

Samuel actually did appear. 219. **Virgile:** Virgil, Roman poet of the first century B.C.,
whose hero, Aeneas, in Book VI of the *Aeneid,* visited the underworld. 220. **Dant:**
Dante, 13th-century Italian poet, whose *Divine Comedy* pictures the poet himself jour-
neying through hell.

230 And bothe we goon abouten oure purchas.
  Taak thou thy part, what that men wol thee yive,
  And I shal myn; thus may we bothe lyve.
  And if that any of us have moore than oother,
  Lat hym be trewe, and parte it with his brother."
   "I graunte," quod the devel, "by my fey."
  And with that word they ryden forth hir wey.
  And right at the entryng of the townes ende,
  To which this somonour shoop hym for to wende,
  They saugh a cart that charged was with hey,
240 Which that a cartere droof forth in his wey.
  Deep was the wey, for which the carte stood.
  The cartere smoot, and cryde as he were wood,
  "Hayt, Brok! hayt, Scot! what spare ye for the stones?
  The feend," quod he, "yow fecche, body and bones,
  As ferforthly as evere were ye foled,
  So muche wo as I have with yow tholed!
  The devel have al, bothe hors and cart and hey!"
   This somonour seyde, "Heere shal we have a pley."
  And neer the feend he drough, as noght ne were,
250 Full prively, and rowned in his ere:
  "Herkne, my brother, herkne, by thy feith!
  Herestow nat how that the cartere seith?
  Hent it anon, for he hath yeve it thee,
  Bothe hey and cart, and eek his caples thre."
   "Nay," quod the devel, "God woot, never a deel!
  It is nat his entente, trust me weel.
  Axe hym thyself, if thou nat trowest me;
  Or elles stynt a while, and thou shalt see."
   This cartere thakketh his hors upon the croupe,
260 And they bigonne to drawen and to stoupe.
  "Heyt! now," quod he, "ther Jhesu Crist yow blesse,
  And al his handwerk, bothe moore and lesse!
  That was wel twight, myn owene lyard boy.
  I pray God save thee, and Seinte Loy!
  Now is my cart out of the slow, pardee!"
   "Lo, brother," quod the feend, "what tolde I thee?
  Heere may ye se, myn owene deere brother,
  The carl spak o thing, but he thoghte another.
  Lat us go forth abouten oure viage;
270 Heere wynne I nothyng upon cariage."

264. Seinte Loy: St. Eligius, here invoked as the patron saint of carriers.

and let us both go about our affairs.   230
You take your part, whatever men will give you,
and I'll take (mine); thus may we both prosper.
And if either gets more than the other,
let him be faithful and divide it with his brother."
    "I agree," quoth the devil, "by my faith."
And with that word they rode forth on their way.
And just at the entrance to the town
to which the summoner had intended to go,
they saw a cart loaded with hay
which a carter was driving along on the track.   240
The track was deep (in mud), by reason of which the cart stood still.
The carter struck (the horses) and cried as if he were mad,
    "Up, Brock! Up, Scot! why d'you let the rocks hold you up?
May the devil," he said, "fetch you, body and bones,
as surely as ever you were foaled,
so much grief have I endured on your account!
The devil take all, horses, cart, and hay!"
    The summoner said (to himself), "Here we'll have some sport."
And he drew near the devil, as if nothing were happening,
and very quietly whispered in his ear: 250
"Listen, my brother, listen, by your faith,
don't you hear what the carter is saying?
Take it at once, for he has given it you,
both hay and cart, and also his three carthorses."
    "No," said the devil, "God knows, not one of them!
It is not his intention, believe me.
Ask him yourself, if you don't trust me;
or else wait a bit and you'll see."
    The carter whacks his horses on the rump,
and they begin to pull and to strain.   260
"Up! now," quoth he, "may Jesus Christ bless you,
and all His handiwork, both great and small!
That was well pulled, my own gray boy.
God and St. Loy save you!
Now my cart is out of the mud, by God!"
    "See, brother," said the devil, "what did I tell you?
Here you can see, my own dear brother,
the fellow spoke one thing, but he thought another.
Let us continue on our journey;
here I'm getting nothing in the way of returns."   270

Whan that they coomen somwhat out of towne,
This somonour to his brother gan to rowne:
"Brother," quod he, "heere woneth an old rebekke,
That hadde almoost as lief to lese hire nekke
As for to yeve a peny of hir good.
I wole han twelf pens, though that she be wood,
Or I wol sompne hire unto oure office;
And yet, God woot, of hire knowe I no vice.
But for thou kanst nat, as in this contree,
280 Wynne thy cost, taak heer ensample of me."
      This somonour clappeth at the wydwes gate.
"Com out," quod he, "thou olde virytrate!
I trowe thou hast som frere or preest with thee."
      "Who clappeth?" seyde this wyf, *"benedicitee!*
God save you, sire, what is youre sweete wille?"
      "I have," quod he, "of somonce here a bille;
Up peyne of cursyng, looke that thou be
To-morn bifore the erchedeknes knee,
T'answere to the court of certeyn thynges."
290   "Now, Lord," quod she, "Crist Jhesu, kyng of kynges,
So wisly helpe me, as I ne may.
I have been syk, and that ful many a day.
I may nat go so fer," quod she, "ne ryde,
But I be deed, so priketh it in my syde.
May I nat axe a libel, sire somonour,
And answere there by my procuratour
To swich thyng as men wole opposen me?"
      "Yis," quod this somonour, "pay anon, lat se,
Twelf pens to me, and I wol thee acquite.
300 I shal no profit han therby but lite;
My maister hath the profit, and nat I.
Com of, and lat me ryden hastily;
Yif me twelf pens, I may no lenger tarye."
      "Twelf pens!" quod she, "now, lady Seinte Marie
So wisly help me out of care and synne,
This wyde world thogh that I sholde wynne,
Ne have I nat twelf pens withinne myn hoold.
Ye knowen wel that I am povre and oold;
Kithe youre almesse on me, povre wrecche."
310   "Nay thanne," quod he, "the foule feend me fecche

When they had come a little beyond the town,
the summoner whispered to his brother:
"Brother," quoth he, "here dwells an old hag,
who would almost rather lose her neck
than give a penny of her money.
I will get twelve pence (from her), however mad she may be,
or else I will summon her to our court;
and yet, God knows, I am aware of no evil she has done.
But since you seem unable, in this district,
to cover your costs, learn from my example here." 280
    The summoner knocks at the widow's gate.
"Come out," said he, "you old reprobate!
I bet you've got some friar or priest (in there) with you."
    "Who knocks?" said this woman, "bless me!
God save you, sir, what is your sweet will?"
    "I have," he said, "a writ of summons here:
upon pain of excommunication, see that you appear
before the archdeacon tomorrow,
to answer for certain things to the court."
    "Now," said she, "Lord Jesus Christ, King of Kings, 290
help me kindly, since I am unable (to help myself).
I have been sick, for many a day.
I can't walk that far," she said, "nor ride,
or it'll kill me, my side pains so.
May I not request a copy of the charge, Sir Summoner,
and answer there through my proxy
to such charges as people will bring against me?"
    "Yes," said the summoner, "pay right away—let's see—
twelve pence to me, and I'll acquit you.
I shall get very little profit from this; 300
my master gets the profit, not I.
Come on! let me get going;
give me twelve pence, I can't wait any longer."
    "Twelve pence!" said she, "now, Lady St. Mary
kindly help me out of trouble and sin:
even if I were to win the whole wide world,
I wouldn't have twelve pence in my house.
You know very well that I am poor and old;
show your charity to me, poor wretch (that I am)."
    "No," said he, "the foul fiend fetch me 310

If I th' excuse, though thou shul be spilt!"
    "Allas!" quod she, "God woot, I have no gilt."
    "Pay me," quod he, "or by the sweete seinte Anne,
As I wol bere awey thy newe panne
For dette which thou owest me of old.
Whan that thou madest thyn housbonde cokewold,
I payde at hoom for thy correccioun."
    "Thou lixt!" quod she, "by my savacioun,
Ne was I nevere er now, wydwe ne wyf,
320 Somoned unto youre court in al my lyf;
Ne nevere I nas but of my body trewe!
Unto the devel blak and rough of hewe
Yeve I thy body and my panne also!"
    And whan the devel herde hire cursen so
Upon hir knees, he seyde in this manere,
"Now, Mabely, myn owene mooder deere,
Is this youre wyl in ernest that ye seye?"
    "The devel," quod she, "so fecche hym er he deye,
And panne and al, but he wol hym repente!"
330   "Nay, olde stot, that is nat myn entente,"
Quod this somonour, "for to repente me
For any thyng that I have had of thee.
I wolde I hadde thy smok and every clooth!"
    "Now, brother," quod the devel, "be nat wrooth;
Thy body and this panne been myne by right.
Thou shalt with me to helle yet to-nyght,
Where thou shalt knowen of oure privetee
Moore than a maister of dyvynytee."
And with that word this foule feend hym hente;
340 Body and soule he with the devel wente
Where as that somonours han hir heritage.
And God, that maked after his ymage
Mankynde, save and gyde us, alle and some,
And leve thise somonours goode men bicome!

316. cokewold: an unfaithful wife was said to have made her husband cuckold.

if I excuse you, even though you may be destroyed!"
   "Alas," she said, "God knows, I'm not guilty."
   "Pay me," said he, "or by sweet St. Anne,
I'll take away your new pan
for the debt which you have long owed me.
When you made your husband cuckold,
I paid for your fine, back home."
   "You lie!" she said, "by my salvation,
I was never until this time, as widow or as wife,
summoned into your court in all my life;   320
I have always been faithful in body!
To the devil black and rough of hue,
I give your body, and my pan too!"
   And when the devil heard her curse so
upon her knees, he said thus:
"Now, Mabel, my dear good lady,
is what you say your real intent?"
   She said: "May the devil take him before he dies,
pan and all, unless he repent!"
   "No, old cow, it's not my intention,"   330
said the summoner, "to repent
for anything that I've had from you.
I wish I had your smock and every (other) piece of your clothes!"
   "Now, brother," said the devil, "don't be angry;
your body and this pan are mine by right.
You shall go with me to hell tonight,
where you shall know about our secrets
more than a master of divinity (knows)."
And with that word, the foul fiend grabbed him;
body and soul he went with the devil   340
where summoners have their heritage.
May God, who made after His (own) image
(all) mankind, save and guide us, one and all,
and grant that these summoners become good men!

SIR THOMAS WYATT (1503–1542)

I FIND NO PEACE

I find no peace, and all my war is done;
I fear and hope; I burn, and freeze like ice;
I fly above the wind, yet can I not arise;
And nought I have, and all the world I seize on.
That looseth nor locketh holdeth me in prison,
And holdeth me not, yet can I 'scape nowise,
Nor letteth me live, nor die, at my devise,
And yet of death it giveth none occasion.
Without eyen, I see; and without tongue, I plain;
10   I desire to perish, and yet I ask health;
I love another, and thus I hate myself;
I feed me in sorrow, and laugh in all my pain.
Likewise displeaseth me both death and life,
And my delight is causer of this strife.

MY GALLEY CHARGÈD WITH FORGETFULNESS

My galley chargèd with forgetfulness
Thorough sharp seas, in winter nights, doth pass
'Tween rock and rock; and eke mine enemy, alas,
That is my lord, steereth with cruelness—
And every oar a thought in readiness,
As though that death were light in such a case.
An endless wind doth tear the sail apace,
Of forcèd sighs and trusty fearfulness;
A rain of tears, a cloud of dark disdain,
10   Hath done the wearied cords great hinderance,
Wreathèd with error and eke with ignorance.
The stars be hid that led me to this pain;
Drownèd is reason, that should me consort,
And I remain despairing of the port.

5. **That:** that which. 6. **'scape nowise:** escape in no manner. 7. **devise:** wish.
9. **eyen:** eyes; **plain:** express pain.

Title. My ship loaded with neglect. 2. **Thorough:** through. 3. **eke:** also; **mine enemy:** love (the abstraction). 13. **consort:** convoy.

THEY FLEE FROM ME

They flee from me that sometime did me seek,
With naked foot stalking in my chamber.
I have seen them gentle, tame, and meek,
That now are wild, and do not remember
That sometime they put themselves in danger
To take bread at my hand; and now they range,
Busily seeking with a continual change.

Thanked be fortune, it hath been otherwise
Twenty times better; but once in speciàl,
In thin array, after a pleasant guise,   10
When her loose gown from her shoulders did fall,
And she me caught in her arms long and small,
Therewith all sweetly did me kiss
And softly said, "Dear heart, how like you this?"

It was no dream; I lay broad waking.
But all is turned thorough my gentleness
Into a strange fashion of forsaking;
And I have leave to go of her goodness,
And she also to use new-fangleness.
But since that I so kindèly am served,   20
I would fain know what she hath deserved.

MY LUTE, AWAKE!

My lute, awake! perform the last
Labor that thou and I shall waste,
And end that I have now begun;
For when this song is sung and past,
My lute, be still, for I have done.

10. after . . . guise: in accordance with a pleasing custom. 12. small: slender.
16. thorough: through. 19. new-fangleness: fickleness.

3. that: that which .

As to be heard where ear is none,
As lead to grave in marble stone,
My song may pierce her heart as soon.
Should we then sigh or sing or moan?
No, no, my lute, for I have done.

The rocks do not so cruelly
Repulse the waves continually
As she my suit and affectiòn,
So that I am past remedy,
Whereby my lute and I have done.

Proud of the spoil that thou hast got
Of simple hearts thorough love's shot,
By whom, unkind, thou hast them won,
Think not he hath his bow forgot,
Although my lute and I have done.

Vengeance shall fall on thy disdain,
That makest but game on earnest pain;
Think not alone under the sun
Unquit to cause thy lovers plain,
Although my lute and I have done.

Perchance thee lie withered and old
The winter nights that are so cold,
Plaining in vain unto the moon:
Thy wishes then dare not be told.
Care then who list, for I have done.

And then may chance thee to repent
The time that thou hast lost and spent
To cause thy lovers sigh and swoon:
Then shalt thou know beauty but lent,
And wish and want as I have done.

6-8. As . . . soon: my song can touch her heart as easily as sound can be heard where there is no ear, or lead (which is soft) can engrave marble. 13. suit: application (for love). 17. thorough: through. 19. bow: traditional equipment of Cupid, son of the goddess of love, with which he shoots arrows at lovers; hence shot of line 17. 22. but game on: only sport of. 24. Unquit: unrevenged; plain: (to) express pain. 26. Perchance thee lie: it may happen that you lie. 30. Care then who list: let him care then who so pleases.

Now cease, my lute, this is the last
Labor that thou and I shall waste,
And ended is that we begun.
Now is this song both sung and past;
My lute, be still, for I have done.   40

FORGET NOT YET

Forget not yet the tried intent
Of such a truth as I have meant;
My great travail so gladly spent,
    Forget not yet.

Forget not yet when first began
The weary life ye know, since when
The suit, the service none tell can,
    Forget not yet.

Forget not yet the great assays,
The cruel wrong, the scornful ways;   10
The painful patience in denays,
    Forget not yet.

Forget not yet, forget not this:
How long ago hath been, and is
The mind that never meant amiss.
    Forget not yet.

Forget not then thine own approved,
The which so long hath thee so loved,
Whose steadfast faith yet never moved;
    Forget not this.   20

38. that: that which.

1. tried intent: proved effort. 2. truth: faithfulness; meant: shown. 3. travail: labor. 7. suit: application (for love); service: the role of a servant (in love). 9. assays: attempts. 11. denays: denials. 17. approved: tested (lover)

EDMUND SPENSER (1552?–1599)

SONNETS

1

Happy ye leaves, whenas those lily hands,
Which hold my life in their dead-doing might,
Shall handle you and hold in love's soft bands,
Like captives trembling at the victor's sight.
And happy lines, on which with starry light
Those lamping eyes will deign sometimes to look
And read the sorrows of my dying sprite,
Written with tears in heart's close bleeding book.
And happy rhymes, bathed in the sacred brook
Of Helicon, whence she derivèd is,
When ye behold that angel's blessèd look,
My soul's long lackèd food, my heaven's bliss.
Leaves, lines, and rhymes, seek her to please alone,
Whom if ye please, I care for other none.

34

Like as a ship that through the ocean wide
By conduct of some star doth make her way;
Whenas a storm hath dimmed her trusty guide,
Out of her course doth wander far astray:
So I, whose star, that wont with her bright ray
Me to direct, with clouds is overcast,
Do wander now in darkness and dismay,
Through hidden perils round about me placed.
Yet hope I well that, when this storm is past,

1. **leaves:** pages. 2. **dead-doing:** death-dealing. 7. **sprite:** spirit. 10. **Helicon:** mountain in Greece, sacred to Apollo and the Muses; here also suggesting Heaven.

3. **guide:** i.e., the star. 5. **wont:** was accustomed.

My Helicè, the lodestar of my life,   10
Will shine again and look on me at last
With lovely light to clear my cloudy grief.
Till then I wander careful, comfortless,
In secret sorrow and sad pensiveness.

45

Leave, lady, in your glass of crystal clean,
Your goodly self for evermore to view;
And in myself, my inward self I mean,
Most lively-like behold your semblant true.
Within my heart, though hardly it can shew
Thing so divine to view of earthly eye,
The fair Idea of your celestial hue
And every part remains immortally.
And were it not that through your cruelty
With sorrow dimmèd and deformed it were,   10
The goodly image of your phys'nomy
Clearer than crystal would therein appear.
But if yourself in me ye plain will see,
Remove the cause by which your fair beams dark'nèd be.

79

Men call you fair, and you do credit it,
For that yourself ye daily such do see;
But the true fair, that is the gentle wit
And virtuous mind, is much more praised of me.
For all the rest, however fair it be,
Shall turn to naught and lose that glorious hue;
But only that is permanent and free
From frail corruption, that doth flesh ensue.
That is true beauty; that doth argue you

10. Helicè: the constellation of the Great Bear; lodestar: polestar, hence, guiding star. 13. careful: full of care.

4. lively-like: lifelike; semblant: image. 11. phys'nomy: face.

1. credit: believe. 2. For that: because. 7. that: refers to wit and mind of lines 3 and 4. 8. that doth flesh ensue: that (referring to corruption) follows flesh. 9. That, that: referring to wit and mind.

10   To be divine and born of heavenly seed,
       Derived from that fair Spirit from whom all true
       And perfect beauty did at first proceed.
       He only fair, and what he fair hath made;
       All other fair, like flowers, untimely fade.

EPITHALAMION

       Ye learnèd sisters, which have oftentimes
       Been to me aiding, others to adorn,
       Whom ye thought worthy of your graceful rhymes,
       That even the greatest did not greatly scorn
       To hear their names sung in your simple lays,
       But joyèd in their praise;
       And when ye list your own mishaps to mourn,
       Which death or love or fortune's wreck did raise,
       Your string could soon to sadder tenor turn,
10   And teach the woods and waters to lament
       Your doleful dreariment:
       Now lay those sorrowful complaints aside
       And, having all your heads with garland crowned,
       Help me mine own love's praises to resound,
       Ne let the same of any be envied;
       So Orpheus did for his bride.
       So I unto myself alone will sing;
       The woods shall to me answer, and my echo ring.

       Early, before the world's light-giving lamp
20   His golden beam upon the hills doth spread,
       Having dispersed the night's uncheerful damp,
       Do ye awake, and with fresh lustyhead
       Go to the bower of my belovèd love,
       My truest turtle dove.
       Bid her awake; for Hymen is awake,
       And long since ready forth his mask to move,
       With his bright tead that flames with many a flake,

Title. Wedding song or poem. 1. sisters: Muses, goddesses who are patrons of the
arts. 5. lays: poems. 9. tenor: tone. 15. Ne: nor. 16. Orpheus: famous Greek musician
whose music charmed the king of the underworld into restoring his dead bride, Eurydice.
22. lustyhead: vigor. 23. bower: chamber. 25. Hymen: god of marriage. 26. mask:
presentation with acting and music. 27. tead: torch; flake: spark.

And many a bachelor to wait on him,
In their fresh garments trim.
Bid her awake, therefore, and soon her dight,   30
For lo! the wishèd day is come at last,
That shall, for all the pains and sorrows past,
Pay to her usury of long delight.
And whilst she doth her dight,
Do ye to her of joy and solace sing,
That all the woods may answer, and your echo ring.

Bring with you all the nymphs that you can hear,
Both of the rivers and the forests green,
And of the sea that neighbors to her near,
All with gay garlands goodly well beseen.   40
And let them also with them bring in hand
Another gay garland
For my fair love, of lilies and of roses,
Bound truelove-wise with a blue silk riband;
And let them make great store of bridal posies,
And let them eke bring store of other flowers,
To deck the bridal bowers.
And let the ground whereas her foot shall tread,
For fear the stones her tender foot should wrong,
Be strewed with fragrant flowers all along,   50
And diapered like the discolored mead;
Which done, do at her chamber door await,
For she will waken straight:
The whiles do ye this song unto her sing,
The woods shall to you answer, and your echo ring.

Ye nymphs of Mulla, which with careful heed
The silver scaly trouts do tend full well,
And greedy pikes which use therein to feed
(Those trouts and pikes all others do excell),
And ye likewise which keep the rushy lake,   60
Where none do fishes take,
Bind up the locks the which hang scattered light,

30. soon her dight: immediately dress herself. 33. usury: interest. 40. beseen: adorned. 46. eke: also. 48. whereas: on which. 51. diapered: decorated; discolored mead: many-colored meadow. 53. straight: at once. 54. The whiles: meanwhile. 56. Mulla: name of a stream near Spenser's house in Ireland; heed: care. 58. use: are accustomed. 62. locks . . . light: that is, the nymphs' locks of hair which are unbound.

And in his waters, which your mirror make,
Behold your faces as the crystal bright,
That when you come whereas my love doth lie,
No blemish she may spy.
And eke ye lightfoot maids which keep the deer
That on the hoary mountain use to tower,
And the wild wolves, which seek them to devour,
70   With your steel darts do chase from coming near:
Be also present here,
To help to deck her, and to help to sing,
That all the woods may answer, and your echo ring.

Wake now, my love, awake! for it is time:
The rosy morn long since left Tithon's bed,
All ready to her silver coach to climb,
And Phoebus gins to show his glorious head.
Hark, how the cheerful birds do chant their lays
And carol of love's praise!
80   The merry lark her matins sings aloft;
The thrush replies; the mavis descant plays;
The ousel shrills; the ruddock warbles soft;
So goodly all agree with sweet consent
To this day's merriment.
Ah! my dear love, why do ye sleep thus long,
When meeter were that ye should now awake
To await the coming of your joyous make,
And hearken to the birds' love-learnèd song,
The dewy leaves among?
90   For they of joy and pleasance to you sing,
That all the woods them answer, and their echo ring.

My love is now awake out of her dream;
And her fair eyes, like stars that dimmèd were
With darksome cloud, now show their goodly beams
More bright than Hesperus his head doth rear.
Come now ye damsels, daughters of delight,
Help quickly her to dight.

63. his: the lake's. 72. deck: dress. 75. Tithon: Tithonus, the lover of Eos, goddess of the dawn, the rosy morn. See p. 233, note on title. 77. Phoebus: god of the sun; gins: begins. 80. matins: morning song (usually associated with church service). 81, 82. mavis, ousel, ruddock: kinds of birds. 81. descant: a soprano melody above the regular tune. 86. meeter: fitter. 87. make: mate. 95. Hesperus: evening star.

But first come ye, fair Hours—which were begot
In Jove's sweet paradise of Day and Night—
Which do the seasons of the year allot,   100
And all that ever in this world is fair
Do make and still repair;
And, ye three handmaids of the Cyprian queen,
The which do still adorn her beauty's pride,
Help to adorn my beautifulest bride.
And as ye her array, still throw between
Some graces to be seen;
And, as ye use to Venus, to her sing,
The whiles the woods shall answer, and your echo ring.

Now is my love all ready forth to come.   110
Let all the virgins therefore well await,
And ye fresh boys that tend upon her groom
Prepare yourselves, for he is coming straight.
Set all your things in seemly good array,
Fit for so joyful day,
The joyfulst day that ever sun did see.
Fair Sun, show forth thy favorable ray,
And let thy lifeful heat not fervent be,
For fear of burning her sunshiny face,
Her beauty to disgrace.   120
O fairest Phoebus, father of the Muse,
If ever I did honor thee aright,
Or sing the thing that mote thy mind delight,
Do not thy servant's simple boon refuse,
But let this day, let this one day be mine,
Let all the rest be thine.
Then I thy sovereign praises loud will sing,
That all the woods shall answer, and their echo ring.

Hark, how the minstrels gin to shrill aloud
Their merry music that resounds from far,   130
The pipe, the tabor, and the trembling croud,
That well agree withouten breach or jar.
But most of all the damsels do delight,
When they their timbrels smite,

98. Hours: Horæ, Greek goddesses in charge of the seasons, who adorned Aphrodite (the Cyprian queen, line 103) as she rose from the sea. 99. Jove: Jupiter, king of the gods in the Roman pantheon. 123. mote: might. 131. tabor: small drum; croud: primitive violin. 134. timbrels: tambourines

And thereunto do dance and carol sweet,
That all the senses they do ravish quite,
The whiles the boys run up and down the street,
Crying aloud with strong confusèd noise,
As if it were one voice.
"Hymen, io Hymen, Hymen!" they do shout,
That even to the heavens their shouting shrill
Doth reach, and all the firmament doth fill;
To which the people standing all about,
As in approvance do thereto applaud,
And loud advance her laud,
And evermore they "Hymen, Hymen," sing,
That all the woods them answer, and their echo ring.

Lo, where she comes along with portly pace
Like Phoebe from her chamber of the East,
Arising forth to run her mighty race,
Clad all in white, that seems a virgin best.
So well it her beseems that ye would ween
Some angel she had been.
Her long loose yellow locks like golden wire,
Sprinkled with pearl, and pearling flowers atween,
Do like a golden mantle her attire;
And, being crownèd with a garland green,
Seem like some maiden queen.
Her modest eyes, abashèd to behold
So many gazers as on her do stare,
Upon the lowly ground affixèd are;
Ne dare lift up her countenance too bold,
But blush to hear her praises sung so loud,
So far from being proud.
Nathless do ye still loud her praises sing,
That all the woods may answer, and your echo ring.

Tell me, ye merchants' daughters, did ye see
So fair a creature in your town before,
So sweet, so lovely, and so mild as she,
Adorned with beauty's grace and virtue's store?

144. approvance: approval. 145. laud: praise. 148. portly: dignified. 149. Phoebe: goddess of the moon. 151, 152. seems, beseems: suits; ween: think. 155. atween: between. 158. Seem: that is, make her seem. 165. Nathless: nevertheless. 170. store: abundance.

Her goodly eyes like sapphires shining bright,
Her forehead ivory white,
Her cheeks like apples which the sun hath rudded,
Her lips like cherries, charming men to bite,
Her breast like to a bowl of cream uncrudded,
Her paps like lilies budded,
Her snowy neck like to a marble tower,
And all her body like a palace fair,
Ascending up with many a stately stair
To honor's seat and chastity's sweet bower.   180
Why stand ye still, ye virgins, in amaze,
Upon her so to gaze,
Whiles ye forget your former lay to sing,
To which the woods did answer, and your echo ring?

But if ye saw that which no eyes can see,
The inward beauty of her lively sprite,
Garnished with heavenly gifts of high degree,
Much more then would ye wonder at that sight
And stand astonished, like to those which read
Medusa's mazeful head.   190
There dwells sweet love and constant chastity,
Unspotted faith and comely womanhood,
Regard of honor and mild modesty;
There virtue reigns as queen in royal throne,
And giveth laws alone,
The which the base affections do obey,
And yield their services unto her will;
Ne thought of thing uncomely ever may
Thereto approach to tempt her mind to ill.
Had ye once seen these her celestial treasures,   200
And unrevealèd pleasures,
Then would ye wonder and her praises sing,
That all the woods should answer, and your echo ring.

Open the temple gates unto my love,
Open them wide that she may enter in,
And all the posts adorn as doth behove,
And all the pillars deck with garlands trim

173. rudded: reddened. 175. uncrudded: uncurdled. 176. paps: nipples. 186. sprite: spirit. 190. Medusa: a monster in Greek mythology whose head bore snakes (hence maze-ful) instead of hair; anyone looking at her was turned to stone. 196. base affections: passions. 206. as doth behove: as is fitting.

For to receive this saint with honor due,
That cometh in to you.
210 With trembling steps and humble reverence
She cometh in before th'Almighty's view.
Of her, ye virgins, learn obedience,
When so ye come into those holy places,
To humble your proud faces.
Bring her up to the high altar, that she may
The sacred ceremonies there partake,
The which do endless matrimony make;
And let the roaring organs loudly play
The praises of the Lord in lively notes,
220 The whiles with hollow throats
The choristers the joyous anthem sing,
That all the woods may answer, and their echo ring.

Behold, whiles she before the altar stands,
Hearing the holy priest that to her speaks
And blesseth her with his two happy hands,
How red roses flush up in her cheeks,
And the pure snow with goodly vermeil stain
Like crimson dyed in grain,
That even the angels, which continually
230 About the sacred altar do remain,
Forget their service and about her fly,
Oft peeping in her face, that seems more fair
The more they on it stare.
But her sad eyes, still fastened on the ground,
Are governèd with goodly modesty
That suffers not one look to glance awry,
Which may let in a little thought unsound.
Why blush ye, love, to give to me your hand,
The pledge of all our band?
240 Sing, ye sweet angels, Alleluya sing,
That all the woods may answer, and your echo ring.

Now all is done; bring home the bride again,
Bring home the triumph of our victory,
Bring home with you the glory of her gain;
With joyance bring her and with jollity.
Never had man more joyful day than this,

227. **vermeil:** vermilion. 228. **dyed in grain:** stained with fast color. 234. **sad:** modest. 239. **band:** bond. 244. **of her gain:** of gaining her.

Whom heaven would heap with bliss.
Make feast therefore now all this livelong day;
This day forever to me holy is.
Pour out the wine without restraint or stay,   250
Pour not by cups, but by the bellyfull,
Pour out to all that wull,
And sprinkle all the posts and walls with wine,
That they may sweat, and drunken be withal.
Crown ye god Bacchus with a coronal,
And Hymen also crown with wreaths of vine;
And let the Graces dance unto the rest,
For they can do it best:
The whiles the maidens do their carol sing,
To which the woods shall answer, and their echo ring.   260

Ring ye the bells, ye young men of the town,
And leave your wonted labors for this day.
This day is holy; do ye write it down,
That ye forever it remember may.
This day the sun is in his chiefest height
With Barnaby the bright,
From whence declining daily by degrees,
He somewhat loseth of his heat and light,
When once the Crab behind his back he sees.
But for this time it ill ordainèd was   270
To choose the longest day in all the year,
And shortest night, when longest fitter were;
Yet never day so long but late would pass.
Ring ye the bells, to make it wear away,
And bonfires make all day,
And dance about them, and about them sing:
That all the woods may answer, and your echo ring.

Ah when will this long weary day have end,
And lend me leave to come unto my love?
How slowly do the hours their numbers spend!   280
How slowly does sad Time his feathers move!
Haste thee, O fairest planet, to thy home

252. **wull:** will. 255. **Bacchus:** god of wine; **coronal:** garland of flowers. 257. **Graces:** three daughters of Zeus, goddesses who add delight to the lives of gods and men; **unto:** on behalf of. 262. **wonted:** usual. 265-266. **This day . . . bright:** the summer solstice, also St. Barnabas' Day. 269. **Crab:** the sun loses some of its heat after it has passed through the zodiacal sign of the Crab, Cancer. 273. **late:** sooner or later. 282. **planet:** sun.

Within the western foam;
Thy tired steeds long since have need of rest.
Long though it be, at last I see it gloom,
And the bright evening star with golden crest
Appear out of the East.
Fair child of beauty, glorious lamp of love,
That all the host of heaven in ranks dost lead,
290   And guidest lovers through the nightès dread,
How cheerfully thou lookest from above,
And seem'st to laugh atween thy twinkling light,
As joying in the sight
Of these glad many, which for joy do sing,
That all the woods them answer, and their echo ring!

Now cease, ye damsels, your delights forepast;
Enough is it that all the day was yours.
Now day is done, and night is nighing fast;
Now bring the bride into the bridal bowers.
300   The night is come, now soon her disarray,
And in her bed her lay;
Lay her in lilies and in violets,
And silken curtains over her display,
And odored sheets, and arras coverlets.
Behold how goodly my fair love does lie
In proud humility:
Like unto Maia, whenas Jove her took
In Tempe, lying on the flowery grass,
'Twixt sleep and wake, after she weary was
310   With bathing in the Acidalian brook.
Now it is night, ye damsels may be gone,
And leave my love alone;
And leave likewise your former lay to sing:
The woods no more shall answer, nor your echo ring.

Now welcome night, thou night so long expected,
That long day's labor dost at last defray,
And all my cares, which cruel Love collected,
Hast summed in one, and cancellèd for aye.
Spread thy broad wing over my love and me,
320   That no man may us see;

285. **it gloom:** it becoming dark. 296. **delights forepast:** bygone delights. 298. **nighing:** coming near. 304. **arras:** tapestried coverlets. 307-310. Maia was a maiden whom Jove seduced in the manner suggested in these lines. Their son was Hermes. 316. **defray:** pay for.

And in thy sable mantle us enwrap,
From fear of peril and foul horror free.
Let no false treason seek us to entrap,
Nor any dread disquiet once annoy
The safety of our joy.
But let the night be calm and quietsome,
Without tempestuous storms or sad affray:
Like as when Jove with fair Alcmena lay,
When he begot the great Tirynthian groom;
Or like as when he with thyself did lie,   330
And begot Majesty.
And let the maids and young men cease to sing;
Ne let the woods them answer, nor their echo ring.

Let no lamenting cries nor doleful tears
Be heard all night within nor yet without;
Ne let false whispers, breeding hidden fears,
Break gentle sleep with misconceivèd doubt.
Let no deluding dreams nor dreadful sights
Make sudden sad affrights;
Ne let house-fires, nor lightning's helpless harms, 340
Ne let the Pouke, nor other evil sprites,
Ne let mischievous witches with their charms,
Ne let hobgoblins, names whose sense we see not,
Fray us with things that be not.
Let not the screech-owl nor the stork be heard,
Nor the night raven that still deadly yells,
Nor damnèd ghosts called up with mighty spells,
Nor grisly vultures make us once affeared.
Ne let the unpleasant choir of frogs still croaking
Make us to wish their choking: 350
Let none of these their dreary accents sing,
Ne let the woods them answer, nor their echo ring.

But let still Silence true night watches keep,
That sacred Peace may in assurance reign,
And timely Sleep, when it is time to sleep,
May pour his limbs forth on your pleasant plain,
The whiles an hundred little wingèd loves,
Like divers feathered doves,

327. **affray:** brawl. 328-329. **Jove . . . groom:** Jove visited Alcmena, wife of Amphitryon of Tiryns, and begot Hercules, the **Tirynthian groom.** 330. **thyself:** night. 340. **helpless:** unpreventable. 341. **Pouke:** Puck, mischievous goblin. 344. **Fray:** frighten. 358. **divers:** various.

Shall fly and flutter round about your bed,
360   And in the secret dark, that none reproves,
Their pretty stealths shall work, and snares shall spread
To filch away sweet snatches of delight,
Concealed through covert night.
Ye sons of Venus, play your sports at will,
For greedy Pleasure, careless of your toys,
Thinks more upon her paradise of joys
Than what ye do, albeit good or ill.
All night therefore attend your merry play,
For it will soon be day.
370   Now none doth hinder you, that say or sing,
Ne will the woods now answer, nor your echo ring.

Who is the same which at my window peeps?
Or whose is that fair face that shines so bright?
Is it not Cynthia, she that never sleeps,
But walks about high heaven all the night?
O fairest goddess, do thou not envỳ
My love with me to spy;
For thou likewise didst love, though now unthought,
And for a fleece of wool, which privily
380   The Latmian shepherd once unto thee brought,
His pleasures with thee wrought.
Therefore to us be favorable now;
And sith of women's labors thou hast charge,
And generation goodly dost enlarge,
Incline thy will t'effect our wishful vow,
And the chaste womb inform with timely seed,
That may our comfort breed.
Till which we cease our hopeful hap to sing,
Ne let the woods us answer, nor our echo ring.

390   And thou great Juno, which with awful might
The laws of wedlock still dost patronize,
And the religion of the faith first-plight
With sacred rites hast taught to solemnize,

374. Cynthia: goddess of the moon. 378. unthought: forgotten. 379. privily: secretly. 380. Latmian shepherd: Endymion, who was so beautiful that even the chaste Cynthia fell in love and slept with him, bearing fifty daughters. 383. sith: since. 384. generation . . . enlarge: cause reproduction. 388. hopeful hap: good fortune. 390. Juno: queen of heaven and protector of women, presiding especially over marriages; awful: awe-inspiring. 392-393, religion . . . solemnize: have taught (us) to sanctify the pledged betrothal with holy ceremonies.

And eke for comfort often callèd art
Of women in their smart:
Eternally bind thou this lovely band,
And all thy blessings unto us impart.
And thou glad Genius, in whose gentle hand
The bridal bower and genial bed remain,
Without blemish or stain,   400
And the sweet pleasures of their love's delight
With secret aid dost succor and supply
Till they bring forth the fruitful progeny:
Send us the timely fruit of this same night.
And thou fair Hebe, and thou Hymen free,
Grant that it may so be;
Till which we cease your further praise to sing,
Ne any woods shall answer, nor your echo ring.

And ye high heavens, the temple of the gods,
In which a thousand torches flaming bright   410
Do burn, that to us wretched earthly clods
In dreadful darkness lend desirèd light;
And all ye powers which in the same remain,
More than we men can feign,
Pour out your blessing on us plenteously,
And happy influence upon us rain,
That we may raise a large posterity,
Which from the earth, which they may long possess
With lasting happiness,
Up to your haughty palaces may mount,   420
And for the guerdon of their glorious merit
May heavenly tabernacles there inherit,
Of blessèd saints for to increase the count.
So let us rest, sweet love, in hope of this,
And cease till then our timely joys to sing;
The woods no more us answer, nor our echo ring.

Song, made in lieu of many ornaments
With which my love should duly have been decked,

394. **callèd art:** (you) are called upon. 395. **Of:** by; **smart:** labor pains. 398.
Genius: the protecting spirit, assigned to a man at the moment of his birth as a guardian,
to whom the bridal bed was sacred. 399. **genial:** conducive to reproduction. 401. **their:**
that is, of the bower and bed. 405. **Hebe:** goddess of youth; **free:** noble, generous.
421. **guerdon:** reward.

Which cutting off through hasty accidents
430   Ye would not stay your due time to expect,
But promised both to recompense,
Be unto her a goodly ornament,
And for short time an endless monument.

SIR WALTER RALEIGH (1552?–1618)

THE PASSIONATE MAN'S PILGRIMAGE

Give me my scallop-shell of quiet,
My staff of faith to walk upon,
My scrip of joy, immortal diet,
My bottle of salvation,
My gown of glory, hope's true gage:
And thus I'll take my pilgrimage.

Blood must be my body's balmer;
No other balm will there be given,
Whilst my soul, like a white palmer,
10   Travels to the land of heaven,
Over the silver mountains,
Where spring the nectar fountains;
And there I'll kiss
The bowl of bliss,
And drink my eternal fill
On every milken hill.
My soul will be a-dry before,
But after, it will ne'er thirst more.

And by the happy blissful way
20   More peaceful pilgrims I shall see,
That have shook off their gowns of clay
And go appareled fresh like me.

429-431. The matter to which these lines refer has never been clearly identified.

Title. Passionate: enduring, suffering. **1. scallop-shell;** badge worn by pilgrim returning from the Holy Land. **3. scrip:** small satchel. **5. gage:** security. **7. balmer:** embalmer. **9. palmer:** kind of pilgrim.

I'll bring them first
To slake their thirst,
And then to taste those nectar suckets,
At the clear wells
Where sweetness dwells,
Drawn up by saints in crystal buckets.

And when our bottles and all we
Are filled with immortality,   30
Then the holy paths we'll travel,
Strewed with rubies thick as gravel,
Ceilings of diamonds, sapphire floors,
High walls of coral, and pearl bowers.

From thence to heaven's bribeless hall
Where no corrupted voices brawl,
No conscience molten into gold,
Nor forged accusers bought and sold,
No cause deferred, nor vain-spent journey,
For there Christ is the king's attorney,   40
Who pleads for all without degrees,
And He hath angels, but no fees.
When the grand twelve million jury
Of our sins and sinful fury,
'Gainst our souls black verdicts give,
Christ pleads His death, and then we live.
Be Thou my speaker, taintless pleader,
Unblotted lawyer, true proceeder,
Thou movest salvation even for alms,
Not with a bribèd lawyer's palms.   50

And this is my eternal plea
To Him that made heaven, earth, and sea:
Seeing my flesh must die so soon,
And want a head to dine next noon,
Just at the stroke when my veins start and spread,
Set on my soul an everlasting head.
Then am I ready, like a palmer fit,
To tread those blest paths which before I writ.

25. **suckets:** preserved fruit. 34. **bowers:** rooms. 35-39: **From thence . . . journey:** allusions to contemporary corruptions and frustrations in the court. 41. **without degrees:** without distinction. 42. **angels:** pun on the coin so called, which bore the figure of the archangel Michael. 48. **Unblotted:** untainted. 54. **want:** need (Raleigh was expecting imminent execution).

THE NYMPH'S REPLY TO THE SHEPHERD

If all the world and love were young,
And truth in every shepherd's tongue,
These pretty pleasures might me move
To live with thee, and be thy love.

Time drives the flocks from field to fold
When rivers rage and rocks grow cold,
And Philomel becometh dumb;
The rest complain of cares to come.

The flowers do fade, and wanton fields
10   To wayward winter reckoning yields;
A honey tongue, a heart of gall,
Is fancy's spring, but sorrow's fall.

Thy gowns, thy shoes, thy beds of roses,
Thy cap, thy kirtle, and thy posies
Soon break, soon wither, soon forgotten:
In folly ripe, in reason rotten.

Thy belt of straw and ivy buds,
Thy coral clasps and amber studs,
All these in me no means can move
20   To come to thee, and be thy love.

But could youth last and love still breed,
Had joys no date, nor age no need,
Then these delights my mind might move
To live with thee, and be thy love.

Title: This is a "reply" to Marlowe's "passionate shepherd." 7. Philomel: the nightingale; dumb: silent. 14. kirtle: skirt or long dress. 22. date: end.

SIR PHILIP SIDNEY (1554–1586)

SONNETS

1

Loving in truth, and fain in verse my love to show,
That the dear She might take some pleasure of my pain,
Pleasure might cause her read, reading might make her know,
Knowledge might pity win, and pity grace obtain,—
I sought fit words to paint the blackest face of woe,
Studying inventions fine, her wits to entertain,
Oft turning others' leaves, to see if thence would flow
Some fresh and fruitful showers upon my sunburned brain.
But words came halting forth, wanting Invention's stay:
Invention, Nature's child, fled step-dame Study's blows,   10
And others' feet still seemed but strangers in my way.
Thus great with child to speak, and helpless in my throes,
Biting my truant pen, beating myself for spite:
"Fool," said my Muse to me, "look in thy heart and write."

31

With how sad steps, O Moon, thou climb'st the skies!
How silently, and with how wan a face!
What! may it be that even in heavenly place
That busy archer his sharp arrows tries?
Sure, if that long-with-love-acquainted eyes
Can judge of love, thou feel'st a lover's case;
I read it in thy looks: thy languished grace,
To me that feel the like, thy state descries.

1. **fain:** desirous. 6. **inventions:** subject matters or ideas, as distinct from words (line 5), the *inventio* and *elocutio* respectively of classical and Renaissance rhetoric— here referring to those of other writers; in line 9, *Invention* refers, by contrast, to his own proper subject. 7. **leaves:** pages. 8. **sunburned:** dried up (by the flames of love). 9. **wanting:** lacking; **stay:** support. 11. **feet:** writings used as guides; metrical units.

4. **busy archer:** Cupid, god of love, who shoots the arrows of love. 8. **descries:** reveals.

Then, even of fellowship, O Moon, tell me,
10   Is constant love deemed there but want of wit?
Are beauties there as proud as here they be?
Do they above love to be loved, and yet
Those lovers scorn whom that love doth possess?
Do they call virtue there ungratefulness?

54

Because I breathe not love to every one,
Nor do not use set colors for to wear,
Nor nourish special locks of vowèd hair,
Nor give each speech a full point of a groan,
The courtly nymphs, acquainted with the moan
Of them who in their lips Love's standard bear,
"What, he!" say they of me. "Now I dare swear
He cannot love; no, no, let him alone."
And think so still, so Stella know my mind;
10   Profess indeed I do not Cupid's art;
But you, fair maids, at length this true shall find,
That his right badge is but worn in the heart:
Dumb swans, not chattering pies, do lovers prove;
They love indeed who quake to say they love.

LEAVE ME, O LOVE

Leave me, O Love, which reachest but to dust;
And thou, my mind, aspire to higher things;
Grow rich in that which never taketh rust;
Whatever fades but fading pleasure brings.
Draw in thy beams, and humble all thy might
To that sweet yoke where lasting freedoms be,
Which breaks the clouds and opens forth the light
That doth both shine and give us sight to see.
O take fast hold; let that light be thy guide
10   In this small course which birth draws out to death,

10. deemed: considered; want: lack. 13. possess: control. 14. read—Do they call ungratefulness virtue?

2. set colors: the colors appointed by the girl. 4. full point: period (i.e., end each speech with a groan, as with a period). 9. And think so still: let them go on thinking thus; so: as long as. 10. Profess: make claim to expertise in. 13. pies: magpies.

4. but: only. 10. course: i.e., life.

And think how evil becometh him to slide
Who seeketh heaven and comes of heavenly breath.
Then farewell world, thy uttermost I see;
Eternal Love, maintain thy life in me.

MICHAEL DRAYTON (1563–1631)

SONNET 61

Since there's no help, come let us kiss and part;
Nay, I have done, you get no more of me;
And I am glad, yea glad with all my heart
That thus so cleanly I myself can free.
Shake hands forever, cancel all our vows;
And, when we meet at any time again,
Be it not seen in either of our brows
That we one jot of former love retain.
Now, at the last gasp of love's latest breath,
When, his pulse failing, passion speechless lies,   10
When faith is kneeling by his bed of death,
And innocence is closing up his eyes:
   Now if thou wouldst, when all have given him over,
   From death to life thou mightst him yet recover.

CHRISTOPHER MARLOWE (1564–1593)

THE PASSIONATE SHEPHERD TO HIS LOVE

Come live with me, and be my love,
And we will all the pleasures prove
That valleys, groves, hills, and fields,
Woods, or steepy mountain yields.

11. evil becometh: ill it befits.

2. prove: try.

And we will sit upon the rocks,
Seeing the shepherds feed their flocks,
By shallow rivers to whose falls
Melodious birds sing madrigals.

And I will make thee beds of roses,
And a thousand fragrant posies;
A cap of flowers, and a kirtle
Embroidered all with leaves of myrtle;

A gown made of the finest wool,
Which from our pretty lambs we pull;
Fair-lined slippers for the cold,
With buckles of the purest gold;

A belt of straw and ivy buds,
With coral clasps and amber studs:
And if these pleasures may thee move,
Come live with me, and be my love.

The shepherds' swains shall dance and sing
For thy delight each May morning:
If these delights thy mind may move,
Then live with me, and be my love.

WILLIAM SHAKESPEARE (1564–1616)

SONGS FROM THE PLAYS

from *Love's Labor's Lost*

SPRING

When daisies pied and violets blue
And lady-smocks all silver-white
And cuckoo-buds of yellow hue
Do paint the meadows with delight,.

8. madrigals: songs, ditties. 11. kirtle: skirt or long dress.

1. pied: with spots of two or more colors. 2, 3. lady-smocks, cuckoo-buds: species
of flowers.

The cuckoo then on every tree
Mocks married men, for thus sings he,
"Cuckoo,
Cuckoo, cuckoo!" O word of fear,
Unpleasing to a married ear!

When shepherds pipe on oaten straws   10
And merry larks are ploughmen's clocks,
When turtles tread, and rooks and daws,
And maidens bleach their summer smocks,
The cuckoo then on every tree
Mocks married men, for thus sings he,
"Cuckoo,
Cuckoo, cuckoo!" O word of fear,
Unpleasing to a married ear!

WINTER

When icicles hang by the wall,
And Dick the shepherd blows his nail,   20
And Tom bears logs into the hall,
And milk comes frozen home in pail;
When blood is nipped and ways be foul,
Then nightly sings the staring owl,
"Tu-whit, tu-who!"
A merry note,
While greasy Joan doth keel the pot.

When all aloud the wind doth blow,
And coughing drowns the parson's saw,
And birds sit brooding in the snow,   30
And Marian's nose looks red and raw;
When roasted crabs hiss in the bowl,
Then nightly sings the staring owl,
"Tu-whit, tu-who!"
A merry note,
While greasy Joan doth keel the pot.

5. cuckoo: herald of spring in England, with a call like its name; traditionally asso-
ciated with cuckoldry, or adultery. 12. turtles: turtle doves; tread: copulate; rooks: large
birds of the crow family; daws: jackdaws. 20. blows his nail: blows on his fingernails
to warm them. 27. keel: cool. 29. saw: proverbial observation. 32. crabs: crab apples.

from *Cymbeline*

Fear no more the heat o' the sun,
Nor the furious winter's rages;
Thou thy worldly task hast done,
Home art gone and ta'en thy wages.
Golden lads and girls all must,
As chimney-sweepers, come to dust.

Fear no more the frown o' the great;
Thou art past the tyrant's stroke;
Care no more to clothe and eat;
10   To thee the reed is as the oak.
The sceptre, learning, physic, must
All follow this and come to dust.

Fear no more the lightning-flash,
Nor the all-dreaded thunder-stone;
Fear not slander, censure rash;
Thou hast finished joy and moan.
All lovers young, all lovers must
Consign to thee and come to dust.

No exorciser harm thee!
20   Nor no witchcraft charm thee!
Ghost unlaid forbear thee!
Nothing ill come near thee!
Quiet consummation have,
And renownèd be thy grave!

Note. These lines are recited by two brothers over the body of a youth (the heroine disguised as a boy) whom they suppose dead. The first stanza is spoken by one brother, the second by the other; in the last two stanzas they alternate lines, but both together recite the final two lines of each of these stanzas.

11. physic: medicine. 14. thunder-stone: thunderbolt. 18. Consign to thee: follow you. 19. exorciser: magician. 21. Ghost . . . thee: may no unappeased spirit trouble you. 23. consummation: death.

SONNETS

18

Shall I compare thee to a summer's day?
Thou art more lovely and more temperate:
Rough winds do shake the darling buds of May,
And summer's lease hath all too short a date.
Sometime too hot the eye of heaven shines,
And often is his gold complexion dimmed;
And every fair from fair sometime declines,
By chance or nature's changing course untrimmed;
But thy eternal summer shall not fade
Nor lose possession of that fair thou ow'st,   10
Nor shall death brag thou wander'st in his shade
When in eternal lines to time thou grow'st.
So long as men can breathe or eyes can see,
So long lives this, and this gives life to thee.

29

When in disgrace with fortune and men's eyes,
I all alone beweep my outcast state,
And trouble deaf heaven with my bootless cries,
And look upon myself, and curse my fate,
Wishing me like to one more rich in hope,
Featured like him, like him with friends possessed,
Desiring this man's art and that man's scope,
With what I most enjoy contented least;
Yet in these thoughts myself almost despising,
Haply I think on thee; and then my state,   10
Like to the lark at break of day arising
From sullen earth, sings hymns at heaven's gate;
For thy sweet love remembered such wealth brings
That then I scorn to change my state with kings.

8. untrimmed: stripped of decoration. **10. thou ow'st:** you possess.

3. bootless: useless. **10. Haply:** by chance.

30

When to the sessions of sweet silent thought
I summon up remembrance of things past,
I sigh the lack of many a thing I sought,
And with old woes new wail my dear time's waste:
Then can I drown an eye, unused to flow,
For precious friends hid in death's dateless night,
And weep afresh love's long-since-canceled woe,
And moan th' expense of many a vanished sight;
Then can I grieve at grievances foregone,
10   And heavily from woe to woe tell o'er
The sad account of fore-bemoanèd moan,
Which I new pay as if not paid before.
But if the while I think on thee, dear friend,
All losses are restored and sorrows end.

64

When I have seen by time's fell hand defaced
The rich-proud cost of outworn buried age;
When sometime lofty towers I see down-razed,
And brass eternal slave to mortal rage;
When I have seen the hungry ocean gain
Advantage on the kingdom of the shore,
And the firm soil win of the watery main,
Increasing store with loss and loss with store;
When I have seen such interchange of state,
10   Or state itself confounded to decay,
Ruin hath taught me thus to ruminate:
That time will come and take my love away.
This thought is as a death, which cannot choose
But weep to have that which it fears to lose.

1. sessions: sittings, as of a court. 4. my dear time's waste: passing of a time valuable to me. 6. dateless: endless. 7. canceled: paid for. 8. expense: loss. 9. foregone: now past. 10. tell: count.

1. fell: cruel. 4. brass: bronze, as used in statuary. 8. store: accumulation. 9. state: condition. 10. state: stateliness.

73

That time of year thou mayst in me behold
When yellow leaves, or none, or few, do hang
Upon those boughs which shake against the cold,
Bare ruined choirs, where late the sweet birds sang.
In me thou see'st the twilight of such day
As after sunset fadeth in the west,
Which by and by black night doth take away,
Death's second self, that seals up all in rest.
In me thou see'st the glowing of such fire
That on the ashes of his youth doth lie   10
As the deathbed whereon it must expire,
Consumed with that which it was nourished by.
This thou perceiv'st, which makes thy love more strong
To love that well which thou must leave ere long.

87

Farewell! thou art too dear for my possessing,
And like enough thou know'st thy estimate:
The charter of thy worth gives thee releasing;
My bonds in thee are all determinate.
For how do I hold thee but by thy granting?
And for that riches where is my deserving?
The cause of this fair gift in me is wanting,
And so my patent back again is swerving.
Thyself thou gav'st, thy own worth then not knowing,
Or me, to whom thou gav'st it, else mistaking;   10
So thy great gift, upon misprision growing,
Comes home again, on better judgment making.
Thus have I had thee, as a dream doth flatter,
In sleep a king, but waking, no such matter.

4. choirs: part of the cathedral where the services are sung.

1. dear: expensive. **2. estimate:** value. **3. charter:** contract. **4. bonds:** rights; **determinate:** at an end, of limited duration. **7. wanting:** lacking. **11. misprision·** misunderstanding.

98

From you have I been absent in the spring,
When proud-pied April, dressed in all his trim,
Hath put a spirit of youth in every thing,
That heavy Saturn laughed and leaped with him.
Yet nor the lays of birds, nor the sweet smell
Of different flowers in odor and in hue,
Could make me any summer's story tell,
Or from their proud lap pluck them where they grew;
Nor did I wonder at the lily's white,
Nor praise the deep vermilion in the rose:
They were but sweet, but figures of delight,
Drawn after you, you pattern of all those.
Yet seemed it winter still, and, you away,
As with your shadow I with these did play.

116

Let me not to the marriage of true minds
Admit impediments: love is not love
Which alters when it alteration finds,
Or bends with the remover to remove.
O, no, it is an ever fixèd mark
That looks on tempests and is never shaken;
It is the star to every wand'ring bark,
Whose worth's unknown, although his height be taken.
Love's not Time's fool, though rosy lips and cheeks
Within his bending sickle's compass come;
Love alters not with his brief hours and weeks,
But bears it out, even to the edge of doom.
If this be error, and upon me proved,
I never writ, nor no man ever loved.

2. proud-pied: splendidly multicolored; **trim:** attire. **4. heavy:** gloomy; **Saturn:** Roman god noted for being cold and austere. **5. lays:** songs. **11. figures:** copies. **12. pattern:** original (from which copies are made). **13. Yet:** now as before; **still:** ever, continuously.

8. his height be taken: the star's elevation may be measured. **11. his:** i. e., Time's. **12. bears it out:** persists. **13. upon:** against.

129

Th' expense of spirit in a waste of shame
Is lust in action; and till action, lust
Is perjured, murd'rous, bloody, full of blame,
Savage, extreme, rude, cruel, not to trust;
Enjoyed no sooner but despisèd straight;
Past reason hunted; and no sooner had,
Past reason hated, as a swallowed bait
On purpose laid to make the taker mad.
Mad in pursuit, and in possession so;
Had, having, and in quest to have, extreme;   10
A bliss in proof; and proved, a very woe;
Before, a joy proposed; behind, a dream.
All this the world well knows, yet none knows well
To shun the heaven that leads men to this hell.

130

My mistress' eyes are nothing like the sun;
Coral is far more red than her lips' red;
If snow be white, why then her breasts are dun;
If hairs be wires, black wires grow on her head.
I have seen roses damasked, red and white,
But no such roses see I in her cheeks;
And in some perfumes is there more delight
Than in the breath that from my mistress reeks.
I love to hear her speak, yet well I know
That music hath a far more pleasing sound;   10
I grant I never saw a goddess go—
My mistress, when she walks, treads on the ground:
And yet, by heaven, I think my love as rare
As any she belied with false compare.

---

1. expense: expenditure. **11. proof:** actuality.

2. Coral: a red, shell-like substance used in jewelry. **3. dun:** grayish brown. **5. damasked:** dappled with red. **8. reeks:** arises (it does not have the modern sense of smelling bad). **14. she:** woman; **belied with false compare:** unduly praised by flattering simile.

146

Poor soul, the center of my sinful earth,
[Thrall to] these rebel powers that thee array:
Why dost thou pine within and suffer dearth,
Painting thy outward walls so costly gay?
Why so large cost, having so short a lease,
Dost thou upon thy fading mansion spend?
Shall worms, inheritors of this excess,
Eat up thy charge? Is this thy body's end?
Then, soul, live thou upon thy servant's loss,
10   And let that pine to aggravate thy store;
Buy terms divine in selling hours of dross;
Within be fed, without be rich no more.
So shalt thou feed on death, that feeds on men,
And death once dead, there's no more dying then.

THOMAS CAMPION (1567–1620)

MY SWEETEST LESBIA

My sweetest Lesbia, let us live and love,
And though the sager sort our deeds reprove,
Let us not weigh them. Heaven's great lamps do dive
Into their west and straight again revive,
But soon as once set is our little light,
Then must we sleep one ever-during night.

If all would lead their lives in love like me,
Then bloody swords and armor should not be;
No drum nor trumpet peaceful sleeps should move,
10   Unless alarm came from the camp of love.
But fools do live and waste their little light,
And seek with pain their ever-during night.

1. **earth:** body. 2. **[Thrall to]:** the text is corrupt at this point; these words seem a reasonable conjecture. 10. **aggravate:** increase.

Title: this poem is partly a translation and partly an imitation of a poem to his mistress, Lesbia, by the Roman poet Catullus (first century B.C.).

When timely death my life and fortune ends,
Let not my hearse be vexed with mourning friends;
But let all lovers, rich in triumph, come
And with sweet pastimes grace my happy tomb;
And Lesbia, close up thou my little light,
And crown with love my ever-during night.

COME, LET US SOUND WITH MELODY

Come, let us sound with melody the praises
Of the kings' King, th' omnipotent Creator,
Author of number, that hath all the world in
    Harmony framèd.

Heaven is His throne perpetually shining,
His divine power and glory; thence He thunders,
One in all, and all still in one abiding,
    Both Father and Son.

O sacred Sprite, invisible, eternal,
Everywhere yet unlimited, that all things   10
Canst in one moment penetrate, revive me,
    O holy Spirit!

Rescue, O rescue me from earthly darkness;
Banish hence all these elemental objects;
Guide my soul that thirsts to the lively fountain
    Of Thy divineness.

Cleanse my soul, O God, Thy bespotted image,
Altered with sin so that heavenly pureness
Cannot acknowledge me, but in Thy mercies,
    O Father of Grace.   20

But when once Thy beams do remove my darkness,
O then I'll shine forth as an angel of light
And record with more than an earthly voice Thy
    Infinite honors.

3. number: verse. 9. Sprite: spirit. 14. elemental objects: earthly parts.

WHEN THOU MUST HOME

When thou must home to shades of underground,
And there arrived, a new admirèd guest,
The beauteous spirits do engirt thee round,
White Iope, blithe Helen, and the rest,
To hear the stories of thy finished love
From that smooth tongue whose music hell can move,

Then wilt thou speak of banqueting delights,
Of masks and revels which sweet youth did make,
Of tourneys and great challenges of knights,
And all these triumphs for thy beauty's sake;
When thou hast told these honors done to thee,
Then tell, O tell, how thou didst murther me.

10

THERE IS A GARDEN IN HER FACE

There is a garden in her face,
Where roses and white lilies grow;
A heavenly paradise is that place,
Wherein all pleasant fruits do flow.
There cherries grow which none may buy,
Till "Cherry-ripe" themselves do cry.

Those cherries fairly do enclose
Of orient pearl a double row,
Which when her lovely laughter shows,
They look like rosebuds filled with snow.
Yet them nor peer nor prince can buy,
Till "Cherry-ripe" themselves do cry.

10

Her eyes like angels watch them still;
Her brows like bended bows do stand,
Threatening with piercing frowns to kill
All that attempt with eye or hand
Those sacred cherries to come nigh,
Till "Cherry-ripe" themselves do cry.

4. Iope: a beautiful woman of uncertain identity, referred to by Propertius, a Latin poet of the first century B.C.; blithe: happy, or possibly in this context "shining." 8. masks: dramatic presentations with songs and dancing. 12. murther: murder.

6, 12, 18. "Cherry-ripe": the cry of a London street salesman. 17. nigh: near.

JOHN DONNE (C. 1572–1631)

THE FLEA

Mark but this flea, and mark in this,
How little that which thou deniest me is;
It sucked me first, and now sucks thee,
And in this flea our two bloods mingled be;
Thou know'st that this cannot be said
A sin, nor shame, nor loss of maidenhead;
    Yet this enjoys before it woo,
      And, pampered, swells with one blood made of two;
      And this, alas, is more than we would do.

Oh stay, three lives in one flea spare,   10
Where we almost, yea, more than married are.
This flea is you and I, and this
Our marriage bed and marriage temple is;
Though parents grudge, and you, we're met,
And cloistered in these living walls of jet.
    Though use make you apt to kill me,
      Let not to that, self-murder added be,
      And sacrilege, three sins in killing three.

Cruel and sudden, hast thou since
Purpled thy nail in blood of innocence?   20
Wherein could this flea guilty be,
Except in that drop which it sucked from thee?
Yet thou triumph'st and say'st that thou
Find'st not thyself, nor me, the weaker now.
    'Tis true, then learn how false fears be:
      Just so much honor, when thou yield'st to me,
      Will waste, as this flea's death took life from thee.

16. use: convention (the convention that the disdain of the cruel mistress is fatal to the lover). 27. Will waste: will be lost.

GO AND CATCH A FALLING STAR

Go and catch a falling star,
  Get with child a mandrake root,
Tell me where all past years are,
  Or who cleft the devil's foot,
Teach me to hear mermaids singing,
  Or to keep off envy's stinging,
      And find
      What wind
Serves to advance an honest mind.

If thou be'st born to strange sights,
  Things invisible to see,
Ride ten thousand days and nights,
  Till age snow white hairs on thee,
Thou, when thou return'st, wilt tell me
All strange wonders that befell thee,
      And swear
      No where
Lives a woman true, and fair.

If thou find'st one, let me know;
  Such a pilgrimage were sweet;
Yet do not, I would not go,
  Though at next door we might meet.
Though she were true when you met her,
All last till you write your letter,
      Yet she
      Will be
False, ere I come, to two, or three.

THE SUN RISING

Busy old fool, unruly sun,
  Why dost thou thus
Through windows and through curtains call on us?
Must to thy motions lovers' seasons run?

2. **mandrake:** the forked root is supposed to resemble the lower half of the human female. 9. **advance:** elevate in status (in court, for instance). 10-11. **If . . . see:** if you have second sight.

Saucy pedantic wretch, go chide
Late schoolboys and sour prentices,
Go tell court-huntsmen that the King will ride,
Call country ants to harvest offices;
Love, all alike, no season knows nor clime,
Nor hours, days, months, which are the rags of time.   10

Thy beams, so reverend and strong
Why shouldst thou think?
I could eclipse and cloud them with a wink,
But that I would not lose her sight so long;
If her eyes have not blinded thine,
Look, and tomorrow late, tell me
Whether both th' Indias of spice and mine
Be where thou left'st them, or lie here with me.
Ask for those kings whom thou saw'st yesterday,
And thou shalt hear, all here in one bed lay.   20

She's all states, and all princes, I:
Nothing else is.
Princes do but play us; compared to this,
All honor's mimic, all wealth alchemy.
Thou, sun, art half as happy as we,
In that the world's contracted thus;
Thine age asks ease, and since thy duties be
To warm the world, that's done in warming us.
Shine here to us, and thou art everywhere:
This bed thy center is, these walls thy sphere.   30

THE GOOD-MORROW

I wonder, by my troth, what thou and I
Did till we loved? Were we not weaned till then,
But sucked on country pleasures, childishly?
Or snorted we in the seven sleepers' den?
'Twas so; but this, all pleasures fancies be.
If ever any beauty I did see,
Which I desired, and got, 'twas but a dream of thee.

9. clime: climate. 23. play: act. 24. alchemy: spurious. Reference to the process by which base metals were to be transformed to gold.

4. **seven sleepers' den:** according to Christian legend, a cave where seven youths escaped persecution by sleeping for 200 years. 5. **but:** except for.

And now good morrow to our waking souls,
Which watch not one another out of fear;
10   For love all love of other sights controls,
And makes one little room an everywhere.
Let sea-discoverers to new worlds have gone;
Let maps to other, worlds on worlds have shown;
Let us possess one world; each hath one, and is one.

My face in thine eye, thine in mine appears,
And true plain hearts do in the faces rest;
Where can we find two better hemispheres
Without sharp north, without declining west?
Whatever dies was not mixed equally;
20   If our two loves be one, or thou and I
Love so alike that none do slacken, none can die.

A VALEDICTION: FORBIDDING MOURNING

As virtuous men pass mildly away,
And whisper to their souls to go,
Whilst some of their sad friends do say,
The breath goes now, and some say, no;

So let us melt and make no noise,
No tear-floods nor sigh-tempests move;
'Twere profanation of our joys
To tell the laity our love.

Moving of th'earth brings harms and fears:
10   Men reckon what it did and meant;
But trepidation of the spheres,
Though greater far, is innocent.

Dull sublunary lovers' love,
Whose soul is sense, cannot admit
Absence, because it doth remove
Those things which elemented it.

13. other: other people.

9. Moving of th'earth: earthquake. 11. trepidation of the spheres: movement in the heavens. 12. innocent: innocuous. 13. sublunary: earthly and therefore subject to change. 16. elemented: comprised.

But we, by a love so much refined
　　That ourselves know not what it is,
Inter-assurèd of the mind,
　　Care less eyes, lips, hands to miss.　　　　　　　20

Our two souls, therefore, which are one,
　　Though I must go, endure not yet
A breach, but an expansion,
　　Like gold to airy thinness beat.

If they be two, they are two so
　　As stiff twin compasses are two;
Thy soul, the fixed foot, makes no show
　　To move, but doth if th'other do.

And though it in the center sit,
　　Yet when the other far doth roam,　　　　　　30
It leans, and hearkens after it,
　　And grows erect as that comes home.

Such wilt thou be to me, who must,
　　Like th'other foot, obliquely run;
Thy firmness makes my circle just,
　　And makes me end where I begun.

A VALEDICTION: OF WEEPING

　　Let me pour forth
My tears before thy face whilst I stay here,
For thy face coins them, and thy stamp they bear;
And by this mintage they are something worth,
　　For thus they be
　　Pregnant of thee.
Fruits of much grief they are, emblems of more:
When a tear falls, that *thou* fall'st which it bore;
So thou and I are nothing then, when on a divers shore

　　On a round ball　　　　　　　　　　　　10
A workman that hath copies by, can lay
An Europe, Afric, and an Asìa,

---

26. compasses: i.e., as used by mathematicians and draftsmen. 35. just: accurate.

9. on a divers shore: on different shores.

And quickly make that which was nothing, all;
    So doth each tear
    Which thee doth wear,
A globe, yea world, by that impression grow,
Till thy tears mixed with mine do overflow
This world; by waters sent from thee, my heaven dissolvèd so.

    O more than moon,
20 Draw not up seas to drown me in thy sphere;
Weep me not dead in thine arms, but forbear
To teach the sea what it may do too soon;
    Let not the wind
    Example find
To do me more harm than it purposeth;
Since thou and I sigh one another's breath,
Whoe'er sighs most is cruellest, and hastes the other's death.

THE CANONIZATION

For God's sake hold your tongue, and let me love,
    Or chide my palsy, or my gout,
My five gray hairs, or ruined fortune flout;
    With wealth your state, your mind with arts improve,
        Take you a course, get you a place,
        Observe his honor, or his grace;
    Or the king's real, or his stampèd face
        Contemplate; what you will, approve,
        So you will let me love.

10 Alas, alas, who's injured by my love?
    What merchant's ships have my sighs drowned?
Who says my tears have overflowed his ground?
    When did my colds a forward spring remove?
        When did the heats which my veins fill
        Add one more to the plaguy bill?

16. world: universe. 20. Draw . . . seas: i.e., as the moon causes a high tide.

5. course: of study; place: position in the royal court. 6. his honor, his grace: titles of nobility. 7. real: real, royal; stampèd face: image on coins. 13. forward: early. 15. plaguy bill: list of people killed by the Plague.

Soldiers find wars, and lawyers find out still
   Litigious men, which quarrels move,
   Though she and I do love.

Call us what you will, we are made such by love;
   Call her one, me another fly;   20
We're tapers too, and at our own cost die;
   And we in us find th' eagle and the dove.
     The Phœnix riddle hath more wit
     By us; we two being one, are it.
So to one neutral thing both sexes fit;
   We die and rise the same, and prove
   Mysterious by this love.

We can die by it, if not live by love;
   And if unfit for tombs and hearse
Our legend be, it will be fit for verse;   30
   And if no piece of chronicle we prove,
     We'll build in sonnets pretty rooms;
     As well a well-wrought urn becomes
The greatest ashes, as half-acre tombs;
   And by these hymns, all shall approve
   Us canonized for love,

And thus invoke us: "You whom reverend love
   Made one another's hermitage;
You, to whom love was peace, that now is rage;
   Who did the whole world's soul contract, and drove   40
     Into the glasses of your eyes
     (So made such mirrors and such spies
That they did all to you epitomize)
   Countries, towns, courts: beg from above
   A pattern of your love!"

23. Phoenix riddle: legend that the bird periodically immolated itself and was regenerated out of its own ashes. 30. legend: life of a saint. 31. chronicle: secular history.

HOLY SONNETS

7

At the round earth's imagined corners, blow
Your trumpets, angels; and arise, arise
From death, you numberless infinities
Of souls, and to your scattered bodies go;
All whom the flood did, and fire shall o'erthrow,
All whom war, dearth, age, agues, tyrannies,
Despair, law, chance hath slain, and you whose eyes
Shall behold God and never taste death's woe.
But let them sleep, Lord, and me mourn a space;
10   For if above all these my sins abound,
'Tis late to ask abundance of Thy grace
When we are there; here on this lowly ground
Teach me how to repent; for that's as good
As if Thou'dst sealed my pardon with Thy blood.

9

If poisonous minerals, and if that tree
Whose fruit threw death on else immortal us,
If lecherous goats, if serpents envious
Cannot be damned, alas, why should I be?
Why should intent or reason, born in me,
Make sins, else equal, in me more heinous?
And mercy being easy and glorious
To God, in His stern wrath why threatens He?
But who am I, that dare dispute with Thee,
10   O God? Oh, of Thine only worthy blood
And my tears, make a heavenly Lethean flood,
And drown in it my sins' black memory.
That Thou remember them, some claim as debt;
I think it mercy, if Thou wilt forget.

5. flood: a reference to Noah's flood; fire: the fire at the Last Judgment.

1. tree: the forbidden tree in the Garden of Eden. 3. lecherous, envious: traditional attributes of these animals. 11. Lethean: of Lethe, river of forgetfulness in Hell. 13. some: Calvinists.

10

Death, be not proud, though some have callèd thee
Mighty and dreadful, for thou art not so;
For those whom thou think'st thou dost overthrow
Die not, poor Death, nor yet canst thou kill me.
From rest and sleep, which but thy pictures be,
Much pleasure; then from thee much more must flow;
And soonest our best men with thee do go,
Rest of their bones, and soul's delivery.
Thou'rt slave to fate, chance, kings, and desperate men,
And dost with poison, war, and sickness dwell;   10
And poppy or charms can make us sleep as well
And better than thy stroke; why swell'st thou then?
One short sleep past, we wake eternally,
And death shall be no more; Death, thou shalt die.

14

Batter my heart, three-personed God; for you
As yet but knock, breathe, shine, and seek to mend;
That I may rise and stand, o'erthrow me, and bend
Your force to break, blow, burn, and make me new.
I, like an usurped town t'another due,
Labor t'admit you, but oh, to no end.
Reason, your viceroy in me, me should defend,
But is captived, and proves weak or untrue.
Yet dearly I love you, and would be lovèd fain,
But am betrothed unto your enemy;   10
Divorce me, untie or break that knot again;
Take me to you, imprison me, for I,
Except you enthrall me, never shall be free,
Nor ever chaste, except you ravish me.

11. poppy: an opiate; charms: magical incantations
9. fain: gladly.

A HYMN TO GOD THE FATHER

Wilt Thou forgive that sin where I begun,
  Which was my sin, though it were done before?
Wilt Thou forgive that sin through which I run,
  And do run still, though still I do deplore?
    When Thou hast done, Thou hast not done,
      For I have more.

Wilt Thou forgive that sin which I have won
  Others to sin, and made my sin their door?
Wilt Thou forgive that sin which I did shun
10 A year or two, but wallowed in a score?
    When Thou hast done, Thou hast not done,
      For I have more.

I have a sin of fear, that when I have spun
  My last thread, I shall perish on the shore;
Swear by Thyself, that at my death Thy Son
  Shall shine as he shines now and heretofore;
    And having done that, Thou hast done;
      I fear no more.

THE ECSTASY

Where, like a pillow on a bed,
  A pregnant bank swelled up to rest
The violet's reclining head,
  Sat we two, one another's best.

Our hands were firmly cémented
  With a fast balm, which thence did spring;
Our eye-beams twisted, and did thread
  Our eyes upon one double string;

---

1. that sin: reference to original sin, passed to him in his conception. **3. run:** ran.
13. sin of fear: despair, according to Aquinas the ultimate sin.

Title: a freeing of the soul, so that it gains knowledge of truths directly, without
recourse to the senses or to reason. 6. fast balm: a resinous-like moisture which fastens.

So to'intergraft our hands, as yet
  Was all our means to make us one;   10
And pictures on our eyes to get
  Was all our propagatiòn.

As 'twixt two equal armies, Fate
  Suspends uncertain victory,
Our souls (which, to advance their state,
  Were gone out) hung 'twixt her and me.

And whilst our souls negotiate there,
  We like sepulchral statues lay;
All day the same our postures were,
  And we said nothing all the day.   20

If any, so by love refined
  That he soul's language understood,
And by good love were grown all mind,
  Within convenient distance stood,

He (though he knew not which soul spake,
  Because both meant, both spake the same)
Might thence a new concoction take,
  And part far purer than he came.

This Ecstasy doth unperplex,
  We said, and tells us what we love;   30
We see by this it was not sex,
  We see we saw not what did move:.

But as all several souls contain
  Mixture of things, they know not what,
Love these mixed souls doth mix again,
  And makes both one, each this and that.

A single violet transplant—
  The strength, the color, and the size:
All which before was poor and scant
  Redoubles still, and multiplies.   40

11. get: beget. 18. sepulchral statues: effigies surmounting a tomb. 27. concoction: a substance refined chemically by heat. 32. did move: i.e., caused us to love. 33. several souls: the soul, though one, was thought to have several natures, combining the intellectual/spiritual and the physical. 40. the subject of the verbs is *all*, referring back to line 38.

When love with one another so
    Interanimates two souls,
That abler soul, which thence doth flow,
    Defects of loneliness controls.

We, then, who are this new soul, know
    Of what we are composed and made,
For th'atomies of which we grow
    Are souls whom no change can invade.

But O alas! so long, so far
    Our bodies why do we forbear?
They'are ours, though they'are not we: we are
    Th'intelligences, they the sphere.

We owe them thanks, because they thus
    Did us to us at first convey,
Yielded their forces, sense, to us,
    Nor are dross to us, but allay.

On man heaven's influence works not so,
    But that it first imprints the air;
So soul into the soul may flow,
    Though it to body first repair.

As our blood labors to beget
    Spirits as like souls as it can,
Because such fingers need to knit
    That subtle knot which makes us man:

So must pure lovers' souls descend
    To'affections, and to faculties
Which sense may reach and apprehend;
    Else a great Prince in prison lies.

---

44. loneliness: separateness (of souls). 47. atomies: atoms. 50. forbear: avoid or deny. 51–52: the analogy is to Ptolemaic astronomy, Christianized, where nine orders of angels (intelligences) rule the nine spheres (the circles of the planets and the stars). 53: thus: cf. lines 5–8. 56. dross: the scum from molten metals; allay: alloy. 57–58: astrological influences on man were thought to be transmitted through the air. 60. repair: goes. 62. spirits: vapors arising from the blood which mediated between body and soul. 66. affections: passions; faculties: powers of action.

To'our bodies turn we then, that so
    Weak men on love revealed may look;   70
Love's mysteries in souls do grow,
    But yet the body is his book.

And if some lover, such as we,
    Have heard this dialogue of one,
Let him still mark us: he shall see
    Small change when we'are to bodies gone.

THE RELIC

When my grave is broke up again
Some second guest to entertain
(For graves have learned that woman-head
To be to more than one a bed),
    And he that digs it spies
A bracelet of bright hair about the bone,
    Will he not let'us alone,
And think that there a loving couple lies,
Who thought that this device might be some way
To make their souls, at the last busy day,   10
Meet at this grave, and make a little stay?

If this fall in a time, or land,
Where mis-devotion doth command,
Then he that digs us up will bring
Us to the Bishop and the King,
    To make us relics; then
Thou shalt be'a Mary Magdalen, and I
    A something else thereby:
All women shall adore us, and some men;
And since at such times miracles are sought,   20
I would have that age by this paper taught
What miracles we harmless lovers wrought.

75. mark: pay attention to.

1-2: This reusing of burial ground was common practice in Donne's time. 3. woman-
head: womanly nature. 10. last busy day: Judgment Day. 12. this: i. e., digging-up of
the speaker's body; fall: happen. 13. an era in which worshiping of idols and relics is
the practice. 17. Mary Magdalen: the repentant prostitute (Luke vii.37-50). 18. A
something else: some other relic, possibly a bone of Christ's. 21. this paper: this poem.

First, we loved well and faithfully,
Yet knew not what we loved, nor why;
Difference of sex no more we knew
Than our guardian angels do;
    Coming and going, we
Perchance might kiss, but not between those meals;
    Our hands ne'er touched the seals
Which nature, injured by late law, sets free:
These miracles we did; but now, alas,
All measure and all language I should pass,
Should I tell what a miracle she was.

30

THE INDIFFERENT

I can love both fair and brown,
Her whom abundance melts, and her whom want betrays,
Her who loves loneness best, and her who masks and plays,
Her whom the country formed, and whom the town,
Her who believes, and her who tries,
Her who still weeps with spongy eyes,
And her who is dry cork, and never cries;
I can love her, and her, and you, and you,
I can love any, so she be not true.

10

Will no other vice content you?
Will it not serve your turn to do as did your mothers?
Or have you all old vices spent, and now would find out others?
Or doth a fear that men are true torment you?
Oh, we are not, be not you so!
Let me, and do you, twenty know.
Rob me, but bind me not, and let me go:
Must I, who came to travail thorough you,
Grow your fixed subject, because you are true?

27–28: i.e., kissed as a greeting, in arriving or departing. 28. **between those meals:** in between those kisses (i.e., the kiss as the food of the soul). 29–30: i.e., we never consummated our love physically, which consummation, though nature allows it, is forbidden by human laws, which are more recent in origin than nature's. 32. **pass:** surpass.

1. **brown:** the conventional Elizabethan beauty was fair. 2. **melts . . . betrays:** i.e., into giving of herself to men. 3. **masks and plays:** putting on a mask to attend balls and dances. 5. **believes . . . tries:** trusts . . . tests (her lover). 17. **travail:** travel; distress; **thorough:** through.

Venus heard me sigh this song,
And by Love's sweetest part, variety, she swore   20
She heard not this till now; and that it should be so no more.
She went, examined, and returned ere long,
And said, "Alas! but two or three
Poor heretics in love there be,
Which think to 'stablish dangerous constancy.
But I have told them, 'Since you will be true,
You shall be true to them who'are false to you.'"

BEN JONSON (1573–1637)

ON MY FIRST SON

Farewell, thou child of my right hand, and joy;
My sin was too much hope of thee, loved boy.
Seven years thou'wert lent to me, and I thee pay,
Exacted by thy fate, on the just day.
O, could I lose all father now! for why
Will man lament the state he should envý,
To have so soon 'scaped world's and flesh's rage
And, if no other misery, yet age?
Rest in soft peace and, asked, say here doth lie
Ben Jonson his best piece of poetry.   10
For whose sake, henceforth, all his vows be such
As what he loves may never like too much.

SONG: TO CELIA

Drink to me only with thine eyes,
    And I will pledge with mine;
Or leave a kiss but in the cup,
    And I'll not look for wine.

19. Venus: goddess of Love. 22. examined: as in an inquisition.

1. child of my right hand: this is the literal translation of the Hebrew name
Benjamin, the child's name. 4. just day: exact day (he became seven years old), i.e., his
birthday. 7. 'scaped: escaped. 10. Jonson his: Jonson's.

Note. This poem is an adaptation of phrases culled from letters of the Greek writer
Philostratus.

The thirst that from the soul doth rise
  Doth ask a drink divine:
But might I of Jove's nectar sup,
  I would not change for thine.

I sent thee late a rosy wreath,
  Not so much honoring thee
As giving it a hope, that there
  It could not withered be.
But thou thereon did'st only breathe,
  And sent'st it back to me;
Since when it grows and smells, I swear,
  Not of itself, but thee.

10

EPITAPH ON SALOMON PAVY,
A CHILD OF QUEEN ELIZABETH'S CHAPEL

Weep with me, all you that read
  This little story:
And know, for whom a tear you shed,
  Death's self is sorry.
'Twas a child, that so did thrive
  In grace and feature,
As Heaven and Nature seemed to strive
  Which owned the creature.
Years he numbered scarce thirteen
  When Fates turned cruel;
Yet three filled zodiacs had he been
  The stage's jewel,
And did act (what now we moan)
  Old men so duly
As, sooth, the Parcae thought him one,
  He played so truly.
So, by error, to his fate

10

3. but: only (a kiss).

7. Jove's nectar: nectar was the drink of the gods, and Jove (Jupiter) the chief god in the Roman pantheon. 8. change: make an exchange.

Title: Salomon Pavy was one of the boy actors of the acting company The Children of Queen Elizabeth's Chapel. 11. three filled zodiacs: i.e., three years. 15. Parcae: the three Fates of Roman mythology.

They all consented;
But viewing him since (alas! too late)
They have repented,   20
And have sought (to give new birth)
In baths to steep him;
But, being so much too good for earth,
Heaven vows to keep him.

SONG: TO CELIA

(from *Volpone*)

Come my Celia, let us prove,
While we may, the sports of love.
Time will not be ours for ever:
He, at length, our good will sever.
Spend not then his gifts in vain:
Suns, that set, may rise again;
But if once we lose this light,
'Tis, with us, perpetual night.
Why should we defer our joys?
Fame and rumor are but toys: 10
Cannot we delude the eyes
Of a few poor household spies?
Or his easier ears beguile,
So removèd by our wile?
'Tis no sin love's fruit to steal,
But the sweet theft to reveal:
To be taken, to be seen,
These have crimes accounted been.

Note. This poem is an adaptation of one by the Roman poet Catullus; it is sung in Jonson's play by Volpone in a (vain) effort to seduce the virtuous wife Celia.

1. prove: try. 13. his: her husband's, whom Volpone has tricked into leaving Celia with him.

ROBERT HERRICK (1591–1674)

DELIGHT IN DISORDER

A sweet disorder in the dress
Kindles in clothes a wantonness:
A lawn about the shoulders thrown
Into a fine distraction;
An erring lace, which here and there
Enthralls the crimson stomacher;
A cuff neglectful, and thereby
Ribbands to flow confusedly;
A winning wave (deserving note)
In the tempestuous petticoat;
A careless shoe-string, in whose tie
I see a wild civility:
Do more bewitch me, than when art
Is too precise in every part.

10

CORINNA'S GOING A-MAYING

Get up, get up for shame! The blooming morn
Upon her wings presents the god unshorn.
    See how Aurora throws her fair,
    Fresh-quilted colors through the air.
    Get up, sweet slug-a-bed, and see
    The dew bespangling herb and tree.
Each flower has wept and bowed toward the East
Above an hour since; yet you not dressed,
    Nay, not so much as out of bed?
    When all the birds have matins said

10

3. **lawn:** linen scarf. 4. **distraction:** confusion. 5. **erring:** wandering. 6. **stomacher:** frontpiece of female dress covering breast and stomach. 8. **Ribbands:** ribbons.

2. **god unshorn:** Apollo, god of the sun. 3. **Aurora:** goddess of the dawn. 10. **matins:** morning prayer.

And sung their thankful hymns, 'tis sin,
Nay, profanation, to keep in,
Whenas a thousand virgins on this day
Spring sooner than the lark, to fetch in May.

Rise, and put on your foliage, and be seen
To come forth, like the springtime, fresh and green,
    And sweet as Flora. Take no care
    For jewels for your gown or hair.
    Fear not; the leaves will strew
    Gems in abundance upon you.   20
Besides, the childhood of the day has kept,
Against you come, some orient pearls unwept.
    Come, and receive them while the light
    Hangs on the dew-locks of the night;
    And Titan on the eastern hill
    Retires himself, or else stands still
Till you come forth. Wash, dress, be brief in praying:
Few beads are best when once we go a-Maying.

Come, my Corinna, come; and coming, mark
How each field turns a street, each street a park   30
    Made green and trimmed with trees; see how
    Devotion gives each house a bough
    Or branch; each porch, each door, ere this,
    An ark, a tabernacle is,
Made up of white-thorn neatly interwove,
As if here were those cooler shades of love.
    Can such delights be in the street
    And open fields, and we not see't?
    Come, we'll abroad; and let's obey
    The proclamation made for May,   40
And sin no more, as we have done, by staying;
But, my Corinna, come, let's go a-Maying.

There's not a budding boy or girl this day
But is got up and gone to bring in May.

14. May: the month and the white hawthorn. 17. Flora: goddess of flowers. 22. Against you come: awaiting your coming. 25. Titan: sun god. 28. beads: prayers. 30. turns: becomes. 34. ark: ark of the covenant, holy object.

A deal of youth ere this is come
Back, and with white-thorn laden home.
Some have dispatched their cakes and cream,
Before that we have left to dream;
And some have wept, and wooed, and plighted troth,
50   And chose their priest, ere we can cast off sloth.
Many a green-gown has been given,
Many a kiss, both odd and even;
Many a glance, too, has been sent
From out the eye, love's firmament;
Many a jest told of the keys betraying
This night, and locks picked; yet we're not a-Maying.

Come, let us go while we are in our prime,
And take the harmless folly of the time.
We shall grow old apace, and die
60   Before we know our liberty.
Our life is short, and our days run
As fast away as does the sun.
And as a vapor or a drop of rain,
Once lost, can ne'er be found again,
So when or you or I are made
A fable, song, or fleeting shade,
All love, all liking, all delight
Lies drowned with us in endless night.
Then, while time serves, and we are but decaying,
70   Come, my Corinna, come, let's go a-Maying.

TO THE VIRGINS, TO MAKE MUCH OF TIME

Gather ye rose-buds while ye may,
    Old Time is still a-flying;
And this same flower that smiles today
    Tomorrow will be dying.

The glorious lamp of heaven, the Sun,
    The higher he's a-getting;
The sooner will his race be run,
    And nearer he's to setting.

48. left: ceased. 51. Many . . . given: many girls have been tumbled on the grass.
65. or . . . or: either . . . or.

That age is best which is the first,
When youth and blood are warmer; 10
But being spent, the worse, and worst
Times, still succeed the former.

Then be not coy, but use your time;
And while ye may, go marry;
For having lost but once your prime,
You may for ever tarry.

GEORGE HERBERT (1593–1633)

JORDAN I

Who says that fictions only and false hair
Become a verse? Is there in truth no beauty?
Is all good structure in a winding stair?
May no lines pass, except they do their duty
Not to a true, but painted chair?

Is it no verse, except enchanted groves
And sudden arbors shadow coarse-spun lines?
Must purling streams refresh a lover's loves?
Must all be veiled, while he that reads, divines,
Catching the sense at two removes? 10

Shepherds are honest people; let them sing:
Riddle who list, for me, and pull for prime;
I envy no man's nightingale or spring;
Nor let them punish me with loss of rhyme,
Who plainly say, My God, My King.

12. still: always.

Title. Jordan: the river that had to be crossed for entry into the Promised Land; subsequently the river in which Christ was baptized. 2. Become: are suitable to. 5. painted chair: compare Plato's contention that art merely imitated an imitation of the real. 7. sudden: suddenly appearing. 12. Riddle . . . prime: as far as I'm concerned let whoever please (list) write ingeniously and draw cards to see who is best (prime: primero, card game).

VIRTUE

Sweet day, so cool, so calm, so bright,
The bridal of the earth and sky:
The dew shall weep thy fall tonight,
    For thou must die.

Sweet rose, whose hue, angry and brave,
Bids the rash gazer wipe his eye:
Thy root is ever in its grave,
    And thou must die.

Sweet spring, full of sweet days and roses,
10 A box where sweets compacted lie:
My music shows ye have your closes,
    And all must die.

Only a sweet and virtuous soul,
Like seasoned timber, never gives;
But though the whole world turn to coal,
    Then chiefly lives.

THE COLLAR

I struck the board and cried, No more!
    I will abroad.
What? shall I ever sigh and pine?
My lines and life are free, free as the road,
  Loose as the wind, and large as store.
    Shall I be still in suit?
Have I no harvest but a thorn
To let me blood, and not restore
What I have lost with cordial fruit?
10   Sure there was wine

2. **bridal:** wedding. 10. **sweets:** perfumes. 11. **ye:** plural—probably referring to days and roses; **closes:** ends of cadences in music. 15. **coal:** ashes.

1. **board:** table. 4. **lines:** appointed lot in life; compare Psalm xvi.6, "The lines are fallen unto me in pleasant places; yea, I have a goodly heritage." 5. **store:** abundance. 6. **in suit:** as a petitioner in the king's court. 8. **To let me blood:** to make me bleed. 9. **cordial:** heart stimulant or restorative.

Before my sighs did dry it; there was corn
  Before my tears did drown it.
  Is the year only lost to me?
  Have I no bays to crown it?
No flowers, no garlands gay? all blasted?
   All wasted?
  Not so, my heart: but there is fruit,
  And thou hast hands.
  Recover all thy sigh-blown age
On double pleasures: leave thy cold dispute   20
Of what is fit and not; forsake thy cage,
  Thy rope of sands,
Which petty thoughts have made, and made to thee
  Good cable, to enforce and draw,
   And be thy law,
  While thou didst wink and wouldst not see.
   Away! Take heed!
   I will abroad.
Call in thy death's-head there; tie up thy fears.
  He that forbears   30
  To suit and serve his need,
  Deserves his load.
But as I raved and grew more fierce and wild
  At every word,
Methought I heard one calling, *Child!*
  And I replied, *My Lord.*

THE PULLEY

  When God at first made man,
Having a glass of blessings standing by,
"Let us," said He, "pour on him all we can.
Let the world's riches, which dispersèd lie,
  Contract into a span."

  So strength first made a way;
Then beauty flowed, then wisdom, honor, pleasure.

---

14. **bays:** crown of bay leaves signifying success. 26. **wink:** close the eyes to a situation. 29. **death's-head:** skull, a *memento mori* (reminder of death). 35. **Methought:** it seemed to me.

  5. **span:** hand's breadth.

When almost all was out, God made a stay,
Perceiving that, alone of all his treasure,
10   Rest in the bottom lay.

"For if I should," said He,
"Bestow this jewel also on my creature,
He would adore My gifts instead of Me,
And rest in nature, not the God of nature;
So both should losers be.

"Yet let him keep the rest,
But keep them with repining restlessness.
Let him be rich and weary, that at least
If goodness lead him not, yet weariness
20   May toss him to My breast."

THE FLOWER

How fresh, O Lord, how sweet and clean
Are Thy returns! Even as the flowers in spring,
To which, besides their own demean,
The late-past frosts tributes of pleasure bring.
Grief melts away
Like snow in May,
As if there were no such cold thing.

Who would have thought my shriveled heart
Could have recovered greenness? It was gone
10   Quite underground, as flowers depart
To see their mother-root when they have blown,
Where they together
All the hard weather,
Dead to the world, keep house unknown.

These are Thy wonders, Lord of power,
Killing and quickening, bringing down to hell
And up to heaven in an hour,

8. made a stay: paused. 17. repining: discontented.

3. demean: domain, demeanor; their intrinsic value. 11 blown: bloomed.

Making a chiming of a passing-bell.
  We say amiss
   This or that is;   20
Thy word is all, if we could spell.

O, that I once past changing were,
Fast in Thy paradise, where no flower can wither!
 Many a spring I shoot up fair,
Offering at heaven, growing and groaning thither;
   Nor doth my flower
   Want a spring shower,
My sins and I joining together.

But while I grow in a straight line,
Still upwards bent, as if heaven were mine own,   30
 Thy anger comes, and I decline:
What frost to that? What pole is not the zone
   Where all things burn,
   When Thou dost turn,
And the least frown of Thine is shown?

And now in age I bud again,
After so many deaths I live and write;
 I once more smell the dew and rain,
And relish versing. O my only light,
   It cannot be   40
   That I am he
On whom Thy tempests fell all night!
These are Thy wonders, Lord of love,
To make us see we are but flowers that glide;
 Which when we once can find and prove,
Thou hast a garden for us where to bide.
   Who would be more,
   Swelling through store,
Forfeit their paradise by their pride.

---

18. Making a chiming . . . -bell: making a varied and gay sound instead of a single-toned mournful sound. 21. spell: interpret properly. 25. Offering at: aiming at. 27. Want. lack. 44. glide: die imperceptibly. 45 prove: experience.

THE ALTAR

A broken ALTAR, Lord, thy servant rears,
Made of a heart, and cémented with tears:
  Whose parts are as thy hand did frame;
  No workman's tool hath touched the same.
        A   HEART   alone
        Is   such   a   stone,
        As   nothing   but
        Thy power doth cut.
        Wherefore each part
10   Of my hard heart
        Meets in this frame,
        To praise thy Name:
That, if I chance to hold my peace,
These stones to praise thee may not cease.
O let thy blessed SACRIFICE be mine,
And sanctify this ALTAR to be thine.

WILLIAM HABINGTON (1605–1654)

TO ROSES IN THE BOSOM OF CASTARA

    Ye blushing virgins happy are
    In the chaste nunnery of her breasts,
    For he'd profane so chaste a fair,
    Whoe'er should call them Cupid's nests.

    Transplanted thus how bright ye grow,
    How rich a perfume do ye yield.
    In some close garden, cowslips so
    Are sweeter than in th'open field.

4. Cf. Exodus xx.25: "And if thou wilt make me an altar of stone, thou shalt not build it of hewen stone: for if thou lift up thy tool upon it, thou has polluted it." 13–14. Cf. Luke xix.40: "I tell you, that if these should hold their peace, the stones would immediately cry out."

3. a fair: a beautiful person.

In those white cloisters live secure
From the rude blasts of wanton breath,   10
Each hour more innocent and pure,
Till you shall wither into death.

Then that which living gave you room,
Your glorious sepulcher shall be;
There wants no marble for a tomb,
Whose breast hath marble been to me.

EDMUND WALLER (1606–1687)

ON A GIRDLE

That which her slender waist confined
Shall now my joyful temples bind;
No monarch but would give his crown,
His arms might do what this has done.

It was my heaven's extremest sphere,
The pale which held that lovely deer.
My joy, my grief, my hope, my love,
Did all within this circle move.

A narrow compass, and yet there
Dwelt all that's good and all that's fair;   10
Give me but what this riband bound;
Take all the rest the sun goes round!

15. wants: needs.

Title. Girdle: sash, worn round the waist. 4. His arms: that is, if his arms. 5. extremest
sphere: outermost of the concentric spheres which were thought to make up the universe.
6. pale: fence. 11. riband: ribbon.

GO, LOVELY ROSE!

Go, lovely rose!
Tell her that wastes her time and me
That now she knows,
When I resemble her to thee,
How sweet and fair she seems to be.

Tell her that's young
And shuns to have her graces spied,
That, hadst thou sprung
In deserts where no men abide,
10   Thou must have uncommended died.

Small is the worth
Of beauty from the light retired;
Bid her come forth:
Suffer herself to be desired,
And not blush so to be admired.

Then die, that she
The common fate of all things rare
May read in thee;
How small a part of time they share
20   That are so wondrous sweet and fair.

4. resemble: compare.

JOHN MILTON (1608–1674)

LYCIDAS

Yet once more, O ye laurels, and once more
Ye myrtles brown, with ivy never sere,
I come to pluck your berries harsh and crude
And with forced fingers rude,
Shatter your leaves before the mellowing year.
Bitter constraint, and sad occasion dear,
Compels me to disturb your season due:
For Lycidas is dead, dead ere his prime,
Young Lycidas, and hath not left his peer.
Who would not sing for Lycidas? he knew   10
Himself to sing, and build the lofty rhyme.
He must not float upon his watery bier
Unwept, and welter to the parching wind,
Without the meed of some melodious tear.

   Begin then, Sisters of the sacred well,
That from beneath the seat of Jove doth spring,
Begin, and somewhat loudly sweep the string.
Hence with denial vain, and coy excuse,
So may some gentle muse
With lucky words favor my destined urn,   20
And as he passes, turn
And bid fair peace be to my sable shroud.

Note. Milton was called upon to contribute to a volume in memory of Edward King at a time when he felt unprepared, and he was reluctant to resume writing poetry. He structured the poem by using the traditional divisions of the pastoral elegy, the main ones being (1) announcement of the death of the "shepherd," (2) previous life of the poet and the departed together, (3) the change after the loss, (4) nature's mourning, (5) questioning of gods and mortals as to responsibility, (6) procession of mourners, and (7) consolation in thinking that the dead "shepherd" is immortal. He twice significantly departs from his models (lines 64-84 and 113-131) to voice private and topical concerns respectively and then explicitly returns to the pastoral convention, with reference to Arethuse and Mincius after the first digression and Alpheus and the Sicilian Muse after the second.

Title. Lycidas: name for Edward King, taken from Virgil's pastoral poetry. 1–2. laurels, myrtles, ivy: plants associated with poetic fame. 2. brown: dark. 6. dear: dire. 13. welter: roll. 15. sisters . . . well: the Muses who live by the Pierian spring, source of poetic inspiration. 19. muse: poet.

For we were nursed upon the self-same hill,
Fed the same flock by fountain, shade, and rill.
Together both, ere the high lawns appeared
Under the opening eye-lids of the morn,
We drove afield, and both together heard
What time the gray-fly winds her sultry horn,
Battening our flocks with the fresh dews of night,
Oft till the star that rose at evening bright
Toward heaven's descent had sloped his westering wheel.
Meanwhile the rural ditties were not mute;
Tempered to the oaten flute,
Rough satyrs danced, and fauns with cloven heel
From the glad sound would not be absent long;
And old Damætas loved to hear our song.

    But O the heavy change now thou art gone,
Now thou art gone, and never must return!
Thee, shepherd, thee the woods and desert caves,
With wild thyme and the gadding vine o'ergrown,
And all their echoes, mourn.
The willows and the hazel copses green
Shall now no more be seen
Fanning their joyous leaves to thy soft lays.
As killing as the canker to the rose,
Or taint-worm to the weanling herds that graze,
Or frost to flowers, that their gay wardrobe wear
When first the white-thorn blows;
Such, Lycidas, thy loss to shepherd's ear.

        Where were ye, Nymphs, when the remorseless deep
Closed o'er the head of your loved Lycidas?
For neither were ye playing on the steep
Where your old bards, the famous Druids, lie,
Nor on the shaggy top of Mona high,
Nor yet where Deva spreads her wizard stream.
Ay me, I fondly dream!
        Had ye been there—for what could that have done?

---

28. **What . . . horn:** i.e., noon. 29. **Battening:** feeding. 36. **Damaetas:** an old shepherd, name taken from Virgil. 40. **gadding:** straying. 45. **canker:** infecting worm. 50. **Nymphs:** minor goddesses of nature. 52. **steep:** mountainside. 53. **Druids:** poetpriests of ancient Britain. 54. **Mona:** Isle of Anglesey, North West Wales. 55. **Deva . . . stream:** the River Dee was thought to have special "divinity." It disembogues into the Irish Sea above Chester, from which Edward King embarked. 56. **fondly:** foolishly.

What could the Muse herself that Orpheus bore,
The Muse herself, for her enchanting son,
Whom universal nature did lament,   60
When by the rout that made the hideous roar,
His gory visage down the stream was sent,
Down the swift Hebrus to the Lesbian shore?
    Alas! what boots it with uncessant care
To tend the homely, slighted, shepherd's trade
And strictly meditate the thankless Muse?
Were it not better done, as others use,
To sport with Amaryllis in the shade
Or with the tangles of Neæra's hair?
Fame is the spur that the clear spirit doth raise   70
(That last infirmity of noble mind)
To scorn delights, and live laborious days;
But the fair guerdon when we hope to find,
And think to burst out into sudden blaze,
Comes the blind Fury with the abhorrèd shears
And slits the thin-spun life. "But not the praise,"
Phœbus replied, and touched my trembling ears:
"Fame is no plant that grows on mortal soil,
Nor in the glistering foil
Set off to the world, nor in broad rumor lies;   80
But lives and spreads aloft by those pure eyes
And perfect witness of all-judging Jove;
As he pronounces lastly on each deed,
Of so much fame in heaven expect thy meed."
    O fountain Arethuse, and thou honored flood,
Smooth-sliding Mincius, crowned with vocal reeds,
That strain I heard was of a higher mood.
But now my oat proceeds,
And listens to the herald of the sea
That came in Neptune's plea;   90

58–63. Muse . . . shore: the Muse Calliope, mother of Orpheus, the Thracian poet, could do nothing for him when a rout of women returning from a Bacchanalian orgy killed him and threw his head into the river Hebrus. His head finally came ashore on the isle of Lesbos. 64. what boots it: what good is it. 65. shepherd's trade: poetry. 66. meditate: study. 67. use: are accustomed to. 68, 69. Amaryllis, Neaera: sporting shepherdesses, names from Virgil. 75. Fury: Atropos, the third of the three Fates. She cuts the thread of life. 77. Phoebus: Apollo, god of poetic inspiration. 79. foil: setting of a jewel. 85. Arethuse: fountain in Sicily, associated with the Greek pastoralist, Theocritus. 86. Mincius: river near the birthplace of the pastoralist Virgil. 88. oat: oaten reed; cf. line 33. 89. herald of the sea: Triton, son of Neptune, god of the sea

He asked the waves, and asked the felon winds,
"What hard mishap hath doomed this gentle swain?"
And questioned every gust of rugged wings
That blows from off each beakèd promontory:
They knew not of his story;
And sage Hippotades their answer brings,
That not a blast was from his dungeon strayed,
The air was calm, and on the level brine
Sleek Panopè with all her sisters played.
It was that fatal and perfidious bark,
Built in the eclipse, and rigged with curses dark,
That sunk so low that sacred head of thine.

    Next Camus, reverend sire, went footing slow,
His mantle hairy, and his bonnet sedge,
Inwrought with figures dim, and on the edge
Like to that sanguine flower inscribed with woe.
"Ah! who hath reft," quoth he, "my dearest pledge?"
Last came, and last did go
The Pilot of the Galilean lake;
Two massy keys he bore of metals twain
(The golden opes, the iron shuts amain);
He shook his mitred locks, and stern bespake:
"How well could I have spared for thee, young swain,
Enow of such as for their bellies' sake
Creep and intrude and climb into the fold!
Of other care they little reckoning make
Than how to scramble at the shearers' feast
And shove away the worthy bidden guest.
Blind mouths! that scarce themselves know how to hold
A sheep-hook, or have learned aught else the least
That to the faithful herdman's art belongs!
What recks it them? What need they? They are sped;
And when they list, their lean and flashy songs
Grate on their scrannel pipes of wretched straw;
The hungry sheep look up, and are not fed,
But, swollen with wind and the rank mist they draw,
Rot inwardly, and foul contagion spread:

    96. Hippotades: Aeolus, god of the winds. **99. Panopè:** leading sea-nymph. **103. Camus:** god of the river Cam; hence, the university of Cambridge. **106. sanguine flower:** hyacinth. **107. pledge:** child. **109. Pilot . . . lake:** St. Peter. **112. mitred:** crowned with a mitre, the bishop's headdress. Peter was the first bishop of Rome. **115. fold:** church. **122. recks . . . sped:** why should they concern themselves? What need have they? They have prospered. **123. list:** please. **124 scrannel:** harsh and feeble.

Besides what the grim wolf with privy paw
Daily devours apace, and nothing said;
But that two-handed engine at the door   130
Stands ready to smite once, and smite no more."
      Return, Alpheus; the dread voice is past
That shrunk thy streams; return, Sicilian Muse,
And call the vales, and bid them hither cast
Their bells and flowerets of a thousand hues.
Ye valleys low, where the mild whispers use
Of shades and wanton winds and gushing brooks,
On whose fresh lap the swart star sparely looks,
Throw hither all your quaint enameled eyes
That on the green turf suck the honeyed showers,   140
And purple all the ground with vernal flowers.
Bring the rathe primrose that forsaken dies,
The tufted crow-toe, and pale jessamine,
The white pink, and the pansy freaked with jet,
The glowing violet,
The musk-rose, and the well-attired woodbine,
With cowslips wan that hang the pensive head,
And every flower that sad embroidery wears;
Bid amaranthus all his beauty shed,
And daffadillies fill their cups with tears,   150
To strew the laureate hearse where Lycid lies.
For so to interpose a little ease,
Let our frail thoughts dally with false surmise.
Ay me! whilst thee the shores and sounding seas
Wash far away, where'er thy bones are hurled,
Whether beyond the stormy Hebrides
Where thou, perhaps, under the whelming tide
Visit'st the bottom of the monstrous world;
Or whether thou, to our moist vows denied,
Sleep'st by the fable of Bellerus old,   160

---

128. wolf: representative of the Roman Catholic Church; privy: secret. 130. two-handed engine: "Over forty guesses about its meaning are on record." (Merritt Hughes, *John Milton: Complete Poems and Major Prose* [New York, 1957], p. 117). 132. Alpheus: river in Arcadia; associated with Arethuse, line 85. 133. Sicilian Muse: pastoral muse; Theocritus lived in Sicily. 136. use: visit. 138. swart star: the dog star Sirius, held responsible for turning vegetation black in summer. 142. rathe: early. 144. freaked with jet: flecked with black. 149. amaranthus: a flower that does not fade. 156. Hebrides: islands off northwestern Scotland. 159. moist vows: tearful prayers. 160. Bellerus: giant associated with Land's End at the tip of Cornwall.

Where the great Vision of the guarded mount
Looks toward Namancos and Bayona's hold:
Look homeward, Angel, now, and melt with ruth;
And, O ye dolphins, waft the hapless youth!
    Weep no more, woeful shepherds, weep no more;
For Lycidas, your sorrow, is not dead,
Sunk though he be beneath the watery floor;
So sinks the day-star in the ocean bed,
And yet anon repairs his drooping head,
170   And tricks his beams, and with new-spangled ore
Flames in the forehead of the morning sky;
So Lycidas sunk low, but mounted high
Through the dear might of Him that walked the waves,
Where other groves and other streams along,
With nectar pure his oozy locks he laves,
And hears the unexpressive nuptial song
In the blessed kingdoms meek of joy and love.
There entertain him all the saints above,
In solemn troops and sweet societies
180   That sing, and singing in their glory move,
And wipe the tears forever from his eyes.
Now, Lycidas, the shepherds weep no more;
Henceforth thou art the genius of the shore,
In thy large recompense, and shalt be good
To all that wander in that perilous flood.
    Thus sang the uncouth swain to the oaks and rills,
While the still morn went out with sandals gray;
He touched the tender stops of various quills,
With eager thought warbling his Doric lay:
190   And now the sun had stretched out all the hills,
And now was dropped into the western bay.
At last he rose, and twitched his mantle blue:
Tomorrow to fresh woods, and pastures new.

161–2. Where . . . hold: Milton thought of St. Michael's Mount on the south coast
of Cornwall as looking toward the Namancos mountains and Bayona, a Spanish stronghold.
163. Angel: Michael; ruth: mercy. 164. dolphins: allusion to a legend of a mythical
drowned sailor whose body was brought ashore by dolphins. 168. day-star: sun. 170.
tricks: adorns. 173. Him: Christ. 176. unexpressive: inexpressible. 183. genius: pro-
tecting spirit. 186. uncouth swain: unknown shepherd. 188. quills: reeds of the shep-
herd's pipe. 189. Doric: the dialect of the Greek pastorals.

ON THE LATE MASSACRE IN PIEMONT

Avenge, O Lord, thy slaughtered saints, whose bones
  Lie scattered on the Alpine mountains cold;
  Even them who kept thy truth so pure of old
  When all our fathers worshipped stocks and stones,
Forget not: in Thy book record their groans
  Who were Thy sheep and in their ancient fold
  Slain by the bloody Piemontese, that rolled
  Mother with infant down the rocks. Their moans
The vales redoubled to the hills, and they
  To Heaven. Their martyred blood and ashes sow   10
  O'er all th' Italian fields where still doth sway
The triple tyrant: that from these may grow
  A hundred-fold, who having learnt Thy way
  Early may fly the Babylonian woe.

WHEN I CONSIDER HOW MY LIGHT IS SPENT

When I consider how my light is spent
  Ere half my days in this dark world and wide,
  And that one talent which is death to hide
  Lodged with me useless, though my soul more bent
To serve therewith my Maker, and present
  My true account, lest He returning chide;
  "Doth God exact day-labor, light denied?"
  I fondly ask. But Patience, to prevent
That murmur, soon replies, "God doth not need
  Either man's work or His own gifts. Who best   10
  Bear His mild yoke, they serve Him best. His state
Is kingly: Thousands at His bidding speed,
  And post o'er land and ocean without rest;
  They also serve who only stand and wait."

1. **slaughtered saints:** the Waldenses, a Protestant group living in Piedmont, Italy, who were massacred by the Catholics under the Duke of Savoy in April, 1655. Milton, serving as Secretary for Foreign Tongues under Cromwell, wrote an official note of protest to the Duke. 4. **When . . . stones:** i.e., in the 12th century, when the Waldenses sect was established, England was, of course, still Catholic and worshipping "images." **10-12. sow . . . grow:** suggestive of the sowing of the dragon's teeth by Cadmus, from which men grew who built the city of Thebes, and also of the parable of the sower, Matthew xiii.3. **12. triple tyrant:** the Pope. **14. Babylonian woe:** the ancient city of Babylon was destroyed because of its iniquity. Conventionally, Babylon became a symbol for the sinful city—here, Milton suggests the Church of Rome.

1-2. **When . . . days:** Milton became blind at age 42. **3. one talent:** ability; unit of money. For the parable of the talents, which is central to the sonnet's meaning, see Matthew xxv.14-30. **8. fondly:** foolishly. **12. Thousands:** i.e., the heavenly angels.

METHOUGHT I SAW MY LATE ESPOUSÈD SAINT

Methought I saw my late espousèd saint
  Brought to me like Alcestis from the grave,
  Whom Jove's great son to her glad husband gave,
  Rescued from death by force though pale and faint.
Mine, as whom washed from spot of child-bed taint
  Purification in the Old Law did save,
  And such, as yet once more I trust to have
  Full sight of her in Heaven without restraint,
Came vested all in white, pure as her mind:
  Her face was veiled, yet to my fancied sight,
  Love, sweetness, goodness, in her person shined
So clear, as in no face with more delight.
  But O, as to embrace me she inclined,
  I waked, she fled, and day brought back my night.

RICHARD LOVELACE (1618–1658)

TO LUCASTA, GOING TO THE WARS

Tell me not, sweet, I am unkind,
That from the nunnery
Of thy chaste breast and quiet mind
To war and arms I fly.

True, a new mistress now I chase,
The first foe in the field,
And with a stronger faith embrace
A sword, a horse, a shield.

Yet this inconstancy is such
As you too shall adore;
I could not love thee, dear, so much,
Loved I not honor more.

---

1. espousèd saint: probably Milton's second wife, Katherine Woodcock, whom he had married after he became blind. She died four months after childbirth, in 1658. **2-3. Alcestis ... Jove's great son:** King Admetus's wife, Alcestis, offered her life for her husband's. In Euripides' play, Hercules wrestles with Death and brings Alcestis back alive from the Underworld. **6. Old Law:** Hebrew law prescribed ritualistic purification of women after childbirth. **10. veiled:** like Alcestis, who could not speak to her husband until the third morning of her return. **14. night:** Milton's blindness.

TO ALTHEA, FROM PRISON

When Love with unconfinèd wings
Hovers within my gates
And my divine Althea brings
To whisper at the grates;
When I lie tangled in her hair
And fettered to her eye:
The birds that wanton in the air
Know no such liberty.

When flowing cups run swiftly round
With no allaying Thames,   10
Our careless heads with roses bound,
Our hearts with loyal flames;
When thirsty grief in wine we steep,
When healths and draughts go free:
Fishes that tipple in the deep
Know no such liberty.

When, like committed linnets, I
With shriller throat shall sing
The sweetness, mercy, majesty,
And glories of my King;   20
When I shall voice aloud, how good
He is, how great should be:
Enlargèd winds that curl the flood
Know no such liberty.

Stone walls do not a prison make,
Nor iron bars a cage;
Minds innocent and quiet take
That for an hermitage.
If I have freedom in my love
And in my soul am free,   30
Angels alone that soar above
Enjoy such liberty.

Title. Lovelace was imprisoned by Parliament in 1642, shortly before the outbreak of the English Civil War, for his Royalist sympathies. 4. grates: prison bars. 7. birds: an alternate version has *gods* here; wanton: sport freely. 10. allaying: alloying, diluting. 14. healths . . . free: toasts are liberally made. 17. committed: caged; linnets: small singing birds. 23. Enlargèd: free; flood: sea.

ANDREW MARVELL (1621–1678)

ON A DROP OF DEW

See how the orient dew,
Shed from the bosom of the morn
Into the blowing roses,
Yet careless of its mansion new—
For the clear region where 'twas born
Round in itself incloses,
And in its little globe's extent
Frames as it can its native element—
How it the purple flower does slight,
10   Scarce touching where it lies,
But gazing back upon the skies,
Shines with a mournful light,
Like its own tear,
Because so long divided from the sphere.
Restless it rolls and unsecure,
Trembling lest it grow impure;
Till the warm sun pity its pain,
And to the skies exhale it back again.
So the soul, that drop, that ray
20   Of the clear fountain of eternal day,
Could it within the human flower be seen,
Remembering still its former height,
Shuns the sweet leaves and blossoms green;
And, recollecting its own light,
Does, in its pure and circling thoughts, express
The greater heaven in an heaven less.

---

1. orient: shining, precious, like a pearl. **6. Round . . . incloses:** incloses itself in its own orb (Herbert J. C. Grierson, *Metaphysical Lyrics and Poems of the Seventeenth Century* [Oxford, 1921], p. 240).

9. How: repeating the **how** of line 1. **14. sphere:** sky.

In how coy a figure wound,
Every way it turns away:
So the world excluding round,
Yet receiving in the day.   30
Dark beneath, but bright above;
Here disdaining, there in love.
How loose and easy hence to go,
How girt and ready to ascend;
Moving but on a point below,
It all about does upwards bend.
Such did the manna's sacred dew distill:
White, and entire, though congealed and chill;
Congealed on earth, but does, dissolving, run
Into the glories of the almighty sun.   40

TO HIS COY MISTRESS

Had we but world enough, and time,
This coyness, lady, were no crime.
We would sit down, and think which way
To walk, and pass our long love's day.
Thou by the Indian Ganges' side
Should'st rubies find; I by the tide
Of Humber would complain. I would
Love you ten years before the Flood;
And you should, if you please, refuse
Till the conversion of the Jews.   10
My vegetable love should grow
Vaster than empires, and more slow.
An hundred years should go to praise
Thine eyes, and on thy forehead gaze;
Two hundred to adore each breast;
But thirty thousand to the rest:

---

30. receiving in: absorbing. 34. girt: prepared. 37. manna: juice from the tree bark which has supposedly been used for food, in particular by the Israelites fleeing from Egypt, when (Exodus xvi.13–15) manna remained after the morning dew evaporated.

7. Humber: river which disembogues at Hull, where Marvell lived. 11. vegetable: growing with primitive insistence.

An age at least to every part,
And the last age should show your heart.
For, lady, you deserve this state,
20   Nor would I love at lower rate.
   But at my back I always hear
Time's wingèd chariot hurrying near;
And yonder all before us lie
Deserts of vast eternity.
Thy beauty shall no more be found,
Nor in thy marble vault shall sound
My echoing song; then worms shall try
That long-preserved virginity;
And your quaint honor turn to dust,
30   And into ashes all my lust.
The grave's a fine and private place,
But none, I think, do there embrace.
   Now, therefore, while the youthful hue
Sits on thy skin like morning dew,
And while thy willing soul transpires
At every pore with instant fires,
Now let us sport us while we may;
And now, like amorous birds of prey,
Rather at once our time devour,
40   Than languish in his slow-chapped power.
Let us roll all our strength and all
Our sweetness up into one ball;
And tear our pleasures with rough strife
Thorough the iron gates of life.
Thus, though we cannot make our sun
Stand still, yet we will make him run.

THE GARDEN

How vainly men themselves amaze
To win the palm, the oak, or bays;
And their incessant labors see
Crowned from some single herb, or tree,
Whose short and narrow-vergèd shade
Does prudently their toils upbraid;

35. transpires: exhales. 40. -chapped: -jawed. 44. Thorough: through.

1. amaze: misdirect their energies. 2. palm, oak, bays: tokens of achievement in war, civil pursuits, and literature, respectively. 5. -vergèd: -limited.

While all flowers and all trees do close
To weave the garlands of repose.

Fair Quiet, have I found thee here,
And Innocence, thy sister dear.   10
Mistaken long, I sought you then
In busy companies of men.
Your sacred plants, if here below,
Only among the plants will grow;
Society is all but rude
To this delicious solitude.

No white nor red was ever seen
So amorous as this lovely green.
Fond lovers, cruel as their flame,
Cut in these trees their mistress' name;   20
Little, alas, they know or heed
How far these beauties hers exceed!
Fair trees! wheres'e'er your barks I wound,
No name shall but your own be found.

When we have run our passion's heat,
Love hither makes his best retreat.
The gods, that mortal beauty chase,
Still in a tree did end their race:
Apollo hunted Daphne so,
Only that she might laurel grow;   30
And Pan did after Syrinx speed,
Not as a nymph, but for a reed.

What wondrous life is this I lead:
Ripe apples drop about my head;
The luscious clusters of the vine
Upon my mouth to crush their wine;
The nectarine and curious peach
Into my hands themselves do reach;
Stumbling on melons as I pass,
Ensnared with flowers, I fall on grass.   40

15. rude: primitive. 17. white, red: colors of female beauty. 18. amorous: lovable.
19. Fond: foolish; flame: ardor. 27-32. The gods . . . reed: Jove preserved Daphne and
Syrinx, from the lust of Apollo and Pan respectively, by changing them into the laurel
and the reed. See Ovid's *Metamorphoses*, I.

Meanwhile, the mind, from pleasure less,
Withdraws into its happiness:
The mind, that ocean where each kind
Does straight its own resemblance find;
Yet it creates, transcending these,
Far other worlds and other seas;
Annihilating all that's made
To a green thought in a green shade.

Here at the fountain's sliding foot,
50   Or at some fruit-tree's mossy root,
Casting the body's vest aside,
My soul into the boughs does glide;
There like a bird it sits and sings,
Then whets and combs its silver wings;
And, till prepared for longer flight,
Waves in its plumes the various light.

Such was that happy garden-state,
While man there walked without a mate;
After a place so pure and sweet,
60   What other help could yet be meet?
But 'twas beyond a mortal's share
To wander solitary there:
Two paradises 'twere in one
To live in paradise alone.

How well the skillful gardener drew
Of flowers and herbs this dial new,
Where from above the milder sun
Does through a fragrant zodiac run;
And, as it works, th'industrious bee
70   Computes its time as well as we.
How could such sweet and wholesome hours
Be reckoned but with herbs and flowers!

41. from pleasure less: turning from inferior pleasures, i.e., of the senses in stanza
5. 43–44. The mind . . . find: the mind contains the ideal forms of all known things.
51. body's vest: i.e., flesh. 54. whets: preens. 60. meet: fitting. 66. dial: sundial, incorpo-
rating the signs of the zodiac.

AN HORATIAN ODE UPON CROMWELL'S RETURN FROM IRELAND

The forward youth that would appear
Must now forsake his Muses dear,
    Nor in the shadows sing
    His numbers languishing.

'Tis time to leave the books in dust
And oil th'unusèd armor's rust,
    Removing from the wall
    The corslet of the hall.

So restless Cromwell could not cease
In the inglorious arts of peace,   10
    But through adventurous war
    Urgèd his active star.

And, like the three-forked lightning, first
Breaking the clouds where it was nursed,
    Did thorough his own side
    His fiery way divide.

For 'tis all one to courage high—
The emulous or enemy;
    And with such, to inclose
    Is more than to oppose.   20

Then burning through the air he went,
And palaces and temples rent;
    And Caesar's head at last
    Did through his laurels blast.

'Tis madness to resist or blame
The force of angry Heaven's flame;
    And, if we would speak true,
    Much to the man is due;

Title. Horatian Ode: *see* Glossary. Cromwell had returned from the suppression of the Irish in 1650 to direct a campaign against the Scots. 2. Muses: the goddesses who traditionally inspire artistic creation. 4. numbers: poetry. 12. active star: destiny. 15. thorough: through. 18. emulous: envious. 19. inclose: curb. 23. Caesar's: i.e., Charles I's. Cromwell had had Charles executed, see line 54.

Who, from his private gardens, where
30   He lived reservèd and austere,
                As if his highest plot
                To plant the bergamot,

Could by industrious valor climb
To ruin the great work of time,
                And cast the kingdom old
                Into another mold.

Though Justice against Fate complain,
And plead the ancient rights in vain;
                But those do hold or break,
40   As men are strong or weak.

Nature, that hateth emptiness,
Allows of penetration less,
                And therefore must make room
                Where greater spirits come.

What field of all the Civil Wars,
Where his were not the deepest scars?
                And Hampton shows what part
                He had of wiser art.

Where, twining subtle fears with hope,
50   He wove a net of such scope,
                That Charles himself might chase
                To Caresbrooke's narrow case.

That thence the royal actor borne
The tragic scaffold might adorn;
                While round, the armèd bands
                Did clap their bloody hands.

He nothing common did or mean
Upon that memorable scene;
                But with his keener eye
60   The axe's edge did try;

32. bergamot: pear tree. 41–42. Nature . . . less: nature abhors a vacuum, and even more strongly refuses to allow two things to occupy the same space. 45. Wars: between Charles (the Royalists) and Cromwell (the Parliamentarians), 1642–46 and 1647–48. 47–52. Hampton . . . case: Charles fled from imprisonment in Hampton Court to Carisbrooke Castle (Caresbrooke), Isle of Wight. The Royalists later claimed that Cromwell (he of line 50) had engineered this escape in order that Charles might give cause for his execution. Charles was executed in 1649. 57. He: the king.

Nor called the gods with vulgar spite
To vindicate his helpless right,
    But bowed his comely head
    Down as upon a bed.

This was that memorable hour
Which first assured the forcèd power.
    So when they did design
    The Capitol's first line,

A bleeding head where they begun,
Did fright the architects to run;   70
    And yet in that the State
    Foresaw its happy fate.

And now the Irish are ashamed
To see themselves in one year tamed;
    So much one man can do,
    That does both act and know.

They can affirm his praises best,
And have, though overcome, confessed
    How good he is, how just,
    And fit for highest trust;   80

Nor yet grown stiffer with command,
But still in the Republic's hand;
    How fit he is to sway
    That can so well obey.

He to the Commons' feet presents
A kingdom for his first year's rents;
    And, what he may, forbears
    His fame, to make it theirs;

And has his sword and spoils ungirt,
To lay them at the public's skirt.   90
    So when the falcon high
    Falls heavy from the sky,

---

66. forcèd power: power gained by force. 68. Capitol's first line: foundations of Rome. 82. still in the Republic's hand: had not yet assumed dictatorial powers. 87. forbears: deflects. 89. ungirt: taken off.

She, having killed, no more does search
But on the next green bough to perch;
   Where, when he first does lure,
   The falconer has her sure.

What may not then our Isle presume
While victory his crest does plume!
   What may not others fear
100   If thus he crown each year!

A Caesar he ere long to Gaul,
To Italy an Hannibal,
   And to all states not free
   Shall climacteric be.

The Pict no shelter now shall find
Within his parti-colored mind;
   But from this valor sad
   Shrink underneath the plaid;

Happy, if in the tufted brake
110   The English hunter him mistake;
   Nor lay his hounds in near
   The Caledonian deer.

But thou the Wars' and Fortune's son
March indefatigably on;
   And for the last effect
   Still keep thy sword erect;

Besides the force it has to fright
The spirits of the shady night,
   The same arts that did gain
120   A power must it maintain.

101–104. **A Caesar . . . be:** before long he will prove conqueror of enslaved states as Caesar to Gaul and Hannibal to Italy; **climacteric:** climax. 105. **Pict.** Scot. 106. **parti-colored:** divided loyalties—to England and Scotland. 107. **sad:** steadfast, sober. 110. **English hunter:** Cromwell; **mistake:** overlook. 112. **Caledonian:** Scottish. 117. **it:** the sword hilt, as a sign of the cross.

HENRY VAUGHAN (1622–1695)

THE WORLD

I saw eternity the other night
Like a great ring of pure and endless light,
    All calm as it was bright;
And round beneath it, time, in hours, days, years,
        Driven by the spheres,
Like a vast shadow moved, in which the world
    And all her train were hurled:
The doting lover in his quaintest strain
        Did there complain;
Near him his lute, his fancy, and his flights,   10
        Wit's sour delights,
With gloves and knots, the silly snares of pleasure
        Yet his dear treasure,
All scattered lay, while he his eyes did pour
        Upon a flower.

The darksome statesman, hung with weights and woe,
Like a thick midnight fog moved there so slow,
    He did nor stay nor go;
Condemning thoughts, like sad eclipses, scowl
        Upon his soul,   20
And clouds of crying witnesses without
        Pursued him with one shout.
Yet digged the mole, and lest his ways be found
        Worked underground,
Where he did clutch his prey (but One did see
        That policy!).

5. spheres: the concentric circles which were thought to make up the universe. 7. train: followers. 8. quaintest strain: cleverest melody. 9. complain: express the pain of passion. 12. knots: love knots, knotted ribbons, for example, which serve as tokens between lovers. 14. pour: weep. 16. darksome: corrupt. 21. without: outside. 23. mole: that is, the statesman; mole is the subject of digged. 25. One: God. 26. policy: strategy.

Churches and altars fed him; perjuries
    Were gnats and flies;
It rained about him blood and tears, but he
    Drank them as free.

The fearful miser on a heap of rust
Sat pining all his life there, did scarce trust
    His own hands with the dust,
Yet would not place one piece above, but lives
    In fear of thieves.
Thousands there were as frantic as himself,
    And hugged each one his pelf:
The downright epicure placed heaven in sense,
    And scorned pretense;
While others, slipped into a wide excess,
    Said little less;
The weaker sort, slight trivial wares enslave,
    Who think them brave;
And poor depisèd truth sat counting by
    Their victory.

Yet some, who all this while did weep and sing,
And sing and weep, soared up into the ring;
    But most would use no wing.
"O fools," said I, "thus to prefer dark night
    Before true light,
To live in grots and caves, and hate the day
    Because it shows the way,
The way which from this dead and dark abode
    Leads up to God,
A way where you might tread the sun, and be
    More bright than he."
But as I did their madness so discuss,
    One whispered thus:
"This ring the Bridegroom did for none provide
    But for His bride."

28. Were gnats and flies: were trifling. 30. as free: freely. 33. dust: gold-dust. 34. above: that is, in heaven. 37. pelf: contemptuous term for money. 38. epicure . . . sense: follower of Epicurus, one who believes that the greatest good lies in the satisfaction of the senses, hence heaven in sense. 39. scorned pretense: scorned Christian aspirations. 40. wide excess: broad self-indulgence. 41. little less: much the same (as the epicure). 43. brave: splendid. 44. sat . . . by: sat by, counting. 51. grots: grottoes, caves.

THE RETREAT

Happy those early days when I
Shined in my angel-infancy:
Before I understood this place
Appointed for my second race,
Or taught my soul to fancy aught
But a white, celestial thought;
When yet I had not walked above
A mile or two from my first love,
And looking back, at that short space,
Could see a glimpse of His bright face;   10
When on some gilded cloud or flower
My gazing soul would dwell an hour,
And in those weaker glories spy
Some shadows of eternity;
Before I taught my tongue to wound
My conscience with a sinful sound,
Or had the black art to dispense
A several sin to every sense,
But felt through all this fleshly dress
Bright shoots of everlastingness.   20
    O how I long to travel back
And tread again that ancient track!
That I might once more reach that plain
Where first I left my glorious train,
From whence th'enlightened spirit sees
That shady city of palm trees.
But, ah, my soul with too much stay
Is drunk, and staggers in the way.
Some men a forward motion love,
But I by backward steps would move;   30
And when this dust falls to the urn,
In that state I came, return.

17. dispense: serve out. 18. several: separate. 24. train: followers, that is, angels.
26. shady city: an image of the heavenly city. 27. stay: remaining (in the flesh). 31. urn:
burial urn.

THE WATERFALL

With what deep murmurs through time's silent stealth
Doth thy transparent, cool, and watery wealth
    Here flowing fall,
    And chide, and call,
As if his liquid, loose retìnue stayed
Lingering, and were of this steep place afraid,
    The common pass
    Where, clear as glass,
    All must descend—
10   Not to an end,
But, quickened by this deep and rocky grave,
Rise to a longer course more bright and brave.

    Dear stream! dear bank, where often I
    Have sat and pleased my pensive eye,
    Why, since each drop of thy quick store
    Runs thither whence it flowed before,
    Should poor souls fear a shade or night,
    Who came, sure, from a sea of light?
    Or since those drops are all sent back
20   So sure to thee, that none doth lack,
    Why should frail flesh doubt any more
    That what God takes he'll not restore?
    O useful element and clear!
    My sacred wash and cleanser here,
    My first consigner unto those
    Fountains of life where the Lamb goes!
    What sublime truths and wholesome themes
    Lodge in thy mystical, deep streams—
    Such as dull man can never find,
30   Unless that Spirit lead his mind
    Which first upon thy face did move,
    And hatched all with His quickening love.
    As this loud brook's incessant fall
    In streaming rings restagnates all,

5. retìnue: following, company. 11. quickened: enlivened. 12. brave: splendid.
20. none doth lack: no drops are missing. 25–26. consigner . . . goes: that is, water, in
his baptism as a child, was the element which first consecrated him to Christ. 30–31. Spirit
. . . move: reference to Genesis i.2—"And the Spirit of God moved upon the face of the
waters." 33. incessant: unceasing. 34. restagnates: inundates.

Which reach by course the bank and then
Are no more seen, just so pass men.
O my invisible estate,
My glorious liberty, still late!
Thou art the channel my soul seeks,
Not this with cataracts and creeks. 40

JOHN DRYDEN (1631–1700)

MAC FLECKNOE

OR A SATIRE UPON THE TRUE-BLUE-PROTESTANT POET, T. S.

All human things are subject to decay,
And when fate summons, monarchs must obey.
This Flecknoe found, who, like Augustus, young
Was called to empire, and had governed long;
In prose and verse, was owned, without dispute
Through all the realms of Nonsense, absolute.
This agèd prince, now flourishing in peace,
And blessed with issue of a large increase,
Worn out with business, did at length debate
To settle the succession of the State; 10
And, pondering which of all his sons was fit
To reign, and wage immortal war with wit,
Cried: " 'Tis resolved; for nature pleads, that he
Should only rule who most resembles me.
Sh—— alone my perfect image bears,
Mature in dullness from his tender years;
Sh—— alone, of all my sons, is he

Title. Richard Flecknoe (d. 1678) was a particularly inept Irish poet and dramatist whom Dryden maliciously chose for his satiric purposes to be the literary father of his contemporary and one-time friend Thomas Shadwell (T.S.); the title means "son of Flecknoe." Shadwell considered himself to be the best poet-playwright of his day and the literary heir of the great Elizabethan-Jacobean poet-playwright Ben Jonson (see line 80). 3. Augustus: Octavian, who later styled himself Augustus, became Emperor of Rome at the age of 32. 12. wit: intelligence and eloquence. 15. Sh——: Shadwell. This use of only the first and second letters of the name suggests, but deliberately does not confer, anonymity upon Dryden's satiric victim, and also permits *double entendre* in line 103.

Who stands confirmed in full stupidity.
The rest to some faint meaning make pretense,
20   But Sh—— never deviates into sense.
Some beams of wit on other souls may fall,
Strike through, and make a lucid interval;
But Sh——'s genuine night admits no ray,
His rising fogs prevail upon the day.
Besides, his goodly fabric fills the eye
And seems designed for thoughtless majesty:
Thoughtless as monarch oaks that shade the plain,
And, spread in solemn state, supinely reign.
Heywood and Shirley were but types of thee,
30   Thou last great prophet of tautology.
Even I, a dunce of more renown than they,
Was sent before but to prepare thy way,
And coarsely clad in Norwich drugget came
To teach the nations in thy greater name.
My warbling lute, the lute I whilom strung
When to King John of Portugal I sung,
Was but the prelude to that glorious day,
When thou on silver Thames didst cut thy way
With well-timed oars before the royal barge,
40   Swelled with the pride of thy celestial charge;
And big with hymn, commander of a host,
The like was ne'er in *Epsom* blankets tossed.
Methinks I see the new Arion sail,
The lute still trembling underneath thy nail.
At thy well-sharpened thumb from shore to shore
The treble squeaks for fear, the basses roar;
Echoes from Pissing Alley "Sh—— call,"
And "Sh——" they resound from A—— Hall.

22. lucid interval: a moment of sense or clarity of thought. 25. goodly fabric: i.e., Shadwell was fat. 28. supinely: passively. 29. Heywood, Shirley: popular playwrights of the preceding generation, but out of style in Dryden's day; types: earlier models. 30. tautology: needless repetition. 32-34. Was sent . . . greater name: a parody of John the Baptist's being sent to prepare for Christ's coming; see Matthew iii.3-4. 33. Norwich drugget: coarse woolen. 35. whilom: formerly. 42. *Epsom* blankets tossed: reference to Shadwell's plays *Epsom Wells* and *The Virtuoso*. In the latter, a would-be wit is tossed in a blanket. 43. Arion: legendary Greek poet. Tossed overboard by sailors who robbed him, he was saved by a dolphin, on whose back he rode to safety—playing all the while on his lyre. 47. Pissing Alley: a side-street so-called near the Strand, close by the Thames.

About thy boat the little fishes throng,
As at the morning toast that floats along.   50
Sometimes, as prince of thy harmonious band,
Thou wield'st thy papers in thy threshing hand.
St. André's feet ne'er kept more equal time,
Not even the feet of thy own *Psyche's* rhyme,
Though they in number as in sense excel:
So just, so like tautology, they fell,
That, pale with envy, Singleton forswore
The lute and sword which he in triumph bore,
And vowed he ne'er would act Villerius more."
Here stopped the good old sire, and wept for joy   60
In silent raptures of the hopeful boy.
All arguments, but most his plays, persuade
That for anointed dullness he was made.

    Close to the walls which fair Augusta bind
(The fair Augusta much to fears inclined),
An ancient fabric raised t'inform the sight
There stood of yore, and Barbican it hight:
A watchtower once; but now, so fate ordains,
Of all the pile an empty name remains.
From its old ruins brothel-houses rise,   70
Scenes of lewd loves, and of polluted joys,
Where their vast courts the mother-strumpets keep,
And, undisturbed by watch, in silence sleep.
Near these a Nursery erects its head,
Where queens are formed, and future heroes bred;
Where unfledged actors learn to laugh and cry,
Where infant punks their tender voices try,
And little Maximins the gods defy.
Great Fletcher never treads in buskins here,

50. toast: i.e., the garbage in the river. 53–54. St. Andre's feet . . . rhyme: St. André was the French choreographer for Shadwell's opera *Psyche*. 55. number: meter. 56. just: evenly. 57. Singleton: one of the royal musicians; forswore: gave up. 59. Villerius: a character in the opera *Siege of Rhodes* (1656) by Sir William Davenant. 63. anointed: consecrated by applying oil, in the manner of English kings. 64–65. Augusta . . . inclined: the City of London (Augusta) in fear of the Popish Plot of 1678, a fabricated tale by one Titus Oates of a plan to assassinate Charles II and put his brother James, a Catholic, on the throne. 66. fabric: building; t'inform the sight: for getting information by seeing (cf. watchtower, line 68). 67. hight: was called. 74. Nursery: an actors' training school. 77. punks: harlots. 78. Maximins: Maximin is the raving tyrant in one of Dryden's own plays. 79. Fletcher: an early seventeenth-century dramatist; buskins: high, thick-soled boots worn by actors in tragedies in the Greek and Roman theaters.

80   Nor greater Jonson dares in socks appear;
      But gentle Simkin just reception finds
      Amidst this monument of vanished minds:
      Pure clinches the suburbian Muse affords,
      And Panton waging harmless war with words.
      Here Flecknoe, as a place to fame well known,
      Ambitiously designed his Sh——'s throne;
      For ancient Dekker prophesied long since
      That in this pile should reign a mighty prince,
      Born for a scourge of wit, and flail of sense;
90   To whom true dullness should some *Psyches* owe,
      But worlds of *Misers* from his pen should flow;
      Humorists and *Hypocrites* it should produce,
      Whole Raymond families, and tribes of Bruce.
           Now Empress Fame had published the renown
      Of Sh——'s coronation through the town.
      Roused by report of Fame, the nations meet,
      From near Bunhill, and distant Watling Street.
      No Persian carpets spread th' imperial way,
      But scattered limbs of mangled poets lay;
100   From dusty shops neglected authors come,
      Martyrs of pies, and relics of the bum.
      Much Heywood, Shirley, Ogleby there lay,
      But loads of Sh—— almost choked the way.
      Bilked stationers for yeomen stood prepared,
      And Herringman was captain of the guard.
      The hoary prince in majesty appeared,
      High on a throne of his own labors reared.
      At his right hand our young Ascanius sate,
      Rome's other hope, and pillar of the state.
110   His brows thick fogs, instead of glories, grace,

---

80. Jonson: see note on title; socks: low shoes worn by actors in comedies in the Greek and Roman theaters. 81. Simkin: a simpleton in low comic drama. 83. clinches: puns; Muse: one of nine Greek goddesses who traditionally inspire artistic creation. 84. Panton: a punster. 87. Dekker: an early seventeenth-century dramatist. 90–93. *Psyches . . .* Bruce: references to some of Shadwell's plays and characters. 97. Bunhill, Watling Street: sites actually close to the Nursery. 101. Martyrs . . . bum: bakers' shops and privies were the recipients of unsold books, which thus got used for very practical purposes (i.e., under pies and as toilet paper). 102. Heywood, Shirley, Ogleby: on the first two, see line 29. The last was a bad versifier who translated Virgil and Homer. 104. Bilked . . . yeomen: disappointed publishers (compare lines 100-103) who acted as guardsmen. 105. Herringman: Dryden's and Shadwell's publisher at the time. 108. Ascanius: son of Aeneas, the progenitor of the Roman Empire; sate: sat. 110. His . . . grace: fogs is the subject of the verb grace.

And lambent dullness played around his face.
As Hannibal did to the altars come,
Sworn by his sire a mortal foe to Rome;
So Sh—— swore, nor should his vow be vain,
That he till death true dullness would maintain;
And in his father's right and realm's defense,
Ne'er to have peace with wit nor truce with sense.
The king himself the sacred unction made,
As king by office, and as priest by trade.
In his sinister hand, instead of ball,   120
He placed a mighty mug of potent ale;
Love's Kingdom to his right he did convey,
At once his scepter and his rule of sway,
Whose righteous lore the prince had practiced young.
And from whose loins recorded *Psyche* sprung.
His temples, last, with poppies were o'erspread,
That nodding seemed to consecrate his head.
Just at that point of time, if fame not lie,
On his left hand twelve reverend owls did fly:
So Romulus, 'tis sung, by Tiber's brook,   130
Presage of sway from twice six vultures took.
Th' admiring throng loud acclamations make
And omens of his future empire take.
The sire then shook the honors of his head,
And from his brows damps of oblivion shed
Full on the filial dullness: long he stood,
Repelling from his breast the raging god;
At length burst out in this prophetic mood:
    "Heavens bless my son, from Ireland let him reign
To far Barbadoes on the western main;   140
Of his dominion may no end be known,
And greater than his father's be his throne;

111. lambent: light and brilliant. 112–113. Hannibal . . . Rome: the Carthaginian general, who had taken an oath as a boy to be an enemy to Rome, almost conquered Rome in 216 B.C. 118. unction: the oil used to anoint a king at the coronation. 120. sinister: left; ball: the traditional symbolic globe carried thus by the king along with the rod (scepter, line 123) after his coronation. 122. *Love's Kingdom:* one of Flecknoe's plays. 126. poppies: suggestive of sleep and dullness. 130–131. Romulus . . . took: the flight of the twelve cultures indicated to Romulus the site (by the river Tiber) upon which he was destined to found Rome. 134. honors: locks of hair. 134–138. These lines parody descriptions in classical literature in which a seer or prophetess "works up" to prophesying. 140. Barbadoes: the easternmost island of the West. Indies. Shadwell's empire will thus be all water.

Beyond *Love's Kingdom* let him stretch his pen!"
He paused, and all the people cried, "Amen."
Then thus continued he: "My son, advance
Still in new impudence, new ignorance.
Success let others teach, learn thou from me
Pangs without birth, and fruitless industry.
Let *Virtuosos* in five years be writ;

150   Yet not one thought accuse thy toil of wit.
Let gentle George in triumph tread the stage,
Make Dorimant betray, and Loveit rage;
Let Cully, Cockwood, Fopling, charm the pit,
And in their folly show the writer's wit.
Yet still thy fools shall stand in thy defense
And justify their author's want of sense.
Let 'em be all by thy own model made
Of dullness, and desire no foreign aid;
That they to future ages may be known,

160   Not copies drawn, but issue of thy own.
Nay, let thy men of wit too be the same,
All full of thee, and differing but in name.
But let no alien S—dl—y interpose,
To lard with wit thy hungry *Epsom* prose.
And when false flowers of rhetoric thou wouldst cull,
Trust nature, do not labor to be dull;
But write thy best, and top; and, in each line,
Sir Formal's oratory will be thine.
Sir Formal, though unsought, attends thy quill,

170   And does thy northern dedications fill.
Nor let false friends seduce thy mind to fame,
By arrogating Jonson's hostile name.

---

149. *Virtuosos:* see note to line 42. 151. gentle George: Sir George Etherege, one of the best of the contemporary Restoration dramatists. The figures in the next two lines are characters in his plays. 153. pit: the section of the theater corresponding to the modern orchestra, in those days cheap. 156. want: lack. 160. issue. children. 163. S — dl — y: Sir Charles Sedley, also a Restoration dramatist who, Dryden suggests here and in the next line, wrote the wittier parts of Shadwell's *Epsom Wells.* 165. cull: select. 168. Sir Formal: a pretentious orator in Shadwell's *The Virtuoso.* 169. quill. pen. 170. northern dedications: Shadwell had dedicated several of his plays to the Duke or Duchess of Newcastle-on-Tyne (in northeast England). 172. arrogating: assuming without justification. 175-176. where Jonson . . . art: in the famous poem prefixed to the First Folio of Shakespeare's plays (1623), Jonson praises Shakespeare's fidelity to nature in his plays and then says: "Yet must I not give Nature all; thy Art,/My gentle Shakespeare, must enjoy a part" (lines 55-56)

Let father Flecknoe fire thy mind with praise,
And uncle Ogleby thy envy raise.
Thou art my blood, where Jonson has no part:
What share have we in nature, or in art?
Where did his wit on learning fix a brand,
And rail at arts he did not understand?
Where made he love in Prince Nicander's vein,
Or swept the dust in *Psyche's* humble strain?   180
Where sold he bargains, "whip-stitch, kiss my arse,"
Promised a play and dwindled to a farce?
When did his Muse from Fletcher scenes purloin,
As thou whole Etherege dost transfuse to thine?
But so transfused, as oil on water's flow,
His always floats above, thine sinks below.
This is thy province, this thy wondrous way,
New humors to invent for each new play:
This is that boasted bias of thy mind,
By which one way, to dullness, 'tis inclined;   190
Which makes thy writings lean on one side still,
And, in all changes, that way bends thy will.
Nor let thy mountain-belly make pretense
Of likeness; thine's a tympany of sense.
A tun of man in thy large bulk is writ,
But sure thou'rt but a kilderkin of wit.
Like mine, thy gentle numbers feebly creep;
Thy tragic Muse gives smiles, thy comic sleep.
With whate'er gall thou set'st thyself to write,
Thy inoffensive satires never bite.   200
In thy felonious heart though venom lies,
It does but touch thy Irish pen and dies.
Thy genius calls thee not to purchase fame
In keen iambics, but mild anagram.
Leave writing plays, and choose for thy command
Some peaceful province in acrostic land.

---

179. in **Prince Nicander's vein:** in the style of Prince Nicander, a character in *Psyche*. 180. **strain:** melody. 181. **sold . . . bargains:** used indecent language in conversation (as in the rest of the line, which parodies one of Shadwell's characters' speeches). 188. **humors:** temperamental biases or inclinations; see the next four lines, which parody Shadwell's Epilogue to *The Humorists*. 194. **likeness:** that is, to Jonson; **tympany:** a wind-bag (produced by gas in the stomach). 195. **tun:** a large wine cask. 196. **kilderkin:** a quarter of a tun. 204: **iambics:** satire. 204–208. **anagram . . . ways:** in these lines Dryden refers to various ingenious patterns of letters and shapes in poems of his time.

There thou mayst wings display and altars raise,
And torture one poor word ten thousand ways.
Or if thou wouldst thy different talents suit,
210   Set thy own songs and sing them to thy lute."
     He said: but his last words were scarcely heard,
For Bruce and Longvil had a trap prepared,
And down they sent the yet declaiming bard.
Sinking he left his drugget robe behind,
Borne upwards by a subterranean wind.
The mantle fell to the young prophet's part,
With double portion of his father's art.

ALEXANDER POPE (1688–1744)

THE RAPE OF THE LOCK

CANTO I

What dire offense from amorous causes springs,
What mighty contests rise from trivial things,
I sing—This verse to Caryll, Muse! is due:

212. Bruce and Longvil: characters in *The Virtuoso*, who dispose of Sir Formal (see line 168) in this way as he orates. 216. mantle . . . part: a parody of Elijah's mantle falling to his heir Elisha; see Kings ii.1–14.

Note. The occasion for the poem was the quarrel that arose between the families of Lord Petre and Arabella Fermor, when the former cut off a lock of the latter's hair. John Caryll, a friend of both and of Pope's, suggested the writing of the poem. It is a mock-epic, using and parodying certain traditional epic features: (1) appeal to the Muse and announcement of theme, (2) supernatural machinery, (3) individual combat in battles, (4) journey to the underworld, (5) history of weapons, (6) elevated diction, (7) catalogues, and (8) Homeric similes (see Glossary).

1, 2. These lines comprise the object of I sing (line 3). 3. Muse: mythical figure who inspires the poet, thought of as female, hence she of line 6 and Goddess of line 7.

This even Belinda may vouchsafe to view;
Slight is the subject, but not so the praise,
If she inspire, and he approve my lays.
    Say what strange motive, Goddess! could compel
A well-bred lord to assault a gentle belle?
O say what stranger cause, yet unexplored,
Could make a gentle belle reject a lord?   10
In tasks so bold, can little men engage,
And in soft bosoms dwells such mighty rage?
    Sol through white curtains shot a timorous ray,
And oped those eyes that must eclipse the day:
Now lap-dogs give themselves the rousing shake,
And sleepless lovers, just at twelve, awake.
Thrice rung the bell, the slipper knocked the ground,
And the pressed watch returned a silver sound.
Belinda still her downy pillow pressed;
Her guardian sylph prolonged the balmy rest.   20
'Twas he had summoned to her silent bed
The morning-dream that hovered o'er her head.
A youth more glittering than a birth-night beau
(That even in slumber caused her cheek to glow)
Seemed to her ear his winning lips to lay,
And thus in whispers said, or seemed to say:
    "Fairest of mortals, thou distinguished care
Of thousand bright inhabitants of air!
If e'er one vision touched thy infant thought,
Of all the nurse and all the priest have taught,   30
Of airy elves by moonlight shadows seen,
The silver token, and the circled green,
Or virgins visited by angel-powers,
With golden crowns and wreaths of heavenly flowers—
Hear and believe! thy own importance know,
Nor bound thy narrow views to things below.
Some secret truths, from learnèd pride concealed,
To maids alone and children are revealed:
What though no credit doubting wits may give?
The fair and innocent shall still believe.   40

4. Belinda: Arabella Fermor; **vouchsafe:** condescend. **6. he:** Caryll; **lays:** songs. **13. Sol:** the sun. **14. those eyes:** Belinda's. **17. slipper . . . ground:** to call the maid. **20. sylph:** one of the contingent of invisible aerial beings guarding Belinda—"The light militia of the lower sky" (line 42). **23. birth-night beau:** gentleman at court resplendently dressed for the Queen's birthday. **32. silver token:** money left by fairies for what they have taken; **circled green:** circular patch of dark green grass said to be caused by fairies.

Know, then, unnumbered spirits round thee fly,
The light militia of the lower sky:
These, though unseen, are ever on the wing,
Hang o'er the box, and hover round the Ring.
Think what an equipage thou hast in air,
And view with scorn two pages and a chair.
As now your own, our beings were of old,
And once enclosed in woman's beauteous mold;
Thence, by a soft transition, we repair
50 From earthly vehicles to these of air.
Think not, when woman's transient breath is fled,
That all her vanities at once are dead:
Succeeding vanities she still regards,
And though she plays no more, o'erlooks the cards.
Her joy in gilded chariots, when alive,
And love of ombre, after death survive.
For when the fair in all their pride expire,
To their first elements their souls retire:
The sprites of fiery termagants in flame
60 Mount up, and take a salamander's name.
Soft yielding minds to water glide away,
And sip, with nymphs, their elemental tea.
The graver prude sinks downward to a gnome,
In search of mischief still on earth to roam.
The light coquettes in sylphs aloft repair,
And sport and flutter in the fields of air.
   "Know further yet; whoever fair and chaste
Rejects mankind, is by some sylph embraced:
For spirits, freed from mortal laws, with ease
70 Assume what sexes and what shapes they please.
What guards the purity of melting maids,
In courtly balls, and midnight masquerades,
Safe from the treacherous friend, the daring spark,
The glance by day, the whisper in the dark,
When kind occasion prompts their warm desires,
When music softens, and when dancing fires?
'Tis but their sylph, the wise celestials know,
Though honor is the word with men below.

44. box: at the theater; Ring: the circular road in Hyde Park, frequented by the fashionable. 45. equipage: body of servants. 46. chair: sedan chair. 55. chariots: carriages. 56. ombre: card game. 57. expire: die. 59. sprites: spirits; termagants: scolding women. 60-63. salamanders: spirits of the fire (as sylphs are spirits of the air); nymphs: spirits of the water; gnome: spirit of the earth.

"Some nymphs there are, too conscious of their face,
For life predestined to the gnomes' embrace. 80
These swell their prospects and exalt their pride,
When offers are disdained, and love denied;
Then gay ideas crowd the vacant brain,
While peers, and dukes, and all their sweeping train,
And garters, stars, and coronets appear,
And in soft sounds, 'Your Grace' salutes their ear.
'Tis these that early taint the female soul,
Instruct the eyes of young coquettes to roll,
Teach infant cheeks a bidden blush to know,
And little hearts to flutter at a beau. 90
  "Oft, when the world imagine women stray,
The sylphs through mystic mazes guide their way,
Through all the giddy circle they pursue,
And old impertinence expel by new.
What tender maid but must a victim fall
To one man's treat, but for another's ball?
When Florio speaks what virgin could withstand,
If gentle Damon did not squeeze her hand?
With varying vanities, from every part,
They shift the moving toyshop of their heart; 100
Where wigs with wigs, with sword-knots sword-knots strive,
Beaux banish beaux, and coaches coaches drive.
This erring mortals levity may call;
Oh, blind to truth! the sylphs contrive it all.
  "Of these am I, who thy protection claim,
A watchful sprite, and Ariel is my name.
Late, as I ranged the crystal wilds of air,
In the clear mirror of thy ruling star
I saw, alas! some dread event impend,
Ere to the main this morning sun descend, 110
But heaven reveals not what, or how, or where:
Warned by the sylph, O pious maid, beware!
This to disclose is all thy guardian can:
Beware of all, but most beware of man!"
  He said; when Shock, who thought she slept too long,
Leaped up, and waked his mistress with his tongue.
'Twas then, Belinda, if report say true,

85. **garters, stars, and coronets:** (wearers of) various emblems of rank. 88. **coquettes:** flirtatious women. 90. **beau:** eligible young man. 93. **giddy circle:** socialite life. 94. **impertinence:** thing of vanity. 95-98. These lines illustrate the means by which the sylphs protect maids: they constantly offer alternative attractions such as **Damon** for **Florio.** 110. **main:** sea. 115. **Shock:** Belinda's dog.

Thy eyes first opened on a billet-doux;
Wounds, charms, and ardors were no sooner read,
120   But all the vision vanished from thy head.
    And now, unveiled, the toilet stands displayed,
Each silver vase in mystic order laid.
First, robed in white, the nymph intent adores,
With head uncovered, the cosmetic powers.
A heavenly image in the glass appears,
To that she bends, to that her eyes she rears;
The inferior priestess, at her altar's side,
Trembling begins the sacred rites of pride.
Unnumbered treasures ope at once, and here
130   The various offerings of the world appear;
From each she nicely culls with curious toil,
And decks the goddess with the glittering spoil.
This casket India's glowing gems unlocks,
And all Arabia breathes from yonder box.
The tortoise here and elephant unite,
Transformed to combs, the speckled and the white.
Here files of pins extend their shining rows,
Puffs, powders, patches, bibles, billet-doux.
Now awful beauty puts on all its arms;
140   The fair each moment rises in her charms,
Repairs her smiles, awakens every grace,
And calls forth all the wonders of her face;
Sees by degrees a purer blush arise,
And keener lightnings quicken in her eyes.
The busy sylphs surround their darling care,
These set the head, and those divide the hair,
Some fold the sleeve, whilst others plait the gown;
And Betty's praised for labors not her own.

CANTO II

Not with more glories, in the ethereal plain,
The sun first rises o'er the purpled main,

118. **billet-doux:** love-letter. 119. **Wounds . . . ardors:** parts of the conventional complaint of lovers, incorporated in the love-letter. 121. **toilet:** the dressing table and its equipment. 123. **nymph:** here, Belinda. 126. **rears:** lifts. 127. **inferior priestess:** Belinda's maid. 128. **rites:** rituals. 131. **culls:** takes; **curious:** careful. 132. **decks:** decorates. 133. **casket:** decorated box. 135-136. **tortoise . . . white:** the lines describe two combs—one of tortoise shell, the other of ivory. 139. **awful:** awe-inspiring. 140. **fair:** fair one. 148. **Betty:** the maid.

1. **ethereal:** heavenly.

Than, issuing forth, the rival of his beams
Launched on the bosom of the silver Thames.
Fair nymphs and well-dressed youths around her shone,
But every eye was fixed on her alone.
On her white breast a sparkling cross she wore,
Which Jews might kiss, and infidels adore.
Her lively looks a sprightly mind disclose,
Quick as her eyes, and as unfixed as those: 10
Favors to none, to all she smiles extends;
Oft she rejects, but never once offends.
Bright as the sun, her eyes the gazers strike,
And, like the sun, they shine on all alike.
Yet graceful ease, and sweetness void of pride,
Might hide her faults, if belles had faults to hide:
If to her share some female errors fall,
Look on her face, and you'll forget 'em all.
    This nymph, to the destruction of mankind,
Nourished two locks, which graceful hung behind   20
In equal curls, and well conspired to deck
With shining ringlets the smooth ivory neck.
Love in these labyrinths his slaves detains,
And mighty hearts are held in slender chains.
With hairy springes we the birds betray,
Slight lines of hair surprise the finny prey,
Fair tresses man's imperial race ensnare,
And beauty draws us with a single hair.
    The adventurous Baron the bright locks admired;
He saw, he wished, and to the prize aspired.   30
Resolved to win, he meditates the way,
By force to ravish, or by fraud betray;
For when success a lover's toil attends,
Few ask, if fraud or force attained his ends.
    For this, ere Phœbus rose, he had implored
Propitious heaven, and every power adored,
But chiefly Love—to Love an altar built,
Of twelve vast French romances, neatly gilt.
There lay three garters, half a pair of gloves;
And all the trophies of his former loves.   40
With tender billet-doux he lights the pyre,

3. **rival:** here, Belinda. 4. **Thames:** river on which stands the city of London and also, upstream, Hampton Court Palace (Canto III, lines 3 and 4), whither the boat is taking Belinda. 8. **infidels:** pagans, in this context, non-Christians. 23. **labyrinths:** coils. 25. **springes:** traps. 26. **finny prey:** fish. 35. **Phœbus:** the sun. 38. **French romances:** French love poems, which were notoriously long. 41. **pyre:** heap of combustible material.

And breathes three amorous sighs to raise the fire.
Then prostrate falls, and begs with ardent eyes
Soon to obtain, and long possess the prize:
The powers gave ear, and granted half his prayer,
The rest the winds dispersed in empty air.
 But now secure the painted vessel glides,
The sunbeams trembling on the floating tides,
While melting music steals upon the sky,
50   And softened sounds along the water die.
Smooth flow the waves, the zephyrs gently play,
Belinda smiled, and all the world was gay.
All but the sylph—with careful thoughts oppressed,
The impending woe sat heavy on his breast.
He summons straight his denizens of air;
The lucid squadrons round the sails repair:
Soft o'er the shrouds aerial whispers breathe,
That seemed but zephyrs to the train beneath.
Some to the sun their insect-wings unfold,
60   Waft on the breeze or sink in clouds of gold;
Transparent forms, too fine for mortal sight,
Their fluid bodies half dissolved in light.
Loose to the wind their airy garments flew,
Thin glittering textures of the filmy dew,
Dipped in the richest tincture of the skies,
Where light disports in ever-mingling dyes,
While every beam new transient colors flings,
Colors that change whene'er they wave their wings.
Amid the circle, on the gilded mast,
70   Superior by the head, was Ariel placed;
His purple pinions opening to the sun,
He raised his azure wand, and thus begun:
 "Ye sylphs and sylphids, to your chief give ear!
Fays, fairies, genii, elves, and dæmons, hear!
Ye know the spheres and various tasks assigned
By laws eternal to the aerial kind.
Some in the fields of purest ether play,
And bask and whiten in the blaze of day.
Some guide the course of wandering orbs on high,
80   Or roll the planets through the boundless sky.
Some less refined, beneath the moon's pale light
Pursue the stars that shoot athwart the night,

51. zephyrs: west winds. 55. denizens: citizens. 56. repair: muster. 58. train: company. 65. tincture: stain. 66. disports: plays. 67. transient: passing. 71 pinions: wings. 74. genii: spirits; dæmons: spirits. 82. stars . . . night: shooting stars.

Or suck the mists in grosser air below,
Or dip their pinions in the painted bow,
Or brew fierce tempests on the wintry main,
Or o'er the glebe distil the kindly rain.
Others on earth o'er human race preside,
Watch all their ways, and all their actions guide:
Of these the chief the care of nations own,
And guard with arms divine the British throne.   90
    "Our humbler province is to tend the fair,
Not a less pleasing, though less glorious care:
To save the powder from too rude a gale,
Nor let the imprisoned essences exhale;
To draw fresh colors from the vernal flowers;
To steal from rainbows e'er they drop in showers
A brighter wash; to curl their waving hairs,
Assist their blushes, and inspire their airs;
Nay oft, in dreams, invention we bestow,
To change a flounce, or add a furbelow.   100
    "This day, black omens threat the brightest fair,
That e'er deserved a watchful spirit's care—
Some dire disaster, or by force, or sleight;
But what, or where, the fates have wrapped in night:
Whether the nymph shall break Diana's law,
Or some frail china jar receive a flaw;
Or stain her honor or her new brocade,
Forget her prayers, or miss a masquerade,
Or lose her heart, or necklace, at a ball;
Or whether heaven has doomed that Shock must fall.   110
Haste, then, ye spirits! to your charge repair:
The fluttering fan be Zephyretta's care;
The drops to thee, Brillantè, we consign;
And, Momentilla, let the watch be thine;
Do thou, Crispissa, tend her favorite lock;
Ariel himself shall be the guard of Shock.
    "To fifty chosen sylphs, of special note,
We trust the important charge, the petticoat:
Oft have we known that seven-fold fence to fail,
Though stiff with hoops, and armed with ribs of whale;   120
Form a strong line about the silver bound,
And guard the wide circumference around.

84. **painted bow:** rainbow. 86. **glebe:** ploughland. 94. **essences:** perfumes. 95. **vernal:** spring. 97. **wash:** color. 100. **flounce:** decoration on a dress; **furbelow:** frill. 101. **threat:** threaten. 103. **or, or:** either, or; **sleight:** trick. 105. **Diana's law:** law of chastity. 113. **drops:** pendant earrings.

"Whatever spirit, careless of his charge,
His post neglects, or leaves the fair at large,
Shall feel sharp vengeance soon o'ertake his sins,
Be stopped in vials, or transfixed with pins;
Or plunged in lakes of bitter washes lie,
Or wedged whole ages in a bodkin's eye;
Gums and pomatums shall his flight restrain,
130   While clogged he beats his silken wings in vain;
Or alum styptics with contracting power
Shrink his thin essence like a riveled flower:
Or, as Ixion fixed, the wretch shall feel
The giddy motion of the whirling mill,
In fumes of burning chocolate shall glow,
And tremble at the sea that froths below!"
    He spoke; the spirits from the sails descend;
Some, orb in orb, around the nymph extend;
Some thrid the mazy ringlets of her hair;
140   Some hang upon the pendants of her ear:
With beating hearts the dire event they wait,
Anxious, and trembling for the birth of Fate.

CANTO III

Close by those meads, forever crowned with flowers,
Where Thames with pride surveys his rising towers,
There stands a structure of majestic frame,
Which from the neighboring Hampton takes its name.
Here Britain's statesmen oft the fall foredoom
Of foreign tyrants and of nymphs at home;
Here thou, great Anna! whom three realms obey,
Dost sometimes counsel take—and sometimes tea.
    Hither the heroes and the nymphs resort,
10   To taste awhile the pleasures of a court;
In various talk the instructive hours they passed,
Who gave the ball, or paid the visit last;

126. vials: small bottles. 127. bitter washes: cosmetic paints. 129. pomatums: perfumed lotions, especially for the hair. 132. riveled: shrivelled. 133. Ixion: figure from Greek mythology tied to a perpetually turning wheel. 139. thrid: weave through.

1. meads: fields. 4. Hampton: see note to Canto II, line 4. 5. foredoom: plan. 7. Anna: Queen Anne (1702-1714).

One speaks the glory of the British Queen,
And one describes a charming Indian screen;
A third interprets motions, looks, and eyes;
At every word a reputation dies.
Snuff, or the fan, supply each pause of chat,
With singing, laughing, ogling, and all that.
Meanwhile, declining from the noon of day,
The sun obliquely shoots his burning ray;   20
The hungry judges soon the sentence sign,
And wretches hang that jurymen may dine;
The merchant from the Exchange returns in peace,
And the long labors of the toilet cease.
Belinda now, whom thirst of fame invites,
Burns to encounter two adventurous knights,
At ombre singly to decide their doom;
And swells her breast with conquests yet to come.
Straight the three bands prepare in arms to join,
Each band the number of the sacred nine.   30
Soon as she spreads her hand, the aerial guard
Descend, and sit on each important card:
First Ariel perched upon a matadore,
Then each, according to the rank they bore;
For sylphs, yet mindful of their ancient race,
Are, as when women, wondrous fond of place.
Behold, four kings in majesty revered,
With hoary whiskers and a forky beard;
And four fair queens whose hands sustain a flower,
The expressive emblem of their softer power;   40
Four knaves in garbs succinct, a trusty band,
Caps on their heads, and halberds in their hand;
And particolored troops, a shining train,
Draw forth to combat on the velvet plain.
The skillful nymph reviews her force with care:
"Let spades be trumps!" she said, and trumps they were.
Now move to war her sable matadores,
In show like leaders of the swarthy Moors.

18. ogling: amorous staring. 23. Exchange: London stock market. 26, 29, 30. Ombre: a card game played by three people, here by the two adventurous knights and Belinda, who hold the three bands of cards, nine in each. 33. matadore: one of the three principal cards in the games of ombre and quadrille. 36. place: rank. 41. knaves: jacks; garbs succinct: tight clothes. 42. halberds: spears. 43. particolored: variously colored. 44. velvet plain: i.e., card table.

Spadillio first, unconquerable lord!
50 Led off two captive trumps, and swept the board.
As many more Manillio forced to yield,
And marched a victor from the verdant field.
Him Basto followed, but his fate more hard
Gained but one trump and one plebeian card.
With his broad saber next, a chief in years,
The hoary majesty of spades appears,
Puts forth one manly leg, to sight revealed,
The rest, his many-colored robe concealed.
The rebel knave, who dares his prince engage,
60 Proves the just victim of his royal rage.
Even mighty Pam, that kings and queens o'erthrew
And mowed down armies in the fights of loo,
Sad chance of war! now destitute of aid,
Falls undistinguished by the victor spade!
    Thus far both armies to Belinda yield;
Now to the Baron fate inclines the field.
His warlike amazon her host invades,
The imperial consort of the crown of spades.
The club's black tyrant first her victim died,
70 Spite of his haughty mien, and barbarous pride:
What boots the regal circle on his head,
His giant limbs, in state unwieldy spread;
That long behind he trails his pompous robe,
And of all monarchs only grasps the globe?
    The Baron now his diamonds pours apace;
The embroidered king who shows but half his face,
And his refulgent queen, with powers combined
Of broken troops an easy conquest find.
' Clubs, diamonds, hearts, in wild disorder seen,
80 With throngs promiscuous strew the level green.
Thus when dispersed a routed army runs,
Of Asia's troops, and Afric's sable sons,
With like confusion different nations fly,
Of various habit, and of various dye,

49, 51, 53, 61. Spadillio, Manillio, Basto, Pam: names of important cards in ombre. 52. verdant: green. 54. plebeian: ordinary. 62. loo: another card game. 67. amazon: one of a tribe of warrior women, here the queen of spades. 70. mien: attitude. 71. What boots: what is the use of. 74. And . . . globe: is the only king (shown) holding the globe. 75. apace: quickly. 77. refulgent: radiant. 82. sable: black.

The pierced battalions disunited fall,
In heaps on heaps; one fate o'erwhelms them all.
    The knave of diamonds tries his wily arts,
And wins (oh shameful chance!) the queen of hearts.
At this, the blood the virgin's cheek forsook,
A livid paleness spreads o'er all her look;   90
She sees, and trembles at the approaching ill,
Just in the jaws of ruin, and codille.
And now (as oft in some distempered state)
On one nice trick depends the general fate.
An ace of hearts steps forth: the king unseen
Lurked in her hand, and mourned his captive queen.
He springs to vengeance with an eager pace,
And falls like thunder on the prostrate ace.
The nymph exulting fills with shouts the sky;
The walls, the woods, and long canals reply.   100
    O thoughtless mortals! ever blind to fate,
Too soon dejected, and too soon elate:
Sudden, these honors shall be snatched away,
And cursed for ever this victorious day.
    For lo! the board with cups and spoons is crowned,
The berries crackle, and the mill turns round;
On shining altars of Japan they raise
The silver lamp; the fiery spirits blaze:
From silver spouts the grateful liquors glide,
While China's earth receives the smoking tide.   110
At once they gratify their scent and taste,
And frequent cups prolong the rich repast.
Straight hover round the fair her airy band;
Some, as she sipped, the fuming liquor fanned,
Some o'er her lap their careful plumes displayed,
Trembling, and conscious of the rich brocade.
Coffee (which makes the politician wise,
And see through all things with his half-shut eyes)
Sent up in vapors to the Baron's brain
New stratagems, the radiant lock to gain.   120
Ah cease, rash youth! desist ere 'tis too late,

89. virgin: Belinda. 92. codille: loss of the game. 95. ace: played by the Baron
(lower in value than Belinda's king). 105. board: table. 106. berries: coffee beans;
mill: coffee mill. 107. altars of Japan: tables finished with a high-gloss varnish in a style
characteristic of Japan. 110. China's earth: china cups.

Fear the just gods, and think of Scylla's fate!
Changed to a bird, and sent to flit in air,
She dearly pays for Nisus' injured hair!
  But when to mischief mortals bend their will,
How soon they find fit instruments of ill!
Just then, Clarissa drew with tempting grace
A two-edged weapon from her shining case:
So ladies in romance assist their knight,
130 Present the spear, and arm him for the fight.
He takes the gift with reverence, and extends
The little engine on his fingers' ends;
This just behind Belinda's neck he spread,
As o'er the fragrant steams she bends her head.
Swift to the lock a thousand sprites repair,
A thousand wings, by turns, blow back the hair,
And thrice they twitched the diamond in her ear,
Thrice she looked back, and thrice the foe drew near.
Just in that instant, anxious Ariel sought
140 The close recesses of the virgin's thought;
As on the nosegay in her breast reclined,
He watched the ideas rising in her mind,
Sudden he viewed, in spite of all her art,
An earthly lover lurking at her heart.
Amazed, confused, he found his power expired,
Resigned to fate, and with a sigh retired.   *scissor*
  The peer now spreads the glittering forfex wide,
To enclose the lock; now joins it, to divide.
Even then, before the fatal engine closed,
150 A wretched sylph too fondly interposed;
Fate urged the shears, and cut the sylph in twain
(But airy substance soon unites again);
The meeting points the sacred hair dissever
From the fair head, forever, and forever!
  Then flashed the living lightning from her eyes,
And screams of horror rend the affrighted skies.
Not louder shrieks to pitying heaven are cast,
When husbands, or when lap-dogs breathe their last;
Or when rich China vessels fallen from high,
160 In glittering dust and painted fragments lie!

lofty lang

  122-124. Scylla's fate . . . hair: Scylla was thus changed after she had clipped a lock
of hair from the head of King Nisus, her father, upon which the safety of the city
depended. **127. Clarissa:** friend (or rival) of Belinda. **128. two-edged weapon:** scissors.
141. nosegay: bunch of flowers. **147. forfex:** scissors. **150. fondly:** foolishly.

"Let wreaths of triumph now my temples twine,"
The victor cried, "the glorious prize is mine!
While fish in streams, or birds delight in air,
Or in a coach and six the British fair,
As long as *Atalantis* shall be read,
Or the small pillow grace a lady's bed,
While visits shall be paid on solemn days,
When numerous wax-lights in bright order blaze,
While nymphs take treats, or assignations give,
So long my honor, name, and praise shall live!"   170
What time would spare, from steel receives its date,
And monuments, like men, submit to fate!
Steel could the labor of the gods destroy,
And strike to dust the imperial towers of Troy;
Steel could the works of mortal pride confound,
And hew triumphal arches to the ground.
What wonder then, fair nymph! thy hairs should feel,
The conquering force of unresisted steel?

CANTO IV

But anxious cares the pensive nymph oppressed,
And secret passions labored in her breast.
Not youthful kings in battle seized alive,
Not scornful virgins who their charms survive,
Not ardent lovers robbed of all their bliss,
Not ancient ladies when refused a kiss,
Not tyrants fierce that unrepenting die,
Not Cynthia when her manteau's pinned awry,
E'er felt such rage, resentment, and despair,
As thou, sad virgin! for thy ravished hair.   10
    For, that sad moment, when the sylphs withdrew
And Ariel weeping from Belinda flew,
Umbriel, a dusky, melancholy sprite,
As ever sullied the fair face of light,
Down to the central earth, his proper scene,
Repaired to search the gloomy Cave of Spleen.
    Swift on his sooty pinions flits the gnome,
And in a vapor reached the dismal dome.

165. *Atalantis:* popular contemporary book about local scandal. 170. Some editors consider that this speech runs to the end of the canto.

8. **manteau:** a loose gown. 16. **Spleen:** bad temper. 17. **gnome:** Umbriel by name (see Canto I, lines 57-64, for explanation of gnomes). 18. **dome:** cave.

No cheerful breeze this sullen region knows,
20   The dreaded east is all the wind that blows.
Here in a grotto, sheltered close from air,
And screened in shades from day's detested glare,
She sighs forever on her pensive bed,
Pain at her side, and Megrim at her head.
    Two handmaids wait the throne: alike in place,
But differing far in figure and in face.
Here stood Ill-Nature like an ancient maid,
Her wrinkled form in black and white arrayed;
With store of prayers, for mornings, nights, and noons,
30   Her hand is filled; her bosom with lampoons.
    There Affectation, with a sickly mien,
Shows in her cheek the roses of eighteen,
Practiced to lisp, and hang the head aside,
Faints into airs, and languishes with pride,
On the rich quilt sinks with becoming woe,
Wrapped in a gown, for sickness and for show.
The fair ones feel such maladies as these,
When each new nightdress gives a new disease.
    A constant vapor o'er the palace flies,
40   Strange phantoms rising as the mists arise;
Dreadful, as hermit's dreams in haunted shades,
Or bright, as visions of expiring maids.
Now glaring fiends, and snakes on rolling spires,
Pale specters, gaping tombs, and purple fires:
Now lakes of liquid gold, Elysian scenes,
And crystal domes, and angels in machines.
    Unnumbered throngs on every side are seen,
Of bodies changed to various forms by Spleen.
Here living tea-pots stand, one arm held out,
50   One bent; the handle this, and that the spout:
A pipkin there, like Homer's tripod walks;
Here sighs a jar, and there a goose pie talks;
Men prove with child, as powerful fancy works,
And maids turned bottles, call aloud for corks.
    Safe passed the gnome through this fantastic band,

20. east: east wind, which brings terribly cold weather in England. **24. Megrim:** headache. **30. lampoons:** malicious satires directed against individuals. **33. Practiced to lisp:** lisping was fashionable in the 18th century. **45. Elysian:** classical equivalent of heavenly. **46. angels in machines:** angel-figures appeared on the stage via machinery. **51. pipkin:** small earthenware jar; **Homer's tripod:** reference to twenty golden-wheeled, self-moving, three-legged stools made by Vulcan, in *Iliad,* XVIII.

A branch of healing spleenwort in his hand.
Then thus addressed the power: "Hail, wayward Queen!
Who rule the sex to fifty from fifteen:
Parent of vapors and of female wit,
Who give the hysteric or poetic fit,   60
On various tempers act by various ways,
Make some take physic, others scribble plays;
Who cause the proud their visits to delay,
And send the godly in a pet to pray.
A nymph there is, that all thy power disdains,
And thousands more in equal mirth maintains.
But oh! if e'er thy gnome could spoil a grace,
Or raise a pimple on a beauteous face,
Like citron-waters matrons' cheeks inflame,
Or change complexions at a losing game;   70
If e'er with airy horns I planted heads,
Or rumpled petticoats, or tumbled beds,
Or caused suspicion when no soul was rude,
Or discomposed the headdress of a prude,
Or e'er to costive lap-dog gave disease,
Which not the tears of brightest eyes could ease:
Hear me, and touch Belinda with chagrin;
That single act gives half the world the spleen."
    The goddess with a discontented air
Seems to reject him, though she grants his prayer.   80
A wondrous bag with both her hands she binds,
Like that where once Ulysses held the winds;
There she collects the force of female lungs,
Sighs, sobs, and passions, and the war of tongues.
A vial next she fills with fainting fears,
Soft sorrows, melting griefs, and flowing tears.
The gnome rejoicing bears her gifts away,
Spreads his black wings, and slowly mounts to day.
    Sunk in Thalestris' arms the nymph he found,
Her eyes dejected and her hair unbound.   90
Full o'er their heads the swelling bag he rent,
And all the furies issued at the vent.

56. spleenwort: kind of fern, thought to be therapeutic. 59. vapors: the "blues."
64. pet: temper. 69. citron-waters: spirits with bad effects on the complexion. 71. airy
horns: imaginary horns worn by deceived husbands. 75. costive: constipated. 77. chagrin:
mental disquietude due to humbling of pride. 82. Ulysses . . . winds. See *Odyssey*, X.
89. Thalestris: friend of Belinda and girl friend of Sir Plume (lines 121-122). 91. rent:
tore. 92. vent: opening.

Belinda burns with more than mortal ire,
And fierce Thalestris fans the rising fire.
"Oh wretched maid!" she spread her hands, and cried
(While Hampton's echoes, "Wretched maid!" replied),
"Was it for this you took such constant care
The bodkin, comb, and essence to prepare?
For this your locks in paper durance bound,
100   For this with torturing irons wreathed around?
For this with fillets strained your tender head,
And bravely bore the double loads of lead?
Gods! shall the ravisher display your hair,
While the fops envy, and the ladies stare!
Honor forbid! at whose unrivaled shrine
Ease, pleasure, virtue, all, our sex resign.
Methinks already I your tears survey,
Already hear the horrid things they say,
Already see you a degraded toast,
110   And all your honor in a whisper lost!
How shall I, then, your helpless fame defend?
'Twill then be infamy to seem your friend!
And shall this prize, the inestimable prize,
Exposed through crystal to the gazing eyes,
And heightened by the diamond's circling rays,
On that rapacious hand forever blaze?
Sooner shall grass in Hyde Park Circus grow,
And wits take lodgings in the sound of Bow,
Sooner let earth, air, sea, to chaos fall,
120   Men, monkeys, lap-dogs, parrots, perish all!"
    She said; then raging to Sir Plume repairs,
And bids her beau demand the precious hairs:
(Sir Plume of amber snuffbox justly vain,
And the nice conduct of a clouded cane)
With earnest eyes, and round unthinking face,
He first the snuffbox opened, then the case,
And thus broke out—"My Lord, why, what the devil?
Z—ds! damn the lock! 'fore Gad, you must be civil!
Plague on't! 'tis past a jest—nay prithee, pox!

---

99. **durance:** captivity. 101. **fillets:** thin bands (binding the hair). 102. **lead:** frame
for arranging the hair. 104. **fops:** foolish, pretentious men. 112. **infamy:** dishonor. 114.
crystal: part of the setting in which the hair is being worn by the Baron. 117. **Circus:**
see note on **Ring,** Canto I, line 44. 118. **wits:** gentlemen; **in . . . Bow:** within earshot of
the bells of St. Mary le Bow, i.e., in the city, where Cockneys, not fashionable people,
reside. 124. **conduct:** handling. 128. **Z—ds!:** God's wounds—swear word; **Gad:** God.

Give her the hair"—he spoke, and rapped his box.   130
    "It grieves me much," replied the peer again,
"Who speaks so well should ever speak in vain.
But by this lock, this sacred lock I swear
(Which never more shall join its parted hair;
Which never more its honors shall renew,
Clipped from the lovely head where late it grew),
That while my nostrils draw the vital air,
This hand, which won it, shall for ever wear."
He spoke, and speaking, in proud triumph spread
The long-contended honors of her head.   140
    But Umbriel, hateful gnome, forbears not so;
He breaks the vial whence the sorrows flow.
Then see! the nymph in beauteous grief appears,
Her eyes half-languishing, half-drowned in tears;
On her heaved bosom hung her drooping head,
Which, with a sigh, she raised; and thus she said:
    "Forever cursed be this detested day,
Which snatched my best, my favorite curl away!
Happy! ah, ten times happy had I been,
If Hampton Court these eyes had never seen!   150
Yet am not I the first mistaken maid,
By love of courts to numerous ills betrayed.
Oh, had I rather unadmired remained
In some lone isle, or distant northern land;
Where the gilt chariot never marks the way,
Where none learn ombre, none e'er taste bohea!
There kept my charms concealed from mortal eye,
Like roses that in deserts bloom and die.
What moved my mind with youthful lords to roam?
Oh, had I stayed, and said my prayers at home!   160
'Twas this the morning omens seemed to tell:
Thrice from my trembling hand the patch-box fell;
The tottering china shook without a wind,
Nay, Poll sat mute, and Shock was most unkind!
A sylph too warned me of the threats of fate,
In mystic visions, now believed too late!
See the poor remnants of these slighted hairs!
My hands shall rend what e'en thy rapine spares:
These in two sable ringlets taught to break,

156. bohea: tea. 162. patch-box: box containing patches worn as beauty spots on the face. 164. Poll: Belinda's parrot.

170 Once gave new beauties to the snowy neck;
The sister-lock now sits uncouth, alone,
And in its fellow's fate foresees its own;
Uncurled it hangs, the fatal shears demands,
And tempts once more, thy sacrilegious hands.
Oh hadst thou, cruel! been content to seize
Hairs less in sight, or any hairs but these!"

CANTO V

She said: the pitying audience melt in tears.
But Fate and Jove had stopped the Baron's ears.
In vain Thalestris with reproach assails,
For who can move when fair Belinda fails?
Not half so fixed the Trojan could remain,
While Anna begged and Dido raged in vain.
Then grave Clarissa graceful waved her fan;
Silence ensued, and thus the nymph began:
"Say why are beauties praised and honored most,
10   The wise man's passion, and the vain man's toast?
Why decked with all that land and sea afford,
Why angels called, and angel-like adored?
Why round our coaches crowd the white-gloved beaux,
Why bows the side-box from its inmost rows;
How vain are all these glories, all our pains,
Unless good sense preserve what beauty gains:
That men may say, when we the front-box grace:
'Behold the first in virtue as in face!'
Oh! if to dance all night, and dress all day,
20   Charmed the smallpox, or chased old age away;
Who would not scorn what housewife's cares produce,
Or who would learn one earthly thing of use?
To patch, nay ogle, might become a saint,
Nor could it sure be such a sin to paint.
But since, alas! frail beauty must decay,
Curled or uncurled, since locks will turn to gray;
Since painted, or not painted, all shall fade,
And she who scorns a man must die a maid;
What then remains but well our power to use,
30   And keep good humor still whate'er we lose?

5, 6. **Trojan:** Æneas, who having been instructed by Jove to leave Carthage, could not be held back by the entreaties of **Dido,** queen of Carthage, and her sister, **Anna.** See *Æneid,* IV, lines 437-443. **23. patch:** apply beauty spots. **24. paint:** paint the face.

And trust me, dear! good humor can prevail,
When airs, and flights, and screams, and scolding fail.
Beauties in vain their pretty eyes may roll;
Charms strike the sight, but merit wins the soul."
   So spoke the dame, but no applause ensued;
Belinda frowned, Thalestris called her prude.
"To arms, to arms!" the fierce virago cries,
And swift as lightning to the combat flies.
All side in parties, and begin the attack;
Fans clap, silks rustle, and tough whalebones crack;   40
Heroes' and heroines' shouts confusedly rise,
And bass and treble voices strike the skies.
No common weapons in their hands are found,
Like gods they fight, nor dread a mortal wound.
   So when bold Homer makes the gods engage,
And heavenly breasts with human passions rage;
'Gainst Pallas, Mars; Latona, Hermes arms;
And all Olympus rings with loud alarms:
Jove's thunder roars, heaven trembles all around,
Blue Neptune storms, the bellowing deeps resound: 50
Earth shakes her nodding towers, the ground gives way,
And the pale ghosts start at the flash of day!
   Triumphant Umbriel on a sconce's height
Clapped his glad wings, and sat to view the fight:
Propped on their bodkin spears, the sprites survey
The growing combat, or assist the fray.
   While through the press enraged Thalestris flies,
And scatters death around from both her eyes,
A beau and witling perished in the throng,
One died in metaphor, and one in song.   60
"O cruel nymph! a living death I bear,"
Cried Dapperwit, and sunk beside his chair.
A mournful glance Sir Fopling upwards cast,
"Those eyes are made so killing"—was his last.
Thus on Maeander's flowery margin lies
The expiring swan, and as he sings he dies.

37. virago: warlike woman, referring to Thalestris. 47. Pallas . . . arms: Mars, god
of war, on the side of the Trojans in the Trojan War, arms himself against Pallas Athene,
goddess of wisdom, friend of the Greeks; Hermes, messenger of the gods, arms himself
against Latona, who also sided with the Trojans. 48. Olympus: home of the gods. 49.
Jove: highest of all the gods in the Roman system. 50. Neptune: God of the sea. 53.
sconce: candlestick. 59. witling: gentleman of small wit, such as Dapperwit, line 62.
64. last: last word. 65. Maeander: a meandering river near Troy.

When bold Sir Plume had drawn Clarissa down,
Chloe stepped in, and killed him with a frown;
She smiled to see the doughty hero slain,
70   But, at her smile, the beau revived again.
Now Jove suspends his golden scales in air,
Weighs the men's wits against the lady's hair;
The doubtful beam long nods from side to side;
At length the wits mount up, the hairs subside.
See, fierce Belinda on the Baron flies,
With more than usual lightning in her eyes;
Nor feared the chief the unequal fight to try,
Who sought no more than on his foe to die.
But this bold lord with manly strength endued,
80   She with one finger and a thumb subdued:
Just where the breath of life his nostrils drew,
A charge of snuff the wily virgin threw;
The gnomes direct, to every atom just,
The pungent grains of titillating dust.
Sudden, with starting tears each eye o'erflows,
And the high dome re-echoes to his nose.
"Now meet thy fate," incensed Belinda cried,
And drew a deadly bodkin from her side.
(The same, his ancient personage to deck,
90   Her great-great-grandsire wore about his neck,
In three seal rings; which after, melted down,
Formed a vast buckle for his widow's gown;
Her infant grandame's whistle next it grew,
The bells she jingled, and the whistle blew;
Then in a bodkin graced her mother's hairs,
Which long she wore, and now Belinda wears.)
"Boast not my fall," he cried, "insulting foe!
Thou by some other shalt be laid as low.
Nor think to die dejects my lofty mind:
100   All that I dread is leaving you behind!
Rather than so, ah, let me still survive,
And burn in Cupid's flames—but burn alive."
"Restore the lock!" she cries; and all around
"Restore the lock!" the vaulted roofs rebound.
Not fierce Othello in so loud a strain

69. doughty: brave. 73. beam: the rod holding the two pairs of the scales. 74. sub-
side: sink. 79. endued: endowed. 88. bodkin: long pin, usually worn in the hair. 105.
Othello: of Shakespeare's play, who believed that the proof of his wife's infidelity lay
in the fact of her loss of her handkerchief, which he angrily demanded of her.

Roared for the handkerchief that caused his pain.
But see how oft ambitious aims are crossed,
And chiefs contend till all the prize is lost!
The lock, obtained with guilt, and kept with pain,
In every place is sought, but sought in vain: 110
With such a prize no mortal must be blessed,
So heaven decrees! with heaven who can contest?

   Some thought it mounted to the lunar sphere,
Since all things lost on earth are treasured there.
There heroes' wits are kept in ponderous vases,
And beaux' in snuff boxes and tweezer-cases.
There broken vows and deathbed alms are found,
And lovers' hearts with ends of riband bound,
The courtier's promises, and sick man's prayers,
The smiles of harlots, and the tears of heirs,   ← *things get*   120
Cages for gnats, and chains to yoke a flea,   *lost.*
Dried butterflies, and tomes of casuistry.

   But trust the Muse—she saw it upward rise,
Though marked by none but quick, poetic eyes
(So Rome's great founder to the heavens withdrew,
To Proculus alone confessed in view):
A sudden star, it shot through liquid air,
And drew behind a radiant trail of hair.
Not Berenice's Locks first rose so bright,
The heavens bespangling with disheveled light.   130
The sylphs behold it kindling as it flies,
And pleased pursue its progress through the skies.

   This the beau monde shall from the Mall survey,
And hail with music its propitious ray.
This the blessed lover shall for Venus take,
And send up vows from Rosamonda's Lake.
This Partridge soon shall view in cloudless skies,

    113. lunar sphere: the innermost of the spheres of the planets which were thought to encircle the earth concentrically. **118. riband:** ribbon. **122. tomes of casuistry:** volumes of subtle and evasive argument. **125–126. Rome's . . . view:** Romulus, founder of Rome, was taken up to heaven in a storm cloud. He later reappeared, but only to the Senator Proculus. **129. Berenice's Locks:** Berenice was an Egyptian queen who sacrificed a lock of hair against the safe return of her husband from war. The lock was later turned into a constellation. **133. the Mall:** road through St. James' Park in London, much frequented by fashionable people (**beau monde**). **134. propitious:** boding well. **135. Venus:** the planet. **136. Rosamonda's Lake:** in St. James' Park, associated with lovers. **137. Partridge:** astrologer, wizard of line 139, who had been the butt of satires a few years before Pope's poem was written.

When next he looks through Galileo's eyes,
And hence the egregious wizard shall foredoom
140   The fate of Louis, and the fall of Rome.
        Then cease, bright nymph! to mourn thy ravished hair,
Which adds new glory to the shining sphere!
Not all the tresses that fair head can boast,
Shall draw such envy as the lock you lost.
For, after all the murders of your eye,
When, after millions slain, yourself shall die:
When those fair suns shall set, as set they must,
And all those tresses shall be laid in dust,
This lock the Muse shall consecrate to fame,
150   And 'midst the stars inscribe Belinda's name.

ON TWO LOVERS STRUCK DEAD BY LIGHTNING

When Eastern lovers feed the funeral fire,
On the same pile the faithful pair expire:
Here pitying Heaven that virtue mutual found,
And blasted both, that it might neither wound.
Hearts so sincere the Almighty saw well-pleased,
Sent his own lightning, and the victims seized.

138. **Galileo's eyes:** telescope. 139. **egregious:** notorious. 140. **fate . . . Rome:** Partridge repeatedly predicted the death of Louis XIV and the fall of the Pope.

Title. The lovers referred to were John Hewet and Sarah Drew, who, while harvesting, were killed by a bolt of lightning on July 31, 1718. When it was suggested to him that the above epitaph would be obscure to country people, Pope composed the following:

Think not, by rigorous judgment seized,
    A pair so faithful could expire:
Victims so pure Heaven saw well-pleased,
    And snatched them in celestial fire.

Live well, and fear no sudden fate:
    When God calls virtue to the grave,
Alike, 'tis justice soon or late,
    Mercy alike to kill or save.

Virtue unmoved can hear the call
    And face the flash that melts the ball.

3. **mutual:** equal.

THOMAS GRAY (1716–1771)

ELEGY

WRITTEN IN A COUNTRY CHURCHYARD

The curfew tolls the knell of parting day,
  The lowing herd wind slowly o'er the lea,
The plowman homeward plods his weary way,
  And leaves the world to darkness and to me.

Now fades the glimmering landscape on the sight,
  And all the air a solemn stillness holds,
Save where the beetle wheels his droning flight,
  And drowsy tinklings lull the distant folds;

Save that from yonder ivy-mantled tower
  The moping owl does to the moon complain   10
Of such, as wandering near her secret bower,
  Molest her ancient solitary reign.

Beneath those rugged elms, that yew-tree's shade,
  Where heaves the turf in many a moldering heap,
Each in his narrow cell for ever laid,
  The rude forefathers of the hamlet sleep.

The breezy call of incense-breathing morn,
  The swallow twittering from the straw-built shed,
The cock's shrill clarion, or the echoing horn,
  No more shall rouse them from their lowly bed.   20

For them no more the blazing hearth shall burn,
  Or busy housewife ply her evening care;
No children run to lisp their sire's return,
  Or climb his knees the envied kiss to share.

1. **curfew:** a bell rung each evening; **knell:** i.e., dying. 2. **lea:** pasture. 16. **rude:** rustic. 23. **lisp:** greet with childish speech.

Oft did the harvest to their sickle yield;
    Their furrow oft the stubborn glebe has broke;
How jocund did they drive their team afield!
    How bowed the woods beneath their sturdy stroke!

Let not Ambition mock their useful toil,
    Their homely joys, and destiny obscure;
Nor Grandeur hear with a disdainful smile
    The short and simple annals of the poor.

The boast of heraldry, the pomp of power,
    And all that beauty, all that wealth e'er gave,
Awaits alike the inevitable hour:
    The paths of glory lead but to the grave.

Nor you, ye proud, impute to these the fault,
    If Memory o'er their tomb no trophies raise,
Where through the long-drawn aisle and fretted vault
    The pealing anthem swells the note of praise.

Can storied urn or animated bust
    Back to its mansion call the fleeting breath?
Can Honor's voice provoke the silent dust,
    Or Flattery soothe the dull, cold ear of Death?

Perhaps in this neglected spot is laid
    Some heart once pregnant with celestial fire;
Hands that the rod of empire might have swayed,
    Or waked to ecstasy the living lyre.

But Knowledge to their eyes her ample page
    Rich with the spoils of time did ne'er unroll;
Chill Penury repressed their noble rage,
    And froze the genial current of the soul.

Full many a gem of purest ray serene,
    The dark unfathomed caves of ocean bear;
Full many a flower is born to blush unseen,
    And waste its sweetness on the desert air.

    26. glebe: clod of earth. **27. jocund:** joyfully. **30. homely:** domestic. **32. annals:** histories. **35. hour:** notice that this is the subject of **awaits. 39. fretted vault:** ceiling with interlacing arches. **41. storied urn:** an urn, containing the ashes of the deceased, with the history inscribed thereon; **animated:** lifelike. **43. provoke:** call to life. **51. Penury:** poverty. **52. genial:** generative.

Some village Hampden, that with dauntless breast
    The little Tyrant of his fields withstood;
Some mute, inglorious Milton here may rest,
    Some Cromwell, guiltless of his country's blood.   60

The applause of listening senates to command,
    The threats of pain and ruin to despise,
To scatter plenty o'er a smiling land,
    And read their history in a nation's eyes,

Their lot forbade; nor circumscribed alone
    Their growing virtues, but their crimes confined:
Forbade to wade through slaughter to a throne,
    And shut the gates of mercy on mankind,

The struggling pangs of conscious truth to hide,
    To quench the blushes of ingenuous shame,   70
Or heap the shrine of Luxury and Pride
    With incense kindled at the Muse's flame.

Far from the madding crowd's ignoble strife,
    Their sober wishes never learned to stray;
Along the cool sequestered vale of life,
    They kept the noiseless tenor of their way.

Yet even these bones from insult to protect,
    Some frail memorial still erected nigh,
With uncouth rhymes and shapeless scultpure decked,
    Implores the passing tribute of a sigh.   80

Their name, their years, spelt by the unlettered Muse,
    The place of fame and elegy supply;
And many a holy text around she strews,
    That teach the rustic moralist to die.

57. **Hampden:** landowner who resisted the levying of unjust taxes by Charles I. 59. **Milton:** the famous seventeenth-century poet, who also served as Cromwell's Latin Secretary. 60. **Cromwell:** leader of the Parliamentarain army in the English Civil Wars of the seventeenth century. He brought about the execution of Charles I and ruled England for a period. 65. **Their lot:** the destiny of the village dead. 65-66. **nor . . . confined:** their lot limited not only their virtues but their crimes. 67-71. **Their lot** (line 65) is the subject of **Forbade;** and **Forbade** governs the infinitives **to wade** (line 67), **shut** (line 68), **to hide** (line 69), **To quench** (line 70), and **heap** (line 71). 72. **Muse's flame:** the Muse was the mythical figure thought to inspire poetry: thus this phrase means inspiration. 73. **madding:** frenzied. 75. **sequestered:** secluded. 76. **tenor:** general course. 79. **uncouth:** unknown; **decked:** decorated. 81. **unlettered Muse:** the inspiration of the illiterate poet.

For who to dumb Forgetfulness a prey,
    This pleasing anxious being e'er resigned,
Left the warm precincts of the cheerful day,
    Nor cast one longing lingering look behind?

On some fond breast the parting soul relies,
90   Some pious drops the closing eye requires;
Ev'n from the tomb the voice of Nature cries,
    Ev'n in our ashes live their wonted fires.

For thee, who, mindful of the unhonored dead,
    Dost in these lines their artless tale relate:
If chance, by lonely contemplation led,
    Some kindred spirit shall inquire thy fate,

Haply some hoary-headed swain may say:
    "Oft have we seen him at the peep of dawn
Brushing with hasty steps the dews away,
100   To meet the sun upon the upland lawn.

"There at the foot of yonder nodding beech,
    That wreathes its old fantastic roots so high,
His listless length at noontide would he stretch
    And pore upon the brook that babbles by.

"Hard by yon wood, now smiling as in scorn,
    Muttering his wayward fancies he would rove,
Now drooping, woeful wan, like one forlorn,
    Or crazed with care, or crossed in hopeless love.

"One morn I missed him on the customed hill,
110   Along the heath, and near his favorite tree;
Another came; nor yet beside the rill,
    Nor up the lawn, nor at the wood was he;

"The next, with dirges due in sad array
    Slow through the church-way path we saw him borne.
Approach and read (for thou canst read) the lay,
    Graved on the stone beneath yon agèd thorn."

86. **being:** the human body. 92. **wonted:** customary. 93. **thee:** the speaker of the poem. 97. **Haply:** by chance; **hoary-headed swain:** white-haired shepherd. 111. **rill:** stream. 113. **The next:** the next thing (we saw); **due:** appropriate. 115. **lay:** poem, the epitaph that follows. 116. **Graved:** engraved; **thorn:** hawthorn.

THE EPITAPH

Here rests his head upon the lap of earth,
*   A youth to Fortune and to Fame unknown.*
Fair Science frowned not on his humble birth,
*   And Melancholy marked him for her own.*   120

Large was his bounty, and his soul sincere;
*   Heaven did a recompense as largely send:*
He gave to Misery all he had, a tear,
*   He gained from Heaven ('twas all he wished) a friend.*

No farther seek his merits to disclose,
*   Or draw his frailties from their dread abode.*
(There they alike in trembling hope repose)
*   The bosom of his Father and his God.*

ODE: ON THE DEATH OF A FAVORITE CAT, DROWNED IN A TUB OF GOLDFISHES

'Twas on a lofty vase's side,
Where China's gayest art had dyed
    The azure flowers that blow;
Demurest of the tabby kind,
The pensive Selima reclined,
    Gazed on the lake below.

Her conscious tail her joy declared;
The fair round face, the snowy beard,
    The velvet of her paws,
Her coat, that with the tortoise vies,   10
Her ears of jet, and emerald eyes,
    She saw; and purred applause.

119. Science: knowledge. 121. bounty: charity.

3. blow: bloom.

Still had she gazed; but 'midst the tide
Two angel forms were seen to glide,
    The genii of the stream:
Their scaly armor's Tyrian hue
Through richest purple to the view
    Betrayed a golden gleam.

The hapless nymph with wonder saw:
A whisker first, and then a claw,
    With many an ardent wish
She stretched in vain to reach the prize.
What female heart can gold despise?
    What cat's averse to fish?

Presumptuous maid! with looks intent
Again she stretched, again she bent,
    Nor knew the gulf between.
(Malignant Fate sat by and smiled)
The slippery verge her feet beguiled,
    She tumbled headlong in.

Eight times emerging from the flood
She mewed to every watery god
    Some speedy aid to send:
No dolphin came, no Nereid stirred;
Nor cruel Tom, nor Susan heard—
    A favorite has no friend!

From hence, ye beauties, undeceived,
Know, one false step is ne'er retrieved,
    And be with caution bold:
Not all that tempts your wandering eyes
And heedless hearts is lawful prize;
    Nor all that glisters, gold.

15. genii: guardian spirits. 16. Tyrian: reference to the purple-crimson dye made from certain mollusks at the ancient Phoenician city of Tyre. 29. verge: edge. 31. eight times: an allusion to the belief that cats have nine lives. 34. dolphin: a reference to the story of Arion, who was saved from the sea by a dolphin; Nereid: sea nymph.

WILLIAM COLLINS (1721–1759)

ODE TO EVENING

If aught of oaten stop or pastoral song
May hope, chaste Eve, to soothe thy modest ear,
   Like thy own solemn springs,
   Thy springs and dying gales,
O nymph reserved, while now the bright-haired sun
Sits in yon western tent, whose cloudy skirts,
   With brede ethereal wove,
   O'erhang his wavy bed;
Now air is hushed, save where the weak-eyed bat
With short shrill shriek flits by on leathern wing,   **10**
   Or where the beetle winds
   His small but sullen horn,
As oft he rises 'midst the twilight path,
Against the pilgrim borne in heedless hum:
   Now teach me, maid composed,
   To breathe some softened strain,
Whose numbers, stealing through thy darkening vale,
May not unseemly with its stillness suit,
   As, musing slow, I hail
   Thy genial loved return!   **20**
For when thy folding-star arising shows
His paly circlet, at his warning lamp
   The fragrant Hours, and elves
   Who slept in flowers the day,
And many a nymph who wreathes her brows with sedge,
And sheds the freshening dew, and, lovelier still,
   The pensive Pleasures sweet,
   Prepare thy shadowy car.
Then lead, calm vot'ress, where some sheety lake
Cheers the lone heath, or some time-hallowed pile   **30**

1. **aught:** any (note); **oaten stop:** a shepherd's reed pipe. 3, 4. **springs:** brooks. 7. **brede:** braid, embroidery. 11. **winds:** blows; **sullen:** of a deep or mournful tone. 14. **pilgrim:** traveler; *borne* modifies *beetle,* line 11. 17. **numbers:** music. 20. **genial:** cheering, enlivening. 21. **folding-star:** evening star, whose rising indicates it is time for the shepherd to put his sheep in their fold. 29. **vot'ress:** votaress, a woman devoted to the religious life.

Or upland fallows gray
Reflect its last cool gleam.
But when chill blustering winds or driving rain
Forbid my willing feet, be mine the hut
　　That from the mountain's side
　　Views wilds, and swelling floods,
And hamlets brown, and dim-discovered spires,
And hears their simple bell, and marks o'er all
　　Thy dewy fingers draw
40　　The gradual dusky veil.
While Spring shall pour his showers, as oft he wont,
And bathe thy breathing tresses, meekest Eve;
　　While Summer loves to sport
　　Beneath thy lingering light;
While sallow Autumn fills thy lap with leaves,
Or Winter, yelling through the troublous air,
　　Affrights thy shrinking train,
　　And rudely rends thy robes:
So long, sure-found beneath the sylvan shed,
50　　Shall Fancy, Friendship, Science, rose-lipped Health,
　　Thy gentlest influence own,
　　And hymn thy favorite name!

WILLIAM BLAKE (1757–1827)

INTRODUCTION TO "SONGS OF INNOCENCE"

Piping down the valleys wild,
Piping songs of pleasant glee,
On a cloud I saw a child,
And he laughing said to me:

"Pipe a song about a Lamb!"
So I piped with merry cheer.

42. breathing tresses: hair which emits sweet odors. 49. sylvan: forest. 51. own: acknowledge.

Note. This poem introduces a group of "Songs" portraying a world of childlike innocence and joy, the state of the new-born soul. Another group, the *Songs of Experience*, in which we find a representation of the materialistic, fallen world, contains certain poems that are counterparts of some of the *Songs of Innocence* (e.g., "The Tiger" contrasts with "The Lamb").

"Piper, pipe that song again."
So I piped; he wept to hear.

"Drop thy pipe, thy happy pipe;
Sing thy songs of happy cheer."   10
So I sung the same again,
While he wept with joy to hear.

"Piper, sit thee down and write
In a book, that all may read."
So he vanished from my sight,
And I plucked a hollow reed,

And I made a rural pen,
And I stained the water clear,
And I wrote my happy songs
Every child may joy to hear.   20

THE LAMB

Little lamb, who made thee?
Dost thou know who made thee?
Gave thee life and bid thee feed
By the stream and o'er the mead;
Gave thee clothing of delight,
Softest clothing, wooly, bright;
Gave thee such a tender voice,
Making all the vales rejoice?
Little lamb, who made thee?
Dost thou know who made thee?   10

Little lamb, I'll tell thee,
Little lamb, I'll tell thee:
He is callèd by thy name,
For He calls Himself a lamb.
He is meek, and He is mild;
He became a little child.
I a child, and thou a lamb:
We are callèd by His name.
Little lamb, God bless thee!
Little lamb, God bless thee!   20

THE CLOD AND THE PEBBLE

"Love seeketh not itself to please,
Nor for itself hath any care,
But for another gives its ease
And builds a Heaven in Hell's despair."

So sung a little clod of clay,
Trodden with the cattle's feet;
But a pebble of the brook
Warbled out these meters meet:

"Love seeketh only self to please,
To bind another to its delight,
Joys in another's loss of ease
And builds a Hell in Heaven's despite."

10

THE SICK ROSE

O rose, thou art sick!
The invisible worm
That flies in the night
In the howling storm

Has found out thy bed
Of crimson joy;
And his dark, secret love
Does thy life destroy.

THE TIGER

Tiger, tiger, burning bright
In the forests of the night,
What immortal hand or eye
Could frame thy fearful symmetry?

In what distant deeps or skies
Burnt the fire of thine eyes?
On what wings dare he aspire?
What the hand dare seize the fire?

And what shoulder, and what art,
Could twist the sinews of thy heart?   10
And when thy heart began to beat,
What dread hand? and what dread feet?

What the hammer? what the chain?
In what furnace was thy brain?
What the anvil? What dread grasp
Dare its deadly terrors clasp?

When the stars threw down their spears,
And watered heaven with their tears,
Did he smile his work to see?
Did he who made the lamb make thee?   20

Tiger, tiger, burning bright
In the forests of the night,
What immortal hand or eye
Dare frame thy fearful symmetry?

LONDON

I wander through each chartered street,
Near where the chartered Thames does flow,
And mark in every face I meet
Marks of weakness, marks of woe.

In every cry of every man,
In every infant's cry of fear,
In every voice, in every ban,
The mind-forged manacles I hear:

How the chimney-sweeper's cry
Every blackening church appalls;   10
And the hapless soldier's sigh
Runs in blood down palace walls;

But most through midnight streets I hear
How the youthful harlot's curse
Blasts the new born infant's tear
And blights with plagues the marriage hearse.

1. **chartered**: granted and legally possessed, as by a charter. 7. **ban**: curse, prohibition, marriage proclamation.

A POISON TREE

I was angry with my friend:
I told my wrath, my wrath did end.
I was angry with my foe:
I told it not, my wrath did grow.

And I watered it in fears,
Night and morning with my tears;
And I sunnèd it with smiles
And with soft deceitful wiles.

And it grew both day and night,
Till it bore an apple bright;
And my foe beheld it shine,
And he knew that it was mine,

And into my garden stole
When the night had veiled the pole:
In the morning glad I see
My foe outstretched beneath the tree.

FROM *MILTON*

And did those feet in ancient time
    Walk upon England's mountains green?
And was the holy Lamb of God
    On England's pleasant pastures seen?

And did the Countenance Divine
    Shine forth upon our clouded hills?
And was Jerusalem builded here
    Among these dark Satanic mills?

Bring me my bow of burning gold!
    Bring me my arrows of desire!
Bring me my spear! O clouds, unfold!
    Bring me my chariot of fire!

I will not cease from mental fight,
    Nor shall my sword sleep in my hand,
Till we have built Jerusalem
    In England's green and pleasant land.

Note. This poem uses the idea that the vision in the last chapters in Revelation was as immediately relevant to England as to Israel.

THE CHIMNEY SWEEPER

A little black thing among the snow,
Crying "'weep! 'weep!" in notes of woe.
"Where are thy father and mother? say!"
"They are both gone up to the church to pray.

"Because I was happy upon the heath,
And smiled among the winter's snow,
They clothed me in the clothes of death,
And taught me to sing the notes of woe.

"And because I am happy and dance and sing,
They think they have done me no injury,   10
And are gone to praise God and his Priest and King,
Who make up a heaven of our misery."

MOCK ON, MOCK ON, VOLTAIRE, ROUSSEAU

Mock on, mock on, Voltaire, Rousseau—
Mock on, mock on: 'tis all in vain!
You throw the sand against the wind,
And the wind blows it back again.

And every sand becomes a gem
Reflected in the beams divine;
Blown back, they blind the mocking eye,
But still in Israel's paths they shine.

The atoms of Democritus
And Newton's particles of light   10
Are sands upon the Red Sea shore,
Where Israel's tents do shine so bright.

2. 'weep: sweep.

1. Voltaire, Rousseau: "prophets" of the French Revolution, first hailed by Blake
but later disowned because of their antiestablishment religious views (Deism). 9–10.
Democritus, Newton: the former a fifth-century B.C. Greek philosopher, the latter the
famous theoretical scientist (1642–1727). 11. a reference to the Israelites' crossing of
the Red Sea in escaping from Pharaoh's host (Exodus xiv)

ROBERT BURNS (1759–1796)

MARY MORISON

O Mary, at thy window be,
It is the wished, the trysted hour!
Those smiles and glances let me see
That make the miser's treasure poor.
How blythely wad I bide the stoure,
A weary slave frae sun to sun,
Could I the rich reward secure,
The lovely Mary Morison.

Yestreen, when to the trembling string
10   The dance gaed through the lighted ha',
To thee my fancy took its wing,
I sat, but neither heard nor saw:
Though this was fair, and that was braw,
And yon the toast of a' the town,
I sighed, and said amang them a',
"Ye are na Mary Morison."

O Mary, canst thou wreck his peace,
Wha for thy sake wad gladly die?
Or canst thou break that heart of his
20   Whase only faut is loving thee?
If love for love thou wilt na gie,
At least be pity to me shown!
A thought ungentle canna be
The thought o' Mary Morison.

2. **trysted:** appointed. 5. **blythely:** gaily; **wad:** would; **bide:** endure; **stoure:** conflict. 6. **frae:** from. 9. **Yestreen:** yesterday evening. 10. **gaed:** went; **ha':** hall. 13. **braw:** excellent. 14. **a':** all. 16. **na:** not. 18. **Wha:** who. 20. **Whase:** whose; **faut:** fault. 21. **gie:** give.

TO A MOUSE, ON TURNING UP HER NEST WITH THE PLOUGH, NOVEMBER, 1785

Wee, sleekit, cowrin, timorous beastie,
O what a panic's in thy breastie!
Thou need na start awa sae hasty,
  Wi' bickering brattle!
I wad be laith to rin an' chase thee
  Wi' murdering pattle!

I'm truly sorry man's dominion
Has broken nature's social union,
An' justifies that ill opinion
  Which makes thee startle   10
At me, thy poor earth-born companion
  An' fellow-mortal!

I doubt na, whyles, but thou may thieve;
What then? poor beastie, thou maun live!
A daimen icker in a thrave
  'S a sma' request;
I'll get a blessin' wi' the lave,
  And never miss 't!

Thy wee bit housie, too, in ruin!
Its silly wa's the win's are strewin!   20
An' naething, now, to big a new ane,
  O' foggage green!
An' bleak December's winds ensuin,
  Baith snell an' keen!

Thou saw the fields laid bare and waste,
An' weary winter comin fast,
An' cozie here, beneath the blast,
  Thou thought to dwell,
Till crash! the cruel coulter past
  Out through thy cell.   30

---

1. **sleekit:** sleek; **cowrin:** cowering. 3. **na:** not; **awa:** away; **sae:** so. 4. **Wi' . . . brattle:** with a scuttling movement. 5. **wad:** would; **laith:** unwilling; **rin:** run. 6. **pattle:** stick. 13. **whyles:** from time to time. 14. **maun:** must. 15. **daimen . . . thrave:** one ear of grain in a whole stack. 16. **'S:** is; **sma':** small. 17. **wi':** with; **lave:** remainder. 20. **silly:** feeble; **wa's:** walls; **win's:** winds. 21. **big:** build; **ane:** one. 22. **foggage:** long grass. 23. **ensuin:** about to follow. 24. **Baith:** both; **snell:** sharp. 29. **coulter:** ploughshare.

That wee bit heap o' leaves an' stibble
Has cost thee mony a weary nibble!
Now thou's turned out, for a' thy trouble,
    But house or hald,
To thole the winter's sleety dribble,
    An' cranreuch cauld!

But, Mousie, thou art no thy lane,
In proving foresight may be vain:
The best laid schemes o' mice an' men
40   Gang aft a-gley,
An' lea'e us nought but grief an' pain
    For promised joy.

Still thou art blest compared wi' me!
The present only toucheth thee;
But och! I backward cast my e'e
    On prospects drear!
An' forward though I canna see,
    I guess an' fear!

A RED, RED ROSE

O, my luve is like a red, red rose
That's newly sprung in June.
O, my luve is like the melodie
That's sweetly played in tune.

As fair art thou, my bonnie lass,
So deep in luve am I,
And I will luve thee still, my dear,
Till a' the seas gang dry.

Till a' the seas gang dry, my dear,
10   And the rocks melt wi' the sun:
And I will luve thee still, my dear,
While the sands o' life shall run.

31. stibble: stubble. 32. mony: many. 33. a': all. 34. But: without; hald: territory.
35. thole: suffer. 36. cranreuch: frost; cauld: cold. 37. no thy lane: not alone. 40. Gang:
go; aft: often; a-gley: astray. 41. lea'e: leave. 45. e'e: eye.

8. a': all; gang: go. 10. wi': with.

And fare thee weel, my only luve,
And fare thee weel a while!
And I will come again, my luve,
Though it were ten thousand mile.

WILLIAM WORDSWORTH (1770–1850)

LINES COMPOSED A FEW MILES ABOVE
TINTERN ABBEY

Five years have past; five summers, with the length
Of five long winters! and again I hear
These waters, rolling from their mountain-springs
With a soft inland murmur.—Once again
Do I behold these steep and lofty cliffs,
That on a wild secluded scene impress
Thoughts of more deep seclusion; and connect
The landscape with the quiet of the sky.
The day is come when I again repose
Here, under this dark sycamore, and view   10
These plots of cottage-ground, these orchard-tufts,
Which at this season, with their unripe fruits,
Are clad in one green hue, and lose themselves
'Mid groves and copses. Once again I see
These hedge-rows, hardly hedge-rows, little lines
Of sportive wood run wild: these pastoral farms,
Green to the very door; and wreaths of smoke
Sent up, in silence, from among the trees!
With some uncertain notice, as might seem
Of vagrant dwellers in the houseless woods,   20
Or of some hermit's cave, where by his fire
The hermit sits alone.
                              These beauteous forms,
Through a long absence, have not been to me
As is a landscape to a blind man's eye:
But oft, in lonely rooms, and 'mid the din
Of towns and cities, I have owed to them
In hours of weariness, sensations sweet,
Felt in the blood, and felt along the heart;

13. weel: well.

And passing even into my purer mind,
30   With tranquil restoration:—feelings too
Of unremembered pleasure: such, perhaps,
As have no slight or trivial influence
On that best portion of a good man's life,
His little, nameless, unremembered acts
Of kindness and of love. Nor less, I trust,
To them I may have owed another gift,
Of aspect more sublime; that blessèd mood,
In which the burthen of the mystery,
In which the heavy and the weary weight
40   Of all this unintelligible world,
Is lightened:—that serene and blessèd mood,
In which the affections gently lead us on,—
Until, the breath of this corporeal frame
And even the motion of our human blood
Almost suspended, we are laid asleep
In body, and become a living soul:
While with an eye made quiet by the power
Of harmony, and the deep power of joy,
We see into the life of things.
                                                    If this
50   Be but a vain belief, yet, oh! how oft—
In darkness and amid the many shapes
Of joyless daylight; when the fretful stir
Unprofitable, and the fever of the world,
Have hung upon the beatings of my heart—
How oft, in spirit, have I turned to thee,
O sylvan Wye! thou wanderer through the woods,
How often has my spirit turned to thee!

And now, with gleams of half-extinguished thought,
With many recognitions dim and faint,
60   And somewhat of a sad perplexity,
The picture of the mind revives again:
While here I stand, not only with the sense
Of present pleasure, but with pleasing thoughts
That in this moment there is life and food
For future years. And so I dare to hope,
Though changed, no doubt, from what I was when first
I came among these hills; when like a roe
I bounded o'er the mountains, by the sides

38. **burthen:** burden.

Of the deep rivers, and the lonely streams,
Wherever nature led: more like a man   70
Flying from something that he dreads than one
Who sought the thing he loved. For nature then
(The coarser pleasures of my boyish days,
And their glad animal movements all gone by)
To me was all in all.—I cannot paint
What then I was. The sounding cataract
Haunted me like a passion: the tall rock,
The mountain, and the deep and gloomy wood,
Their colors and their forms, were then to me
An appetite; a feeling and a love,   80
That had no need of a remoter charm,
By thought supplied, nor any interest
Unborrowed from the eye.—That time is past,
And all its aching joys are now no more,
And all its dizzy raptures. Not for this
Faint I, nor mourn nor murmur; other gifts
Have followed; for such loss, I would believe,
Abundant recompense. For I have learned
To look on nature, not as in the hour
Of thoughtless youth; but hearing oftentimes   90
The still, sad music of humanity,
Nor harsh nor grating, though of ample power
To chasten and subdue. And I have felt
A presence that disturbs me with the joy
Of elevated thoughts; a sense sublime
Of something far more deeply interfused,
Whose dwelling is the light of setting suns,
And the round ocean and the living air,
And the blue sky, and in the mind of man:
A motion and a spirit, that impels   100
All thinking things, all objects of all thought,
And rolls through all things. Therefore am I still
A lover of the meadows and the woods
And mountains; and of all that we behold
From this green earth; of all the mighty world
Of eye, and ear,—both what they half create,
And what perceive; well pleased to recognize
In nature and the language of the sense
The anchor of my purest thoughts, the nurse,

86. **Faint I:** am I discouraged. 106-107. **both what . . . what perceive:** the senses in part receive and in part create their impressions.

110   The guide, the guardian of my heart, and soul
       Of all my moral being.
                                   Nor perchance,
       If I were not thus taught, should I the more
       Suffer my genial spirits to decay:
       For thou art with me here upon the banks
       Of this fair river; thou my dearest Friend,
       My dear, dear Friend; and in thy voice I catch
       The language of my former heart, and read
       My former pleasures in the shooting lights
       Of thy wild eyes. Oh! yet a little while
120   May I behold in thee what I was once,
       My dear, dear Sister! and this prayer I make,
       Knowing that Nature never did betray
       The heart that loved her; 'tis her privilege,
       Through all the years of this our life, to lead
       From joy to joy: for she can so inform
       The mind that is within us, so impress
       With quietness and beauty, and so feed
       With lofty thoughts, that neither evil tongues,
       Rash judgments, nor the sneers of selfish men,
130   Nor greetings where no kindness is, nor all
       The dreary intercourse of daily life,
       Shall e'er prevail against us, or disturb
       Our cheerful faith that all which we behold
       Is full of blessings. Therefore let the moon
       Shine on thee in thy solitary walk;
       And let the misty mountain-winds be free
       To blow against thee: and, in after years,
       When these wild ecstasies shall be matured
       Into a sober pleasure; when thy mind
140   Shall be a mansion for all lovely forms,
       Thy memory be as a dwelling-place
       For all sweet sounds and harmonies; oh! then,
       If solitude, or fear, or pain, or grief,
       Should be thy portion, with what healing thoughts
       Of tender joy wilt thou remember me,
       And these my exhortations! Nor, perchance—
       If I should be where I no more can hear
       Thy voice, nor catch from thy wild eyes these gleams
       Of past existence—wilt thou then forget
150   That on the banks of this delightful stream

113. genial: innate. **115. Friend:** his sister Dorothy.

We stood together; and that I, so long
A worshipper of Nature, hither came
Unwearied in that service: rather say
With warmer love—oh! with far deeper zeal
Of holier love. Nor wilt thou then forget,
That after many wanderings, many years
Of absence, these steep woods and lofty cliffs,
And this green pastoral landscape, were to me
More dear, both for themselves and for thy sake!

SHE DWELT AMONG THE UNTRODDEN WAYS

She dwelt among the untrodden ways
   Beside the springs of Dove,
A maid whom there were none to praise
   And very few to love:

A violet by a mossy stone
   Half-hidden from the eye!
—Fair as a star, when only one
   Is shining in the sky.

She lived unknown, and few could know
   When Lucy ceased to be;   10
But she is in her grave, and, oh,
   The difference to me!

A SLUMBER DID MY SPIRIT SEAL

A slumber did my spirit seal;
   I had no human fears:
She seemed a thing that could not feel
   The touch of earthly years.

No motion has she now, no force;
   She neither hears nor sees;
Rolled round in earth's diurnal course,
   With rocks, and stones, and trees.

2. springs of Dove: the source of the river Dove.

7. diurnal: daily.

MY HEART LEAPS UP

My heart leaps up when I behold
   A rainbow in the sky:
So was it when my life began;
So is it now I am a man;
So be it when I shall grow old,
   Or let me die!
The Child is father of the Man;
And I could wish my days to be
Bound each to each by natural piety

COMPOSED UPON WESTMINSTER BRIDGE

SEPTEMBER 3, 1802

Earth has not anything to show more fair:
Dull would he be of soul who could pass by
A sight so touching in its majesty:
This City now doth, like a garment, wear
The beauty of the morning; silent, bare,
Ships, towers, domes, theaters, and temples lie
Open unto the fields, and to the sky;
All bright and glittering in the smokeless air.
Never did sun more beautifully steep
In his first splendor, valley, rock, or hill;
Ne'er saw I, never felt, a calm so deep!
The river glideth at his own sweet will:
Dear God! the very houses seem asleep;
And all that mighty heart is lying still!

10

IT IS A BEAUTEOUS EVENING

It is a beauteous evening, calm and free,
The holy time is quiet as a nun
Breathless with adoration; the broad sun
Is sinking down in its tranquillity;

9. **natural piety:** as distinguished from religious piety.

Title. Westminster Bridge is one of the bridges crossing the river Thames in London,
near the Houses of Parliament.

The gentleness of heaven broods o'er the sea:
Listen! the mighty being is awake,
And doth with his eternal motion make
A sound like thunder—everlastingly.
Dear Child! dear Girl! that walkest with me here,
If thou appear untouched by solemn thought,   10
Thy nature is not therefore less divine:
Thou liest in Abraham's bosom all the year;
And worship'st at the temple's inner shrine,
God being with thee when we know it not.

LONDON, 1802

Milton! thou shouldst be living at this hour:
England hath need of thee: she is a fen
Of stagnant waters: altar, sword, and pen,
Fireside, the heroic wealth of hall and bower,
Have forfeited their ancient English dower
Of inward happiness. We are selfish men;
Oh! raise us up, return to us again;
And give us manners, virtue, freedom, power.
Thy soul was like a star, and dwelt apart;
Thou hadst a voice whose sound was like the sea.   10
Pure as the naked heavens, majestic, free,
So didst thou travel on life's common way,
In cheerful godliness; and yet thy heart
The lowliest duties on herself did lay.

THE WORLD IS TOO MUCH WITH US

The world is too much with us; late and soon,
Getting and spending, we lay waste our powers:
Little we see in Nature that is ours;
We have given our hearts away, a sordid boon!
The sea that bares her bosom to the moon;
The winds that will be howling at all hours,

9. **Child:** Wordsworth's natural daughter Caroline. 12. **Abraham's bosom:** in a state of heavenly peace.

5. **dower:** legacy.

4. **boon:** normally means gift, here exchange.

And are up-gathered now like sleeping flowers;
For this, for everything, we are out of tune:
It moves us not.—Great God! I'd rather be
10   A pagan suckled in a creed outworn;
So might I, standing on this pleasant lea,
Have glimpses that would make me less forlorn;
Have sight of Proteus rising from the sea;
Or hear old Triton blow his wreathèd horn.

THE SOLITARY REAPER

Behold her, single in the field,
Yon solitary Highland lass!
Reaping and singing by herself;
Stop here, or gently pass!
Alone she cuts and binds the grain,
And sings a melancholy strain;
O listen! for the vale profound
Is overflowing with the sound.

No nightingale did ever chaunt
10   More welcome notes to weary bands
Of travellers in some shady haunt,
Among Arabian sands:
A voice so thrilling ne'er was heard
In spring-time from the cuckoo-bird,
Breaking the silence of the seas
Among the farthest Hebrides.

Will no one tell me what she sings?—
Perhaps the plaintive numbers flow
For old, unhappy, far-off things,
20   And battles long ago:
Or is it some more humble lay,
Familiar matter of to-day?
Some natural sorrow, loss, or pain,
That has been, and may be again?

13. Proteus: a sea god who could change his form or shape. 14. Triton: a sea god, usually pictured carrying a conch-shell trumpet.

7. profound: deep. 14. cuckoo-bird: one of the heralds of spring. 16. Hebrides: a group of islands off the northwest coast of Scotland. 17. Will . . . sings: the Highland girl (cf. line 2) is singing in a language unfamiliar to the poet. 18. numbers: poetic lines. 21. lay: poem or song.

Whate'er the theme, the maiden sang
As if her song could have no ending;
I saw her singing at her work,
And o'er the sickle bending;—
I listened, motionless and still;
And, as I mounted up the hill,   30
The music in my heart I bore
Long after it was heard no more.

ODE:
INTIMATIONS OF IMMORTALITY FROM RECOLLECTIONS OF EARLY CHILDHOOD

I

There was a time when meadow, grove, and stream,
The earth, and every common sight,
      To me did seem
      Apparelled in celestial light,
The glory and the freshness of a dream.
It is not now as it hath been of yore;—
      Turn wheresoe'er I may,
      By night or day,
The things which I have seen I now can see no more.

II

      The rainbow comes and goes,   10
      And lovely is the rose,
      The moon doth with delight
Look round her when the heavens are bare;
      Waters on a starry night
      Are beautiful and fair;
   The sunshine is a glorious birth;
   But yet I know, where'er I go,
That there hath past away a glory from the earth.

III

Now, while the birds thus sing a joyous song,
      And while the young lambs bound   20
         As to the tabor's sound,

Note. Wordsworth used the last three lines of "My Heart Leaps Up" as an epigraph.

21. tabor: small drum, used like a tambourine to beat time to dancing.

To me alone there came a thought of grief:
A timely utterance gave that thought relief,
  And I again am strong:
The cataracts blow their trumpets from the steep;
No more shall grief of mine the season wrong;
I hear the echoes through the mountains throng,
The winds come to me from the fields of sleep,
  And all the earth is gay;
30   Land and sea
 Give themselves up to jollity,
  And with the heart of May
Doth every beast keep holiday;—
  Thou child of joy,
Shout round me, let me hear thy shouts, thou happy shepherd-boy!

IV

Ye blessèd creatures, I have heard the call
 Ye to each other make; I see
The heavens laugh with you in your jubilee;
 My heart is at your festival,
40   My head hath its coronal,
The fulness of your bliss, I feel—I feel it all.
 Oh evil day! if I were sullen
 While earth herself is adorning,
  This sweet May-morning,
 And the children are culling
  On every side,
 In a thousand valleys far and wide,
 Fresh flowers; while the sun shines warm,
And the babe leaps up on his mother's arm:—
50   I hear, I hear, with joy I hear!
 —But there's a tree, of many, one,
A single field which I have looked upon,
Both of them speak of something that is gone:
 The pansy at my feet
 Doth the same tale repeat:
Whither is fled the visionary gleam?
Where is it now, the glory and the dream?

25. **cataracts:** waterfalls; **steep:** mountainside. 40. **coronal:** crown (of flowers).

V

Our birth is but a sleep and a forgetting:
The soul that rises with us, our life's star,
  Hath had elsewhere its setting,   60
    And cometh from afar:
  Not in entire forgetfulness,
  And not in utter nakedness,
But trailing clouds of glory do we come
  From God, who is our home:
Heaven lies about us in our infancy!
Shades of the prison-house begin to close
  Upon the growing boy,
But he beholds the light, and whence it flows,
  He sees it in his joy;   70
The youth, who daily farther from the east
  Must travel, still is Nature's priest,
  And by the vision splendid
  Is on his way attended;
At length the man perceives it die away,
And fade into the light of common day.

VI

Earth fills her lap with pleasures of her own;
Yearnings she hath in her own natural kind,
And, even with something of a mother's mind,
  And no unworthy aim,   80
  The homely nurse doth all she can
To make her foster-child, her inmate man,
  Forget the glories he hath known,
And that imperial palace whence he came.

VII

Behold the child among his new-born blisses,
A six year's darling of a pigmy size!
See, where 'mid work of his own hand he lies,
Fretted by sallies of his mother's kisses,
With light upon him from his father's eyes!
See, at his feet, some little plan or chart,   90
Some fragment from his dream of human life,

81. homely: familiar and unpretentious. **88. Fretted by sallies:** bothered by the advances (?); checkered over, with the sense of confining, by the advances (?).

Shaped by himself with newly-learnèd art;
  A wedding or a festival,
  A mourning or a funeral;
    And this hath now his heart,
    And unto this he frames his song:
      Then will he fit his tongue
To dialogues of business, love, or strife;
    But it will not be long

100   Ere this be thrown aside,
      And with new joy and pride
The little actor cons another part;
Filling from time to time his "humorous stage"
With all the persons, down to palsied age,
That life brings with her in her equipage;
    As if his whole vocation
    Were endless imitation.

VIII

Thou, whose exterior semblance doth belie
  Thy soul's immensity;

110 Thou best philosopher, who yet dost keep
Thy heritage, thou eye among the blind,
That, deaf and silent, read'st the eternal deep,
Haunted for ever by the eternal mind,—
    Mighty prophet! Seer blest!
    On whom those truths do rest,
Which we are toiling all our lives to find,
In darkness lost, the darkness of the grave;
Thou, over whom thy immortality
Broods like the day, a master o'er a slave,

120 A presence which is not to be put by;
Thou little child, yet glorious in the might
Of heaven-born freedom on thy being's height,
Why with such earnest pains dost thou provoke
The years to bring the inevitable yoke,
Thus blindly with thy blessedness at strife?
Full soon thy soul shall have her earthly freight,
And custom lie upon thee with a weight,
Heavy as frost, and deep almost as life!

102. **cons**: studies. 103. **"humorous stage"**: A quotation from an Elizabethan poet and playwright, Ben Jonson (1573?-1637): an allusion to the theater that exhibits mankind as governed by four basic temperaments (or humors). 105. **equipage**: coach. 108. **exterior . . . belie**: appearance gives the wrong impression of.

IX

O joy! that in our embers
Is something that doth live,   130
That nature yet remembers
What was so fugitive!
The thought of our past years in me doth breed
Perpetual benediction: not indeed
For that which is most worthy to be blest;
Delight and liberty, the simple creed
Of childhood, whether busy or at rest,
With new-fledged hope still fluttering in his breast:—
Not for these I raise
The song of thanks and praise;   140
But for those obstinate questionings
Of sense and outward things,
Fallings from us, vanishings;
Blank misgivings of a creature
Moving about in worlds not realized,
High instincts before which our mortal nature
Did tremble like a guilty thing surprised:
But for those first affections,
Those shadowy recollections,
Which, be they what they may,   150
Are yet the fountain light of all our day,
Are yet a master light of all our seeing;
Uphold us, cherish, and have power to make
Our noisy years seem moments in the being
Of the eternal silence: truths that wake,
To perish never;
Which neither listlessness, nor mad endeavor,
Nor man nor boy,
Nor all that is at enmity with joy,
Can utterly abolish or destroy!   160
Hence in a season of calm weather
Though inland far we be,
Our souls have sight of that immortal sea
Which brought us hither,
Can in a moment travel thither,
And see the children sport upon the shore,
And hear the mighty waters rolling evermore.

132. fugitive: fleeting. 145. realized: actualized.

X

Then sing, ye birds, sing, sing a joyous song!
    And let the young lambs bound
170   As to the tabor's sound!
We in thought will join your throng,
    Ye that pipe and ye that play,
    Ye that through your hearts today
    Feel the gladness of the May!
What though the radiance which was once so bright
Be now forever taken from my sight,
  Though nothing can bring back the hour
Of splendor in the grass, of glory in the flower;
    We will grieve not, rather find
180   Strength in what remains behind;
    In the primal sympathy
    Which having been must ever be;
    In the soothing thoughts that spring
    Out of human suffering;
    In the faith that looks through death,
In years that bring the philosophic mind.

XI

And O, ye fountains, meadows, hills, and groves,
Forebode not any severing of our loves!
Yet in my heart of hearts I feel your might;
190 I only have relinquished one delight
To live beneath your more habitual sway.
I love the brooks which down their channels fret,
Even more than when I tripped lightly as they;
The innocent brightness of a new-born day
    Is lovely yet;
The clouds that gather round the setting sun
Do take a sober coloring from an eye
That hath kept watch o'er man's mortality;
Another race hath been, and other palms are won.
200 Thanks to the human heart by which we live,
Thanks to its tenderness, its joys, and fears,
To me the meanest flower that blows can give
Thoughts that do often lie too deep for tears.

181. **primal sympathy:** original feeling (for nature). 188. **Forebode not:** have no forebodings about. 192. **fret:** run. 199. **palms:** honors. 202. **meanest:** lowliest; **blows:** blossoms.

SAMUEL TAYLOR COLERIDGE (1772–1834)

THE RIME OF THE ANCIENT MARINER

PART I

An ancient mariner
meeteth three gallants
bidden to a wedding-
feast, and detaineth
one.

It is an ancient mariner,
And he stoppeth one of three.
"By thy long gray beard and glittering eye,
Now wherefore stopp'st thou me?

"The bridegroom's doors are opened wide,
And I am next of kin;
The guests are met, the feast is set:
May'st hear the merry din."

He holds him with his skinny hand,
"There was a ship," quoth he.   **10**
"Hold off! unhand me, gray-beard loon!"
Eftsoons his hand dropped he.

The wedding-guest
is spellbound by the
eye of the old sea-
faring man, and
constrained to hear
his tale.

He holds him with his glittering eye—
The wedding-guest stood still,
And listens like a three years' child:
The mariner hath his will.

The wedding-guest sat on a stone:
He cannot choose but hear;
And thus spake on that ancient man,
The bright-eyed mariner.   **20**

"The ship was cheered, the harbor cleared,
Merrily did we drop
Below the kirk, below the hill,
Below the lighthouse top.

12. eftsoons: immediately. **23. kirk:** church.

*The mariner tells how
the ship sailed south-
ward with a good wind
and fair weather, till
it reached the Line.*

"The sun came up upon the left,
Out of the sea came he!
And he shone bright, and on the right
Went down into the sea.

30

"Higher and higher every day,
Till over the mast at noon—"
The wedding-guest here beat his breast,
For he heard the loud bassoon.

*The wedding-guest
heareth the bridal
music; but the
mariner continueth
his tale.*

The bride hath paced into the hall,
Red as a rose is she;
Nodding their heads before her goes
The merry minstrelsy.

The wedding-guest he beat his breast,
Yet he cannot choose but hear;
And thus spake on that ancient man,
The bright-eyed mariner.

40

*The ship driven by a
storm toward the south
pole.*

"And now the storm-blast came, and he
Was tyrannous and strong:
He struck with his o'ertaking wings,
And chased us south along.

"With sloping masts and dipping prow,
As who pursued with yell and blow
Still treads the shadow of his foe,
And forward bends his head,
The ship drove fast, loud roared the blast,
And southward aye we fled.

50

"And now there came both mist and snow,
And it grew wondrous cold:
And ice, mast-high, came floating by,
As green as emerald.

*The land of ice and
of fearful sounds,
where no living thing
was to be seen.*

"And through the drifts the snowy clifts
Did send a dismal sheen:
Nor shapes of men nor beasts we ken—
The ice was all between.

30. Indicates they had reached the equator. 55. clifts: cliffs.

"The ice was here, the ice was there,
The ice was all around: 60
It cracked and growled, and roared and howled,
Like noises in a swound!

Till a great sea-bird,
called the albatross,
came through the
snow-fog, and was
received with great
joy and hospitality.

"At length did cross an albatross,
Thorough the fog it came;
As if it had been a Christian soul,
We hailed it in God's name.

"It ate the food it ne'er had eat,
And round and round it flew.
The ice did split with a thunder-fit;
The helmsman steered us through!   70

And lo! the albatross
proveth a bird of good
omen, and followeth
the ship as it returned
northward through fog
and floating ice.

"And a good south wind sprung up behind;
The albatross did follow,
And every day, for food or play,
Came to the mariners' hollo!

"In mist or cloud, on mast or shroud,
It perched for vespers nine;
Whiles all the night, through fog-smoke white,
Glimmered the white moon-shine."

The ancient mariner
inhospitably killeth
the pious bird of good
omen.

"God save thee, ancient mariner!
From the fiends that plague thee thus!—   80
Why look'st thou so?"—"With my crossbow
I shot the albatross!"

PART II

"The sun now rose upon the right:
Out of the sea came he,
Still hid in mist, and on the left
Went down into the sea.

62. swound: swoon; faint. 74. hollo: cry of invitation. 75. shroud: rope attached to
the mast. 76. vespers: evening prayer.

"And the good south wind still blew behind,
But no sweet bird did follow,
Nor any day for food or play
Came to the mariners' hollo!

His shipmates cry out
against the ancient
mariner for killing
the bird of good luck.

"And I had done a hellish thing,
And it would work 'em woe:
For all averred, I had killed the bird
That made the breeze to blow.
'Ah wretch!' said they, 'the bird to slay,
That made the breeze to blow!'

But when the fog
cleared off, they
justify the same, and
thus make themselves
accomplices in the
crime.

"Nor dim nor red, like God's own head,
The glorious sun uprist:
Then all averred, I had killed the bird
That brought the fog and mist.
''Twas right,' said they, 'such birds to slay
That bring the fog and mist.'

The fair breeze
continues; the ship
enters the Pacific
Ocean, and sails
northward, even till
it reaches the Line.
The ship hath been
suddenly becalmed.

"The fair breeze blew, the white foam flew,
The furrow followed free;
We were the first that ever burst
Into that silent sea.

"Down dropped the breeze, the sails dropped
        down,
'Twas sad as sad could be;
And we did speak only to break
The silence of the sea!

"All in a hot and copper sky,
The bloody sun, at noon,
Right up above the mast did stand,
No bigger than the moon.

"Day after day, day after day,
We stuck, nor breath nor motion;
As idle as a painted ship
Upon a painted ocean.

And the albatross
begins to be avenged.

"Water, water, everywhere,
And all the boards did shrink;   120
Water, water, everywhere,
Nor any drop to drink.

"The very deep did rot: O Christ!
That ever this should be!
Yea, slimy things did crawl with legs
Upon the slimy sea.

A Spirit had followed
them; one of the invis-
ible inhabitants of this
planet, neither departed
souls nor angels; con-
cerning whom the
learned Jew, Josephus,
and the Platonic Con-
stantinopolitan, Mi-
chael Psellus, may be
consulted. They are
very numerous, and
there is no climate or
element without one
or more.

"About, about, in reel and rout
The death-fires danced at night;
The water, like a witch's oils,
Burnt green, and blue, and white.   130

"And some in dreams assurèd were
Of the Spirit that plagued us so;
Nine fathom deep he had followed us
From the land of mist and snow.

"And every tongue, through utter drought,
Was withered at the root;
We could not speak, no more than if
We had been choked with soot.

The shipmates, in their
sore distress, would
fain throw the whole
guilt on the ancient
mariner: in sign
whereof they hang the
dead sea-bird round
his neck.

"Ah! well-a-day! what evil looks
Had I from old and young!   140
Instead of the cross, the albatross
About my neck was hung."

PART III

The ancient mariner
beholdeth a sign in the
element afar off.

"There passed a weary time. Each throat
Was parched, and glazed each eye.
A weary time! a weary time!
How glazed each weary eye,
When looking westward, I beheld
A something in the sky.

127. **reel and rout:** dancelike movements. 128. **death-fires:** weird lights on mast or rigging, caused by static electricity but regarded by sailors as an omen.

"At first it seemed a little speck,
150   And then it seemed a mist;
It moved and moved, and took at last
A certain shape, I wist.

"A speck, a mist, a shape, I wist!
And still it neared and neared:
As if it dodged a water-sprite,
It plunged and tacked and veered.

At its nearer
approach, it seemeth
him to be a ship; and
at a dear ransom he
160 *freeth his speech from*
the bonds of thirst

"With throats unslaked, with black lips baked,
We could nor laugh nor wail;
Through utter drought all dumb we stood!
I bit my arm, I sucked the blood,
And cried, 'A sail! a sail!'

A flash of joy;

"With throats unslaked, with black lips baked,
Agape they heard me call:
Gramercy! they for joy did grin,
And all at once their breath drew in,
As they were drinking all.

And horror follows.
For can it be a ship
that comes onward
without wind or tide?
170

" 'See! see! (I cried) she tacks no more!
Hither to work us weal;
Without a breeze, without a tide,
She steadies with upright keel!'

"The western wave was all a-flame;
The day was well nigh done!
Almost upon the western wave
Rested the broad bright sun;
When that strange shape drove suddenly
Betwixt us and the sun.

It seemeth him but
the skeleton of a ship.

"And straight the sun was flecked with bars
(Heaven's Mother send us grace!),
As if through a dungeon-grate he peered
180   With broad and burning face.

152. wist: knew. **164. Gramercy:** an exclamation meaning "many thanks." **168.**
weal: good.

"Alas! (thought I, and my heart beat loud)
How fast she nears and nears!
Are those her sails that glance in the sun,
Like restless gossameres?

And its ribs are seen
as bars on the face of
the setting sun. The
specter-woman and
her death-mate, and
no other on board the
skeleton-ship.

"Are those her ribs through which the sun
Did peer, as through a grate?
And is that woman all her crew?
Is that a Death? and are there two?
Is Death that woman's mate?

Like vessel, like crew!

"Her lips were red, her looks were free,   190
Her locks were yellow as gold:
Her skin was as white as leprosy,
The nightmare Life-in-Death was she,
Who thicks man's blood with cold.

Death and Life-in-
Death have diced for
the ship's crew, and
she (the latter)
winneth the ancient
mariner.

"The naked hulk alongside came,
And the twain were casting dice;
'The game is done! I've won! I've won!'
Quoth she, and whistles thrice.

No twilight within the
courts of the sun.

"The sun's rim dips; the stars rush out:
At one stride comes the dark;   200
With far-heard whisper, o'er the sea,
Off shot the specter-bark.

At the rising of the
moon,

"We listened and looked sideways up!
Fear at my heart, as at a cup,
My life-blood seemed to sip!
The stars were dim, and thick the night,
The steersman's face by his lamp gleamed white;
From the sails the dew did drip —
Till clomb above the eastern bar
The hornèd moon, with one bright star   210
Within the nether tip.

One after another,

"One after one, by the star-dogged moon,
Too quick for groan or sigh,
Each turned his face with a ghastly pang,
And cursed me with his eye.

184. **gossameres:** spider webs. 190. **free:** noble.

*His shipmates drop
down dead.*

"Four times fifty living men
(And I heard nor sigh nor groan),
With heavy thump, a lifeless lump,
They dropped down one by one.

220   *But Life-in-Death
begins her work on
the ancient mariner.*

"The souls did from their bodies fly,—
They fled to bliss or woe!
And every soul, it passed me by,
Like the whizz of my cross-bow!"

PART IV

*The wedding-guest
feareth that a spirit
is talking to him.*

"I fear thee, ancient mariner!
I fear thy skinny hand!
And thou art long, and lank, and brown,
As is the ribbed sea-sand.

*But the ancient
mariner assureth him
of his bodily life, and*
230   *proceedeth to relate
his horrible penance.*

"I fear thee and thy glittering eye,
And thy skinny hand, so brown."—
"Fear not, fear not, thou wedding-guest!
This body dropped not down.

"Alone, alone, all, all alone,
Alone on a wide, wide sea!
And never a saint took pity on
My soul in agony.

*He despiseth the
creatures of the calm,*

"The many men, so beautiful!
And they all dead did lie:
And a thousand thousand slimy things
Lived on; and so did I.

240   *And envieth that they
should live, and so
many lie dead.*

"I looked upon the rotting sea,
And drew my eyes away;
I looked upon the rotting deck,
And there the dead men lay.

"I looked to heaven, and tried to pray;
But or ever a prayer had gushed,
A wicked whisper came, and made
My heart as dry as dust.

245. or: before.

"I closed my lids, and kept them close,
And the balls like pulses beat;
For the sky and the sea, and the sea and   250
     the sky
Lay like a load on my weary eye,
And the dead were at my feet.

But the curse liveth
for him in the eye of
the dead men.

"The cold sweat melted from their limbs,
Nor rot nor reek did they:
The look with which they looked on me
Had never passed away.

"An orphan's curse would drag to hell
A spirit from on high;
But oh! more horrible than that
Is the curse in a dead man's eye!   260
Seven days, seven nights, I saw that curse,
And yet I could not die.

In his loneliness and
fixedness he yearneth
toward the journeying
moon, and the stars
that still sojourn, yet
still move onward; and
everywhere the blue
sky belongs to them,
and is their appointed
rest, and their native
country and their own
natural homes, which
they enter unan-
nounced, as lords that
are certainly expected
and yet there is a silent
joy at their arrival.

"The moving moon went up the sky,
And nowhere did abide:
Softly she was going up,
And a star or two beside—

"Her beams bemocked the sultry main,
Like April hoar-frost spread;
But where the ship's huge shadow lay,
The charmèd water burned alway   270
A still and awful red.

"Beyond the shadow of the ship,
I watched the water-snakes:
They moved in tracks of shining white,
And when they reared, the elfish light
Fell off in hoary flakes.

By the light of the
moon he beholdeth
God's creatures of the
great calm.

"Within the shadow of the ship
I watched their rich attire:
Blue glossy green, and velvet black,
They coiled and swam; and every track   280
Was a flash of golden fire.

Their beauty and their
happiness.

"O happy living things! no tongue
Their beauty might declare:
A spring of love gushed from my heart,

*He blesseth them in
his heart.*

And I blessed them unaware:
Sure my kind saint took pity on me,
And I blessed them unaware.

*The spell begins to
break.*

290

"The selfsame moment I could pray;
And from my neck so free
The albatross fell off, and sank
Like lead into the sea."

PART V

"Oh sleep! it is a gentle thing,
Beloved from pole to pole!
To Mary Queen the praise be given!
She sent the gentle sleep from Heaven,
That slid into my soul.

*By grace of the Holy
Mother, the ancient
mariner is refreshed
with rain.*

300

"The silly buckets on the deck,
That had so long remained,
I dreamed that they were filled with dew;
And when I awoke, it rained.

"My lips were wet, my throat was cold,
My garments all were dank;
Sure I had drunken in my dreams,
And still my body drank.

"I moved, and could not feel my limbs:
I was so light—almost
I thought that I had died in sleep,
And was a blessèd ghost.

*He heareth sounds and
310 seeth strange sights
and commotions in the
sky and the element.*

"And soon I heard a roaring wind:
It did not come anear;
But with its sound it shook the sails,
That were so thin and sere.

"The upper air burst into life!
And a hundred fire-flags sheen,
To and fro they were hurried about!
And to and fro, and in and out,
The wan stars danced between.

297. silly: simple. 314. sheen: shone.

"And the coming wind did roar more loud,
And the sails did sigh like sedge;
And the rain poured down from one black   320
    cloud;
The moon was at its edge.

"The thick black cloud was cleft, and still
The moon was at its side:
Like waters shot from some high crag,
The lightning fell with never a jag,
A river steep and wide.

"The loud wind never reached the ship,
Yet now the ship moved on!
Beneath the lightning and the moon
The dead men gave a groan.   330

*The bodies of the
ship's crew are
inspired, and the ship
moves on;*

"They groaned, they stirred, they all uprose,
Nor spake, nor moved their eyes;
It had been strange, even in a dream,
To have seen those dead men rise.

"The helmsman steered, the ship moved on;
Yet never a breeze up blew;
The mariners all 'gan work the ropes,
Where they were wont to do;
They raised their limbs like lifeless tools—
We were a ghastly crew.   340

"The body of my brother's son
Stood by me, knee to knee:
The body and I pulled at one rope,
But he said nought to me."

*But not by the souls
of the men, nor by
dæmons of earth or
middle air, but by a
blessed troop of
angelic spirits, sent
down by the invocation
of the guardian saint.*

"I fear thee, ancient mariner!"
"Be calm, thou wedding-guest!
'Twas not those souls that fled in pain,
Which to their corses came again,
But a troop of spirits blest:

319. sedge: reeds. 348. corses: corpses.

350
"For when it dawned—they dropped their arms,
And clustered round the mast;
Sweet sounds rose slowly through their mouths,
And from their bodies passed.

"Around, around, flew each sweet sound,
Then darted to the sun;
Slowly the sounds came back again,
Now mixed, now one by one.

360
"Sometimes a-dropping from the sky
I heard the sky-lark sing;
Sometimes all little birds that are,
How they seemed to fill the sea and air
With their sweet jargoning!

"And now 'twas like all instruments,
Now like a lonely flute;
And now it is an angel's song,
That makes the heavens be mute.

370
"It ceased; yet still the sails made on
A pleasant noise till noon,
A noise like of a hidden brook
In the leafy month of June,
That to the sleeping woods all night
Singeth a quiet tune.

"Till noon we quietly sailed on,
Yet never a breeze did breathe:
Slowly and smoothly went the ship,
Moved onward from beneath.

The lonesome Spirit
from the south pole
carries on the ship as
far as the Line, in
380 *obedience to the*
angelic troop, but still
requireth vengeance.

"Under the keel nine fathom deep,
From the land of mist and snow,
The Spirit slid: and it was he
That made the ship to go.
The sails at noon left off their tune,
And the ship stood still also.

362. jargoning: warbling.

"The sun, right up above the mast,
Had fixed her to the ocean:
But in a minute she 'gan stir,
With a short uneasy motion—
Backwards and forwards half her length
With a short uneasy motion.

"Then like a pawing horse let go,
She made a sudden bound: 390
It flung the blood into my head,
And I fell down in a swound.

*The Polar Spirit's
fellow-dæmons, the
invisible inhabitants
of the element, take
part in his wrong; and
two of them relate
one to the other, that
penance long and
heavy for the ancient
mariner hath been
accorded to the Polar
Spirit, who returneth
southward.*

"How long in that same fit I lay,
I have not to declare;
But ere my living life returned,
I heard and in my soul discerned
Two voices in the air.

" 'Is it he?' quoth one, 'Is this the man?
By Him who died on cross,
With his cruel bow he laid full low   400
The harmless albatross.

" 'The Spirit who bideth by himself
In the land of mist and snow,
He loved the bird that loved the man
Who shot him with his bow.'

"The other was a softer voice,
As soft as honey-dew:
Quoth he, 'The man hath penance done,
And penance more will do.' "

PART VI

First Voice

" 'But tell me, tell me! speak again,   410
Thy soft response renewing—
What makes that ship drive on so fast?
What is the ocean doing?'

392. swound: faint. 394. have not to declare: cannot say.

Second Voice

" 'Still as a slave before his lord,
The ocean hath no blast;
His great bright eye most silently
Up to the moon is cast—

" 'If he may know which way to go;
For she guides him smooth or grim.
See, brother, see! how graciously
She looketh down on him.'

First Voice

" 'But why drives on that ship so fast,
Without or wave or wind?'

Second Voice

" 'The air is cut away before,
And closes from behind.

" 'Fly, brother, fly! more high, more high!
Or we shall be belated:
For slow and slow that ship will go,
When the mariner's trance is abated.'

"I woke, and we were sailing on
As in a gentle weather:
'Twas night, calm night, the moon was high;
The dead men stood together.

"All stood together on the deck,
For a charnel-dungeon fitter:
All fixed on me their stony eyes,
That in the moon did glitter.

"The pang, the curse, with which they died,
Had never passed away:
I could not draw my eyes from theirs,
Nor turn them up to pray.

"And now this spell was snapped: once more
I viewed the ocean green,
And far forth, yet little saw
Of what had else been seen—

420

*The mariner hath
been cast into a
trance; for the angelic
power causeth the
vessel to drive north-
ward faster than
human life could
endure.*

430   *The supernatural
motion is retarded;
the mariner awakes,
and his penance
begins anew.*

440

*The curse is finally
expiated.*

"Like one, that on a lonesome road
Doth walk in fear and dread,
And having once turned round walks on,
And turns no more his head:
Because he knows a frightful fiend   450
Doth close behind him tread.

"But soon there breathed a wind on me,
Nor sound nor motion made:
Its path was not upon the sea,
In ripple or in shade.

"It raised my hair, it fanned my cheek
Like a meadow-gale of spring—
It mingled strangely with my fears,
Yet it felt like a welcoming.

"Swiftly, swiftly flew the ship,   460
Yet she sailed softly too:
Sweetly, sweetly blew the breeze—
On me alone it blew.

And the ancient
mariner beholdeth
his native country.

"Oh! dream of joy! is this indeed
The light-house top I see?
Is this the hill? is this the kirk?
Is this mine own countree?

"We drifted o'er the harbor-bar,
And I with sobs did pray—
O let me be awake, my God!   470
Or let me sleep alway.

"The harbor-bay was clear as glass,
So smoothly it was strewn!
And on the bay the moonlight lay,
And the shadow of the moon.

"The rock shone bright, the kirk no less,
That stands above the rock:
The moonlight steeped in silentness
The steady weathercock.

480

The angelic spirits
leave the dead bodies,

"And the bay was white with silent light,
Till rising from the same,
Full many shapes, that shadows were,
In crimson colors came.

"A little distance from the prow
Those crimson shadows were:
I turned my eyes upon the deck—
Oh, Christ! what saw I there!

490   *And appear in their*
own forms of light.

"Each corse lay flat, lifeless and flat,
And, by the holy rood!
A man all light, a seraph-man,
On every corse there stood.

"This seraph-band, each waved his hand:
It was a heavenly sight!
They stood as signals to the land,
Each one a lovely light;

"This seraph-band, each waved his hand,
No voice did they impart—
No voice; but oh! the silence sank
Like music on my heart.

500

"But soon I heard the dash of oars,
I heard the pilot's cheer;
My head was turned perforce away,
And I saw a boat appear.

"The pilot and the pilot's boy,
I heard them coming fast:
Dear Lord in Heaven! it was a joy
The dead men could not blast.

510

"I saw a third—I heard his voice:
It is the hermit good!
He singeth loud his godly hymns
That he makes in the wood.
He'll shrieve my soul, he'll wash away
The albatross's blood."

489. **rood**: cross. 490. **seraph**: one of the highest of the orders of angels. 512. **shrieve**: absolve.

PART VII

The hermit of the
wood,

"This hermit good lives in that wood
Which slopes down to the sea.
How loudly his sweet voice he rears!
He loves to talk with marineres
That come from a far countree.

"He kneels at morn, and noon, and eve—
He hath a cushion plump: 520
It is the moss that wholly hides
The rotted old oak-stump.

"The skiff-boat neared: I heard them talk,
'Why, this is strange, I trow!
Where are those lights so many and fair,
That signal made but now?'

Approacheth the ship
with wonder.

" 'Strange, by my faith!' the hermit said—
'And they answered not our cheer!
The planks look warped! and see those sails,
How thin they are and sere!   530
I never saw aught like to them,
Unless perchance it were

" 'Brown skeletons of leaves that lag
My forest-brook along;
When the ivy-tod is heavy with snow,
And the owlet whoops to the wolf below,
That eats the she-wolf's young.'

" 'Dear Lord! it hath a fiendish look—
(The pilot made reply)
I am a-feared'—'Push on, push on!'   540
Said the hermit cheerily.

"The boat came closer to the ship,
But I nor spake nor stirred;
The boat came close beneath the ship,
And straight a sound was heard.

524. I trow: I believe. 528. cheer: hail. 535. ivy-tod: clump of ivy.

The ship suddenly
sinketh.

· "Under the water it rumbled on,
Still louder and more dread:
It reached the ship, it split the bay;
The ship went down like lead.

550   *The ancient mariner*
is saved in the pilot's
boat.

"Stunned by that loud and dreadful sound,
Which sky and ocean smote,
Like one that hath been seven days drowned
My body lay afloat;
But swift as dreams, myself I found
Within the pilot's boat.

"Upon the whirl, where sank the ship,
The boat spun round and round;
And all was still, save that the hill
Was telling of the sound.

560

"I moved my lips—the pilot shrieked
And fell down in a fit;
The holy hermit raised his eyes,
And prayed where he did sit.

"I took the oars: the pilot's boy,
Who now doth crazy go,
Laughed loud and long, and all the while
His eyes went to and fro.
'Ha! ha!' quoth he, 'full plain I see,
The Devil knows how to row.'

570

"And now, all in my own countree,
I stood on the firm land!
The hermit stepped forth from the boat,
And scarcely he could stand.

The ancient mariner
earnestly entreateth
the hermit to shrieve
him; and the penance
of life falls on him.

" 'O shrieve me, shrieve me, holy man!'
The hermit crossed his brow.
'Say quick,' quoth he, 'I bid thee say—
What manner of man art thou?'

575. crossed his brow: made the sign of the cross.

"Forthwith this frame of mine was wrenched
With a woeful agony,
Which forced me to begin my tale;   580
And then it left me free.

And ever and anon
throughout his future
life an agony
constraineth him to
travel from land to
land;

"Since then, at an uncertain hour,
That agony returns:
And till my ghastly tale is told,
This heart within me burns.

"I pass, like night, from land to land;
I have strange power of speech;
That moment that his face I see,
I know the man that must hear me:
To him my tale I teach.   590

"What loud uproar bursts from that door!
The wedding-guests are there:
But in the garden-bower the bride
And bride-maids singing are:
And hark the little vesper bell
Which biddeth me to prayer!

"O wedding-guest! this soul hath been
Alone on a wide, wide sea:
So lonely 'twas, that God himself
Scarce seemèd there to be.   600

"O sweeter than the marriage-feast,
'Tis sweeter far to me,
To walk together to the kirk
With a goodly company!—

"To walk together to the kirk,
And all together pray,
While each to his great Father bends,
Old men, and babes, and loving friends,
And youths and maidens gay!

And to teach, by his
own example, love
and reverence to all
things that God made
and loveth.

"Farewell, farewell! but this I tell   610
To thee, thou wedding-guest!
He prayeth well, who loveth well
Both man and bird and beast.

"He prayeth best, who loveth best
All things both great and small;
For the dear God who loveth us,
He made and loveth all."

The mariner, whose eye is bright,
Whose beard with age is hoar,
620   Is gone: and now the wedding-guest
Turned from the bridegroom's door.

He went like one that hath been stunned,
And is of sense forlorn:
A sadder and a wiser man,
He rose the morrow morn.

KUBLA KHAN

In Xanadu did Kubla Khan
A stately pleasure-dome decree:
Where Alph, the sacred river, ran
Through caverns measureless to man
      Down to a sunless sea.
So twice five miles of fertile ground
With walls and towers were girdled round:
And here were gardens bright with sinuous rills,
Where blossomed many an incense-bearing tree;
10   And here were forests ancient as the hills,
Enfolding sunny spots of greenery.

But oh! that deep romantic chasm which slanted
Down the green hill athwart a cedarn cover!
A savage place! as holy and enchanted
As e'er beneath a waning moon was haunted
By woman wailing for her demon-lover!

Note. In a note Coleridge describes how the following fragment was composed when he awoke from an opium dream (the opium had been prescribed for a physical ailment) which he had upon falling asleep after reading in Samuel Purchas's *Pilgrimage* (a seventeenth-century "travelogue"). The transcription of the complete vision was interrupted by a business visitor who detained the poet for an hour, after which he could recover practically no more.

1. **Xanadu:** a place in China. 3. **Alph:** fictitious river, associated with Alpheus, which according to legend runs underground to emerge later as a fountain. 13. **athwart . . . cover:** across a cedar grove.

And from this chasm, with ceaseless turmoil seething,
As if this earth in fast thick pants were breathing,
A mighty fountain momently was forced,
Amid whose swift half-intermitted burst   20
Huge fragments vaulted like rebounding hail,
Or chaffy grain beneath the thresher's flail:
And 'mid these dancing rocks at once and ever
It flung up momently the sacred river.
Five miles meandering with a mazy motion
Through wood and dale the sacred river ran,
Then reached the caverns measureless to man,
And sank in tumult to a lifeless ocean:
And 'mid this tumult Kubla heard from far
Ancestral voices prophesying war!   30

    The shadow of the dome of pleasure
    Floated midway on the waves;
    Where was heard the mingled measure
    From the fountain and the caves.
It was a miracle of rare device,
A sunny pleasure-dome with caves of ice!

    A damsel with a dulcimer
    In a vision once I saw:
    It was an Abyssinian maid,
    And on her dulcimer she played,   40
    Singing of Mount Abora.
    Could I revive within me
    Her symphony and song,
    To such a deep delight 'twould win me,
That with music loud and long,
I would build that dome in air,
That sunny dome! those caves of ice!
And all who heard should see them there,
And all should cry, "Beware! Beware!
His flashing eyes, his floating hair!   50
Weave a circle round him thrice,
And close your eyes with holy dread,
For he on honey-dew hath fed,
And drunk the milk of Paradise."

37. **dulcimer:** metal stringed instrument played with small hammers. 41. **Mount Abora:** no actual mountain; the word is a compound of literary memories.

DEJECTION: AN ODE

> Late, late yestreen I saw the new Moon,
> With the old Moon in her arms;
> And I fear, I fear, my Master dear!
> We shall have a deadly storm.
> *Ballad of Sir Patrick Spence*

I

Well! If the bard was weather-wise, who made
   The grand old ballad of Sir Patrick Spence,
   This night, so tranquil now, will not go hence
Unroused by winds that ply a busier trade
Than those which mould yon cloud in lazy flakes,
Or the dull sobbing draft that moans and rakes
Upon the strings of this Aeolian lute,
     Which better far were mute.
   For lo! the new moon winter-bright!
   And overspread with phantom light
    (With swimming phantom light o'erspread,
    But rimmed and circled by a silver thread),
I see the old moon in her lap, foretelling
   The coming-on of rain and squally blast.
And oh! that even now the gust were swelling,
   And the slant night-shower driving loud and fast!
Those sounds which oft have raised me, whilst they awed,
    And sent my soul abroad,
   Might now perhaps their wonted impulse give,
   Might startle this dull pain, and make it move and live!

II

A grief without a pang, void, dark, and drear,
   A stifled, drowsy, unimpassioned grief,
Which finds no natural outlet, no relief,
    In word, or sigh, or tear—
O Lady! in this wan and heartless mood,
To other thoughts by yonder throstle wooed,
   All this long eve, so balmy and serene,
Have I been gazing on the western sky,
   And its peculiar tint of yellow green:

---

7. Aeolian lute: a harp whose strings vibrate to currents of air, named after Aeolus, god of the winds. 19. wonted: accustomed. 26. throstle: thrush.

And still I gaze—and with how blank an eye!   30
And those thin clouds above, in flakes and bars,
That give away their motion to the stars—
Those stars that glide behind them or between,
Now sparkling, now bedimmed, but always seen:
Yon crescent moon, as fixed as if it grew
In its own cloudless, starless lake of blue—
I see them all so excellently fair:
I see, not feel, how beautiful they are!

III

My genial spirits fail;
And what can these avail   40
To lift the smothering weight from off my breast?
It were a vain endeavor,
Though I should gaze forever
On that green light that lingers in the west:
I may not hope from outward forms to win
The passion and the life, whose fountains are within.

IV

O Lady! we receive but what we give,
And in our life alone does Nature live:
Ours is her wedding garment, ours her shroud!
And would we aught behold, of higher worth,   50
Than that inanimate cold world allowed
To the poor loveless ever-anxious crowd,
Ah! from the soul itself must issue forth
A light, a glory, a fair luminous cloud
Enveloping the Earth—
And from the soul itself must there be sent
A sweet and potent voice, of its own birth,
Of all sweet sounds the life and element!

V

O pure of heart! thou need'st not ask of me
What this strong music in the soul may be!   60
What, and wherein it doth exist,
This light, this glory, this fair luminous mist,
This beautiful and beauty-making power.

39. genial: enlivening, vital. 50. aught: anything.

Joy, virtuous Lady! Joy that ne'er was given,
Save to the pure, and in their purest hour,
Life, and Life's effluence, cloud at once and shower,
Joy, Lady! is the spirit and the power
Which wedding Nature to us gives in dower,
    A new Earth and new Heaven
70   Undreamt of by the sensual and the proud—
Joy is the sweet voice, Joy the luminous cloud—
      We in ourselves rejoice!
And thence flows all that charms or ear or sight,
    All melodies the echoes of that voice,
All colors a suffusion from that light.

VI

There was a time when, though my path was rough,
    This joy within me dallied with distress,
And all misfortunes were but as the stuff
    Whence Fancy made me dreams of happiness:
80   For hope grew round me, like the twining vine,
And fruits, and foliage, not my own, seemed mine.
But now afflictions bow me down to earth:
Nor care I that they rob me of my mirth.
      But oh! each visitation
Suspends what nature gave me at my birth,
    My shaping spirit of Imagination.
For not to think of what I needs must feel,
    But to be still and patient all I can;
And haply by abstruse research to steal
90   From my own nature all the natural man—
This was my sole resource, my only plan:
Till that which suits a part infects the whole,
And now is almost grown the habit of my soul.

VII

Hence, viper thoughts, that coil around my mind,
    Reality's dark dream!
I turn from you, and listen to the wind,
    Which long has raved unnoticed. What a scream
Of agony by torture lengthened out
That lute sent forth! Thou Wind, that rav'st without,
100   Bare crag, or mountain tairn, or blasted tree,

66. effluence: a flowing out. 68. in dower: as a bridal gift. 89. haply: by good
fortune. 100. tairn: tarn (a small mountain lake).

Or pine grove whither woodman never clomb,
Or lonely house long held the witches' home,
   Methinks were fitter instruments for thee,
Mad lutanist! who in this month of showers,
Of dark-brown gardens, and of peeping flowers,
Mak'st devils' yule, with worse than wintry song,
The blossoms, buds, and timorous leaves among.
   Thou actor, perfect in all tragic sounds!
Thou mighty poet, e'en to frenzy bold!
     What tell'st thou now about?   110
    'Tis of the rushing of an host in rout,
  With groans of trampled men with smarting wounds—
At once they groan with pain, and shudder with the cold!
But hush! there is a pause of deepest silence!
   And all that noise, as of a rushing crowd,
With groans and tremulous shudderings: all is over—
   It tells another tale, with sounds less deep and loud:
     A tale of less affright,
     And tempered with delight,
As Otway's self had framed the tender lay—   120
     'Tis of a little child
     Upon a lonesome wild,
Not far from home, but she hath lost her way:
And now moans low in bitter grief and fear,
And now screams loud, and hopes to make her mother hear.

VIII

'Tis midnight, but small thoughts have I of sleep:
Full seldom may my friend such vigils keep!
Visit her, gentle Sleep! with wings of healing,
   And may this storm be but a mountain-birth,
May all the stars hang bright above her dwelling,   130
   Silent as though they watched the sleeping Earth!
     With light heart may she rise,
     Gay fancy, cheerful eyes,
   Joy lift her spirit, joy attune her voice;
To her may all things live, from pole to pole,
Their life the eddying of her living soul!
    O simple spirit, guided from above,
   Dear Lady! friend devoutest of my choice,
'Thus mayest thou ever, evermore rejoice.

106. devils' yule: an unnatural Christmas. 120: Otway: seventeenth-century English dramatist; lay: poem, song.

WALTER SAVAGE LANDOR (1775–1864)

ROSE AYLMER

Ah what avails the sceptered race,
    Ah what the form divine!
What every virtue, every grace!
    Rose Aylmer, all were thine.

Rose Aylmer, whom these wakeful eyes
    May weep, but never see,
A night of memories and of sighs
    I consecrate to thee.

PAST RUINED ILION HELEN LIVES

Past ruined Ilion Helen lives,
    Alcestis rises from the shades;
Verse calls them forth—'tis verse that gives
    Immortal youth to mortal maids.

Soon shall oblivion's deepening veil
    Hide all the peopled hills you see,
The gay, the proud, while lovers hail
    In distant ages you and me.

The tear for fading beauty check,
10   For passing glory cease to sigh:
One form shall rise above the wreck,
    One name, Ianthe, shall not die.

Title. Rose Aylmer: daughter of Lord Aylmer (hence **sceptered race** of line 1); she was a friend of the poet's.

Title. **Ilion:** Troy; **Helen:** the most beautiful woman in the world, cause of the Trojan war and destruction of Troy. **2. Alcestis:** wife of King Admetus; she offered her life for her husband's, but was brought back from death by Hercules. **12. Ianthe:** the poet's friend.

GEORGE GORDON, LORD BYRON (1788–1824)

THE DESTRUCTION OF SENNACHERIB

I

The Assyrian came down like the wolf on the fold,
And his cohorts were gleaming in purple and gold;
And the sheen of their spears was like stars on the sea
When the blue wave rolls nightly on deep Galilee.

II

Like the leaves of the forest when summer is green,
That host with their banners at sunset were seen;
Like the leaves of the forest when autumn hath blown,
That host on the morrow lay withered and strown.

III

For the Angel of Death spread his wings on the blast,
And breathed in the face of the foe as he passed;   10
And the eyes of the sleepers waxed deadly and chill,
And their hearts but once heaved, and forever grew still!

IV

And there lay the steed with his nostril all wide,
But through it there rolled not the breath of his pride;
And the foam of his gasping lay white on the turf,
And cold as the spray of the rock-beating surf.

V

And there lay the rider, distorted and pale,
With the dew on his brow and the rust on his mail;
And the tents were all silent, the banners alone,
The lances unlifted, the trumpet unblown.   20

Title: Sennacherib was an Assyrian king whose army, while besieging Jerusalem in 701 B.C., was slain by pestilence. See II Kings xix.35: 2. cohorts: band of warriors.

VI

And the widows of Ashur are loud in their wail,
And the idols are broke in the temple of Baal;
And the might of the Gentile, unsmote by the sword,
Hath melted like snow in the glance of the Lord!

PERCY BYSSHE SHELLEY (1792–1822)

HYMN TO INTELLECTUAL BEAUTY

I

The awful shadow of some unseen power
  Floats though unseen among us,—visiting
  This various world with as inconstant wing
As summer winds that creep from flower to flower,—
Like moonbeams that behind some piny mountain shower,
    It visits with inconstant glance
    Each human heart and countenance;
Like hues and harmonies of evening,—
    Like clouds in starlight widely spread,—
10   Like memory of music fled,—
    Like aught that for its grace may be
Dear, and yet dearer for its mystery.

II

Spirit of Beauty, that dost consecrate
  With thine own hues all thou dost shine upon
  Of human thought or form,—where art thou gone?
Why dost thou pass away and leave our state,
This dim vast vale of tears, vacant and desolate?
    Ask why the sunlight not for ever
    Weaves rainbows o'er yon mountain river,
20 Why aught should fail and fade that once is shown,
    Why fear and dream and death and birth
    Cast on the daylight of this earth
    Such gloom,—why man has such a scope
For love and hate, despondency and hope?

21. Ashur: Assyria. 22. Baal: god of the Assyrians.

Title. Intellectual Beauty: beauty conceived by the intellect rather than experienced by the senses. 1. awful: awe-inspiring.

III

No voice from some sublimer world hath ever
  To sage or poet these responses given—
  Therefore the names of Demon, Ghost, and Heaven,
Remain the records of their vain endeavor,
Frail spells—whose uttered charm might not avail to sever,
    From all we hear and all we see,   30
    Doubt, chance, and mutability.
Thy light alone—like mist o'er mountains driven,
    Or music by the night wind sent
    Through strings of some still instrument,
    Or moonlight on a midnight stream,
Gives grace and truth to life's unquiet dream.

IV

Love, hope, and self-esteem, like clouds depart
  And come, for some uncertain moments lent.
  Man were immortal, and omnipotent,
Didst thou, unknown and awful as thou art,   40
Keep with thy glorious train firm state within his heart.
    Thou messenger of sympathies,
    That wax and wane in lovers' eyes—
Thou—that to human thought art nourishment,
    Like darkness to a dying flame!
    Depart not as thy shadow came,
    Depart not—lest the grave should be,
Like life and fear, a dark reality.

V

While yet a boy I sought for ghosts, and sped
  Through many a listening chamber, cave, and ruin,   50
  And starlight wood, with fearful steps pursuing
Hopes of high talk with the departed dead.
I called on poisonous names with which our youth is fed;
    I was not heard—I saw them not—
    When musing deeply on the lot
Of life, at that sweet time when winds are wooing
    All vital things that wake to bring
    News of birds and blossoming,—

29. charm: incantation.

Sudden, thy shadow fell on me;
60   I shrieked, and clasped my hands in ecstasy!

VI

I vowed that I would dedicate my powers
    To thee and thine—have I not kept the vow?
    With beating heart and streaming eyes, even now
I call the phantoms of a thousand hours
Each from his voiceless grave: they have in visioned bowers
        Of studious zeal or love's delight
        Outwatched with me the envious night—
They know that never joy illumed my brow
        Unlinked with hope that thou wouldst free
70   This world from its dark slavery,
        That thou—O awful Loveliness,
Wouldst give whate'er these words cannot express.

VII

The day becomes more solemn and serene
    When noon is past—there is a harmony
    In autumn, and a luster in its sky,
Which through the summer is not heard or seen,
As if it could not be, as if it had not been!
        Thus let thy power, which like the truth
        Of nature on my passive youth
80   Descended, to my onward life supply
        Its calm—to one who worships thee,
        And every form containing thee,
Whom, Spirit fair, thy spells did bind
To fear himself, and love all human kind.

OZYMANDIAS

I met a traveller from an antique land
Who said: Two vast and trunkless legs of stone
Stand in the desert . . . Near them, on the sand,
Half sunk, a shattered visage lies, whose frown,
And wrinkled lip, and sneer of cold command,
Tell that its sculptor well those passions read
Which yet survive, stamped on these lifeless things,

Title. Ozymandias: a pharaoh, ruler of Egypt. 7-8. survive . . . fed: outlive the
sculptor (mocked: imitated) and the pharaoh.

The hand that mocked them, and the heart that fed;
And on the pedestal these words appear:
"My name is Ozymandias, king of kings: 10
Look on my works, ye Mighty, and despair!"
Nothing beside remains. Round the decay
Of that colossal wreck, boundless and bare
The lone and level sands stretch far away.

ODE TO THE WEST WIND

I

O wild West Wind, thou breath of autumn's being,
Thou, from whose unseen presence the leaves dead
Are driven, like ghosts from an enchanter fleeing,

Yellow, and black, and pale, and hectic red,
Pestilence-stricken multitudes: O thou,
Who chariotest to their dark wintry bed

The wingèd seeds, where they lie cold and low,
Each like a corpse within its grave, until
Thine azure sister of the spring shall blow

Her clarion o'er the dreaming earth, and fill   10
(Driving sweet buds like flocks to feed in air)
With living hues and odors plain and hill;

Wild Spirit, which art moving everywhere;
Destroyer and preserver; hear, oh hear!

II

Thou on whose stream, mid the steep sky's commotion,
Loose clouds like earth's decaying leaves are shed,
Shook from the tangled boughs of Heaven and Ocean,

Angels of rain and lightning: there are spread
On the blue surface of thine aery surge,
Like the bright hair uplifted from the head   20

Of some fierce Maenad, even from the dim verge
Of the horizon to the zenith's height,
The locks of the approaching storm. Thou dirge

Of the dying year, to which this closing night
Will be the dome of a vast sepulchre,
Vaulted with all thy congregated might

Of vapors, from whose solid atmosphere
Black rain, and fire, and hail will burst: oh hear!

III

Thou who didst waken from his summer dreams
30   The blue Mediterranean, where he lay,
Lulled by the coil of his crystàlline streams,

Beside a pumice isle in Baiae's bay,
And saw in sleep old palaces and towers
Quivering within the wave's intenser day,

All overgrown with azure moss and flowers
So sweet, the sense faints picturing them! Thou
For whose path the Atlantic's level powers

Cleave themselves into chasms, while far below
The sea-blooms and the oozy woods which wear
40   The sapless foliage of the ocean, know

Thy voice, and suddenly grow gray with fear,
And tremble and despoil themselves: oh hear!

IV

If I were a dead leaf thou mightest bear;
If I were a swift cloud to fly with thee;
A wave to pant beneath thy power, and share

The impulse of thy strength, only less free
Than thou, O uncontrollable! If even
I were as in my boyhood, and could be

---

21. Maenad: nymph in the train of Bacchus, god of wine. **31. coil:** movement.
32. Baiae: village on west coast of Italy.

The comrade of thy wanderings over Heaven,
As then, when to outstrip thy skiey speed   50
Scarce seemed a vision; I would ne'er have striven

As thus with thee in prayer in my sore need.
Oh, lift me as a wave, a leaf, a cloud!
I fall upon the thorns of life! I bleed!

A heavy weight of hours has chained and bowed
One too like thee: tameless, and swift, and proud.

V

Make me thy lyre, even as the forest is:
What if my leaves are falling like its own!
The tumult of thy mighty harmonies

Will take from both a deep, autumnal tone,   60
Sweet though in sadness. Be thou, Spirit fierce,
My spirit! Be thou me, impetuous one!

Drive my dead thoughts over the universe
Like withered leaves to quicken a new birth!
And, by the incantation of this verse,

Scatter, as from an unextinguished hearth
Ashes and sparks, my words among mankind!
Be through my lips to unawakened earth

The trumpet of a prophecy! O Wind,
If winter comes, can spring be far behind?   70

THE INDIAN SERENADE

I arise from dreams of thee
In the first sweet sleep of night,
When the winds are breathing low,
And the stars are shining bright:
I arise from dreams of thee,
And a spirit in my feet
Hath led me—who knows how?
To thy chamber-window, Sweet!

10   The wandering airs, they faint
On the dark, the silent stream—
The Champak odors fail
Like sweet thoughts in a dream;
The nightingale's complaint,
It dies upon her heart;—
As I must on thine,
Oh, belovèd as thou art!

Oh, lift me from the grass!
I die! I faint! I fail!
Let thy love in kisses rain
20   On my lips and eyelids pale.
My cheek is cold and white, alas!
My heart beats loud and fast;—
Oh! press it close to thine again,
Where it will break at last.

ENGLAND IN 1819

An old, mad, blind, despised, and dying king;
Princes, the dregs of their dull race, who flow
Through public scorn,—mud from a muddy spring:
Rulers, who neither see, nor feel, nor know,
But, leech-like, to their fainting country cling
Till they drop, blind in blood, without a blow;
A people starved and stabbed in the untilled field;
An army which liberticide and prey
Makes as a two-edged sword to all who wield;
10   Golden and sanguine laws which tempt and slay;
Religion Christless, Godless—a book sealed;
A Senate,—Time's worst statute unrepealed,—
Are graves from which a glorious Phantom may
Burst, to illumine our tempestuous day.

11. **Champak:** Indian tree of the magnolia family.

8. **liberticide:** killing of liberty. 10. **golden and sanguine:** based on gold and blood.

STANZAS WRITTEN IN DEJECTION, NEAR NAPLES

I

The sun is warm, the sky is clear,
  The waves are dancing fast and bright,
Blue isles and snowy mountains wear
  The purple noon's transparent might;
  The breath of the moist earth is light
Around its unexpanded buds;
  Like many a voice of one delight,
The winds, the birds, the ocean floods,
The City's voice itself is soft, like Solitude's.

II

I see the Deep's untrampled floor   10
  With green and purple seaweeds strown;
I see the waves upon the shore,
  Like light dissolved in star-showers, thrown.
  I sit upon the sands alone—
The lightning of the noontide ocean
  Is flashing round me, and a tone
Arises from its measured motion;
How sweet! did any heart now share in my emotion.

III

Alas! I have nor hope nor health,
  Nor peace within nor calm around,   20
Nor that content surpassing wealth
  The sage in meditation found,
  And walked with inward glory crowned—
Nor fame, nor power, nor love, nor leisure.
  Others I see whom these surround—
Smiling they live, and call life pleasure;
To me that cup has been dealt in another measure.

IV

Yet now despair itself is mild,
  Even as the winds and waters are;

30 I could lie down like a tired child,
    And weep away the life of care
    Which I have borne and yet must bear,
    Till death like sleep might steal on me,
    And I might feel in the warm air
    My cheek grow cold, and hear the sea
    Breathe o'er my dying brain its last monotony.

V

    Some might lament that I were cold,
    As I, when this sweet day is gone,
    Which my lost heart, too soon grown old,
40   Insults with this untimely moan;
    They might lament—for I am one
    Whom men love not—and yet regret,
    Unlike this day, which, when the sun
    Shall on its stainless glory set,
    Will linger, though enjoyed, like joy in memory yet.

JOHN KEATS (1795–1821)

ON FIRST LOOKING INTO CHAPMAN'S HOMER

    Much have I travelled in the realms of gold,
    And many goodly states and kingdoms seen;
    Round many western islands have I been
    Which bards in fealty to Apollo hold.
    Oft of one wide expanse had I been told
    That deep-browed Homer ruled as his demesne;
    Yet did I never breathe its pure serene
    Till I heard Chapman speak out loud and bold:
    Then felt I like some watcher of the skies
10 When a new planet swims into his ken;

4. bards . . . Apollo: poets owing allegiance to the god of poetry. **6. demesne:** possession. **7. serene:** atmosphere. **8. Chapman:** George Chapman, who had translated the *Iliad* and the *Odyssey* in the early seventeenth century.

Or like stout Cortez when with eagle eyes
He stared at the Pacific—and all his men
Looked at each other with a wild surmise—
Silent, upon a peak in Darien.

WHEN I HAVE FEARS THAT I MAY CEASE TO BE

When I have fears that I may cease to be
Before my pen has gleaned my teeming brain,
Before high-pilèd books, in charactery,
Hold like rich garners the full-ripened grain;
When I behold, upon the night's starred face,
Huge cloudy symbols of a high romance,
And think that I may never live to trace
Their shadows, with the magic hand of chance;
And when I feel, fair creature of an hour,
That I shall never look upon thee more,   10
Never have relish in the faery power
Of unreflecting love;—then on the shore
Of the wide world I stand alone, and think
Till love and fame to nothingness do sink.

BRIGHT STAR, WOULD I WERE STEADFAST AS THOU ART—

Bright star, would I were steadfast as thou art—
Not in lone splendor hung aloft the night
And watching, with eternal lids apart,
Like nature's patient, sleepless eremite,
The moving waters at their priestlike task
Of pure ablution round earth's human shores,
Or gazing on the new soft-fallen mask
Of snow upon the mountains and the moors—

11. **Cortez:** Hernando Cortez, Spanish conqueror of Mexico, whom Keats here seems to equate with Balboa, discoverer of the Pacific Ocean. 14 **Darien:** former name of Panama.

3. **charactery:** writing. 4 **garners:** granaries.

4. **eremite:** hermit.

No—yet still steadfast, still unchangeable,
10   Pillowed upon my fair love's ripening breast,
To feel forever its soft fall and swell,
Awake forever in a sweet unrest,
Still, still to hear her tender-taken breath,
And so live ever—or else swoon to death.

THE EVE OF ST. AGNES

I

St. Agnes' Eve—Ah, bitter chill it was!
The owl, for all his feathers, was a-cold;
The hare limped trembling through the frozen grass,
And silent was the flock in woolly fold:
Numb were the beadsman's fingers, while he told
His rosary, and while his frosted breath,
Like pious incense from a censer old,
Seemed taking flight for heaven, without a death,
Past the sweet Virgin's picture, while his prayer he saith.

II

10   His prayer he saith, this patient, holy man;
Then takes his lamp, and riseth from his knees,
And back returneth, meager, barefoot, wan,
Along the chapel aisle by slow degrees:
The sculptured dead, on each side, seem to freeze,
Imprisoned in black, purgatorial rails:
Knights, ladies, praying in dumb oratories,
He passeth by; and his weak spirit fails
To think how they may ache in icy hoods and mails.

III

Northward he turneth through a little door,
20   And scarce three steps, ere music's golden tongue
Flattered to tears this agèd man and poor;

Title. The night before the feast day of St. Agnes; i.e., the night before January 21.
5. beadsman: a man employed to pray for people's souls. **16. oratories:** chapels.

But no—already had his deathbell rung:
The joys of all his life were said and sung:
His was harsh penance on St. Agnes' Eve:
Another way he went, and soon among
Rough ashes sat he for his soul's reprieve,
And all night kept awake, for sinners' sake to grieve.

IV

That ancient beadsman heard the prelude soft;
And so it chanced, for many a door was wide,
From hurry to and fro. Soon, up aloft,   30
The silver, snarling trumpets 'gan to chide:
The level chambers, ready with their pride,
Were glowing to receive a thousand guests:
The carvèd angels, ever eager-eyed,
Stared, where upon their heads the cornice rests,
With hair blown back, and wings put crosswise on their breasts.

V

At length burst in the argent revelry,
With plume, tiara, and all rich array,
Numerous as shadows haunting faerily
The brain, new stuffed, in youth, with triumphs gay   40
Of old romance. These let us wish away,
And turn, sole-thoughted, to one lady there,
Whose heart had brooded, all that wintry day,
On love, and winged St. Agnes' saintly care,
As she had heard old dames full many times declare.

VI

They told her how, upon St. Agnes' Eve,
Young virgins might have visions of delight,
And soft adorings from their loves receive
Upon the honeyed middle of the night,
If ceremonies due they did aright;   50
As, supperless to bed they must retire,
And couch supine their beauties, lily white;
Nor look behind, nor sideways, but require
Of heaven with upward eyes for all that they desire.

37. **argent:** silver.

VII

Full of this whim was thoughtful Madeline:
The music, yearning like a god in pain,
She scarcely heard: her maiden eyes divine,
Fixed on the floor, saw many a sweeping train
Pass by—she heeded not at all: in vain
60   Came many a tiptoe, amorous cavalier,
And back retired, not cooled by high disdain;
But she saw not: her heart was otherwhere:
She sighed for Agnes' dreams, the sweetest of the year.

VIII

She danced along with vague, regardless eyes,
Anxious her lips, her breathing quick and short:
The hallowed hour was near at hand: she sighs
Amid the timbrels, and the thronged resort
Of whisperers in anger, or in sport;
'Mid looks of love, defiance, hate, and scorn,
70   Hoodwinked with faery fancy; all amort,
Save to St. Agnes and her lambs unshorn,
And all the bliss to be before tomorrow morn.

IX

So, purposing each moment to retire,
She lingered still. Meantime, across the moors,
Had come young Porphyro, with heart on fire
For Madeline. Beside the portal doors,
Buttressed from moonlight, stands he, and implores
All saints to give him sight of Madeline,
But for one moment in the tedious hours,
80   That he might gaze and worship all unseen;
Perchance speak, kneel, touch, kiss—in sooth such things have been.

X

He ventures in: let no buzzed whisper tell:
All eyes be muffled, or a hundred swords

67. **timbrels:** tambourines; **resort:** group. 70. **Hoodwinked:** beguiled; **amort:** as if dead, oblivious. 71. **lambs unshorn:** lambs were offered to St. Agnes on her day; the wool was subsequently woven by nuns. 77. **Buttressed . . . moonlight:** shadowed by the projecting wall supports. 81. **in sooth:** truly. 82-90. There is a vendetta between Porphyro's family (**lineage,** line 88) and Madeline's.

Will storm his heart, love's feverous citadel:
For him, those chambers held barbarian hordes,
Hyena foemen, and hot-blooded lords,
Whose very dogs would execrations howl
Against his lineage: not one breast affords
Him any mercy, in that mansion foul,
Save one old beldame, weak in body and in soul.   90

XI

Ah, happy chance! the agèd creature came,
Shuffling along with ivory-headed wand,
To where he stood, hid from the torch's flame,
Behind a broad hall-pillar, far beyond
The sound of merriment and chorus bland:
He startled her; but soon she knew his face,
And grasped his fingers in her palsied hand,
Saying, "Mercy, Porphyro! hie thee from this place:
They are all here tonight, the whole blood-thirsty race!

XII

"Get hence! get hence! there's dwarfish Hildebrand;   100
He had a fever late, and in the fit
He cursèd thee and thine, both house and land:
Then there's that old Lord Maurice, not a whit
More tame for his gray hairs—Alas me! flit!
Flit like a ghost away."—"Ah, Gossip dear,
We're safe enough; here in this armchair sit,
And tell me how"—"Good saints! not here, not here;
Follow me, child, or else these stones will be thy bier."

XIII

He followed through a lowly archèd way,
Brushing the cobwebs with his lofty plume,   110
And as she muttered "Well-a—well-a-day!"
He found him in a little moonlight room,
Pale, latticed, chill, and silent as a tomb.
"Now tell me where is Madeline," said he,
"O tell me Angela, by the holy loom
Which none but secret sisterhood may see,
When they St. Agnes' wool are weaving piously."

90. **beldame:** old woman. 92. **wand:** walking stick. 105. **Gossip:** long-standing friend.

XIV

"St. Agnes! Ah! it is St. Agnes' Eve——
Yet men will murder upon holy days:
Thou must hold water in a witch's sieve,
And be liege-lord of all the elves and fays,
To venture so: it fills me with amaze
To see thee, Porphyro!—St. Agnes' Eve!
God's help! my lady fair the conjuror plays
This very night: good angels her deceive!
But let me laugh awhile, I've mickle time to grieve."

XV

Feebly she laugheth in the languid moon,
While Porphyro upon her face doth look,
Like puzzled urchin on an agèd crone
Who keepeth closed a wondrous riddle-book,
As spectacled she sits in chimney nook.
But soon his eyes grew brilliant, when she told
His lady's purpose; and he scarce could brook
Tears, at the thought of those enchantments cold,
And Madeline asleep in lap of legends old.

XVI

Sudden a thought came like a full-blown rose,
Flushing his brow, and in his painèd heart
Made purple riot: then doth he propose
A stratagem, that makes the beldame start:
"A cruel man and impious thou art:
Sweet lady, let her pray, and sleep, and dream
Alone with her good angels, far apart
From wicked men like thee. Go, go!—I deem
Thou canst not surely be the same that thou didst seem."

XVII

"I will not harm her, by all saints I swear,"
Quoth Porphyro: "O may I ne'er find grace
When my weak voice shall whisper its last prayer,
If one of her soft ringlets I displace,
Or look with ruffian passion in her face:

124. conjuror plays: is trying to evoke the vision of her lover, Porphyro. **125.** good
. . . deceive: may the good angels assist her in procuring the vision, which is actually
an illusion. **126.** mickle: much. **133.** brook: hold back.

Good Angela, believe me by these tears;   150
Or I will, even in a moment's space,
Awake, with horrid shout, my foemen's ears,
And beard them, though they be more fanged than wolves and bears."

XVIII

"Ah! why wilt thou affright a feeble soul?
A poor, weak, palsy-stricken, churchyard thing,
Whose passing-bell may ere the midnight toll;
Whose prayers for thee, each morn and evening,
Were never missed."—Thus plaining, doth she bring
A gentler speech from burning Porphyro;
So woeful, and of such deep sorrowing,   160
That Angela gives promise she will do
Whatever he shall wish, betide her weal or woe.

XIX

Which was, to lead him, in close secrecy,
Even to Madeline's chamber, and there hide
Him in a closet, of such privacy
That he might see her beauty unespied,
And win perhaps that night a peerless bride,
While legioned faeries paced the coverlet,
And pale enchantment held her sleepy-eyed.
Never on such a night have lovers met,   170
Since Merlin paid his Demon all the monstrous debt.

XX

"It shall be as thou wishest," said the dame:
"All cates and dainties shall be storèd there
Quickly on this feast-night: by the tambour frame
Her own lute thou wilt see: no time to spare,
For I am slow and feeble, and scarce dare
On such a catering trust my dizzy head.
Wait here, my child, with patience; kneel in prayer
The while: Ah! thou must needs the lady wed,
Or may I never leave my grave among the dead."   180

153. beard: defy. 156. passing-bell: bell that will mark her death. 158. plaining: complaining. 162. betide . . . woe: come what may. 171. Merlin . . . debt: Merlin, a magician in Arthurian legend, sired by a devil; the meaning of the line is unclear 173. cates: delicacies. 174. tambour frame: frame for embroidery.

XXI

So saying, she hobbled off with busy fear.
The lover's endless minutes slowly passed;
The dame returned, and whispered in his ear
To follow her; with agèd eyes aghast
From fright of dim espial. Safe at last,
Through many a dusky gallery, they gain
The maiden's chamber, silken, hushed, and chaste;
Where Porphyro took covert, pleased amain.
His poor guide hurried back with agues in her brain.

XXII

190
Her faltering hand upon the balustrade,
Old Angela was feeling for the stair,
When Madeline, St. Agnes' charmèd maid,
Rose, like a missioned spirit, unaware:
With silver taper's light, and pious care,
She turned, and down the agèd gossip led
To a safe level matting. Now prepare,
Young Porphyro, for gazing on that bed;
She comes, she comes again, like ring-dove frayed and fled.

XXIII

200
Out went the taper as she hurried in;
Its little smoke, in pallid moonshine, died:
She closed the door, she panted, all akin
To spirits of the air, and visions wide:
No uttered syllable, or, woe betide!
But to her heart, her heart was voluble,
Paining with eloquence her balmy side;
As though a tongueless nightingale should swell
Her throat in vain, and die, heart-stifled, in her dell.

XXIV

210
A casement high and triple-arched there was,
All garlanded with carven imageries
Of fruits, and flowers, and bunches of knot-grass,
And diamonded with panes of quaint device,
Innumerable of stains and splendid dyes,

188. amain: greatly. **193. missioned:** summoned. **198. frayed:** frightened. **201. akin:** literally, related to, but here, receptive. **208. casement:** window. **211. device:** family emblems.

As are the tiger-moth's deep-damasked wings;
And in the midst, 'mong thousand heraldries,
And twilight saints, and dim emblazonings,
A shielded scutcheon blushed with blood of queens and kings.

XXV

Full on this casement shone the wintry moon,
And threw warm gules on Madeline's fair breast,
As down she knelt for heaven's grace and boon;
Rose-bloom fell on her hands, together pressed,   220
And on her silver cross soft amethyst,
And on her hair a glory, like a saint:
She seemed a splendid angel, newly dressed,
Save wings, for heaven:—Porphyro grew faint:
She knelt, so pure a thing, so free from mortal taint.

XXVI

Anon his heart revives: her vespers done,
Of all its wreathèd pearls her hair she frees;
Unclasps her warmèd jewels one by one;
Loosens her fragrant bodice; by degrees
Her rich attire creeps rustling to her knees: 230
Half-hidden, like a mermaid in sea-weed,
Pensive awhile she dreams awake, and sees,
In fancy, fair St. Agnes in her bed,
But dares not look behind, or all the charm is fled.

XXVII

Soon, trembling in her soft and chilly nest,
In sort of wakeful swoon, perplexed she lay,
Until the poppied warmth of sleep oppressed
Her soothèd limbs, and soul fatigued away;
Flown, like a thought, until the morrow-day;
Blissfully havened both from joy and pain;   240
Clasped like a missal where swart Paynims pray;
Blinded alike from sunshine and from rain,
As though a rose should shut, and be a bud again.

213. **deep-damasked:** rose-colored. 214-216. **heraldries, emblazonings, scutcheon:** representations of coats of arms in the stained-glass window. 218. **gules:** heraldic term for red. 222. **glory:** halo. 237. **poppied:** drugged. 239-242. **Flown, havened, clasped, blinded: soul** is the subject of these verbs; **missal:** prayer book; **swart Paynims:** black pagans; **blinded:** protected.

XXVIII

Stolen to this paradise, and so entranced,
Porphyro gazed upon her empty dress,
And listened to her breathing, if it chanced
To wake into a slumberous tenderness;
Which when he heard, that minute did he bless,
And breathed himself: then from the closet crept,
250   Noiseless as fear in a wide wilderness,
And over the hushed carpet, silent, stepped,
And 'tween the curtains peeped, where, lo!—how fast she slept.

XXIX

Then by the bedside, where the faded moon
Made a dim, silver twilight, soft he set
A table, and, half anguished, threw thereon
A cloth of woven crimson, gold, and jet:—
O for some drowsy Morphean amulet!
The boisterous, midnight, festive clarion,
The kettle-drum, and far-heard clarinet,
260   Affray his ears, though but in dying tone:—
The hall door shuts again, and all the noise is gone

XXX

And still she slept an azure-lidded sleep,
In blanchèd linen, smooth, and lavendered,
While he from forth the closet brought a heap
Of candied apple, quince, and plum, and gourd;
With jellies soother than the creamy curd,
And lucent syrups, tinct with cinnamon;
Manna and dates, in argosy transferred
From Fez; and spicèd dainties, every one,
270   From silken Samarcand to cedared Lebanon

XXXI

These delicates he heaped with glowing hand
On golden dishes and in baskets bright

247. **wake . . . tenderness:** to fall into the rhythmic breathing of sleep. 257.
Morphean amulet: a charm which produced sleep (Morpheus was the god of sleep).
265. **gourd:** melon. 266. **soother:** smoother. 267. **lucent:** shining. 268. **manna:** sweet
gummy juice; **argosy:** large ship or fleet of ships. 269–270. **Fez, Samarcand, Lebanon:**
places in Morocco, central Asia, and the Levant

Of wreathèd silver: sumptuous they stand
In the retirèd quiet of the night,
Filling the chilly room with perfume light.——
"And now, my love, my seraph fair, awake!
Thou art my heaven, and I thine eremite:
Open thine eyes for meek St. Agnes' sake,
Or I shall drowse beside thee, so my soul doth ache."

XXXII

Thus whispering, his warm, unnervèd arm   280
Sank in her pillow. Shaded was her dream
By the dusk curtains:——'twas a midnight charm
Impossible to melt as icèd stream:
The lustrous salvers in the moonlight gleam;
Broad golden fringe upon the carpet lies:
It seemed he never, never could redeem
From such a steadfast spell his lady's eyes;
So mused awhile, entoiled in woofèd phantasies.

XXXIII

Awakening up, he took her hollow lute,——
Tumultuous,——and, in chords that tenderest be,   290
He played an ancient ditty, long since mute,
In Provence called, "La belle dame sans mercy":
Close to her ear touching the melody;——
Wherewith disturbed, she uttered a soft moan:
He ceased—she panted quick—and suddenly
Her blue affrayèd eyes wide open shone:
Upon his knees he sank, pale as smooth-sculptured stone.

XXXIV

Her eyes were open, but she still beheld,
Now wide awake, the vision of her sleep:
There was a painful change, that nigh expelled   300
The blisses of her dream so pure and deep,
At which fair Madeline began to weep,

276. seraph: an angel of the highest rank. 277. eremite: hermit. 288. entoiled . . . phantasies: entangled in woven dreams. 292. Provence . . . mercy": Provence, a southern province of France, was the locale in which Medieval love poems such as "The Beautiful Lady Without Pity" were composed and sung. Keats used this title for one of his own poems.

And moan forth witless words with many a sigh;
While still her gaze on Porphyro would keep;
Who knelt, with joinèd hands and piteous eye,
Fearing to move or speak, she looked so dreamingly.

XXXV

"Ah, Porphyro!" said she, "but even now
Thy voice was at sweet tremble in mine ear,
Made tuneable with every sweetest vow;
310 And those sad eyes were spiritual and clear:
How changed thou art! how pallid, chill, and drear!
Give me that voice again, my Porphyro,
Those looks immortal, those complainings dear!
Oh leave me not in this eternal woe,
For if thou diest, my Love, I know not where to go."

XXXVI

Beyond a mortal man impassioned far
At these voluptuous accents, he arose,
Ethereal, flushed, and like a throbbing star
Seen mid the sapphire heaven's deep repose;
320 Into her dream he melted, as the rose
Blendeth its odor with the violet,—
Solution sweet: meantime the frost-wind blows
Like love's alarum pattering the sharp sleet
Against the window-panes; St. Agnes' moon hath set.

XXXVII

'Tis dark: quick pattereth the flaw-blown sleet:
"This is no dream, my bride, my Madeline!"
'Tis dark: the icèd gusts still rave and beat:
"No dream, alas! alas! and woe is mine!
Porphyro will leave me here to fade and pine.—
330 Cruel! what traitor could thee hither bring?
I curse not, for my heart is lost in thine,
Though thou forsakest a deceivèd thing;—
A dove forlorn and lost with sick unprunèd wing."

XXXVIII

"My Madeline! sweet dreamer! lovely bride!
Say, may I be for aye thy vassal blessed?

325. **flaw-blown:** gust-blown.

Thy beauty's shield, heart-shaped and vermeil dyed?
Ah, silver shrine, here will I take my rest
After so many hours of toil and quest,
A famished pilgrim,—saved by miracle.
Though I have found, I will not rob thy nest 340
Saving of thy sweet self; if thou think'st well
To trust, fair Madeline, to no rude infidel.

XXXIX

"Hark! 'tis an elfin-storm from faery land,
Of haggard seeming, but a boon indeed:
Arise—arise! the morning is at hand;—
The bloated wassaillers will never heed:—
Let us away, my love, with happy speed;
There are no ears to hear, or eyes to see,—
Drowned all in Rhenish and the sleepy mead:
Awake! arise! my love, and fearless be, 350
For o'er the southern moors I have a home for thee."

XL

She hurried at his words, beset with fears,
For there were sleeping dragons all around,
At glaring watch, perhaps, with ready spears—
Down the wide stairs a darkling way they found.—
In all the house was heard no human sound.
A chain-drooped lamp was flickering by each door;
The arras, rich with horseman, hawk, and hound,
Fluttered in the besieging wind's uproar;
And the long carpets rose along the gusty floor. 360

XLI

They glide, like phantoms, into the wide hall;
Like phantoms, to the iron porch, they glide;
Where lay the porter, in uneasy sprawl,
With a huge empty flagon by his side:
The wakeful bloodhound rose, and shook his hide,
But his sagacious eye an inmate owns;
By one, and one, the bolts full easy slide:—
The chains lie silent on the footworn stones;—
The key turns, and the door upon its hinges groans.

336. vermeil: vermilion. **344. haggard:** wild. **349. Rhenish:** wine; **mead:** liquor made from honey. **358. arras:** tapestry. **366. owns:** recognizes.

XLII

370   And they are gone: aye, ages long ago
      These lovers fled away into the storm.
      That night the Baron dreamt of many a woe,
      And all his warrior-guests, with shade and form
      Of witch, and demon, and large coffin-worm,
      Were long be-nightmared. Angela the old
      Died palsy-twitched, with meager face deform;
      The beadsman, after thousand avès told,
For aye unsought-for slept among his ashes cold.

ODE TO A NIGHTINGALE

I

My heart aches, and a drowsy numbness pains
    My sense, as though of hemlock I had drunk,
Or emptied some dull opiate to the drains
    One minute past, and Lethe-wards had sunk:
'Tis not through envy of thy happy lot,
    But being too happy in thine happiness—
        That thou, light-wingèd Dryad of the trees,
            In some melodious plot
Of beechen green, and shadows numberless,
10   Singest of summer in full-throated ease.

II

O, for a draught of vintage! that hath been
    Cooled a long age in the deep-delvèd earth,
Tasting of Flora and the country green,
    Dance, and Provençal song, and sunburnt mirth!
O for a beaker full of the warm South,
    Full of the true, the blushful Hippocrene,
        With beaded bubbles winking at the brim,
            And purple-stainèd mouth;
That I might drink, and leave the world unseen,
20   And with thee fade away into the forest dim:

377. avès: "Hail Mary's."

2. hemlock: poisonous drug. 4. Lethe-wards: towards the river of forgetfulness, in Hades. 7. Dryad: wood nymph. 13. Flora: goddess of flowers. 14. Provençal song: love poetry from Provence, a province in the south of France. 16. Hippocrene: the fountain of the muses on Mt. Helicon.

III

Fade far away, dissolve, and quite forget
   What thou among the leaves hast never known,
The weariness, the fever, and the fret
   Here, where men sit and hear each other groan;
Where palsy shakes a few, sad, last gray hairs,
     Where youth grows pale, and specter-thin, and dies;
       Where but to think is to be full of sorrow
        And leaden-eyed despairs,
     Where Beauty cannot keep her lustrous eyes,
      Or new Love pine at them beyond tomorrow.   30

IV

Away! away! for I will fly to thee,
   Not charioted by Bacchus and his pards,
But on the viewless wings of Poesy,
   Though the dull brain perplexes and retards:
Already with thee! tender is the night,
     And haply the Queen-Moon is on her throne,
       Clustered around by all her starry fays;
        But here there is no light,
     Save what from heaven is with the breezes blown
      Through verdurous glooms and winding mossy ways.   40

V

I cannot see what flowers are at my feet,
   Nor what soft incense hangs upon the boughs,
But, in embalmèd darkness, guess each sweet
   Wherewith the seasonable month endows
The grass, the thicket, and the fruit tree wild;
     White hawthorn, and the pastoral eglantine;
       Fast-fading violets covered up in leaves;
        And mid-May's eldest child,
     The coming musk-rose, full of dewy wine,
      The murmurous haunt of flies on summer eves.   50

---

32. **Bacchus . . . pards:** the god of wine and the leopards that drew his chariot.
36. **haply:** perhaps. 40. **verdurous:** green. 43. **embalmèd:** fragrant.

VI

Darkling I listen; and, for many a time
　　I have been half in love with easeful Death,
Called him soft names in many a musèd rhyme,
　　To take into the air my quiet breath;
Now more than ever seems it rich to die,
　　To cease upon the midnight with no pain,
　　　　While thou art pouring forth thy soul abroad
　　　　　　In such an ecstasy!
　　Still wouldst thou sing, and I have ears in vain—
60　　　　To thy high requiem become a sod.

VII

Thou was not born for death, immortal Bird!
　　No hungry generations tread thee down;
The voice I hear this passing night was heard
　　In ancient days by emperor and clown:
Perhaps the self-same song that found a path
　　Through the sad heart of Ruth, when, sick for home,
　　　　She stood in tears amid the alien corn;
　　　　　　The same that oft-times hath
　　Charmed magic casements, opening on the foam
70　　　　Of perilous seas, in faery lands forlorn.

VIII

Forlorn! the very word is like a bell
　　To toll me back from thee to my sole self!
Adieu! the fancy cannot cheat so well
　　As she is famed to do, deceiving elf.
Adieu! adieu! thy plaintive anthem fades
　　Past the near meadows, over the still stream
　　　　Up the hill-side; and now 'tis buried deep
　　　　　　In the next valley-glades:
　　Was it a vision, or a waking dream?
80　　　　Fled is that music:—Do I wake or sleep?

51. darkling: in the dark. **66. Ruth:** Ruth worked in the fields of a foreign country after her husband's death; see Ruth ii. **67. corn:** grain. **69. casements:** windows. **73. fancy:** the imagination.

ODE ON A GRECIAN URN

I

Thou still unravished bride of quietness,
    Thou foster-child of silence and slow time,
Sylvan historian, who canst thus express
    A flowery tale more sweetly than our rhyme:
What leaf-fringed legend haunts about thy shape
    Of deities or mortals, or of both,
        In Tempe or the dales of Arcady?
What men or gods are these? What maidens loath?
    What mad pursuit? What struggle to escape?
        What pipes and timbrels? What wild ecstasy?   10

II

Heard melodies are sweet, but those unheard
    Are sweeter; therefore, ye soft pipes, play on;
Not to the sensual ear, but, more endeared,
    Pipe to the spirit, ditties of no tone:
Fair youth, beneath the trees, thou canst not leave
    Thy song, nor ever can those trees be bare;
        Bold Lover, never, never canst thou kiss,
Though winning near the goal—yet, do not grieve;
    She cannot fade, though thou hast not thy bliss,
        Forever wilt thou love, and she be fair!   20

III

Ah, happy, happy boughs! that cannot shed
    Your leaves, nor ever bid the spring adieu;
And, happy melodist, unwearièd,
    Forever piping songs forever new;
More happy love! more happy, happy love!
    Forever warm and still to be enjoyed,
        Forever panting, and forever young;
All breathing human passion far above,
    That leaves a heart high-sorrowful and cloyed,
        A burning forehead, and a parching tongue.   30

3. **Sylvan:** woodland. 7. **Tempe, Arcady:** idyllic pastoral areas in Greece. **10.** timbrels: tambourines.

IV

Who are these coming to the sacrifice?
  To what green altar, O mysterious priest,
Lead'st thou that heifer lowing at the skies,
    And all her silken flanks with garlands dressed?
What little town by river or sea shore,
    Or mountain-built with peaceful citadel,
      Is emptied of this folk, this pious morn?
And, little town, thy streets forevermore
    Will silent be; and not a soul to tell
40   Why thou are desolate, can e'er return.

V

O Attic shape! Fair attitude! with brede
  Of marble men and maidens overwrought,
With forest branches and the trodden weed;
    Thou, silent form, dost tease us out of thought
As doth eternity: Cold Pastoral!
    When old age shall this generation waste,
      Thou shalt remain, in midst of other woe
Than ours, a friend to man, to whom thou say'st,
    "Beauty is truth, truth beauty,—that is all
50   Ye know on earth, and all ye need to know."

TO AUTUMN

I

Season of mists and mellow fruitfulness,
  Close bosom-friend of the maturing sun;
Conspiring with him how to load and bless
  With fruit the vines that round the thatch-eaves run;
To bend with apples the mossed cottage-trees,
  And fill all fruit with ripeness to the core;
    To swell the gourd, and plump the hazel shells
With a sweet kernel; to set budding more,
  And still more, later flowers for the bees,
10   Until they think warm days will never cease,
        For summer has o'er-brimmed their clammy cells.

---

41. **Attic:** Grecian; **brede:** pattern. 42. **overwrought:** superimposed. 49. In many editions, quotation marks have been placed around "Beauty is truth, truth beauty." For a discussion of lines 49-50, see Appendix I.

II

Who hath not seen thee oft amid thy store?
  Sometimes whoever seeks abroad may find
Thee sitting careless on a granary floor,
  Thy hair soft-lifted by the winnowing wind;
Or on a half-reaped furrow sound asleep,
  Drowsed with the fume of poppies, while thy hook
    Spares the next swath and all its twinèd flowers:
And sometimes like a gleaner thou dost keep
  Steady thy laden head across a brook;   20
  Or by a cider-press, with patient look,
    Thou watchest the last oozings hours by hours.

III

Where are the songs of spring? Aye, where are they?
  Think not of them, thou hast thy music too,—
While barrèd clouds bloom the soft-dying day,
  And touch the stubble-plains with rosy hue;
Then in a wailful choir the small gnats mourn
  Among the river sallows, borne aloft
    Or sinking as the light wind lives or dies;
And full-grown lambs loud bleat from hilly bourn;   30
  Hedge-crickets sing; and now with treble soft
  The redbreast whistles from a garden-croft;
    And gathering swallows twitter in the skies.

LA BELLE DAME SANS MERCI

"O what can ail thee, knight-at-arms,
  Alone and palely loitering?
The sedge has withered from the lake,
  And no birds sing.

"O what can ail thee, knight-at-arms,
  So haggard and so woe-begone?
The squirrel's granary is full,
  And the harvest's done.

12. store: plenty. 28. sallows: willows. 30. bourn: domain. 32. garden-croft: a
small enclosed field.

Title. The beautiful lady without pity.

"I see a lily on thy brow
    With anguish moist and fever dew;
And on thy cheek a fading rose
    Fast withereth too."

"I met a lady in the meads,
    Full beautiful, a faery's child;
Her hair was long, her foot was light,
    And her eyes were wild.

"I made a garland for her head,
    And bracelets too, and fragrant zone;
She looked at me as she did love,
    And made sweet moan.

"I set her on my pacing steed,
    And nothing else saw all day long;
For sidelong would she bend, and sing
    A faery's song.

"She found me roots of relish sweet,
    And honey wild, and manna dew,
And sure in language strange she said,
    'I love thee true.'

"She took me to her elfin grot,
    And there she wept, and sighed full sore;
And there I shut her wild wild eyes
    With kisses four.

"And there she lullèd me asleep,
    And there I dreamed,—Ah! woe betide!
The latest dream I ever dreamed
    On the cold hill's side.

"I saw pale kings and princes too,
    Pale warriors, death-pale were they all;
They cried: 'La belle dame sans merci
    Hath thee in thrall!'

13. meads: fields. **18. zone:** belt. **26. manna dew:** sweet gummy juice. **29. grot:** cave.

"I saw their starved lips in the gloam,
 With horrid warning gapèd wide,
And I awoke and found me here,
 On the cold hill's side.

"And this is why I sojourn here,
 Alone and palely loitering,
Though the sedge is withered from the lake,
 And no birds sing."

RALPH WALDO EMERSON (1803–1882)

BRAHMA

If the red slayer think he slays,
 Or if the slain think he is slain,
They know not well the subtle ways
 I keep, and pass, and turn again.

Far or forgot to me is near;
 Shadow and sunlight are the same;
The vanished gods to me appear;
 And one to me are shame and fame.

They reckon ill who leave me out;
 When me they fly, I am the wings;
I am the doubter and the doubt,   10
 And I the hymn the Brahmin sings.

The strong gods pine for my abode,
 And pine in vain the sacred Seven;
But thou, meek lover of the good!
 Find me, and turn thy back on heaven.

Title. Brahma: Hindu god, maker of the Universe. **1. red slayer:** death. **4. I:** Brahma. **9. reckon ill:** figure things badly. **10. fly:** flee from. **12. Brahmin:** high-caste worshipper of Brahma. **13. strong gods:** gods of fire, sky, and death. **14. Seven:** highest saints.

DAYS

Daughters of Time, the hypocritic Days,
Muffled and dumb like barefoot dervishes,
And marching single in an endless file,
Bring diadems and fagots in their hands.
To each they offer gifts after his will,
Bread, kingdoms, stars, and sky that holds them all.
I, in my pleachèd garden, watched the pomp,
Forgot my morning wishes, hastily
Took a few herbs and apples, and the Day
Turned and departed silent. I too late
Under her solemn fillet saw the scorn.

10

ALFRED, LORD TENNYSON (1809–1892)

THE LOTOS-EATERS

"Courage!" he said, and pointed toward the land,
"This mounting wave will roll us shoreward soon."
In the afternoon they came unto a land
In which it seemèd always afternoon.
All round the coast the languid air did swoon,
Breathing like one that hath a weary dream.
Full-faced above the valley stood the moon;
And, like a downward smoke, the slender stream
Along the cliff to fall and pause and fall did seem.

10   A land of streams! some, like a downward smoke,
Slow-dropping veils of thinnest lawn, did go;
And some through wavering lights and shadows broke,
Rolling a slumbrous sheet of foam below.
They saw the gleaming river seaward flow

2. dervishes: Moslems dedicated to lives of poverty. **4. diadems:** ornamented head-gear; **fagots:** bundles of twigs. **7. pleachèd:** interlaced with branches. **11. fillet:** headband.

Title. The Lotos-Eaters were the inhabitants of an island at which Ulysses and his crew stopped on the way home from Troy. Eating the lotos flower brought about for-getfulness. **1. he:** Ulysses (see headnote to Tennyson's "Ulysses." p. 231). **11. lawn:** fine linen.

From the inner land; far off, three mountain-tops,
Three silent pinnacles of agèd snow,
Stood sunset-flushed; and, dewed with showery drops,
Up-clomb the shadowy pine above the woven copse.
The charmèd sunset lingered low adown
In the red West: through mountain clefts the dale   20
Was seen far inland, and the yellow down
Bordered with palm, and many a winding vale
And meadow, set with slender galingale;
A land where all things always seemed the same!
And round about the keel with faces pale,
Dark faces pale against that rosy flame,
The mild-eyed melancholy Lotos-eaters came.

Branches they bore of that enchanted stem,
Laden with flower and fruit, whereof they gave
To each, but whoso did receive of them   30
And taste, to him the gushing of the wave
Far, far away did seem to mourn and rave
On alien shores; and if his fellow spake,
His voice was thin, as voices from the grave;
And deep-asleep he seemed, yet all awake,
And music in his ears his beating heart did make.

They sat them down upon the yellow sand,
Between the sun and moon upon the shore;
And sweet it was to dream of Fatherland,
Of child, and wife, and slave; but evermore   40
Most weary seemed the sea, weary the oar,
Weary the wandering fields of barren foam.
Then some one said, "We will return no more";
And all at once they sang, "Our island home
Is far beyond the wave; we will no longer roam."

CHORIC SONG

I

There is sweet music here that softer falls
Than petals from blown roses on the grass,
Or night-dews on still waters between walls

18. **Up-clomb:** climbed up; **copse:** small wood. 21. **down:** high ground. 23. **galin-gale:** species of plant. 25. **keel:** of the mariners' boat. 44. **island home:** Ithaca. 47. **blown roses:** roses past their prime.

Of shadowy granite, in a gleaming pass;
50 Music that gentlier on the spirit lies,
Than tired eyelids upon tired eyes;
Music that brings sweet sleep down from the blissful skies.
Here are cool mosses deep,
And through the moss the ivies creep,
And in the stream the long-leaved flowers weep,
And from the craggy ledge the poppy hangs in sleep.

II

Why are we weighed upon with heaviness,
And utterly consumed with sharp distress,
While all things else have rest from weariness?
60 All things have rest: why should we toil alone—
We only toil, who are the first of things—
And make perpetual moan,
Still from one sorrow to another thrown;
Nor ever fold our wings,
And cease from wanderings,
Nor steep our brows in slumber's holy balm;
Nor hearken what the inner spirit sings,
"There is no joy but calm!"
Why should we only toil, the roof and crown of things?

III

70 Lo! in the middle of the wood,
The folded leaf is wooed from out the bud
With winds upon the branch, and there
Grows green and broad, and takes no care,
Sun-steeped at noon, and in the moon
Nightly dew-fed; and turning yellow
Falls, and floats adown the air.
Lo! sweetened with the summer light,
The full-juiced apple, waxing over-mellow,
Drops in a silent autumn night.
80 All its allotted length of days
The flower ripens in its place,
Ripens and fades, and falls, and hath no toil,
Fast-rooted in the fruitful soil.

IV

Hateful is the dark-blue sky,
Vaulted o'er the dark-blue sea.
Death is the end of life; ah why
Should life all labor be?
Let us alone. Time driveth onward fast,
And in a little while our lips are dumb.
Let us alone. What is it that will last?   90
All things are taken from us, and become
Portions and parcels of the dreadful past.
Let us alone. What pleasure can we have
To war with evil? Is there any peace
In ever climbing up the climbing wave?
All things have rest, and ripen toward the grave
In silence—ripen, fall, and cease:
Give us long rest or death, dark death, or dreamful ease.

V

How sweet it were, hearing the downward stream,
With half-shut eyes ever to seem   100
Falling asleep in a half-dream!
To dream and dream, like yonder amber light,
Which will not leave the myrrh-bush on the height;
To hear each other's whispered speech;
Eating the Lotos day by day,
To watch the crisping ripples on the beach,
And tender curving lines of creamy spray;
To lend our hearts and spirits wholly
To the influence of mild-mannered melancholy;
To muse and brood and live again in memory,   110
With those old faces of our infancy
Heaped over with a mound of grass,
Two handfuls of white dust, shut in an urn of brass!

VI

Dear is the memory of our wedded lives,
And dear the last embraces of our wives
And their warm tears: but all hath suffered change:
For surely now our household hearths are cold:
Our sons inherit us: our looks are strange:

And we should come like ghosts to trouble joy.
120   Or else the island princes over-bold
Have eat our substance, and the minstrel sings
Before them of the ten years' war in Troy,
And our great deeds, as half-forgotten things.
Is there confusion in the little isle?
Let what is broken so remain.
The Gods are hard to reconcile:
'Tis hard to settle order once again.
There *is* confusion worse than death,
Trouble on trouble, pain on pain,
130   Long labor unto agèd breath,
Sore task to hearts worn out by many wars
And eyes grown dim with gazing on the pilot-stars.

VII

But, propped on beds of amaranth and moly,
How sweet—while warm airs lull us, blowing lowly—
With half-dropped eyelid still,
Beneath a heaven dark and holy,
To watch the long bright river drawing slowly
His waters from the purple hill—
To hear the dewy echoes calling
140   From cave to cave through the thick-twined vine—
To watch the emerald-colored water falling
Through many a woven acanthus-wreath divine!
Only to hear and see the far-off sparkling brine,
Only to hear were sweet, stretched out beneath the pine.

VIII

The Lotos blooms below the barren peak:
The Lotos blows by every winding creek:
All day the wind breathes low with mellower tone:
Through every hollow cave and alley lone
Round and round the spicy downs the yellow Lotos-dust is blown.
150   We have had enough of action, and of motion we,
Rolled to starboard, rolled to larboard, when the surge was seething free,
Where the wallowing monster spouted his foam-fountains in the sea.
Let us swear an oath, and keep it with an equal mind,

---

121. eat our substance: consumed our wealth. **133. amaranth:** a flower that does not fade; **moly:** a magic herb. **142. acanthus:** plant with large leaves. **146. blows:** blossoms.

In the hollow Lotos-land to live and lie reclined
On the hills like Gods together, careless of mankind.
For they lie beside their nectar, and the bolts are hurled
Far below them in the valleys, and the clouds are lightly curled
Round their golden houses, girdled with the gleaming world;
Where they smile in secret, looking over wasted lands,
Blight and famine, plague and earthquake, roaring deeps and fiery sands,   160
Clanging fights, and flaming towns, and sinking ships, and praying hands.
But they smile, they find a music centered in a doleful song
Steaming up, a lamentation and an ancient tale of wrong,
Like a tale of little meaning though the words are strong;
Chanted from an ill-used race of men that cleave the soil,
Sow the seed, and reap the harvest with enduring toil,
Storing yearly little dues of wheat and wine and oil;
Till they perish and they suffer—some, 'tis whispered—down in hell
Suffer endless anguish, others in Elysian valleys dwell,
Resting weary limbs at last on beds of asphodel.   170
Surely, surely, slumber is more sweet than toil, the shore
Than labor in the deep mid-ocean, wind and wave and oar;
Oh, rest ye, brother mariners, we will not wander more.

MORTE D'ARTHUR

So all day long the noise of battle rolled
Among the mountains by the winter sea;
Until King Arthur's table, man by man,
Had fallen in Lyonnesse about their lord,
King Arthur; then, because his wound was deep,
The bold Sir Bedivere uplifted him,
Sir Bedivere, the last of all his knights,
And bore him to a chapel nigh the field,
A broken chancel with a broken cross,
That stood on a dark strait of barren land.   10
On one side lay the ocean, and on one

156. bolts: thunderbolts. 167. dues: harvests. 169. Elysian valleys: where the virtu-
ous Greeks went after death. 170. asphodel: flower associated with the Elysian fields.

Title. Death of Arthur. 3. table: the celebrated Round Table, i.e., King Arthur's
company of knights. 4. Lyonnesse: legendary country off the southwest coast of England.
9. chancel: part of the church containing the altar.

Lay a great water, and the moon was full.
   Then spake King Arthur to Sir Bedivere:
"The sequel of today unsolders all
The goodliest fellowship of famous knights
Whereof this world holds record. Such a sleep
They sleep—the men I loved. I think that we
Shall never more, at any future time,
Delight our souls with talk of knightly deeds,

20 Walking about the gardens and the halls
Of Camelot, as in the days that were.
I perish by this people which I made,—
Though Merlin sware that I should come again
To rule once more—but let what will be, be,
I am so deeply smitten through the helm
That without help I cannot last till morn.
Thou therefore take my brand Excalibur,
Which was my pride: for thou rememberest how
In those old days, one summer noon, an arm

30 Rose up from out the bosom of the lake,
Clothed in white samite, mystic, wonderful,
Holding the sword—and how I rowed across
And took it, and have worn it, like a king;
And, wheresoever I am sung or told
In aftertime, this also shall be known:
But now delay not: take Excalibur,
And fling him far into the middle mere:
Watch what thou seest, and lightly bring me word."
   To him replied the bold Sir Bedivere:

40 "It is not meet, Sir King, to leave thee thus,
Aidless, alone, and smitten through the helm.
A little thing may harm a wounded man.
Yet I thy hest will all perform at full,
Watch what I see, and lightly bring thee word."
   So saying, from the ruined shrine he stepped
And in the moon athwart the place of tombs,
Where lay the mighty bones of ancient men,
Old knights, and over them the sea-wind sang
Shrill, chill, with flakes of foam. He, stepping down

---

21. Camelot: King Arthur's capital. 23. Merlin: the magician in Arthur's court; sware: swore. 27. brand: sword. 31. samite: heavy silk. 37. mere: lake (cf. line 12). 38. lightly: quickly. 40. meet: proper. 43. hest: command. 46. athwart: across.

By zig-zag paths, and juts of pointed rock,   50
Came on the shining levels of the lake.
  There drew he forth the brand Excalibur,
And o'er him, drawing it, the winter moon,
Brightening the skirts of a long cloud, ran forth
And sparkled keen with frost against the hilt:
For all the haft twinkled with diamond sparks,
Myriads of topaz-lights, and jacinth-work
Of subtlest jewelry. He gazed so long
That both his eyes were dazzled, as he stood,
This way and that dividing the swift mind,   60
In act to throw: but at the last it seemed
Better to leave Excalibur concealed
There in the many-knotted waterflags,
That whistled stiff and dry about the marge.
So strode he back slow to the wounded king.
  Then spake King Arthur to Sir Bedivere:
"Hast thou performed my mission which I gave?
What is it thou hast seen? or what hast heard?"
  And answer made the bold Sir Bedivere:
"I heard the ripple washing in the reeds,   70
And the wild water lapping on the crag."
  To whom replied King Arthur, faint and pale:
"Thou hast betrayed thy nature and thy name,
Not rendering true answer, as beseemed
Thy fealty, nor like a noble knight:
For surer sign had followed, either hand,
Or voice, or else a motion of the mere.
This is a shameful thing for men to lie.
Yet now, I charge thee, quickly go again
As thou art lief and dear, and do the thing   80
I bade thee, watch, and lightly bring me word."
  Then went Sir Bedivere the second time
Across the ridge, and paced beside the mere,
Counting the dewy pebbles, fixed in thought;
But when he saw the wonder of the hilt,
How curiously and strangely chased, he smote
His palms together, and he cried aloud:
  "And if indeed I cast the brand away,
Surely a precious thing, one worthy note,
Should thus be lost for ever from the earth,   90

74-75. beseemed/Thy fealty: as was proper to your oath. 80. lief: beloved. 86.
curiously: cleverly; chased: ornamented.

Which might have pleased the eyes of many men.
What good should follow this, if this were done?
What harm, undone? deep harm to disobey,
Seeing obedience is the bond of rule.
Were it well to obey then, if a king demand
An act unprofitable, against himself?
The king is sick, and knows not what he does.
What record, or what relic of my lord
Should be to aftertime, but empty breath
100 And rumors of a doubt? but were this kept,
Stored in some treasure-house of mighty kings,
Some one might show it at a joust of arms,
Saying, 'King Arthur's sword, Excalibur,
Wrought by the lonely Maiden of the Lake.
Nine years she wrought it, sitting in the deeps
Upon the hidden bases of the hills.'
So might some old man speak in the aftertime
To all the people, winning reverence.
But now much honor and much fame were lost."
110   So spake he, clouded with his own conceit,
And hid Excalibur the second time,
And so strode back slow to the wounded king.
    Then spoke King Arthur, breathing heavily:
"What is it thou hast seen? or what hast heard?"
    And answer made the bold Sir Bedivere:
"I heard the water lapping on the crag,
And the long ripple washing in the reeds."
    To whom replied King Arthur, much in wrath:
"Ah, miserable and unkind, untrue,
120 Unknightly, traitor-hearted! Woe is me!
Authority forgets a dying king,
Laid widowed of the power in his eye
That bowed the will. I see thee what thou art,
For thou, the latest-left of all my knights,
In whom should meet the offices of all,
Thou wouldst betray me for the precious hilt;
Either from lust of gold, or like a girl
Valuing the giddy pleasure of the eyes.
Yet, for a man may fail in duty twice,
130 And the third time may prosper, get thee hence:
But, if thou spare to fling Excalibur,

110. conceit: fancy. 129. for: because.

I will arise and slay thee with my hands."
   Then quickly rose Sir Bedivere, and ran,
And, leaping down the ridges lightly, plunged
Among the bulrush-beds, and clutched the sword,
And strongly wheeled and threw it. The great brand
Made lightnings in the splendor of the moon,
And flashing round and round, and whirled in an arch,
Shot like a streamer of the northern morn,
Seen where the moving isles of winter shock   140
By night, with noises of the northern sea.
So flashed and fell the brand Excalibur:
But ere he dipped the surface, rose an arm
Clothed in white samite, mystic, wonderful,
And caught him by the hilt, and brandished him
Three times, and drew him under in the mere.
And lightly went the other to the king.
   Then spoke King Arthur, drawing thicker breath:
"Now see I by thine eyes that this is done.
Speak out: what is it thou hast heard, or seen?"   150
   And answer made the bold Sir Bedivere:
"Sir King, I closed mine eyelids, lest the gems
Should blind my purpose, for I never saw,
Nor shall see, here or elsewhere, till I die,
Not though I live three lives of mortal men,
So great a miracle as yonder hilt.
Then with both hands I flung him, wheeling him;
But when I looked again, behold an arm,
Clothed in white samite, mystic, wonderful,
That caught him by the hilt, and brandished him   160
Three times, and drew him under in the mere."
   And answer made King Arthur, breathing hard:
"My end draws nigh; 'tis time that I were gone.
Make broad thy shoulders to receive my weight,
And bear me to the margin; yet I fear
My wound hath taken cold, and I shall die."
   So saying, from the pavement he half rose,
Slowly, with pain, reclining on his arm,
And looking wistfully with wide blue eyes
As in a picture. Him Sir Bedivere   170
Remorsefully regarded through his tears,

---

139. **streamer . . . morn:** northern lights. 140. **moving . . . winter:** icebergs;
shock: collide. 167. **pavement:** floor of the chapel.

And would have spoken, but he found not words,
Then took with care, and kneeling on one knee,
O'er both his shoulders drew the languid hands,
And rising bore him through the place of tombs.
    But, as he walked, King Arthur panted hard,
Like one that feels a nightmare on his bed
When all the house is mute. So sighed the king,
Muttering and murmuring at his ear, "Quick, quick!
180   I fear it is too late, and I shall die."
But the other swiftly strode from ridge to ridge,
Clothed with his breath, and looking, as he walked,
Larger than human on the frozen hills.
He heard the deep behind him, and a cry
Before. His own thought drove him like a goad.
Dry clashed his harness in the icy caves
And barren chasms, and all to left and right
The bare black cliff clanged round him, as he based
His feet on juts of slippery crag that rang
190   Sharp-smitten with the dint of armèd heels—
And on a sudden, lo! the level lake,
And the long glories of the winter moon.
    Then saw they how there hove a dusky barge,
Dark as a funeral scarf from stem to stern,
Beneath them; and descending they were ware
That all the decks were dense with stately forms
Black-stoled, black-hooded, like a dream—by these
Three queens with crowns of gold—and from them rose
A cry that shivered to the tingling stars,
200   And, as it were one voice, an agony
Of lamentation, like a wind that shrills
All night in a waste land where no one comes,
Or hath come, since the making of the world.
    Then murmured Arthur, "Place me in the barge,"
And to the barge they came. There those three queens
Put forth their hands, and took the king, and wept.
But she, that rose the tallest of them all
And fairest, laid his head upon her lap,
And loosed the shattered casque, and chafed his hands,
210   And called him by his name, complaining loud,
And dropping bitter tears against his brow

184. **deep:** sea. 193. **hove:** came in sight. 195. **ware:** aware. 209. **casque:** helmet.
210. **complaining:** mourning.

Striped with dark blood: for all his face was white
And colorless, and like the withered moon
Smote by the fresh beam of the springing east;
And all his greaves and cuisses dashed with drops
Of onset; and the light and lustrous curls—
That made his forehead like a rising sun
High from the dais-throne—were parched with dust;
Or, clotted into points and hanging loose,
Mixed with the knightly growth that fringed his lips.   220
So like a shattered column lay the king;
Not like that Arthur who, with lance in rest,
From spur to plume a star of tournament,
Shot through the lists at Camelot, and charged
Before the eyes of ladies and of kings.

   Then loudly cried the bold Sir Bedivere:
"Ah! my Lord Arthur, whither shall I go?
Where shall I hide my forehead and my eyes?
For now I see the true old times are dead,
When every morning brought a noble chance,   230
And every chance brought out a noble knight.
Such times have been not since the light that led
The holy Elders with the gift of myrrh.
But now the whole Round Table is dissolved
Which was an image of the mighty world;
And I, the last, go forth companionless,
And the days darken round me, and the years,
Among new men, strange faces, other minds."

   And slowly answered Arthur from the barge:
"The old order changeth, yielding place to new,   240
And God fulfills Himself in many ways,
Lest one good custom should corrupt the world.
Comfort thyself: what comfort is in me?
I have lived my life, and that which I have done
May He within Himself make pure! but thou,
If thou shouldst never see my face again,
Pray for my soul. More things are wrought by prayer
Than this world dreams of. Wherefore, let thy voice
Rise like a fountain for me night and day.
For what are men better than sheep or goats   250

215. **greaves and cuisses:** armor protecting shins and thighs. 215-216. **drops/of
onset:** drops (of blood) from the attack. 232-233. **light . . . myrrh:** reference to the star
of Bethlehem and the journey of the three Magi, who brought the myrrh, a fragrant herb.

That nourish a blind life within the brain,
If, knowing God, they lift not hands of prayer
Both for themselves and those who call them friend?
For so the whole round earth is every way
Bound by gold chains about the feet of God.
But now farewell. I am going a long way
With these thou seèst—if indeed I go—
(For all my mind is clouded with a doubt)
To the island-valley of Avilion;
260   Where falls not hail, or rain, or any snow,
Nor ever wind blows loudly; but it lies
Deep-meadowed, happy, fair with orchard-lawns
And bowery hollows crowned with summer sea,
Where I will heal me of my grievous wound."

So said he, and the barge with oar and sail
Moved from the brink, like some full-breasted swan
That, fluting a wild carol ere her death,
Ruffles her pure cold plume, and takes the flood
With swarthy webs. Long stood Sir Bedivere
270   Revolving many memories, till the hull
Looked one black dot against the verge of dawn,
And on the mere the wailing died away.

ULYSSES

It little profits that an idle king,
By this still hearth, among these barren crags,
Matched with an agèd wife, I mete and dole
Unequal laws unto a savage race,
That hoard, and sleep, and feed, and know not me.
I cannot rest from travel: I will drink
Life to the lees: all times I have enjoyed
Greatly, have suffered greatly, both with those
That loved me, and alone; on shore, and when
10   Through scudding drifts the rainy Hyades

259. **Avilion:** Avalon, the Celtic equivalent of the Elysian Fields, the legendary place where the virtuous Greeks went after death. 267. **fluting . . . death:** reference to the idea that a swan sings only just prior to its death.

Title. Ulysses or Odysseus is the hero of Homer's *Odyssey,* which describes the ten years' homecoming from the Trojan War of this Grecian king, who ruled the island of Ithaca. 3. **mete and dole:** administer. 7. **lees:** dregs. 10. **scudding drifts:** driving rain; **Hyades:** stars that supposedly cause the rain.

Vexed the dim sea: I am become a name;
For always roaming with a hungry heart
Much have I seen and known: cities of men
And manners, climates, councils, governments,
Myself not least, but honored of them all;
And drunk delight of battle with my peers,
Far on the ringing plains of windy Troy.
I am a part of all that I have met;
Yet all experience is an arch wherethrough
Gleams that untravelled world whose margin fades   20
For ever and for ever when I move.
How dull it is to pause, to make an end,
To rust unburnished, not to shine in use!
As though to breathe were life! Life piled on life
Were all too little, and of one to me
Little remains: but every hour is saved
From that eternal silence, something more,
A bringer of new things; and vile it were
For some three suns to store and hoard myself,
And this gray spirit yearning in desire   30
To follow knowledge like a sinking star,
Beyond the utmost bound of human thought.

    This is my son, mine own Telemachus,
To whom I leave the scepter and the isle—
Well-loved of me, discerning to fulfil
This labor, by slow prudence to make mild
A rugged people, and through soft degrees
Subdue them to the useful and the good.
Most blameless is he, centered in the sphere
Of common duties, decent not to fail   40
In offices of tenderness, and pay
Meet adoration to my household gods,
When I am gone. He works his work, I mine.

    There lies the port; the vessel puffs her sail:
There gloom the dark broad seas. My mariners,
Souls that have toiled, and wrought, and thought with me—
That ever with a frolic welcome took
The thunder and the sunshine, and opposed
Free hearts, free foreheads—you and I are old;
Old age hath yet his honor and his toil.   50
Death closes all: but something ere the end,

29. suns: years. 42. Meet: proper.

Some work of noble note, may yet be done,
Not unbecoming men that strove with Gods.
The lights begin to twinkle from the rocks:
The long day wanes: the slow moon climbs: the deep
Moans round with many voices. Come, my friends,
'Tis not too late to seek a newer world.
Push off, and sitting well in order smite
The sounding furrows; for my purpose holds
60   To sail beyond the sunset, and the baths
Of all the western stars, until I die.
It may be that the gulfs will wash us down:
It may be we shall touch the Happy Isles,
And see the great Achilles, whom we knew.
Though much is taken, much abides; and though
We are not now that strength which in old days
Moved earth and heaven, that which we are, we are:
One equal temper of heroic hearts,
Made weak by time and fate, but strong in will
70   To strive, to seek, to find, and not to yield.

TITHONUS

The woods decay, the woods decay and fall,
The vapors weep their burthen to the ground,
Man comes and tills the field and lies beneath,
And after many a summer dies the swan.
Me only cruel immortality
Consumes: I wither slowly in thine arms,
Here at the quiet limit of the world,
A white-haired shadow roaming like a dream
The ever-silent spaces of the East,
10   Far-folded mists, and gleaming halls of morn.
        Alas! for this gray shadow, once a man—
So glorious in his beauty and thy choice,
Who madest him thy chosen, that he seemed

62. gulfs: whirlpools. 63. Happy Isles: the Elysian Fields, where virtuous Greeks went after death. 64. Achilles: foremost Greek hero in the Trojan War.

Title. Tithonus: a mortal beloved by the goddess of the dawn (Eos), who granted him eternal life (see lines 15-16, etc.) but not eternal youth (see line 18). 4. swan: noted for its longevity. 6. thine arms: those of the goddess of the dawn.

To his great heart none other than a God!
I asked thee, "Give me immortality."
Then didst thou grant mine asking with a smile,
Like wealthy men who care not how they give.
But thy strong Hours indignant worked their wills,
And beat me down and marred and wasted me,
And though they could not end me, left me maimed   20
To dwell in presence of immortal youth,
Immortal age beside immortal youth,
And all I was, in ashes. Can thy love,
Thy beauty, make amends, though even now,
Close over us, the silver star, thy guide,
Shines in those tremulous eyes that fill with tears
To hear me? Let me go; take back thy gift:
Why should a man desire in any way
To vary from the kindly race of men,
Or pass beyond the goal of ordinance   30
Where all should pause, as is most meet for all?

   A soft air fans the cloud apart; there comes
A glimpse of that dark world where I was born.
Once more the old mysterious glimmer steals
From thy pure brows, and from thy shoulders pure,
And bosom beating with a heart renewed.
Thy cheek begins to redden through the gloom,
Thy sweet eyes brighten slowly close to mine,
Ere yet they blind the stars, and the wild team
Which love thee, yearning for thy yoke, arise,   40
And shake the darkness from their loosened manes,
And beat the twilight into flakes of fire.

   Lo! ever thus thou growest beautiful
In silence, then, before thine answer given,
Departest, and thy tears are on my cheek.

   Why wilt thou ever scare me with thy tears,
And make me tremble lest a saying learnt,
In days far-off, on that dark earth, be true?
"The Gods themselves cannot recall their gifts."

   Ay me! ay me! with what another heart   50
In days far-off, and with what other eyes

24. make amends: compensate. 25. close: not the verb, but the adverb; silver star: morning star, usually Venus. 29. kindly: natural, pleasant. 30. goal of ordinance: the life-span normally allotted to man. 39. team: the horses that draw the chariot of the dawn.

I used to watch—if I be he that watched—
The lucid outline forming round thee; saw
The dim curls kindle into sunny rings;
Changed with thy mystic change, and felt my blood
Glow with the glow that slowly crimsoned all
Thy presence and thy portals, while I lay,
Mouth, forehead, eyelids, growing dewy-warm
With kisses balmier than half-opening buds
₆₀ Of April, and could hear the lips that kissed
Whispering I knew not what of wild and sweet,
Like that strange song I heard Apollo sing,
While Ilion like a mist rose into towers.

Yet hold me not for ever in thine East:
How can my nature longer mix with thine?
Coldly thy rosy shadows bathe me, cold
Are all thy lights, and cold my wrinkled feet
Upon thy glimmering thresholds, when the steam
Floats up from those fields about the homes
₇₀ Of happy men that have the power to die,
And grassy barrows of the happier dead.
Release me, and restore me to the ground;
Thou seèst all things, thou wilt see my grave:
Thou wilt renew thy beauty morn by morn;
I earth in earth forget these empty courts,
And thee returning on thy silver wheels.

BREAK, BREAK, BREAK

Break, break, break,
    On thy cold gray stones, O Sea!
And I would that my tongue could utter
    The thoughts that arise in me.

O, well for the fisherman's boy,
    That he shouts with his sister at play!
O, well for the sailor lad,
    That he sings in his boat on the bay!

57. portals: gates (of the dawn). 62-63. Apollo . . . Ilion: Apollo, god of poetry and music, tended the flocks of Laomedon, father of Tithonus, while Poseidon built the walls of Troy (Ilion). 71 barrows: tombs. 75. courts: courts of the sun.

And the stately ships go on
   To their haven under the hill;   10
But O, for the touch of a vanished hand,
   And the sound of a voice that is still!

Break, break, break,
   At the foot of thy crags, O Sea!
But the tender grace of a day that is dead
   Will never come back to me.

CROSSING THE BAR

Sunset and evening star,
   And one clear call for me!
And may there be no moaning of the bar,
   When I put out to sea,

But such a tide as moving seems asleep,
   Too full for sound and foam,
When that which drew from out the boundless deep
   Turns again home.

Twilight and evening bell,
   And after that the dark!   10
And may there be no sadness of farewell,
   When I embark;

For though from out our bourne of time and place
   The flood may bear me far,
I hope to see my Pilot face to face
   When I have crossed the bar.

TEARS, IDLE TEARS,
I KNOW NOT WHAT THEY MEAN

Tears, idle tears, I know not what they mean,
Tears from the depth of some divine despair
Rise in the heart, and gather to the eyes,
In looking on the happy autumn fields,
And thinking of the days that are no more.

Title: **bar:** sand-bar. 13. **bourne:** realm.

Fresh as the first beam glittering on a sail,
That brings our friends up from the underworld,
Sad as the last which reddens over one
That sinks with all we love below the verge;
So sad, so fresh, the days that are no more.

Ah, sad and strange as in dark summer dawns
The earliest pipe of half-awakened birds
To dying ears, when unto dying eyes
The casement slowly grows a glimmering square;
So sad, so strange, the days that are no more.

Dear as remembered kisses after death,
And sweet as those by hopeless fancy feigned
On lips that are for others; deep as love,
Deep as first love, and wild with all regret;
O death in life, the days that are no more!

NOW SLEEPS THE CRIMSON PETAL, NOW THE WHITE

Now sleeps the crimson petal, now the white;
Nor waves the cypress in the palace walk;
Nor winks the gold fin in the porphyry font:
The fire-fly wakens; waken thou with me.

Now droops the milk-white peacock like a ghost,
And like a ghost she glimmers on to me.

Now lies the earth all Danaë to the stars,
And all thy heart lies open unto me.

Now slides the silent meteor on, and leaves
A shining furrow, as thy thoughts in me.

Now folds the lily all her sweetness up,
And slips into the bosom of the lake.
So fold thyself, my dearest, thou, and slip
Into my bosom and be lost in me.

9. **verge:** horizon. 14. **casement:** window.

3. **winks:** flickers; **porphyry:** a hard red stone; **font:** basin. 7. **Danaë:** legendary Greek princess seduced by Zeus in the form of a shower of gold. 10. **thy thoughts:** thoughts of you.

ROBERT BROWNING (1812–1889)

SOLILOQUY OF THE SPANISH CLOISTER

I

Gr-r-r—there go, my heart's abhorrence!
  Water your damned flower-pots, do!
If hate killed men, Brother Lawrence,
  God's blood, would not mine kill you!
What? your myrtle-bush wants trimming?
  Oh, that rose has prior claims—
Needs its leaden vase filled brimming?
  Hell dry you up with its flames!

II

At the meal we sit together:
  Salve tibi! I must hear   10
Wise talk of the kind of weather,
  Sort of season, time of year:
Not a plenteous cork-crop: scarcely
  Dare we hope oak-galls, I doubt:
What's the Latin name for "parsley"?
  What's the Greek name for Swine's Snout?

III

Whew! We'll have our platter burnished,
  Laid with care on our own shelf!
With a fire-new spoon we're furnished,
  And a goblet for ourself,   20
Rinsed like something sacrificial
  Ere 'tis fit to touch our chaps—
Marked with L. for our initial!
  (He-he! There his lily snaps!)

Title. cloister: monastery. **10.** *Salve tibi:* hail to thee (these words and the other italicized words in this stanza are supposedly Brother Lawrence's). **14.** *oak-galls:* growths on oak trees, used commercially. **19. fire-new:** brand-new. **22. chaps:** cheeks.

IV

Saint, forsooth! While brown Dolores
    Squats outside the Convent bank
With Sanchicha, telling stories,
    Steeping tresses in the tank,
Blue-black, lustrous, thick like horsehairs,
    —Can't I see his dead eye glow,
Bright as 'twere a Barbary corsair's?
    (That is, if he'd let it show!)

V

When he finishes refection,
    Knife and fork he never lays
Cross-wise, to my recollection,
    As do I, in Jesu's praise.
I the Trinity illustrate,
    Drinking watered orange-pulp—
In three sips the Arian frustrate;
    While he drains his at one gulp.

VI

Oh, those melons? If he's able
    We're to have a feast! so nice!
One goes to the Abbot's table,
    All of us get each a slice.
How go on your flowers? None double?
    Not one fruit-sort can you spy?
Strange!—And I, too, at such trouble,
    Keep them close-nipped on the sly!

VII

There's a great text in Galatians,
    Once you trip on it, entails
Twenty-nine distinct damnations,
    One sure, if another fails:

28. **tresses:** hair. 31. **Barbary corsair:** pirate from the northern coast of Africa.
33. **refection:** meal. 39. **Arian:** Arianism was a heresy of the fourth century whose
adherents denied the doctrine of the Trinity. 46. **fruit-sort:** blossom that will develop into
a fruit. 49. **Galatians:** St. Paul's Letter to the Galatians, v. 19 ff., gives a list of the sins
of the flesh.

If I trip him just a-dying,
　　Sure of heaven as sure can be,
Spin him round and send him flying
　　Off to hell, a Manichee?

VIII

Or, my scrofulous French novel
　　On gray paper with blunt type!
Simply glance at it, you grovel
　　Hand and foot in Belial's gripe: 　　　　　　60
If I double down its pages
　　At the woeful sixteenth print,
When he gathers his greengages,
　　Ope a sieve and slip it in't?

IX

Or, there's Satan!—one might venture
　　Pledge one's soul to him, yet leave
Such a flaw in the indenture
　　As he'd miss till, past retrieve,
Blasted lay that rose-acacia
　　We're so proud of! *Hy, Zy, Hine*— 　　　　70
'St, there's Vespers! *Plena gratiâ*
　　Ave, Virgo! Gr-r-r—you swine!

MY LAST DUCHESS

FERRARA

That's my last Duchess painted on the wall,
Looking as if she were alive. I call
That piece a wonder, now: Frà Pandolf's hands
Worked busily a day, and there she stands.

56. **Manichee:** Manicheanism was a third-century heresy according to which Good and Evil were separate and equal powers. 57. **scrofulous:** morally corrupt. 60. **Belial:** a devil. 62. **woeful:** awful, in the sense of lurid; **print:** illustration. 64. **sieve:** basket. 66. **Pledge:** make a deal (with Satan). 67. **indenture:** deed of contract (with Satan). 68. **he'd:** i.e., Satan would. 70. *Hy, Zy, Hine:* meaning doubtful; possibly a curse on Lawrence or the sound of vespers or the vesper bells. 71. *Plena gratiâ:* full of grace. 72. *Ave, Virgo:* Hail, Virgin.

Ferrara: the speaker of the poem is the Duke of Ferrara, who is addressing the agent of his future father-in-law. 3. **Frà Pandolf:** Brother Pandolf, an imaginary painter.

Will't please you sit and look at her? I said
"Frà Pandolf" by design, for never read
Strangers like you that pictured countenance,
The depth and passion of its earnest glance,
But to myself they turned (since none puts by
The curtain I have drawn for you, but I)
And seemed as they would ask me, if they durst,
How such a glance came there; so, not the first
Are you to turn and ask thus. Sir, 'twas not
Her husband's presence only, called that spot
Of joy into the Duchess' cheek: perhaps
Frà Pandolf chanced to say, "Her mantle laps
Over my lady's wrist too much," or "Paint
Must never hope to reproduce the faint
Half-flush that dies along her throat": such stuff
Was courtesy, she thought, and cause enough
For calling up that spot of joy. She had
A heart—how shall I say?—too soon made glad,
Too easily impressed; she liked whate'er
She looked on, and her looks went everywhere.
Sir, 'twas all one! My favor at her breast,
The dropping of the daylight in the West,
The bough of cherries some officious fool
Broke in the orchard for her, the white mule
She rode with round the terrace—all and each
Would draw from her alike the approving speech,
Or blush, at least. She thanked men,—good! but thanked
Somehow—I know not how—as if she ranked
My gift of a nine-hundred-years-old name
With anybody's gift. Who'd stoop to blame
This sort of trifling? Even had you skill
In speech—(which I have not)—to make your will
Quite clear to such an one, and say, "Just this
Or that in you disgusts me; here you miss,
Or there exceed the mark"—and if she let
Herself be lessoned so, nor plainly set
Her wits to yours, forsooth, and made excuse,
—E'en then would be some stooping; and I choose
Never to stoop. Oh sir, she smiled, no doubt,
Whene'er I passed her; but who passed without

11. **durst:** dared. 42. **stooping:** lowering of dignity.

Much the same smile? This grew; I gave commands:
Then all smiles stopped together. There she stands
As if alive. Will't please you rise? We'll meet
The company below, then. I repeat,
The Count your master's known munificence
Is ample warrant that no just pretense 50
Of mine for dowry will be disallowed;
Though his fair daughter's self, as I avowed
At starting, is my object. Nay, we'll go
Together down, sir. Notice Neptune, though,
Taming a sea-horse, thought a rarity,
Which Claus of Innsbruck cast in bronze for me!

THE BISHOP ORDERS HIS TOMB
AT SAINT PRAXED'S CHURCH

ROME, 15—

Vanity, saith the preacher, vanity!
Draw round my bed: is Anselm keeping back?
Nephews—sons mine . . . ah God, I know not! Well—
She, men would have to be your mother once,
Old Gandolf envied me, so fair she was!
What's done is done, and she is dead beside,
Dead long ago, and I am Bishop since,
And as she died so must we die ourselves,
And thence ye may perceive the world's a dream.
Life, how and what is it? As here I lie 10
In this state-chamber, dying by degrees,
Hours and long hours in the dead night, I ask,
"Do I live, am I dead?" Peace, peace seems all.
Saint Praxed's ever was the church for peace;
And so, about this tomb of mine. I fought
With tooth and nail to save my niche, ye know:
—Old Gandolf cozened me, despite my care;

49. **munificence:** generosity. 56. **Claus of Innsbruck:** fictitious sculptor.

Title. St. Praxed: a virgin saint. 1. **Vanity . . . vanity:** reference to the words of the Preacher, son of King David, in Ecclesiastes i.2. 2. and 3. **Anselm, Nephews—sons:** Anselm is one of the illegitimate sons (cf. lines 36, 45, 53, 64, etc.) euphemistically referred to here as nephews. 5. **Gandolf:** imaginary predecessor of the imaginary bishop. 16. **niche:** a recess of the tomb. 17. **cozened:** cheated.

Shrewd was that snatch from out the corner south
He graced his carrion with, God curse the same!
20   Yet still my niche is not so cramped but thence
One sees the pulpit o' the epistle-side,
And somewhat of the choir, those silent seats,
And up into the aery dome where live
The angels, and a sunbeam's sure to lurk:
And I shall fill my slab of basalt there,
And 'neath my tabernacle take my rest,
With those nine columns round me, two and two,
The odd one at my feet where Anselm stands:
Peach-blossom marble all, the rare, the ripe
30   As fresh-poured red wine of a mighty pulse.
—Old Gandolf with his paltry onion-stone,
Put me where I may look at him! True peach,
Rosy and flawless: how I earned the prize!
Draw close: that conflagration of my church
—What then? So much was saved if aught were missed!
My sons, ye would not be my death? Go dig
The white-grape vineyard where the oil-press stood,
Drop water gently till the surface sink,
And if ye find . . . ah God, I know not, I! . . .
40   Bedded in store of rotten fig-leaves soft,
And corded up in a tight olive-frail,
Some lump, ah God, of *lapis lazuli*,
Big as a Jew's head cut off at the nape,
Blue as a vein o'er the Madonna's breast . . .
Sons, all have I bequeathed you, villas, all,
That brave Frascati villa with its bath,
So, let the blue lump poise between my knees,
Like God the Father's globe on both his hands
Ye worship in the Jesu Church so gay,
50   For Gandolf shall not choose but see and burst!
Swift as a weaver's shuttle fleet our years:
Man goeth to the grave, and where is he?

21. epistle-side: the south side of the church, from which the epistles are read.
22. choir: part of the church where the services are sung. 25. I: the sculptured effigy of
himself; basalt: dark-colored rock. 26. tabernacle: stone canopy over the tomb. 31. onion-
stone: cheap marble. 35. if . . . missed: what if something were missed. 41. olive-frail:
olive basket. 42. *lapis lazuli*: semi-precious blue stone. 46. Frascati: fashionable suburb
of Rome. 49. Jesu Church: name of a church in Rome. 51. Swift . . . years: allusion
to Job vii.6.

Did I say basalt for my slab, sons? Black—
'Twas ever antique-black I meant! How else
Shall ye contrast my frieze to come beneath?
The bas-relief in bronze ye promised me,
Those Pans and Nymphs ye wot of, and perchance
Some tripod, thyrsus, with a vase or so,
The Savior at his sermon on the mount,
Saint Praxed in a glory, and one Pan   60
Ready to twitch the Nymph's last garment off,
And Moses with the tables . . . but I know
Ye mark me not! What do they whisper thee,
Child of my bowels, Anselm? Ah, ye hope
To revel down my villas while I gasp
Bricked o'er with beggar's moldy travertine
Which Gandolf from his tomb-top chuckles at!
Nay, boys, ye love me—all of jasper, then!
'Tis jasper ye stand pledged to, lest I grieve
My bath must needs be left behind, alas!   70
One block, pure green as a pistachio-nut,
There's plenty jasper somewhere in the world—
And have I not Saint Praxed's ear to pray
Horses for ye, and brown Greek manuscripts,
And mistresses with great smooth marbly limbs?
—That's if ye carve my epitaph aright,
Choice Latin, picked phrase, Tully's every word,
No gaudy ware like Gandolf's second line—
Tully, my masters? Ulpian serves his need!
And then how I shall lie through centuries,   80
And hear the blessed mutter of the mass,
And see God made and eaten all day long,
And feel the steady candle-flame, and taste
Good strong thick stupefying incense-smoke!
For as I lie here, hours of the dead night,
Dying in state and by such slow degrees,
I fold my arms as if they clasped a crook,

55. frieze: sculptured border. **56. bas-relief:** sculpture in which the figures stand out only a little from the background. **57. Pans and Nymphs:** minor pagan gods and goddesses of nature; **wot:** know. **58. tripod:** stool associated with the pagan god Apollo; **thyrsus:** staff of Bacchus, god of wine. **60. glory:** halo. **62. tables:** tablets on which the Commandments were inscribed. **65. revel down:** squander away to pay for their revelry. **66. travertine:** light-colored limestone. **68. jasper:** green ornamental stone. **77. Tully:** Cicero, model for fine Latin prose. **79. Ulpian:** writer of inferior Latin prose. **82. made . . . eaten:** i.e., the mass. **87. crook:** symbolic bishop's staff.

And stretch my feet forth straight as stone can point,
And let the bedclothes, for a mortcloth, drop
90   Into great laps and folds of sculptor's-work:
And as yon tapers dwindle, and strange thoughts
Grow, with a certain humming in my ears,
About the life before I lived this life,
And this life too, popes, cardinals and priests,
Saint Praxed at his sermon on the mount,
Your tall pale mother with her talking eyes,
And new-found agate urns as fresh as day,
And marble's language, Latin pure, discreet,
—Aha, ELUCESCEBAT quoth our friend?
100   No Tully, said I, Ulpian at the best!
Evil and brief hath been my pilgrimage.
All *lapis*, all, sons! Else I give the Pope
My villas! Will ye ever eat my heart?
Ever your eyes were as a lizard's quick,
They glitter like your mother's for my soul,
Or ye would heighten my impoverished frieze,
Piece out its starved design, and fill my vase
With grapes, and add a vizor and a term,
And to the tripod ye would tie a lynx
110   That in his struggle throws the thyrsus down,
To comfort me on my entablature
Whereon I am to lie till I must ask,
"Do I live, am I dead?" There, leave me, there!
For ye have stabbed me with ingratitude
To death—ye wish it—God, ye wish it! Stone—
Gritstone, a-crumble! Clammy squares which sweat
As if the corpse they keep were oozing through—
And no more *lapis* to delight the world!
Well go! I bless ye. Fewer tapers there,
120   But in a row: and, going, turn your backs
—Ay, like departing altar-ministrants,
And leave me in my church, the church for peace,
That I may watch at leisure if he leers—
Old Gandolf, at me, from his onion-stone,
As still he envied me, so fair she was!

89. mortcloth: cloth draped over dead body. **99. ELUCESCEBAT:** Ulpian's spelling for the word meaning "he was illustrious," which in Ciceronian Latin would have been "elucebat." **108. vizor:** mask; **term:** bust of the Roman God Terminus. **109. lynx:** animal associated with Bacchus. **111. entablature:** dais. **116. Gritstone:** sandstone.

MEETING AT NIGHT

The gray sea and the long black land;
And the yellow half-moon large and low;
And the startled little waves that leap
In fiery ringlets from their sleep,
As I gain the cove with pushing prow,
And quench its speed i' the slushy sand.

Then a mile of warm sea-scented beach;
Three fields to cross till a farm appears;
A tap at the pane, the quick sharp scratch
And blue spurt of a lighted match,   10
And a voice less loud, through its joys and fears,
Than the two hearts beating each to each!

PARTING AT MORNING

Round the cape of a sudden came the sea,
And the sun looked over the mountain's rim:
And straight was a path of gold for him,
And the need of a world of men for me.

LOVE AMONG THE RUINS

I

Where the quiet-colored end of evening smiles
        Miles and miles
On the solitary pastures where our sheep
        Half-asleep
Tinkle homeward through the twilight, stray or stop
        As they crop—
Was the site once of a city great and gay
        (So they say),
Of our country's very capital, its prince
        Ages since   10
Held his court in, gathered councils, wielding far
        Peace or war.

3. him: sun.

II

Now,—the country does not even boast a tree,
    As you see,
To distinguish slopes of verdure, certain rills
    From the hills
Intersect and give a name to (else they run
    Into one),
Where the domed and daring palace shot its spires
20   Up like fires
O'er the hundred-gated circuit of a wall
    Bounding all,
Made of marble, men might march on nor be pressed,
    Twelve abreast.

III

And such plenty and perfection, see, of grass
    Never was!
Such a carpet as, this summer-time, o'erspreads
    And embeds
Every vestige of the city, guessed alone,
30   Stock or stone—
Where a multitude of men breathed joy and woe
    Long ago;
Lust of glory pricked their hearts up, dread of shame
    Struck them tame;
And that glory and that shame alike, the gold
    Bought and sold.

IV

Now,—the single little turret that remains
    On the plains,
By the caper overrooted, by the gourd
40   Overscored,
While the patching houseleek's head of blossom winks
    Through the chinks—
Marks the basement whence a tower in ancient time
    Sprang sublime,
And a burning ring, all round, the chariots traced
    As they raced,
And the monarch and his minions and his dames
    Viewed the games.

    15. rills: streams. **39. caper:** prickly bush. **41. houseleek:** small cactus-like plant,
commonly found growing on roofs. **47. minions:** favorites.

V

And I know, while thus the quiet-colored eve
    Smiles to leave   50
To their folding, all our many-tinkling fleece
    In such peace,
And the slopes and rills in undistinguished gray
    Melt away—
That a girl with eager eyes and yellow hair
    Waits me there
In the turret whence the charioteers caught soul
    For the goal,
When the king looked, where she looks now, breathless, dumb
    Till I come.   60

VI

But he looked upon the city, every side,
    Far and wide,
All the mountains topped with temples, all the glades'
    Colonnades.
All the causeys, bridges, aqueducts,—and then,
    All the men!
When I do come, she will speak not, she will stand,
    Either hand
On my shoulder, give her eyes the first embrace
    Of my face,   70
Ere we rush, ere we extinguish sight and speech
    Each on each.

VII

In one year they sent a million fighters forth
    South and north,
And they built their gods a brazen pillar high
    As the sky,
Yet reserved a thousand chariots in full force—
    Gold, of course.
Oh heart! oh blood that freezes, blood that burns!
    Earth's returns   80
For whole centuries of folly, noise and sin!
    Shut them in,
With their triumphs and their glories and the rest!
    Love is best.

65. **causeys:** causeways, raised roads.

ROBERT BROWNING

A TOCCATA OF GALUPPI'S

I

Oh, Galuppi, Baldassaro, this is very sad to find!
I can hardly misconceive you; it would prove me deaf and blind;
But although I take your meaning, 'tis with such a heavy mind!

II

Here you come with your old music, and here's all the good it brings.
What, they lived once thus at Venice where the merchants were the kings,
Where St. Mark's is, where the Doges used to wed the sea with rings?

III

Ay, because the sea's the street there; and 'tis arched by . . . what you call
. . . Shylock's bridge with houses on it, where they kept the carnival:
I was never out of England—it's as if I saw it all!

IV

10 Did young people take their pleasure when the sea was warm in May?
Balls and masks begun at midnight, burning ever to mid-day
When they made up fresh adventures for the morrow, do you say?

V

Was a lady such a lady, cheeks so round and lips so red,—
On her neck the small face buoyant, like a bell-flower on its bed,
O'er the breast's superb abundance where a man might base his head?

VI

Well, and it was graceful of them—they'd break talk off and afford
—She, to bite her mask's black velvet—he, to finger on his sword,
While you sat and played toccatas, stately at the clavichord?

Title. Toccata: a "touch piece," a musical composition full of chords and running passages, often designed for virtuoso performance; Galuppi: Baldassaro Galuppi, an eighteenth-century Venetian composer and performer. 6. St. Mark's: cathedral in Venice; Doges . . . rings: each year the chief magistrate, the Doge, threw a ring into the Adriatic to symbolize the marriage of Venice, which relied on sea commerce for its wealth, with the sea. 8. Shylock's bridge: the Rialto, one of the bridges over the Grand Canal, referred to in The Merchant of Venice. 11. masks: masquerades. 16. afford: make room for (Galuppi's music). 18. clavichord: a keyboard instrument.

VII

What? Those lesser thirds so plaintive, sixths diminished, sigh on sigh,
Told them something? Those suspensions, those solutions—"Must we die?"   20
Those commiserating sevenths—"Life might last! we can but try!"

VIII

"Were you happy?"—"Yes."—"And are you still as happy?"—"Yes. And you?"
—"Then, more kisses!"—"Did *I* stop them, when a million seemed so few?"
Hark! the dominant's persistence, till it must be answered to!

IX

So an octave struck the answer. Oh, they praised you, I dare say!
"Brave Galuppi! that was music! good alike at grave and gay!
I can always leave off talking, when I hear a master play."

X

Then they left you for their pleasure: till in due time, one by one,
Some with lives that came to nothing, some with deeds as well undone,
Death stepped tacitly and took them where they never see the sun.   30

XI

But when I sit down to reason, think to take my stand nor swerve,
While I triumph o'er a secret wrung from nature's close reserve,
In you come with your cold music till I creep through every nerve.

XII

Yes, you like a ghostly cricket, creaking where a house was burned:
"Dust and ashes, dead and done with, Venice spent what Venice earned.
The soul, doubtless, is immortal—where a soul can be discerned.

XIII

"Yours for instance: you know physics, something of geology,
Mathematics are your pastime; souls shall rise in their degree;
Butterflies may dread extinction,—you'll not die, it cannot be!

XIV

"As for Venice and her people, merely born to bloom and drop,   40
Here on earth they bore their fruitage, mirth and folly were the crop:
What of soul was left, I wonder, when the kissing had to stop?

19–25. thirds, sixths, diminished, suspensions, sevenths, dominant, octave: technical musical terms, whose emotional significance is made explicit by the context.

XV

"Dust and ashes!" So you creak it, and I want the heart to scold.
Dear dead women, with such hair, too—what's become of all the gold
Used to hang and brush their bosoms? I feel chilly and grown old.

A GRAMMARIAN'S FUNERAL

SHORTLY AFTER THE REVIVAL OF LEARNING IN EUROPE

Let us begin and carry up this corpse,
    Singing together.
Leave we the common crofts, the vulgar thorpes
    Each in its tether
Sleeping safe on the bosom of the plain,
    Cared-for till cock-crow:
Look out if yonder be not day again
    Rimming the rock-row!
That's the appropriate country; there, man's thought,
10   Rarer, intenser,
Self-gathered for an outbreak, as it ought,
    Chafes in the censer.
Leave we the unlettered plain its herd and crop;
    Seek we sepulture
On a tall mountain, citied to the top,
    Crowded with culture!
All the peaks soar, but one the rest excels;
    Clouds overcome it;
No! yonder sparkle is the citadel's
20   Circling its summit.
Thither our path lies; wind we up the heights:
    Wait ye the warning?
Our low life was the level's and the night's;
    He's for the morning.
Step to a tune, square chests, erect each head,
    'Ware the beholders!
This is our master, famous, calm, and dead,
    Borne on our shoulders.

Title: The grammarian of this poem is an imaginary dead scholar who spent his life investigating the precise effects of certain Greek particles (words like articles, prepositions, conjunctions); see lines 129–131. 3. crofts: small enclosed fields; thorpes: villages. 12. i.e., is irritated by its confinement. 14. sepulture: burial place. 22. i.e., to begin the funeral procession.

Sleep, crop and herd! sleep, darkling thorpe and croft,
    Safe from the weather!   30
He, whom we convoy to his grave aloft,
    Singing together,
He was a man born with thy face and throat,
    Lyric Apollo!
Long he lived nameless: how should spring take note
    Winter would follow?
Till Io, the little touch, and youth was gone!
    Cramped and diminished,
Moaned he, "New measures, other feet anon!
    My dance is finished?"   40
No, that's the world's way: (keep the mountainside,
    Make for the city!)
He knew the signal, and stepped on with pride
    Over men's pity;
Left play for work, and grappled with the world
    Bent on escaping:
"What's in the scroll," quoth he, "thou keepest furled?
    Show me their shaping,
Theirs who most studied man, the bard and sage,—
    Give!"—So he gowned him,   50
Straight got by heart that book to its last page:
    Learnèd, we found him.
Yea, but we found him bald too, eyes like lead,
    Accents uncertain:
"Time to taste life," another would have said,
    "Up with the curtain!"
This man said rather, "Actual life comes next?
    Patience a moment!
Grant I have mastered learning's crabbed text,
    Still there's the comment.   60
Let me know all! Prate not of most or least,
    Painful or easy!
Even to the crumbs I'd fain eat up the feast,
    Ay, nor feel queasy."
Oh, such a life as he resolved to live,
    When he had learned it,
When he had gathered all books had to give!
    Sooner, he spurned it.

34. Apollo: Greek god of music and poetry. 39. measures: rhythms. 50. gowned him: put on his robes of learning. 59. crabbed: obscure or difficult. 60. comment: commentary on a text. 61. Prate: babble or prattle. 63. fain: gladly. 68. Sooner: any earlier (than his having learned everything); it: the *life* of line 65.

Image the whole, then execute the parts—
70   Fancy the fabric
Quite, ere you build, ere steel strike fire from quartz,
        Ere mortar dab brick!

(Here's the town gate reached: there's the marketplace
        Gaping before us.)
Yea, this in him was the peculiar grace
        (Hearten our chorus!)
That before living he'd learn how to live—
        No end to learning:
Earn the means first—God surely will contrive
80   Use for our earning.
Others mistrust and say, "But time escapes:
        Live now or never!"
He said, "What's time? Leave Now for dogs and apes!
        Man has Forever."
Back to his book then: deeper drooped his head:
        Calculus racked him:
Leaden before, his eyes grew dross of lead:
        Tussis attacked him.
"Now, master, take a little rest!"—not he!
90   (Caution redoubled,
Step two abreast, the way winds narrowly!)
        Not a whit troubled,
Back to his studies, fresher than at first,
        Fierce as a dragon
He (soul-hydroptic with a sacred thirst)
        Sucked at the flagon.
Oh, if we draw a circle premature,
        Heedless of far gain,
Greedy for quick returns of profit, sure
100   Bad is our bargain!
Was it not great? did not he throw on God
        (He loves the burthen)
God's task to make the heavenly period
        Perfect the earthen?
Did not he magnify the mind, show clear
        Just what it all meant?
He would not discount life, as fools do here,

---

70. Fancy: see in the mind's eye; fabric: structure. 71. Quite: entirely, completely. 86. *Calculus*: disease of the bladder. 87. dross: the scum from molten metals. 88. *Tussis*: bronchitis. 95. hydroptic: thirsty. 107. discount: sell cheaply, at a discount.

Paid by instalment.
He ventured neck or nothing—heaven's success
    Found, or earth's failure: 110
"Wilt thou trust death or not?" He answered "Yes!
    Hence with life's pale lure!"
That low man seeks a little thing to do,
    Sees it and does it:
This high man, with a great thing to pursue,
    Dies ere he knows it.
That low man goes on adding one to one,
    His hundred's soon hit:
This high man, aiming at a million,
    Misses an unit.   120
That, has the world here—should he need the next,
    Let the world mind him!
This, throws himself on God, and unperplexed
    Seeking shall find Him.
So, with the throttling hands of death at strife,
    Ground he at grammar;
Still, through the rattle, parts of speech were rife:
    While he could stammer
He settled *Hoti's* business—let it be!—
    Properly based *Oun*—   130
Gave us the doctrine of the enclitic *De,*
    Dead from the waist down.
Well, here's the platform, here's the proper place:
    Hail to your purlieus,
All ye highfliers of the feathered race,
    Swallows and curlews!
Here's the top peak; the multitude below
    Live, for they can, there:
This man decided not to Live but Know—
    Bury this man there?   140
Here—here's his place, where meteors shoot, clouds form,
    Lightnings are loosened,
Stars come and go! Let joy break with the storm,
    Peace let the dew send!
Lofty designs must close in like effects:
    Loftily lying,
Leave him—still loftier than the world suspects,
    Living and dying.

127. **rattle:** death rattle. 129–131: *Hoti* and *De* are Greek particles, *Oun* an adverb; **enclitic:** a word attached to a preceding word, as *not* in *cannot.* 134. **purlieus:** haunts or environs.

ANDREA DEL SARTO

(CALLED "THE FAULTLESS PAINTER")

But do not let us quarrel any more,
No, my Lucrezia; bear with me for once:
Sit down and all shall happen as you wish.
You turn your face, but does it bring your heart?
I'll work then for your friend's friend, never fear,
Treat his own subject after his own way,
Fix his own time, accept too his own price,
And shut the money into this small hand
When next it takes mine. Will it? tenderly?
10   Oh, I'll content him,—but tomorrow, Love!
I often am much wearier than you think,
This evening more than usual, and it seems
As if—forgive now—should you let me sit
Here by the window with your hand in mine
And look a half-hour forth on Fiesole,
Both of one mind, as married people use,
Quietly, quietly the evening through,
I might get up tomorrow to my work
Cheerful and fresh as ever. Let us try.
20   Tomorrow, how you shall be glad for this!
Your soft hand is a woman of itself,
And mine the man's bared breast she curls inside.
Don't count the time lost, neither; you must serve
For each of the five pictures we require:
It saves a model. So! keep looking so,
My serpentining beauty, rounds on rounds!
—How could you ever prick those perfect ears,
Even to put the pearl there! oh, so sweet—
My face, my moon, my everybody's moon,
30   Which everybody looks on and calls his,
And, I suppose, is looked on by in turn,
While she looks—no one's: very dear, no less.
You smile? why, there's my picture ready made,
There's what we painters call our harmony!
A common grayness silvers everything,—

Title: Andrea del Sarto (1486–1530), one of the great Florentine Renaissance painters, though not so great as Rafael, Michelangelo, and Leonardo da Vinci, all mentioned in the poem. 2. Lucrezia: Lucrezia del Fede, Andrea's wife. 15. Fiesole: a village to the northeast of Florence. 16. use: are accustomed to do.

All in a twilight, you and I alike
—You, at the point of your first pride in me
(That's gone you know),—but I, at every point;
My youth, my hope, my art, being all toned down
To yonder sober pleasant Fiesole.   40
There's the bell clinking from the chapel-top;
That length of convent wall across the way
Holds the trees safer, huddled more inside;
The last monk leaves the garden; days decrease,
And autumn grows, autumn in everything.
Eh? the whole seems to fall into a shape
As if I saw alike my work and self
And all that I was born to be and do,
A twilight-piece. Love, we are in God's hand.
How strange now looks the life He makes us lead: 50
So free we seem, so fettered fast we are!
I feel He laid the fetter: let 'it lie!
This chamber for example—turn your head—
All that's behind us! You don't understand
Nor care to understand about my art,
But you can hear at least when people speak:
And that cartoon, the second from the door
—It is the thing, Love! so such thing should be—
Behold Madonna!—I am bold to say.
I can do with my pencil what I know,   60
What I see, what at bottom of my heart
I wish for, if I ever wish so deep—
Do easily, too—when I say perfectly,
I do not boast, perhaps: yourself are judge,
Who listened to the Legate's talk last week,
And just as much they used to say in France.
At any rate 'tis easy, all of it!
No sketches first, no studies, that's long past:
I do what many dream of all their lives,
—Dream? strive to do, and agonize to do,   70

---

57. **cartoon:** drawing for a painting, tapestry, mosaic, etc., of the same size as the work to be executed. 65. **Legate:** a representative of the Pope. 66. Andrea had gone to Fontainebleu, in France (line 150), some seven years earlier, at the invitation of King Francis I (line 149), where he painted pictures for the King. After a year, Lucrezia, who had remained in Florence, asked him to come home (lines 166, 172). He received the King's permission to go, upon promising to return to France, and was given money to purchase works of art for Francis; but Lucrezia persuaded Andrea to break his promise, and he immorally used the King's money to adorn his own house (lines 212–218).

And fail in doing. I could count twenty such
On twice your fingers, and not leave this town,
Who strive—you don't know how the others strive
To paint a little thing like that you smeared
Carelessly passing with your robes afloat, —
Yet do much less, so much less, Someone says,
(I know his name, no matter)—so much less!
Well, less is more, Lucrezia: I am judged.
There burns a truer light of God in them,
80 In their vexed, beating, stuffed, and stopped-up brain,
Heart, or whate'er else, than goes on to prompt
This low-pulsed, forthright craftsman's hand of mine.
Their works drop groundward, but themselves, I know,
Reach many a time a heaven that's shut to me,
Enter and take their place there sure enough,
Though they come back and cannot tell the world.
My works are nearer heaven, but I sit here.
The sudden blood of these men! at a word—
Praise them, it boils, or blame them, it boils too.
90 I, painting from myself and to myself,
Know what I do, am unmoved by men's blame
Or their praise either. Somebody remarks
Morello's outline there is wrongly traced,
His hue mistaken; what of that? or else,
Rightly traced and well ordered; what of that?
Speak as they please, what does the mountain care?
Ah, but a man's reach should exceed his grasp,
Or what's a heaven for? All is silver-gray,
Placid and perfect with my art: the worse!
100 I know both what I want and what might gain,
And yet how profitless to know, to sigh
"Had I been two, another and myself,
Our head would have o'erlooked the world!" No doubt.
Yonder's a work now, of that famous youth
The Urbinate who died five years ago.
('Tis copied, George Vasari sent it me.)
Well, I can fancy how he did it all,
Pouring his soul, with kings and popes to see,

---

93. **Morello:** the highest peak of the Apennines in the area of Florence. 105. **the Urbinate:** the painter Rafael (1483–1520), who was a native of Urbino, a city some sixty miles east of Florence. 106. **George Vasari:** a pupil of Andrea's, famous as the author of *Lives of the Painters* (1550), a book from which Browning took his data for this poem.

Reaching, that heaven might so replenish him,
Above and through his art—for it gives way;   110
That arm is wrongly put—and there again—
A fault to pardon in the drawing's lines,
Its body, so to speak: its soul is right,
He means right—that, a child may understand.
Still, what an arm! and I could alter it:
But all the play, the insight and the stretch—
Out of me, out of me! And wherefore out?
Had you enjoined them on me, given me soul,
We might have risen to Rafael, I and you!
Nay, Love, you did give all I asked, I think—   120
More than I merit, yes, by many times.
But had you—oh, with the same perfect brow,
And perfect eyes, and more than perfect mouth,
And the low voice my soul hears, as a bird
The fowler's pipe, and follows to the snare—
Had you, with these the same, but brought a mind!
Some women do so. Had the mouth there urged
"God and the glory! never care for gain.
The present by the future, what is that?
Live for fame, side by side with Agnolo!   130
Rafael is waiting: up to God, all three!"
I might have done it for you. So it seems:
Perhaps not. All is as God overrules.
Beside, incentives come from the soul's self;
The rest avail not. Why do I need you?
What wife had Rafael, or has Agnolo?
In this world, who can do a thing, will not;
And who would do it, cannot, I perceive:
Yet the will's somewhat—somewhat, too, the power—
And thus we half-men struggle. At the end,   140
God, I conclude, compensates, punishes.
'Tis safer for me, if the award be strict,
That I am something underrated here,
Poor this long while, despised, to speak the truth.
I dared not, do you know, leave home all day,
For fear of chancing on the Paris lords.
The best is when they pass and look aside;

118. enjoined: imposed, as a penance. 125. fowler's pipe: bird-catcher's imitation of a bird call to lure the bird to the net or trap. 130. Agnolo: Michelangelo (1475–1564). 146. Paris lords: see note to line 66.

But they speak sometimes; I must bear it all.
Well may they speak! That Francis, that first time,
150   And that long festal year at Fontainebleau!
I surely then could sometimes leave the ground,
Put on the glory, Rafael's daily wear,
In that humane great monarch's golden look,—
One finger in his beard or twisted curl
Over his mouth's good mark that made the smile,
One arm about my shoulder, round my neck,
The jingle of his gold chain in my ear,
I painting proudly with his breath on me,
All his court round him, seeing with his eyes,
160   Such frank French eyes, and such a fire of souls
Profuse, my hand kept plying by those hearts,—
And, best of all, this, this, this face beyond,
This in the background, waiting on my work,
To crown the issue with a last reward!
A good time, was it not, my kingly days?
And had you not grown restless . . . but I know—
'Tis done and past; 'twas right, my instinct said;
Too live the life grew, golden and not gray,
And I'm the weak-eyed bat no sun should tempt
170   Out of the grange whose four walls make his world.
How could it end in any other way?
You called me, and I came home to your heart.
The triumph was—to reach and stay there; since
I reached it ere the triumph, what is lost?
Let my hands frame your face in your hair's gold,
You beautiful Lucrezia that are mine!
"Rafael did this, Andrea painted that;
The Roman's is the better when you pray,
But still the other's Virgin was his wife"—
180   Men will excuse me. I am glad to judge
Both pictures in your presence; clearer grows
My better fortune, I resolve to think.
For, do you know, Lucrezia, as God lives,
Said one day Agnolo, his very self,
To Rafael . . . I have known it all these years . . .
(When the young man was flaming out his thoughts
Upon a palace wall for Rome to see,
Too lifted up in heart because of it)

149. that Francis: see note to line 66. 178. the Roman's: Rafael's.

"Friend, there's a certain sorry little scrub
Goes up and down our Florence, none cares how,   190
Who, were he set to plan and execute
As you are, pricked on by your popes and kings,
Would bring the sweat into that brow of yours!"
To Rafael's!—And indeed the arm is wrong.
I hardly dare . . . yet, only you to see,
Give the chalk here—quick, thus the line should go!
Ay, but the soul! he's Rafael! rub it out!
Still, all I care for, if he spoke the truth,
(What he? why, who but Michel Agnolo?
Do you forget already words like those?)   200
If really there was such a chance, so lost,—
Is, whether you're—not grateful—but more pleased.
Well, let me think so. And you smile indeed!
This hour has been an hour! Another smile?
If you would sit thus by me every night
I should work better, do you comprehend?
I mean that I should earn more, give you more.
See, it is settled dusk now: there's a star,
Morello's gone, the watch-lights show the wall,
The cue-owls speak the name we call them by.   210
Come from the window, Love,—come in, at last,
Inside the melancholy little house
We built to be so gay with. God is just.
King Francis may forgive me. Oft at nights,
When I look up from painting, eyes tired out,
The walls become illumined, brick from brick
Distinct, instead of mortar, fierce bright gold,
That gold of his I did cement them with!
Let us but love each other. Must you go?
That Cousin here again? he waits outside?   220
Must see you—you, and not with me? Those loans?
More gaming debts to pay? you smiled for that?
Well, let smiles buy me! have you more to spend?
While hand and eye and something of a heart
Are left me, work's my ware, and what's it worth?
I'll pay my fancy. Only let me sit
The gray remainder of the evening out,
Idle, you call it, and muse perfectly
How I could paint, were I but back in France,

218. see note to line 66. 220. that Cousin: a euphemism for Lucrezia's lover.

230   One picture, just one more—the Virgin's face,
        Not yours this time! I want you at my side
        To hear them—that is, Michel Agnolo—
        Judge all I do and tell you of its worth.
        Will you? Tomorrow satisfy your friend.
        I take the subjects for his corridor,
        Finish the portrait out of hand—there, there,
        And throw him in another thing or two
        If he demurs; the whole should prove enough
        To pay for this same Cousin's freak. Beside,
240   What's better, and what's all I care about,
        Get you the thirteen scudi for the ruff!
        Love, does that please you? Ah, but what does he,
        The Cousin? what does he to please you more?
              I am grown peaceful as old age tonight.
        I regret little, I would change still less.
        Since there my past life lies, why alter it?
        The very wrong to Francis!—it is true
        I took his coin, was tempted and complied,
        And built this house and sinned, and all is said.
250   My father and my mother died of want.
        Well, had I riches of my own? you see
        How one gets rich! Let each one bear his lot.
        They were born poor, lived poor, and poor they died:
        And I have labored somewhat in my time
        And not been paid profusely. Some good son
        Paint my two hundred pictures—let him try!
        No doubt, there's something strikes a balance. Yes,
        You loved me quite enough, it seems tonight.
        This must suffice me here. What would one have?
260   In heaven, perhaps, new chances, one more chance—
        Four great walls in the New Jerusalem,
        Meted on each side by the angel's reed,
        For Leonard, Rafael, Agnolo and me
        To cover—the three first without a wife,
        While I have mine! So—still they overcome
        Because there's still Lucrezia,—as I choose.

        Again the Cousin's whistle! Go, my Love.

---

239. freak: whim or fancy. 241. scudi: Italian coins, so called from the image of
a shield (*scudo*) on them. 261. Cf. Revelations xxi.15–17. 262. Meted: measured; reed:
used as a measuring rod. 263. Leonard: Leonardo da Vinci (1452–1519).

PORPHYRIA'S LOVER

The rain set early in tonight,
　　The sullen wind was soon awake;
It tore the elm-tops down for spite,
　　And did its worst to vex the lake:
　　I listened with heart fit to break.
When glided in Porphyria; straight
　　She shut the cold out and the storm,
And kneeled and made the cheerless grate
　　Blaze up, and all the cottage warm;
　　Which done, she rose, and from her form   10
Withdrew the dripping cloak and shawl,
　　And laid her soiled gloves by, untied
Her hat and let the damp hair fall,
　　And, last, she sat down by my side
　　And called me. When no voice replied,
She put my arm about her waist,
　　And made her smooth white shoulder bare,
And all her yellow hair displaced,
　　And, stooping, made my cheek lie there,
　　And spread, o'er all, her yellow hair,   20
Murmuring how she loved me—she,
　　Too weak, for all her heart's endeavor,
To set its struggling passion free
　　From pride, and vainer ties dissever,
　　And give herself to me, forever.
But passion sometimes would prevail,
　　Nor could tonight's gay feast restrain
A sudden thought of one so pale
　　For love of her, and all in vain:
　　So she was come through wind and rain.   30
Be sure I looked up at her eyes,
　　Happy and proud: at last I knew
Porphyria worshipped me. Surprise
　　Made my heart swell; and still it grew,
　　While I debated what to do.
That moment she was mine, mine, fair,
　　Perfectly pure and good: I found
A thing to do, and all her hair
　　In one long yellow string I wound
　　Three times her little throat around,   40

And strangled her. No pain felt she;
    I am quite sure she felt no pain.
As a shut bud that holds a bee,
    I warily oped her lids: again
    Laughed the blue eyes without a stain.
And I untightened next the tress
    About her neck: her cheek once more
Blushed bright beneath my burning kiss.
    I propped her head up as before,
50   Only this time my shoulder bore
Her head, which droops upon it still:
    The smiling, rosy, little head,
So glad it has its utmost will,
    That all it scorned at once is fled,
    And I, its love, am gained instead!
Porphyria's love: she guessed not how
    Her darling one wish would be heard;
And thus we sit together now,
    And all night long we have not stirred,
60   And yet God has not said a word!

WALT WHITMAN (1819–1892)

WHEN LILACS LAST IN THE DOORYARD BLOOMED

I

When lilacs last in the dooryard bloomed,
And the great star early drooped in the western sky in the night,
I mourned, and yet shall mourn with ever-returning spring.

Ever-returning spring, trinity sure to me you bring,
Lilac blooming perennial and drooping star in the west,
And thought of him I love.

6. **him:** President Lincoln, assassinated April, 1865.

II

O powerful western fallen star!
O shades of night—O moody, tearful night!
O great star disappeared—O the black murk that hides the star!
O cruel hands that hold me powerless—O helpless soul of me!   10
O harsh surrounding cloud that will not free my soul.

III

In the dooryard fronting an old farm-house near the white-washed
    palings,
Stands the lilac-bush tall-growing with heart-shaped leaves of rich
    green,
With many a pointed blossom rising delicate, with the perfume
    strong I love,
With every leaf a miracle—and from this bush in the dooryard,
With delicate-colored blossoms and heart-shaped leaves of rich
    green,
A sprig with its flower I break.

IV

In the swamp in secluded recesses,
A shy and hidden bird is warbling a song.

Solitary the thrush,   20
The hermit withdrawn to himself, avoiding the settlements,
Sings by himself a song.

Song of the bleeding throat,
Death's outlet song of life (for well, dear brother, I know,
If thou wast not granted to sing thou would'st surely die).

V

Over the breast of the spring, the land, amid cities,
Amid lanes and through old woods, where lately the violets peeped
    from the ground, spotting the gray debris,
Amid the grass in the fields each side of the lanes, passing the
    endless grass,
Passing the yellow-speared wheat, every grain from its shroud in
    the dark-brown fields uprisen,
Passing the apple-tree blows of white and pink in the orchards,   30
Carrying a corpse to where it shall rest in the grave,
Night and day journeys a coffin.

VI

Coffin that passes through lanes and streets,
Through day and night with the great cloud darkening the land,
With the pomp of the inlooped flags with the cities draped in
    black,
With the show of the States themselves as of crepe-veiled women
    standing,
With processions long and winding and the flambeaus of the night,
With the countless torches lit, with the silent sea of faces and the
    unbared heads,
With the waiting depot, the arriving coffin, and the somber faces,
40   With dirges through the night, with the thousand voices rising
    strong and solemn,
With all the mournful voices of the dirges poured around the
    coffin,
The dim-lit churches and the shuddering organs—where amid these
    you journey,
With the tolling tolling bells' perpetual clang,
Here, coffin that slowly passes,
I give you my sprig of lilac.

VII

(Nor for you, for one alone,
Blossoms and branches green to coffins all I bring,
For fresh as the morning, thus would I chant a song for you O
    sane and sacred death.

All over bouquets of roses,
50   O death, I cover you over with roses and early lilies,
But mostly and now the lilac that blooms the first,
Copious I break, I break the sprigs from the bushes,
With loaded arms I come, pouring for you,
For you and the coffins all of you O death.)

VIII

O western orb sailing the heaven,
Now I know what you must have meant as a month since I walked,
As I walked in silence the transparent shadowy night,
As I saw you had something to tell as you bent to me night after
    night,
As you drooped from the sky low down as if to my side (while
    the other stars all looked on),

37. flambeaus: torches.

As we wandered together the solemn night (for something I know   60
    not what kept me from sleep),
As the night advanced, and I saw on the rim of the west how full
    you were of woe,
As I stood on the rising ground in the breeze in the cool transparent
    night,
As I watched where you passed and was lost in the netherward
    black of the night,
As my soul in its trouble dissatisfied sank, as where you, sad orb,
Concluded, dropped in the night, and was gone.

IX

Sing on there in the swamp,
O singer bashful and tender, I hear your notes, I hear your call,
I hear, I come presently, I understand you,
But a moment I linger, for the lustrous star has detained me,
The star, my departing comrade, holds and detains me.   70

X

O how shall I warble myself for the dead one there I loved?
And how shall I deck my song for the large sweet soul that has
    gone?
And what shall my perfume be for the grave of him I love?

Sea-winds blown from east and west,
Blown from the eastern sea and blown from the western sea, till
    there on the prairies meeting,
These and with these and the breath of my chant,
I'll perfume the grave of him I love.

XI

O what shall I hang on the chamber walls?
And what shall the pictures be that I hang on the walls,
To adorn the burial-house of him I love?   80

Pictures of growing spring and farms and homes,
With the fourth-month eve at sundown, and the gray smoke lucid
    and bright,
With floods of the yellow gold of the gorgeous, indolent, sinking
    sun, burning, expanding the air,
With the fresh sweet herbage under foot, and the pale green leaves
    of the trees prolific,

63. **netherward:** downward. 72. **deck:** adorn.

In the distance the flowing glaze, the breast of the river, with a
    wind-dapple here and there,
With ranging hills on the banks, with many a line against the sky,
    and shadows,
And the city at hand with dwellings so dense, and stacks of
    chimneys,
And all the scenes of life and the workshops, and the workmen
    homeward returning.

XII

Lo, body and soul—this land,
90 My own Manhattan with spires, and the sparkling and hurrying
    tides, and the ships,
The varied and ample land, the South and the North in the light,
    Ohio's shores and flashing Missouri,
And ever the far-spreading prairies covered with grass and corn.
Lo, the most excellent sun so calm and haughty,
The violet and purple morn with just-felt breezes,
The gentle soft-born measureless light,
The miracle spreading, bathing all, the fulfilled noon,
The coming eve delicious, the welcome night and the stars,
Over my cities shining all, enveloping man and land.

XIII

Sing on, sing on you gray-brown bird,
100 Sing from the swamps, the recesses, pour your chant from the
    bushes,
Limitless out of the dusk, out of the cedars and pines.

Sing on dearest brother, warble your reedy song,
Loud human song, with voice of uttermost woe.

O liquid and free and tender!
O wild and loose to my soul—O wondrous singer!
You only I hear—yet the star holds me (but will soon depart),
Yet the lilac with mastering odor holds me.

XIV

Now while I sat in the day and looked forth,
In the close of the day with its light and the fields of spring, and

106 and 107. yet: still.

the farmers preparing their crops,
In the large unconscious scenery of my land with its lakes and
    forests,   110
In the heavenly aerial beauty (after the perturbed winds and the
    storms),
Under the arching heavens of the afternoon swift passing, and the
    voices of children and women,
The many-moving sea-tides, and I saw the ships how they sailed,
And the summer approaching with richness, and the fields all busy
    with labor,
And the infinite separate houses, how they all went on, each with
    its meals and minutia of daily usages,
And the streets how their throbbings throbbed, and the cities pent
    —lo, then and there,
Falling upon them all and among them all, enveloping me with
    the rest,
Appeared the cloud, appeared the long black trail,
And I knew death, its thought, and the sacred knowledge of death.

Then with the knowledge of death as walking one side of me,   120
And the thought of death close-walking the other side of me,
And I in the middle as with companions, and as holding the hands
    of companions,
I fled forth to the hiding receiving night that talks not,
Down to the shores of the water, the path by the swamp in the
    dimness,
To the solemn shadowy cedars and ghostly pines so still.

And the singer so shy to the rest received me,
The gray-brown bird I know received us comrades three,
And he sang the carol of death, and a verse for him I love.

From deep secluded recesses,
From the fragrant cedars and the ghostly pines so still,   130
Came the carol of the bird.

And the charm of the carol rapt me,
As I held as if by their hands my comrades in the night,
And the voice of my spirit tallied the song of the bird.

Come lovely and soothing death,
Undulate round the world, serenely arriving, arriving,

116. pent: confined. **136. *Undulate:*** move with the motion of a wave.

In the day, in the night, to all, to each,
Sooner or later delicate death.

Praised be the fathomless universe,
140   For life and joy, and for objects and knowledge curious,
And for love, sweet love—but praise! praise! praise!
For the sure-enwinding arms of cool-enfolding death.

Dark mother always gliding near with soft feet,
Have none chanted for thee a chant of fullest welcome?
Then I chant it for thee, I glorify thee above all,
I bring thee a song that when thou must indeed come, come
    unfalteringly.

Approach strong deliveress,
When it is so, when thou hast taken them, I joyously sing the dead,
Lost in the loving floating ocean of thee,
150   Laved in the flood of thy bliss, O death.
From me to thee glad serenades,
Dances for thee I propose saluting thee, adornments and feastings
    for thee,
And the sights of the open landscape and the high-spread sky are
    fitting,
And life and the fields, and the huge and thoughtful night.

The night in silence under many a star,
The ocean shore and the husky whispering wave whose voice I
    know,
And the soul turning to thee, O vast and well-veiled death,
And the body gratefully nestling close to thee.

Over the tree-tops I float thee a song,
160   Over the rising and sinking waves, over the myriad fields and the
    prairies wide,
Over the dense-packed cities all and the teeming wharves and ways,
I float this carol with joy, with joy to thee, O death.

XV

To the tally of my soul,
Loud and strong kept up the gray-brown bird,
With pure deliberate notes spreading, filling the night.

---

160. myriad: countless. **163. tally:** record.

Loud in the pines and cedars dim,
Clear in the freshness moist and the swamp-perfume,
And I with my comrades there in the night.

While my sight that was bound in my eyes unclosed,
As to long panoramas of visions.   170

And I saw askant the armies,
I saw as in noiseless dreams hundreds of battle-flags,
Borne through the smoke of the battles and pierced with missiles
    I saw them,
And carried hither and yon through the smoke, and torn and
    bloody,
And at last but a few shreds left on the staffs (and all in silence),
And the staffs all splintered and broken.
I saw battle-corpses, myriads of them,
And the white skeletons of young men, I saw them,
I saw the debris and debris of all the slain soldiers of the war,
But I saw they were not as was thought,   180
They themselves were fully at rest, they suffered not,
The living remained and suffered, the mother suffered,
And the wife and the child and the musing comrade suffered,
And the armies that remained suffered.

XVI

Passing the visions, passing the night,
Passing, unloosing the hold of my comrades' hands,
Passing the song of the hermit bird and the tallying song of my
    soul,
Victorious song, death's outlet song, yet varying, ever-altering song,
As low and wailing, yet clear the notes, rising and falling, flooding
    the night,
Sadly sinking and fainting, as warning and warning, and yet again   190
    bursting with joy,
Covering the earth and filling the spread of the heaven,
As that powerful psalm in the night I heard from recesses,
Passing, I leave thee lilac with heart-shaped leaves,
I leave thee there in the dooryard, blooming, returning with spring.

I cease from my song for thee,
From my gaze on thee in the west, fronting the west, communing
    with thee,
O comrade lustrous with silver face in the night.

171. askant: with misgivings.

Yet each to keep and all, retrievements out of the night,
The song, the wondrous chant of the gray-brown bird,
200　And the tallying chant, the echo aroused in my soul,
With the lustrous and drooping star with the countenance full
　　of woe,
With the holders holding my hand nearing the call of the bird,
Comrades mine and I in the midst, and their memory ever to keep,
　　for the dead I loved so well,
For the sweetest, wisest soul of all my days and lands—and this for
　　his dear sake,
Lilac and star and bird twined with the chant of my soul,
There in the fragrant pines and the cedars dusk and dim.

MATTHEW ARNOLD (1822–1888)

TO MARGUERITE

Yes! in the sea of life enisled,
With echoing straits between us thrown,
Dotting the shoreless watery wild,
We mortal millions live *alone*.
The islands feel the enclasping flow,
And then their endless bounds they know.

But when the moon their hollows lights,
And they are swept by balms of spring,
And in their glens, on starry nights,
10　The nightingales divinely sing;
And lovely notes, from shore to shore,
Across the sounds and channels pour—

Oh! then a longing like despair
Is to their farthest caverns sent;
For surely once, they feel, we were
Parts of a single continent!
Now round us spreads the watery plain—
Oh might our marges meet again!

Who ordered, that their longing's fire
Should be, as soon as kindled, cooled?   20
Who renders vain their deep desire?—
A God, a God their severance ruled!
And bade betwixt their shores to be
The unplumbed, salt, estranging sea.

THE SCHOLAR GYPSY

Go, for they call you, shepherd, from the hill;
    Go, shepherd, and untie the wattled cotes.
        No longer leave thy wistful flock unfed,
        Nor let thy bawling fellows rack their throats,
            Nor the cropped herbage shoot another head.
                But when the fields are still,
        And the tired men and dogs all gone to rest,
            And only the white sheep are sometimes seen
            Cross and recross the strips of moon-blanched green,
        Come, shepherd, and again begin the quest.   10

Here, where the reaper was at work of late,
    In this high field's dark corner, where he leaves
        His coat, his basket, and his earthen cruse,
        And in the sun all morning binds the sheaves,
            Then here, at noon, comes back his stores to use—
                Here will I sit and wait,

Title. Arnold's note—"There was very lately a lad in the University of Oxford, who was by his poverty forced to leave his studies there; and at last to join himself to a company of vagabond gypsies. Among these extravagant people, by the insinuating subtilty of his carriage, he quickly got so much of their love and esteem as that they discovered to him their mystery. After he had been a pretty while well exercised in the trade, there chanced to ride by a couple of scholars, who had formerly been of his acquaintance. They quickly spied out their old friend among the gypsies; and he gave them an account of the necessity which drove him to that kind of life, and told them that the people he went with were not such impostors as they were taken for, but that they had a traditional kind of learning among them, and could do wonders by the power of imagination, their fancy binding that of others: that himself had learned much of their art, and when he had compassed the whole secret, he intended, he said, to leave their company, and give the world an account of what he had learned." Arnold took this passage from J. Glanvill's *Vanity of Dogmatizing,* 1661. **1-10.** The speaker is addressing a fictitious shepherd who is assisting him in his quest for traces of the Scholar Gypsy, who, he suggests, still haunts the Oxford countryside. **2. wattled cotes:** sheep pens. **13. cruse·** jug.

While to my ear from uplands far away
 The bleating of the folded flocks is borne,
  With distant cries of reapers in the corn—
20 All the live murmur of a summer's day.

Screened is this nook o'er the high, half-reaped field,
 And here till sun-down, shepherd, will I be.
  Through the thick corn the scarlet poppies peep,
 And round green roots and yellowing stalks I see
  Pale pink convolvulus in tendrils creep;
   And air-swept lindens yield
 Their scent, and rustle down their perfumed showers
  Of bloom on the bent grass where I am laid,
  And bower me from the August sun with shade;
30 And the eye travels down to Oxford's towers.

And near me on the grass lies Glanvill's book;
 Come, let me read the oft-read tale again:
  The story of the Oxford scholar poor,
 Of pregnant parts and quick inventive brain,
  Who, tired of knocking at preferment's door,
   One summer morn forsook
 His friends, and went to learn the gypsy lore,
  And roamed the world with that wild brotherhood,
  And came, as most men deemed, to little good,
40 But came to Oxford and his friends no more.

But once, years after, in the country lanes,
 Two scholars, whom at college erst he knew,
  Met him, and of his way of life inquired;
 Whereat he answered that the gypsy crew,
  His mates, had arts to rule as they desired
   The workings of men's brains,
 And they can bind them to what thoughts they will.
  "And I," he said, "the secret of their art,
  When fully learned, will to the world impart;
50 But it needs heaven-sent moments for this skill."

  18. folded flocks: flocks in their folds. 19. corn: wheat or other grain. 34. Of pregnant parts: intellectually promising. 35. preferment: advancement in an ecclesiastical position. 42. erst: formerly.

This said, he left them, and returned no more.
  But rumors hung about the countryside,
    That the lost scholar long was seen to stray,
  Seen by rare glimpses, pensive and tongue-tied,
    In hat of antique shape, and cloak of gray,
      The same the gypsies wore.
  Shepherds had met him on the Hurst in spring;
    At some lone alehouse in the Berkshire moors,
    On the warm ingle-bench, the smock-frocked boors
  Had found him seated at their entering;   60

But, 'mid their drink and clatter, he would fly.
  And I myself seem half to know thy looks,
    And put the shepherds, wanderer! on thy trace;
  And boys who in lone wheatfields scare the rooks
    I ask if thou hast passed their quiet place;
      Or in my boat I lie
  Moored to the cool bank in the summer heats,
    'Mid wide grass meadows which the sunshine fills,
    And watch the warm, green-muffled Cumner hills,
  And wonder if thou haunt'st their shy retreats.   70

For most, I know, thou lov'st retired ground.
  Thee, at the ferry, Oxford riders blithe,
    Returning home on summer nights, have met
  Crossing the stripling Thames at Bablock-hithe,
    Trailing in the cool stream thy fingers wet,
      As the slow punt swings round:
  And leaning backward in a pensive dream,
    And fostering in thy lap a heap of flowers
    Plucked in shy fields and distant Wychwood bowers,
  And thine eyes resting on the moonlit stream.   80

And then they land, and thou art seen no more.
  Maidens, who from the distant hamlets come
    To dance around the Fyfield elm in May,
  Oft through the darkening fields have seen thee roam,
    Or cross a stile into the public way.

---

57. **Hurst:** name of a hill near Oxford. Other place names in the poem, except those in the last two stanzas, are in this general environment. 59. **ingle:** fireside; **boors:** rustics. 62. **thy:** the speaker here and henceforth addresses the Scholar Gypsy.

Oft thou hast given them store
Of flowers: the frail-leafed, white anemone,
　　Dark bluebells drenched with dews of summer eves,
　　And purple orchises with spotted leaves—
90　　　But none hath words she can report of thee.

And, above Godstow Bridge, when hay-time's here
In June, and many a scythe in sunshine flames,
　　Men who through those wide fields of breezy grass,
　　Where black-winged swallows haunt the glittering Thames,
　　　To bathe in the abandoned lasher pass,
　　　　Have often passed thee near,
　　Sitting upon the river bank o'ergrown;
　　Marked thine outlandish garb, thy figure spare,
　　Thy dark vague eyes, and soft abstracted air;
100　　But when they came from bathing, thou wast gone.

At some lone homestead in the Cumner hills,
　　Where at her open door the housewife darns,
　　　Thou hast been seen, or hanging on a gate,
　　To watch the threshers in the mossy barns.
　　　Children, who early range these slopes and late
　　　　For cresses from the rills,
　　Have known thee watching, all an April day,
　　The springing pastures and the feeding kine;
　　And marked thee, when the stars come out and shine,
110　　Through the long dewy grass move slow away.

In autumn, on the skirts of Bagley Wood,
　　Where most the gypsies by the turf-edged way
　　　Pitch their smoked tents, and every bush you see
　　With scarlet patches tagged and shreds of gray,
　　　Above the forest-ground called Thessaly,
　　　　The blackbird picking food
　　Sees thee, nor stops his meal, nor fears at all;
　　So often has he known thee past him stray
　　Rapt, twirling in thy hand a withered spray,
120　　And waiting for the spark from heaven to fail.

---

95. lasher: pool below a weir; pass is the verb of which men (line 93) is the sub-
ject. 106. cresses: water cress; rills: streams.

And once, in winter, on the causeway chill,
  Where home through flooded fields foot-travellers go,
    Have I not passed thee on the wooden bridge
  Wrapped in thy cloak and battling with the snow,
    Thy face toward Hinksey and its wintry ridge?
      And thou hast climbed the hill
  And gained the white brow of the Cumner range;
    Turned once to watch, while thick the snowflakes fall,
    The line of festal light in Christ Church hall;
  Then sought thy straw in some sequestered grange.   130

But what—I dream! Two hundred years are flown
  Since first thy story ran through Oxford halls,
    And the grave Glanvill did the tale inscribe
  That thou wert wandered from the studious walls
    To learn strange arts, and join a gypsy tribe;
      And thou from earth art gone
  Long since, and in some quiet churchyard laid:
    Some country nook, where o'er thy unknown grave
    Tall grasses and white flowering nettles wave,
  Under a dark red-fruited yew-tree's shade.   140

—No, no, thou hast not felt the lapse of hours.
  For what wears out the life of mortal men?
    'Tis that from change to change their being rolls;
  'Tis that repeated shocks, again, again,
    Exhaust the energy of strongest souls,
      And numb the elastic powers.
  Till, having used our nerves with bliss and teen,
    And tired upon a thousand schemes our wit,
    To the just-pausing Genius we remit
  Our worn-out life, and are—what we have been.   150

Thou hast not lived, why shouldst thou perish, so?
  Thou hadst *one* aim, *one* business, and *one* desire;
    Else wert thou long since numbered with the dead—
  Else hadst thou spent, like other men, thy fire.
    The generations of thy peers are fled,
      And we ourselves shall go;

129. **Christ Church hall:** the dining hall of Christ Church, an Oxford college.
147. **teen:** sorrow, vexation. 149. **just-pausing Genius:** the soul of the world.

But thou possessest an immortal lot,
  And we imagine thee exempt from age
  And living as thou liv'st on Glanvill's page,
160 Because thou hadst—what we, alas! have not.

For early didst thou leave the world, with powers
  Fresh, undiverted to the world without,
    Firm to their mark, not spent on other things;
  Free from the sick fatigue, the languid doubt,
    Which much to have tried, in much been baffled, brings.
      O life unlike to ours!
  Who fluctuate idly without term or scope,
    Of whom each strives, nor knows for what he strives,
    And each half lives a hundred different lives;
170 Who wait like thee, but not, like thee, in hope.

Thou waitest for the spark from heaven; and we,
  Light half-believers of our casual creeds,
    Who never deeply felt, nor clearly willed,
  Whose insight never has borne fruit in deeds,
    Whose vague resolves never have been fulfilled;
      For whom each year we see
  Breeds new beginnings, disappointments new;
    Who hesitate and falter life away,
    And lose tomorrow the ground won to-day—
180 Ah! do not we, wanderer, await it too?

Yes, we await it, but it still delays,
  And then we suffer; and amongst us One,
    Who most has suffered, takes dejectedly
  His seat upon the intellectual throne;
    And all his store of sad experience he
      Lays bare of wretched days;
  Tells us his misery's birth and growth and signs,
    And how the dying spark of hope was fed,
    And how the breast was soothed, and how the head,
190 And all his hourly varied anodynes.

This for our wisest: and we others pine,
  And wish the long unhappy dream would end,

182. **One:** no one is certain as to whom Arnold is referring; proposed candidates have been Goethe, Tennyson, Carlyle, and Coleridge. 190. **anodynes:** pain killers.

And waive all claim to bliss, and try to bear,
With close-lipped patience for our only friend,
    Sad patience, too-near-neighbor to despair.
      But none has hope like thine.
Thou through the fields and through the woods dost stray,
    Roaming the countryside, a truant boy,
    Nursing thy project in unclouded joy,
And every doubt long blown by time away.   200

O born in days when wits were fresh and clear,
    And life ran gaily as the sparkling Thames;
      Before this strange disease of modern life,
    With its sick hurry, its divided aims,
      Its heads o'ertaxed, its palsied hearts, was rife—
        Fly hence, our contact fear!
Still fly, plunge deeper in the bowering wood!
    Averse, as Dido did with gesture stern
    From her false friend's approach in Hades turn,
Wave us away, and keep thy solitude.   210

Still nursing the unconquerable hope,
    Still clutching the inviolable shade,
      With a free onward impulse brushing through,
    By night, the silvered branches of the glade—
      Far on the forest-skirts, where none pursue,
        On some mild pastoral slope
Emerge, and resting on the moonlit pales,
    Freshen thy flowers, as in former years,
    With dew, or listen with enchanted ears,
From the dark dingles, to the nightingales.   220

But fly our paths, our feverish contact fly!
    For strong the infection of our mental strife,
      Which, though it gives no bliss, yet spoils for rest;
    And we should win thee from thy own fair life,
      Like us distracted, and like us unblessed.
        Soon, soon thy cheer would die,
Thy hopes grow timorous, and unfixed thy powers,

---

205. rife: prevalent. 208–209. Dido . . . Hades: Æneas, hero of Virgil's *Æneid*, deserted Dido, Queen of Carthage, who thereupon killed herself. Later, in Hades, which he visited as a living mortal, her shade shunned him. 217. pales: fence uprights. 220. dingles: hollows.

And thy clear aims be cross and shifting made;
And then thy glad perennial youth would fade,
230   Fade, and grow old at last, and die like ours.

Then fly our greetings, fly our speech and smiles!
      —As some grave Tyrian trader from the sea
      Descried at sunrise an emerging prow
Lifting the cool-haired creepers stealthily,
      The fringes of a southward-facing brow
            Among the Ægean isles;
And saw the merry Grecian coaster come,
      Freighted with amber grapes and Chian wine,
      Green bursting figs, and tunnies steeped in brine;
240   And knew the intruders on his ancient home,

The young light-hearted masters of the waves;
And snatched his rudder, and shook out more sail;
      And day and night held on indignantly
O'er the blue Midland waters with the gale,
      Betwixt the Syrtes and soft Sicily,
            To where the Atlantic raves
Outside the western straits; and unbent sails
      There, where down cloudy cliffs, through sheets of foam,
      Shy traffickers, the dark Iberians come;
250   And on the beach undid his corded bales.

THYRSIS

A MONODY

To commemorate the author's friend, Arthur Hugh Clough,
who died at Florence, 1861

How changed is here each spot man makes or fills!
In the two Hinkseys nothing keeps the same;

228. cross: crossed. 232. Tyrian: Phoenician—this people had been the masters of
the Mediterranean Sea (the Midland waters, line 244) before the Greeks. 233. descried:
observed. 234. cool-haired creepers: foliage overhanging the harbor. 238. Chian: Greek.
239. tunnies: tuna fish. 245. Syrtes: gulfs of North coast of Africa. 249. Iberians:
Spaniards or Portuguese.

Note. This elegy is based on the conventional pastoral elegy; see the note to Milton's
Lycidas. Thyrsis and Corydon (lines 77 and 80) are conventional pastoral names which
the poet uses here for Clough and himself respectively.

2. Hinkseys: villages in the environment of Oxford. Most of the other places referred
to in the poem are from this area.

The village-street its haunted mansion lacks,
 And from the sign is gone Sibylla's name,
  And from the roofs the twisted chimney-stacks.
   Are ye too changed, ye hills?
 See, 'tis no foot of unfamiliar men
  Tonight from Oxford up your pathway strays!
  Here came I often, often, in old days:
 Thyrsis and I; we still had Thyrsis then.   10

Runs it not here, the track by Childsworth Farm,
 Past the high wood, to where the elm tree crowns
  The hill behind whose ridge the sunset flames?
 The signal-elm, that looks on Ilsley Downs,
  The Vale, the three lone weirs, the youthful Thames?—
   This winter eve is warm,
 Humid the air; leafless, yet soft as spring,
  The tender purple spray on copse and briers;
  And that sweet city with her dreaming spires,
 She needs not June for beauty's heightening, 20

Lovely all times she lies, lovely tonight!
 Only, methinks, some loss of habit's power
  Befalls me wandering through this upland dim.
 Once passed I blindfold here, at any hour;
  Now seldom come I, since I came with him.
   That single elm tree bright
 Against the west—I miss it! is it gone?
  We prized it dearly; while it stood, we said,
  Our friend, the Gypsy Scholar, was not dead;
 While the tree lived, he in these fields lived on. 30

Too rare, too rare, grow now my visits here;
 But once I knew each field, each flower, each stick;
  And with the country-folk acquaintance made
 By barn in threshing-time, by new-built rick.
  Here, too, our shepherd-pipes we first assayed.
   Ah me! this many a year

---

4. sign: inn sign. 18. spray: small branch; copse: small wood. 29. Gypsy Scholar: see Arnold's note to the previous poem. 35. shepherd-pipes . . . assayed: literally, we tried our flutes; in the pastoral convention, poets are referred to as shepherds, their art as piping; they habitually had piping contests, hence lines 80 and 81.

My pipe is lost, my shepherd's holiday!
   Needs must I lose them, needs with heavy heart
   Into the world and wave of men depart;
40 But Thyrsis of his own will went away.

It irked him to be here, he could not rest.
   He loved each simple joy the country yields,
      He loved his mates; but yet he could not keep,
   For that a shadow loured on the fields,
      Here with the shepherds and the silly sheep.
         Some life of men unblessed
   He knew, which made him droop, and filled his head.
   He went; his piping took a troubled sound
   Of storms that rage outside our happy ground;
50 He could not wait their passing, he is dead.

So, some tempestuous morn in early June,
   When the year's primal burst of bloom is o'er,
      Before the roses and the longest day—
   When garden-walks, and all the grassy floor
      With blossoms red and white of fallen May
         And chestnut-flowers are strewn—
   So have I heard the cuckoo's parting cry,
      From the wet field, through the vexed garden-trees,
      Come with the volleying rain and tossing breeze:
60 *The bloom is gone, and with the bloom go I!*

Too quick despairer, wherefore wilt thou go?
   Soon will the high Midsummer pomps come on,
      Soon will the musk carnations break and swell,
   Soon shall we have gold-dusted snapdragon,
      Sweet-William with his homely cottage-smell,
         And stocks in fragrant blow;
   Roses that down the alleys shine afar,
      And open, jasmine-muffled lattices,
      And groups under the dreaming garden-trees,
70 And the full moon, and the white evening star.

He hearkens not! light comer, he is flown!
   What matters it? next year he will return,

---

40. Thyrsis . . . away: Clough resigned his fellowship at Oxford in 1848. 43. keep:
live there. 45. silly: innocent.

And we shall have him in the sweet spring days,
With whitening hedges, and uncrumpling fern,
And blue-bells trembling by the forest-ways,
And scent of hay new-mown.
But Thyrsis never more we swains shall see;
See him come back, and cut a smoother reed,
And blow a strain the world at last shall heed—
For Time, not Corydon, hath conquered thee.   80

Alack, for Corydon no rival now!—
But when Sicilian shepherds lost a mate,
Some good survivor with his flute would go,
Piping a ditty sad for Bion's fate,
And cross the unpermitted ferry's flow,
And relax Pluto's brow,
And make leap up with joy the beauteuous head
Of Proserpine, among whose crownèd hair
Are flowers, first opened on Sicilian air,
And flute his friend, like Orpheus, from the dead.   90

O easy access to the hearer's grace
When Dorian shepherds sang to Proserpine!
For she herself had trod Sicilian fields,
She knew the Dorian water's gush divine,
She knew each lily white which Enna yields,
Each rose with blushing face;
She loved the Dorian pipe, the Dorian strain.
But ah, of our poor Thames she never heard!
Her foot the Cumner cowslips never stirred;
And we should tease her with our plaint in vain.   100

Well! wind-dispersed and vain the words will be,
Yet, Thyrsis, let me give my grief its hour
In the old haunt, and find our tree-topped hill!

84. Piping . . . fate: reference to "Lament for Bion," a pastoral elegy written in the second century B.C., by Moschus, a fellow Greek-Sicilian poet. 85–90. And cross . . . dead: Arnold imagines a poet passing over the river Styx, boundary of Hades, across which the living were not allowed to go. Pluto and Proserpine were king and queen of Hades. Orpheus, the Greek hero, had, while living, once entered Hades and with his music charmed Pluto into permitting him to attempt to restore his wife Eurydice to the land of the living. 92. Dorian: Sicilian Greek. 95. Enna: Sicilian town, near which Proserpine was captured by Pluto.

Who, if not I, for questing here hath power?
I know the wood which hides the daffodil,
    I know the Fyfield tree,
I know what white, what purple fritillaries
    The grassy harvest of the river-fields,
    Above by Ensham, down by Sandford, yields,
110   And what sedged brooks are Thames's tributaries;

I know these slopes; who knows them if not I?—
    But many a dingle on the loved hillside,
        With thorns once studded, old, white-blossomed trees,
    Where thick the cowslips grew, and, far descried,
        High towered the spikes of purple orchises,
            Hath since our day put by
    The coronals of that forgotten time;
        Down each green bank hath gone the ploughboy's team,
        And only in the hidden brookside gleam
120   Primroses, orphans of the flowery prime.

Where is the girl, who, by the boatman's door,
    Above the locks, above the boating throng,
        Unmoored our skiff, when, through the Wytham flats,
    Red loosestrife and blond meadow-sweet among,
        And darting swallows, and light water-gnats,
            We tracked the shy Thames shore?
    Where are the mowers, who, as the tiny swell
        Of our boat passing heaved the river-grass,
        Stood with suspended scythe to see us pass?—
130   They all are gone, and thou art gone as well.

Yes, thou art gone! and round me too the night
    In ever-nearing circle weaves her shade.
        I see her veil draw soft across the day,
    I feel her slowly chilling breath invade
        The cheek grown thin, the brown hair sprent with gray;
            I feel her finger light
    Laid pausefully upon life's headlong train;
        The foot less prompt to meet the morning dew,
        The heart less bounding at emotion new,
140   And hope, once crushed, less quick to spring again.

107. fritillaries: flowers. 112. dingle: hollow. 114. descried: observed. 117.
coronals: crowns of flowers. 124. loosestrife: flowers. 135. sprent: sprinkled.

And long the way appears, which seemed so short
  To the unpractised eye of sanguine youth;
    And high the mountain-tops, in cloudy air,
  The mountain-tops where is the throne of Truth,
    Tops in life's morning sun so bright and bare!
      Unbreachable the fort
  Of the long-battered world uplifts its wall;
    And strange and vain the earthly turmoil grows,
    And near and real the charm of thy repose,
  And night as welcome as a friend would fall.   150

But hush! the upland hath a sudden loss
  Of quiet!—Look, adown the dusk hillside,
    A troop of Oxford hunters going home,
  As in old days, jovial and talking, ride!
    From hunting with the Berkshire hounds they come.
      Quick! let me fly, and cross
  Into yon further field!—'Tis done; and see,
    Backed by the sunset, which doth glorify
    The orange and pale violet evening sky,
  Bare on its lonely ridge, the Tree! the Tree!   160

I take the omen! Eve lets down her veil,
  The white fog creeps from bush to bush about,
    The west unflushes, the high stars grow bright,
  And in the scattered farms the lights come out.
    I cannot reach the Signal-Tree to-night,
      Yet, happy omen, hail!
  Hear it from thy broad lucent Arnovale
    (For there thine earth-forgetting eyelids keep
    The morningless and unawakening sleep
  Under the flowery oleanders pale),   170

Hear it, O Thyrsis, still our Tree is there!—
  Ah vain! These English fields, this upland dim,
    These brambles pale with mist engarlanded,
  That lone, sky-pointing tree, are not for him.
    To a boon southern country he is fled,
      And now in happier air,

167. **lucent**: bright; **Arnovale**: the valley of the Arno, the river upon which Florence stands, where Clough was buried.

Wandering with the great Mother's train divine
(And purer or more subtle soul than thee,
I trow, the mighty Mother doth not see!)
180   Within a folding of the Apennine,

Thou hearest the immortal strains of old.
Putting his sickle to the perilous grain
In the hot cornfield of the Phrygian king,
For thee the Lityerses song again
Young Daphnis with his silver voice doth sing;
Sings his Sicilian fold,
His sheep, his hapless love, his blinded eyes;
And how a call celestial round him rang,
And heavenward from the fountain-brink he sprang,
190   And all the marvel of the golden skies.

There thou art gone, and me thou leavest here
Sole in these fields; yet will I not despair:
Despair I will not, while I yet descry
'Neath the mild canopy of English air
That lonely Tree against the western sky.
Still, still these slopes, 'tis clear,
Our Gypsy Scholar haunts, outliving thee!
Fields where soft sheep from cages pull the hay,
Woods with anemones in flower till May,
200   Know him a wanderer still; then why not me?

A fugitive and gracious light he seeks,
Shy to illumine; and I seek it too.
This does not come with houses or with gold,
With place, with honor and a flattering crew;
'Tis not in the world's market bought and sold—
But the smooth-slipping weeks
Drop by, and leave its seeker still untired;

177. great Mother's train: the entourage of Rhea, Greek goddess of the earth, Mother Nature. 179. trow: believe. 180. Apennine: mountain range near Florence. 181–190. Two stories about Daphnis, the Sicilian shepherd with the silver voice, are alluded to here. One is of the reaping contest with Lityerses, king of Phrygia (Troy), who habitually killed those he defeated. The other is of Daphnis's translation to heaven by his father, the Greek god Hermes, after he had been blinded by a nymph he had betrayed. At the place where Daphnis had risen to heaven, Hermes caused a fountain to spring, with which the verse here seems to identify Daphnis. 193. descry: observe.

Out of the heed of mortals he is gone,
He wends unfollowed, he must house alone;
Yet on he fares, by his own heart inspired.   **210**

Thou too, O Thyrsis, on like quest wast bound;
Thou wanderest with me for a little hour!
Men gave thee nothing; but this happy quest,
If men esteemed thee feeble, gave thee power,
If men procured thee trouble, gave thee rest.
And this rude Cumner ground,
Its fir-topped Hurst, its farms, its quiet fields,
Here cam'st thou in thy jocund youthful time,
Here was thine height of strength, thy golden prime!
And still the haunt beloved a virtue yields.   **220**

What though the music of thy rustic flute
Kept not for long its happy, country tone;
Lost it too soon, and learnt a stormy note
Of men contention-tossed, of men who groan,
Which tasked thy pipe too sore, and tired thy throat—
It failed, and thou wast mute!
Yet hadst thou always visions of our light,
And long with men of care thou couldst not stay,
And soon thy foot resumed its wandering way,
Left human haunt, and on alone till night.   **230**

Too rare, too rare, grow now my visits here!
'Mid city-noise, not, as with thee of yore,
Thyrsis! in reach of sheep-bells is my home.
—Then through the great town's harsh, heart-wearying roar,
Let in thy voice a whisper often come,
To chase fatigue and fear:
Why faintest thou? I wandered till I died.
Roam on! the light we sought is shining still.
Dost thou ask proof? Our Tree yet crowns the hill,
Our Scholar travels yet the loved hillside.   **240**

217. **Hurst:** wooded hill near Oxford.

DOVER BEACH

The sea is calm tonight.
The tide is full, the moon lies fair
Upon the straits; on the French coast the light
Gleams and is gone; the cliffs of England stand,
Glimmering and vast, out in the tranquil bay.
Come to the window, sweet is the night air!

Only, from the long line of spray
Where the sea meets the moon-blanched land,
Listen! you hear the grating roar

10   Of pebbles which the waves draw back, and fling,
At their return, up the high strand,
Begin, and cease, and then again begin,
With tremulous cadence slow, and bring
The eternal note of sadness in.

Sophocles long ago
Heard it on the Ægean, and it brought
Into his mind the turbid ebb and flow
Of human misery; we
Find also in the sound a thought,

20   Hearing it by this distant northern sea.

The Sea of Faith
Was once, too, at the full, and round earth's shore
Lay like the folds of a bright girdle furled.
But now I only hear
Its melancholy, long, withdrawing roar,
Retreating, to the breath
Of the night wind, down the vast edges drear
And naked shingles of the world.

Ah, love, let us be true

30   To one another! for the world, which seems

Title. English seaport on the Channel, from which the lights of France are visible
some twenty miles away across the Strait.

15, 16. **Sophocles . . . Ægean:** in his *Antigone*, Sophocles, the Greek tragedian, com-
pares the curse on the house of Oedipus with the force of the sea; the Ægean Sea lies off
the east coast of Greece. 23. **girdle:** sash of a woman's dress. 28. **shingles:** pebbly beaches.

To lie before us like a land of dreams,
So various, so beautiful, so new,
Hath really neither joy, nor love, nor light,
Nor certitude, nor peace, nor help for pain;
And we are here as on a darkling plain,
Swept with confused alarms of struggle and flight,
Where ignorant armies clash by night.

GEORGE MEREDITH (1828–1909)

from *MODERN LOVE*

1

By this he knew she wept with waking eyes:
That, at his hand's light quiver by her head,
The strange low sobs that shook their common bed
Were called into her with a sharp surprise,
And strangled mute, like little gaping snakes,
Dreadfully venomous to him. She lay
Stone-still, and the long darkness flowed away
With muffled pulses. Then, as midnight makes
Her giant heart of Memory and Tears
Drink the pale drug of silence, and so beat   10
Sleep's heavy measure, they from head to feet
Were moveless, looking through their dead black years,
By vain regret scrawled over the blank wall.
Like sculptured effigies they might be seen
Upon their marriage-tomb, the sword between;
Each wishing for the sword that severs all.

47

We saw the swallows gathering in the sky,
And in the osier-isle we heard them noise.

Note. This is the first of a sequence of sixteen-line sonnets describing a marriage that is disintegrating.

14. effigies: likenesses. 15. sword between: allusion to medieval tales in which chastity was thus ensured.

2. osier-isle: island with willows.

We had not to look back on summer joys,
Or forward to a summer of bright dye:
But in the largeness of the evening earth
Our spirits grew as we went side by side.
The hour became her husband and my bride.
Love that had robbed us so, thus blessed our dearth!
The pilgrims of the year waxed very loud
In multitudinous chatterings, as the flood
Full brown came from the West, and like pale blood
Expanded to the upper crimson cloud.
Love that had robbed us of immortal things
This little moment mercifully gave,
Where I have seen across the twilight wave
The swan sail with her young beneath her wings.

50

Thus piteously Love closed what he begat:
The union of this ever-diverse pair!
These two were rapid falcons in a snare,
Condemned to do the flitting of the bat.
Lovers beneath the singing sky of May
They wandered once, clear as the dew on flowers;
But they fed not on the advancing hours:
Their hearts held cravings for the buried day.
Then each applied to each that fatal knife,
Deep questioning, which probes to endless dole.
Ah, what a dusty answer gets the soul
When hot for certainties in this our life!—
In tragic hints here see what evermore
Moves dark as yonder midnight ocean's force,
Thundering like ramping hosts of warrior horse,
To throw that faint thin line upon the shore!

---

9. pilgrims of the year: the swallows. **10. flood:** river.

1. begat: generated. **10. dole:** grief. **15. ramping:** rampaging.

LUCIFER IN STARLIGHT

On a starred night Prince Lucifer uprose.
Tired of his dark dominion swung the fiend
Above the rolling ball, in cloud part screened,
Where sinners hugged their spectre of repose—
Poor prey to his hot fit of pride were these.
And now upon his western wing he leaned,
Now his huge bulk o'er Afric's sands careened,
Now the black planet shadowed Arctic snows.
Soaring through wider zones that pricked his scars
With memory of the old revolt from Awe,   10
He reached a middle height, and at the stars,
Which are the brain of heaven, he looked, and sank.
Around the ancient track marched, rank on rank,
The army of unalterable law.

EMILY DICKINSON (1830–1886)

AFTER GREAT PAIN

After great pain, a formal feeling comes—
The Nerves sit ceremonious, like Tombs—
The stiff Heart questions was it He, that bore,
And Yesterday, or Centuries before?

The Feet, mechanical, go round—
Of Ground, or Air, or Ought—
A Wooden way
Regardless grown,
A Quartz contentment, like a stone—

This is the Hour of Lead—   10
Remembered, if outlived,
As Freezing persons, recollect the Snow—
First—Chill—then Stupor—then the letting go—

Title: Lucifer, literally "bringer of light," is identified with Satan, before that rebel archangel's fall from Heaven; also identified with the planet Venus when it is the morning star. 8. black planet: i.e., Lucifer.

I HEARD A FLY BUZZ

I heard a Fly buzz—when I died—
The Stillness in the Room
Was like the Stillness in the Air—
Between the Heaves of Storm—

The Eyes around—had wrung tnem dry—
And Breaths were gathering firm
For that last Onset—when the King
Be witnessed—in the Room—

I willed my Keepsakes—Signed away
What portion of me be
Assignable—and then it was
There interposed a Fly—

With Blue—uncertain stumbling Buzz—
Between the light—and me—
And then the Windows failed—and then
I could not see to see—

IT WAS NOT DEATH

It was not Death, for I stood up,
And all the Dead, lie down—
It was not Night, for all the Bells
Put out their Tongues, for Noon.

It was not Frost, for on my Flesh
I felt Siroccos—crawl—
Nor Fire—for just my Marble feet
Could keep a Chancel, cool—

And yet, it tasted, like them all,
The Figures I have seen
Set orderly, for Burial,
Reminded me, of mine—

6. Siroccos: hot winds. 8. Chancel: part of a church near the altar.

As if my life were shaven,
And fitted to a frame,
And could not breathe without a key,
And 'twas like Midnight, some—

When everything that ticked—has stopped—
And Space stares all around—
Or Grisly frosts—first Autumn morns,
Repeal the Beating Ground—   20

But, most, like Chaos—Stopless—cool—
Without a Chance, or Spar—
Or even a Report of Land—
To justify—Despair.

BECAUSE I COULD NOT STOP FOR DEATH

Because I could not stop for Death—
He kindly stopped for me—
The Carriage held but just Ourselves—
And Immortality.

We slowly drove—He knew no haste
And I had put away
My labor and my leisure too,
For His Civility—

We passed the School, where Children strove
At Recess—in the Ring—   10
We passed the Fields of Gazing Grain—
We passed the Setting Sun—

Or rather—He passed Us—
The Dews drew quivering and chill—
For only Gossamer, my Gown—
My Tippet—only Tulle—

20. **Repeal:** stop (the heart of the ground, understood).

15. **Gossamer:** thin filmy cloth. 16. **Tippet:** shawl; **Tulle:** silk

We paused before a House that seemed
A Swelling of the Ground—
The Roof was scarcely visible—
20   The Cornice—in the Ground—

Since then—'tis Centuries—and yet
Feels shorter than the Day
I first surmised the Horses' Heads
Were toward Eternity—

A NARROW FELLOW IN THE GRASS

A narrow Fellow in the Grass
Occasionally rides—
You may have met Him—did you not
His notice sudden is—

The Grass divides as with a Comb—
A spotted shaft is seen—
And then it closes at your feet
And opens further on—

He likes a Boggy Acre
10   A Floor too cool for Corn—
Yet when a Boy, and Barefoot
I more than once at Noon
Have passed, I thought, a Whip lash
Unbraiding in the Sun
When stooping to secure it
It wrinkled, and was gone—

Several of Nature's People
I know, and they know me—
I feel for them a transport
20   Of cordiality—

But never met this Fellow
Attended, or alone
Without a tighter breathing
And Zero at the Bone—

20. Cornice: molding along the top of a wall.

FURTHER IN SUMMER

Further in Summer than the Birds
Pathetic from the Grass
A minor Nation celebrates
Its unobtrusive Mass.

No Ordinance be seen
So gradual the Grace
A pensive Custom it becomes
Enlarging Loneliness.

Antiquest felt at Noon
When August burning low   10
Arise this spectral Canticle
Repose to typify

Remit as yet no Grace
No Furrow on the Glow
Yet a Druidic Difference
Enhances Nature now

GO NOT TOO NEAR A HOUSE OF ROSE

Go not too near a House of Rose—
The depredation of a Breeze
Or inundation of a Dew
Alarms its walls away—

Nor try to tie the Butterfly,
Nor climb the Bars of Ecstasy,
In insecurity to lie
Is Joy's insuring quality.

5. Ordinance: ritual. 9. Antiquest: most ancient. 11. Canticle: chant. 15. Druidic: of the Druids, an ancient pre-Christian order of priests.

2. depredation: plundering. 3. inundation: flooding.

THERE'S A CERTAIN SLANT OF LIGHT

There's a certain Slant of light,
Winter Afternoons—
That oppresses, like the Heft
Of Cathedral Tunes—

Heavenly Hurt, it gives us—
We can find no scar,
But internal difference,
Where the Meanings, are—

None may teach it—Any—
'Tis the Seal Despair—
An imperial affliction
Sent us of the Air—

When it comes, the Landscape listens—
Shadows—hold their breath—
When it goes, 'tis like the Distance
On the look of Death—

PAIN HAS AN ELEMENT OF BLANK

Pain—has an Element of Blank—
It cannot recollect
When it begun—or if there were
A time when it was not—

It has no Future—but itself—
Its Infinite contain
Its Past—enlightened to perceive
New Periods—of Pain.

3. Heft: weight.

WILD NIGHTS

Wild Nights—Wild Nights!
Were I with thee
Wild Nights should be
Our luxury!

Futile—the Winds—
To a Heart in port—
Done with the Compass—
Done with the Chart!

Rowing in Eden—
Ah, the Sea!   10
Might I but moor—Tonight—
In Thee!

ALGERNON CHARLES SWINBURNE (1837–1909)

HYMN TO PROSERPINE

AFTER THE PROCLAMATION IN ROME OF THE CHRISTIAN FAITH
VICISTI, GALILÆE

I have lived long enough, having seen one thing, that love hath
    an end;
Goddess and maiden and queen, be near me now and befriend.
Thou art more than the day or the morrow, the seasons that laugh
    or that weep;

Title. Proserpine: Queen of the underworld, daughter of the fertility goddess, Ceres; thus associated with death, sleep, and the earth. **Epigraph. Vicisti, Galilæe:** "Thou hast conquered, O Galilean," words said to have been addressed to Christ by Julian the Apostate, Roman Emperor 361-63, on his deathbed. He had unsuccessfully attempted to revive paganism in Rome. **1. I:** the speaker is a Roman poet of the fourth century A.D. **2. Goddess . . . queen.** Proserpine.

For these give joy and sorrow; but thou, Proserpina, sleep.
Sweet is the treading of wine, and sweet the feet of the dove;
But a goodlier gift is thine than foam of the grapes or love.
Yea, is not even Apollo, with hair and harpstring of gold,
A bitter God to follow, a beautiful God to behold?
I am sick of singing: the bays burn deep and chafe: I am fain
10   To rest a little from praise and grievous pleasure and pain.
For the Gods we know not of, who give us our daily breath,
We know they are cruel as love or life, and lovely as death.
O Gods dethroned and deceased, cast forth, wiped out in a day!
From your wrath is the world released, redeemed from your chains,
        men say.
New Gods are crowned in the city; their flowers have broken your rods;
They are merciful, clothed with pity, the young compassionate Gods.
But for me their new device is barren, the days are bare;
Things long past over suffice, and men forgotten that were.
Time and the Gods are at strife; ye dwell in the midst thereof,
20   Draining a little life from the barren breasts of love.
I say to you, cease, take rest; yea, I say to you all, be at peace,
Till the bitter milk of her breast and the barren bosom shall cease.
Wilt thou yet take all, Galilean? but these thou shalt not take,
The laurel, the palms and the pæan, the breasts of the nymphs in
        the brake;
Breasts more soft than a dove's, that tremble with tenderer breath;
And all the wings of the Loves, and all the joy before death;
All the feet of the hours that sound as a single lyre,
Dropped and deep in the flowers, with strings that flicker like fire.
More than these wilt thou give, things fairer than all these things?
30   Nay, for a little we live, and life hath mutable wings.
A little while and we die; shall life not thrive as it may?
For no man under the sky lives twice, outliving his day.
And grief is a grievous thing, and a man hath enough of his tears:
Why should he labor, and bring fresh grief to blacken his years?
Thou hast conquered, O pale Galilean; the world has grown gray
        from thy breath;

---

7. **Apollo:** God of music, poetry, the sun, and other things; here especially music
and poetry. 9. **bays:** laurel leaves, worn on the head as a sign of achievement in poetry;
fain: desirous. 17. **device:** their sign, i.e., the cross. 23. **Galilean:** Christ. 24. **laurel . . .
pæan:** emblems of human achievements; **brake:** thicket. 30. **mutable:** changeable.

We have drunken of things Lethean, and fed on the fulness of
   death.
Laurel is green for a season, and love is sweet for a day;
But love grows bitter with treason, and laurel outlives not May.
Sleep, shall we sleep after all? for the world is not sweet in the
   end;
For the old faiths loosen and fall, the new years ruin and rend.   40
Fate is a sea without shore, and the soul is a rock that abides;
But her ears are vexed with the roar and her face with the foam
   of the tides.
O lips that the live blood faints in, the leavings of rack and rods!
O ghastly glories of saints, dead limbs of gibbeted Gods!
Though all men abase them before you in spirit, and all knees
   bend,
I kneel not, neither adore you, but standing, look to the end.
All delicate days and pleasant, all spirits and sorrows are cast
Far out with the foam of the present that sweeps to the surf of
   the past:
Where beyond the extreme sea-wall, and between the remote
   sea-gates,
Waste water washes, and tall ships founder, and deep death waits: 50
Where, mighty with deepening sides, clad about with the seas as
   with wings,
And impelled of invisible tides, fulfilled of unspeakable things,
White-eyed and poisonous-finned, shark-toothed and serpentine-
   curled,
Rolls, under the whitening wind of the future, the wave of the
   world.
The depths stand naked in sunder behind it, the storms flee away;
In the hollow before it the thunder is taken and snared as a prey;
In its sides is the north-wind bound; and its salt is of all men's tears;
With light of ruin, and sound of changes, and pulse of years:
With travail of day after day, and with trouble of hour upon hour;
And bitter as blood is the spray; and the crests are as fangs that
   devour: 60

36. **Lethean:** of Lethe, the river of forgetfulness. 43. **rack and rods:** instruments of torture. 44. **gibbeted:** hung. 45. **abase them:** humble themselves; **you:** the saints. 55. **sunder:** division.

And its vapor and storm of its steam as the sighing of spirits to be;
And its noise as the noise in a dream; and its depth as the roots of
    the sea:
And the height of its heads as the height of the utmost stars of the air:
And the ends of the earth at the might thereof tremble, and time
    is made bare.
Will ye bridle the deep sea with reins, will ye chasten the high
    sea with rods?
Will ye take her to chain her with chains, who is older than all
    ye Gods?
All ye as a wind shall go by, as a fire shall ye pass and be passed;
Ye are Gods, and behold, ye shall die, and the waves be upon
    you at last.
In the darkness of time, in the deeps of the years, in the changes
    of things,
Ye shall sleep as a slain man sleeps, and the world shall forget you
70   for kings.
Though the feet of thine high priests tread where thy lords and
    our forefathers trod,
Though these that were Gods are dead, and thou being dead art
    a God,
Though before thee the throned Cytherean be fallen, and hidden
    her head,
Yet thy kingdom shall pass, Galilean, thy dead shall go down to
    thee dead.
Of the maiden thy mother men sing as a goddess with grace clad
    around;
Thou art throned where another was king; where another was
    queen she is crowned.
Yea, once we had sight of another: but now she is queen, say these.
Not as thine, not as thine was our mother, a blossom of flowering
    seas,
Clothed round with the world's desire as with raiment, and fair
    as the foam,
80   And fleeter than kindled fire, and a goddess and mother of Rome.
For thine came pale and a maiden, and sister to sorrow; but ours,
Her deep hair heavily laden with odor, and color of flowers,

---

65. ye: the saints. 71. thine: Christ's. 72. Gods: pagan gods. 73. Cytherean: Venus, goddess of love. 75. maiden: Virgin Mary. 77, 78, 80. another, mother, mother of Rome: all refer to Venus, who emerged from the sea and was the mother of Æneas, founder of Rome.

White rose of the rose-white water, a silver splendor, a flame,
Bent down unto us that besought her, and earth grew sweet with
     her name.
For thine came weeping, a slave among slaves, and rejected; but she
Came flushed from the full-flushed wave, and imperial, her foot
     on the sea.
And the wonderful waters knew her, the winds and the viewless
     ways,
And the roses grew rosier, and bluer the sea-blue stream of the bays.
Ye are fallen, our lords, by what token? we wist that ye should
     not fall.
Ye were all so fair that are broken; and one more fair than ye all.   90
But I turn to her still, having seen she shall surely abide in the end;
Goddess and maiden and queen, be near me now and befriend.
O daughter of earth, of my mother, her crown and blossom of
     birth,
I am also, I also thy brother; I go as I came unto earth.
In the night where thine eyes are as moons are in heaven, the
     night where thou art,
Where the silence is more than all tunes, where sleep overflows
     from the heart,
Where the poppies are sweet as the rose in our world, and the
     red rose is white,
And the wind falls faint as it blows with the fume of the flowers
     of the night,
And the murmur of spirits that sleep in the shadow of Gods
     from afar
Grows dim in thine ears and deep as the deep dim soul of a
     star,   100
In the sweet low light of thy face, under heavens untrod by the
     sun,
Let my soul with their souls find place, and forget what is done
     and undone.
Thou art more than the Gods who number the days of our
     temporal breath;
For these give labor and slumber; but thou, Prosperina, death.
Therefore now at thy feet I abide for a season in silence. I
     know
I shall die as my fathers died, and sleep as they sleep; even so.
For the glass of the years is brittle wherein we gaze for a span;

---

84. **besought:** prayed to. 89. **token:** visible means; **wist:** thought. 90, 91: **one, her:**
Proserpine. 103. **Gods:** Christ and His saints.

A little soul for a little bears up this corpse which is man.
So long I endure, no longer; and laugh not again, neither weep.
110   For there is no God found stronger than death; and death is a
      sleep.

THE GARDEN OF PROSERPINE

Here, where the world is quiet;
    Here, where all trouble seems
Dead winds' and spent waves' riot
    In doubtful dreams of dreams;
I watch the green field growing
For reaping folk and sowing,
For harvest-time and mowing,
    A sleepy world of streams.

I am tired of tears and laughter,
10   And men that laugh and weep,
Of what may come hereafter
    For men that sow to reap:
I am weary of days and hours,
Blown buds of barren flowers,
Desires and dreams and powers
    And everything but sleep.

Here life has death for neighbor,
    And far from eye or ear
Wan waves and wet winds labor,
20   Weak ships and spirits steer;
They drive adrift, and whither
They wot not who make thither;
But no such winds blow hither,
    And no such things grow here.

No growth of moor or coppice,
    No heather-flower or vine,

Title. Proserpine: daughter of Ceres, goddess of fruitfulness: she was abducted into the underworld by Pluto, where she spent the winter of each year, returning to the upper world in the spring. See lines 59-60. **1. Here:** the underworld. **14. blown:** blossomed. **22. wot:** know. **25. coppice:** small wood.

But bloomless buds of poppies,
   Green grapes of Proserpine,
Pale beds of blowing rushes,
   Where no leaf blooms or blushes   30
Save this whereout she crushes
   For dead men deadly wine.

Pale, without name or number,
   In fruitless fields of corn,
They bow themselves and slumber
   All night till light is born;
And like a soul belated,
In hell and heaven unmated,
By cloud and mist abated
   Comes out of darkness morn.   40

Though one were strong as seven,
   He too with death shall dwell,
Nor wake with wings in heaven,
   Nor weep for pains in hell;
Though one were fair as roses,
His beauty clouds and closes;
And well though love reposes,
   In the end it is not well.

Pale, beyond porch and portal,
   Crowned with calm leaves, she stands   50
Who gathers all things mortal
   With cold immortal hands;
Her languid lips are sweeter
Than love's, who fears to greet her,
To men that mix and meet her
   From many times and lands.

She waits for each and other,
   She waits for all men born;
Forgets the earth her mother,
   The life of fruits and corn;   60

34. **corn:** grain. 37. **belated:** tardy. 39. **abated:** diminished. 49. **porch and portal:** the gates of the underworld.

And spring and seed and swallow
Take wing for her and follow
Where summer song rings hollow
    And flowers are put to scorn.

There go the loves that wither,
    The old loves with wearier wings;
And all dead years draw thither,
    And all disastrous things:
Dead dreams of days forsaken,
Blind buds that snows have shaken,
Wild leaves that winds have taken,
    Red strays of ruined springs.

We are not sure of sorrow,
    And joy was never sure;
Today will die tomorrow;
    Time stoops to no man's lure;
And love, grown faint and fretful,
With lips but half regretful
Sighs, and with eyes forgetful
    Weeps that no loves endure.

From too much love of living,
    From hope and fear set free,
We thank with brief thanksgiving
    Whatever gods may be
That no life lives for ever;
That dead men rise up never;
That even the weariest river
    Winds somewhere safe to sea.

Then star nor sun shall waken,
    Nor any change of light:
Nor sound of waters shaken,
    Nor any sound or sight:
Nor wintry leaves nor vernal,
Nor days nor things diurnal;
Only the sleep eternal
    In an eternal night.

70

80

90

68. disastrous things: things that have come to disaster. 76. lure: a bunch of feathers
baited with food used to recall the hawk in falconry. 94. diurnal: daily.

THOMAS HARDY (1840–1928)

HAP

If but some vengeful god would call to me
From up the sky, and laugh: "Thou suffering thing,
Know that thy sorrow is my ecstasy,
That thy love's loss is my hate's profiting!"

Then would I bear it, clench myself, and die,
Steeled by the sense of ire unmerited;
Half-eased in that a Powerfuller than I
Had willed and meted me the tears I shed.

But not so. How arrives it joy lies slain,
And why unblooms the best hope ever sown?   10
—Crass Casualty obstructs the sun and rain,
And dicing Time for gladness casts a moan. . . .
These purblind Doomsters had as readily strown
Blisses about my pilgrimage as pain.

THE DARKLING THRUSH

I leant upon a coppice gate
    When Frost was spectre-gray,
And Winter's dregs made desolate
    The weakening eye of day.
The tangled bine-stems scored the sky
    Like strings of broken lyres,

Title. Hap: chance. 8. meted: measured out. 9. How arrives it: how does it come
about. 11. Crass Casualty: crude chance. 13. purblind Doomsters: half-blind settlers
of our fate.

Title. Darkling: in the dark. 1. coppice: small wood. 5. bine-stems: stems of the
woodbine, a wild vine; scored: scratched.

And all mankind that haunted nigh
    Had sought their household fires.

The land's sharp features seemed to be
10   The Century's corpse outleant,
His crypt the cloudy canopy,
    The wind his death-lament.
The ancient pulse of germ and birth
    Was shrunken hard and dry,
And every spirit upon earth
    Seemed fervourless as I.

At once a voice arose among
    The bleak twigs overhead
In a full-hearted evensong
20   Of joy illimited;
An aged thrush, frail, gaunt, and small,
    In blast-beruffled plume,
Had chosen thus to fling his soul
    Upon the growing gloom.

So little cause for carolings
    Of such ecstatic sound
Was written on terrestrial things
    Afar or nigh around,
That I could think there trembled through
30   His happy good-night air
Some blessed Hope, whereof he knew
    And I was unaware.

CHANNEL FIRING

That night your great guns, unawares,
Shook all our coffins as we lay,
And broke the chancel window-squares,
We thought it was the Judgment-day

7. **haunted nigh:** lived nearby. 10. **Century's corpse:** the poem was written in December 1900, which Hardy apparently thought was the end of the nineteenth century; **outleant:** spread out. 11. **crypt:** burial place. 13. **pulse:** rhythm; **germ:** seed. 20. **illimited:** unlimited.

Title. Refers to naval gunnery practice in the English Channel; the poem was written four months before the outbreak of the first world war. 3. **chancel:** the part of the church near the altar.

And sat upright. While drearisome
Arose the howl of wakened hounds:
The mouse let fall the altar-crumb,
The worms drew back into the mounds,

The glebe cow drooled. Till God called, "No;
It's gunnery practice out at sea   10
Just as before you went below;
The world is as it used to be:

"All nations striving strong to make
Red war yet redder. Mad as hatters
They do no more for Christès sake
Than you who are helpless in such matters.

"That this is not the judgment-hour
For some of them's a blessed thing,
For if it were they'd have to scour
Hell's floor for so much threatening. . . .   20

"Ha, ha. It will be warmer when
I blow the trumpet (if indeed
I ever do; for you are men,
And rest eternal sorely need)."

So down we lay again. "I wonder,
Will the world ever saner be,"
Said one, "than when He sent us under
In our indifferent century!"

And many a skeleton shook his head.
"Instead of preaching forty year,"   30
My neighbour Parson Thirdly said,
"I wish I had stuck to pipes and beer."

Again the guns disturbed the hour,
Roaring their readiness to avenge,
As far inland as Stourton Tower,
And Camelot, and starlit Stonehenge.

9. glebe cow: cow in a small field. **35. Stourton:** in Sømerset and Wilts, with a tower dating from the 18th century commemorating Alfred the Great's raising his standard against the Danes in 879. **36. Camelot:** legendary capital of King Arthur; **Stonehenge:** prehistoric stone circle on Salisbury Plain.

THE CONVERGENCE OF THE TWAIN

(LINES ON THE LOSS OF THE "TITANIC")

I

In a solitude of the sea
Deep from human vanity,
And the Pride of Life that planned her, stilly couches she.

II

Steel chambers, late the pyres
Of her salamandrine fires,
Cold currents thrid, and turn to rhythmic tidal lyres.

III

Over the mirrors meant
To glass the opulent
The sea-worm crawls—grotesque, slimed, dumb, indifferent.

IV

10   Jewels in joy designed
To ravish the sensuous mind
Lie lightless, all their sparkles bleared and black and blind.

V

Dim moon-eyed fishes near
Gaze at the gilded gear
And query: "What does this vaingloriousness down here?" . . .

VI

Well: while was fashioning
This creature of cleaving wing,
The Immanent Will that stirs and urges everything

Title. The coming together of the two; "Titanic": the "unsinkable" luxury liner
which, on April 15, 1912, on her maiden voyage from England to America, hit an iceberg
and sank, with considerable loss of life. 3. stilly: quietly. 4-5. pyres . . . fires: i.e., the
furnaces. 6. thrid: thread. 16. was fashioning: was being made. 18. Immanent Will:
Hardy's name for the supreme power in the universe.

VII

Prepared a sinister mate
For her—so gaily great —
A Shape of Ice, for the time far and dissociate.   20

VIII

And as the smart ship grew
In stature, grace, and hue,
In shadowy silent distance grew the Iceberg too.

IX

Alien they seemed to be:
No mortal eye could see
The intimate welding of their later history,

X

Or sign that they were bent
By paths coincident
On being anon twin halves of one august event,   30

XI

Till the Spinner of the Years
Said "Now!" And each one hears,
And consummation comes, and jars two hemispheres.

"AH, ARE YOU DIGGING ON MY GRAVE?"

"Ah, are you digging on my grave
    My loved one?—planting rue?"
—"No: yesterday he went to wed
One of the brightest wealth has bred.
'It cannot hurt her now,' he said,
    'That I should not be true.' "

"Then who is digging on my grave?
    My nearest dearest kin?"
—"Ah, no: they sit and think, 'What use!

21. **dissociate:** apart. 29. **coincident:** coming together. 33. **consummation:** fulfillment.

2. **rue:** a plant associated with grief.

10 What good will planting flowers produce?
No tendance of her mound can loose
    Her spirit from Death's gin.' "

"But some one digs upon my grave?
    My enemy?—prodding sly?"
—"Nay: when she heard you had passed the Gate
That shuts on all flesh soon or late,
She thought you no more worth her hate,
    And cares not where you lie."

"Then, who is digging on my grave?
20   Say—since I have not guessed!"
—"O it is I, my mistress dear,
Your little dog, who still lives near,
And much I hope my movements here
    Have not disturbed your rest?"

"Ah, yes! *You* dig upon my grave . . .
    Why flashed it not on me
That one true heart was left behind!
What feeling do we ever find
To equal among human kind
30   A dog's fidelity!"

"Mistress, I dug upon your grave
    To bury a bone, in case
I should be hungry near this spot
When passing on my daily trot.
I am sorry, but I quite forgot
    It was your resting-place."

THE OXEN

Christmas Eve, and twelve of the clock.
    "Now they are all on their knees,"
An elder said as we sat in a flock
    By the embers in hearthside ease.

11. **tendance of:** attending to. 12. **gin:** trap.

We pictured the meek mild creatures where
　　They dwelt in their strawy pen,
Nor did it occur to one of us there
　　To doubt they were kneeling then.

So fair a fancy few would weave
　　In these years! Yet, I feel,
If someone said on Christmas Eve,
　　"Come; see the oxen kneel,

"In the lonely barton by yonder coomb
　　Our childhood used to know,"
I should go with him in the gloom,
　　Hoping it might be so.

AFTERWARDS

When the Present has latched its postern behind my tremulous stay,
　　And the May month flaps its glad green leaves like wings,
Delicate-filmed as new-spun silk, will the neighbours say,
　　"He was a man who used to notice such things"?

If it be in the dusk when, like an eyelid's soundless blink,
　　The dewfall-hawk comes crossing the shades to alight
Upon the wind-warped upland thorn, a gazer may think,
　　"To him this must have been a familiar sight."

If I pass during some nocturnal blackness, mothy and warm,
　　When the hedgehog travels furtively over the lawn,
One may say, "He strove that such innocent creatures should come
　　　　to no harm,
　　But he could do little for them; and now he is gone."

13. **barton:** farmyard; **coomb:** valley.

1. **postern:** gate; **tremulous:** quivering. 7. **thorn:** hawthorn.

If, when hearing that I have been stilled at last, they stand at the
    door,
  Watching the full-starred heavens that winter sees,
Will this thought rise on those who will meet my face no more,
    "He was one who had an eye for such mysteries"?

And will any say when my bell of quittance is heard in the gloom,
    And a crossing breeze cuts a pause in its outrollings,
Till they rise again, as they were a new bell's boom,
20   "He hears it not now, but used to notice such things"?

IN TIME OF "THE BREAKING OF NATIONS"

I

Only a man harrowing clods
    In a slow silent walk
With an old horse that stumbles and nods
    Half asleep as they stalk.

II

Only thin smoke without flame
    From the heaps of couch-grass;
Yet this will go onward the same
    Though Dynasties pass.

III

Yonder a maid and her wight
10   Come whispering by:
War's annals will fade into night
    Ere their story die.

17. bell of quittance: funeral bell.

Title. Allusion to Jeremiah li. 20, in which the Lord threatens the destruction of na-
tions. The poem was written during World War I. 1. harrowing clods: breaking up pieces
of earth. 6. couch-grass: coarse grass. 8. Dynasties: lines of hereditary rulers. 9. wight:
man. 11. annals: histories.

NEUTRAL TONES

We stood by a pond that winter day,
And the sun was white, as though chidden of God,
And a few leaves lay on the starving sod;
    —They had fallen from an ash, and were gray.

Your eyes on me were as eyes that rove
Over tedious riddles of years ago;
And some words played between us to and fro
    On which lost the more by our love.

The smile on your mouth was the deadest thing
Alive enough to have strength to die;   10
And a grin of bitterness swept thereby
    Like an ominous bird a-wing. . . .

Since then, keen lessons that love deceives,
And wrings with wrong, have shaped to me
Your face, and the God-curst sun, and a tree,
    And a pond edged with grayish leaves.

NEW YEAR'S EVE

"I have finished another year," said God,
    "In grey, green, white, and brown;
I have strewn the leaf upon the sod,
Sealed up the worm within the clod,
    And let the last sun down."

"And what's the good of it?" I said,
    "What reasons made you call
From formless void this earth we tread,
When nine-and-ninety can be read
    Why nought should be at all?   10

"Yea, Sire; why shaped you us, 'who in
    This tabernacle groan'—

2. chidden of: scolded by. 3. sod: earth. 12. ominous: menacing. 14. wrings: distresses.

3. sod: earth. 8. void: emptiness. 12. tabernacle: temple, literally tent or temporary shelter. The quotation is from 2 Corinthians v.4.

> If ever a joy be found herein,
> Such joy no man had wished to win
>   If he had never known!"
>
> Then he: "My labours—logicless—
>   You may explain; nor I:
> Sense-sealed I have wrought, without a guess
> That I evolved a Consciousness
20   To ask for reasons why.
>
> "Strange that ephemeral creatures who
>   By my own ordering are,
> Should see the shortness of my view,
> Use ethic tests I never knew,
>   Or made provision for!"
>
> He sank to raptness as of yore,
>   And opening New Year's Day
> Wove it by rote as theretofore,
> And went on working evermore
30   In his unweeting way.

GERARD MANLEY HOPKINS (1844–1889)

THE WINDHOVER:

TO CHRIST OUR LORD

> I caught this morning morning's minion, king-
>   dom of daylight's dauphin, dapple-dawn-drawn Falcon, in his riding
>   Of the rolling level underneath him steady air, and striding
> High there, how he rung upon the rein of a wimpling wing
> In his ecstasy! then off, off forth on swing,
>   As a skate's heel sweeps smooth on a bow-bend: the hurl and gliding
>   Rebuffed the big wind. My heart in hiding
> Stirred for a bird,—the achieve of, the mastery of the thing!

21. ephemeral: short-lived. 24. ethic: moral. 26. raptness: self-absorption; of yore: of old. 28. by rote: mechanically. 30. unweeting: oblivious.

Title. Windhover: a kestrel, a species of hawk that hovers in the air and drops upon its prey. 1. minion: favorite. 2. dauphin: crown prince; dapple-: streaked. 4. rung: moved in a ring; wimpling: undulating.

Brute beauty and valour and act, oh, air, pride, plume here
  Buckle! AND the fire that breaks from thee then, a billion   10
Times told lovelier, more dangerous, O my chevalier!

No wonder of it: shéer plód makes plough down sillion
Shine, and blue-bleak embers, ah my dear,
  Fall, gall themselves, and gash gold-vermilion.

PIED BEAUTY

Glory be to God for dappled things—
  For skies of couple-colour as a brinded cow;
    For rose-moles all in stipple upon trout that swim;
Fresh-firecoal chestnut-falls; finches' wings;
  Landscape plotted and pieced—fold, fallow, and plough;
    And áll trádes, their gear and tackle and trim.

All things counter, original, spare, strange;
  Whatever is fickle, freckled (who knows how?)
    With swift, slow; sweet, sour; adazzle, dim;
He fathers-forth whose beauty is past change: 10
    Praise him.

SPRING AND FALL:

TO A YOUNG CHILD

Márgarét, are you gríeving
Over Goldengrove unleaving?
Leáves, líke the things of man, you
With your fresh thoughts care for, can you?

11. chevalier: horseman. 12. sillion: furrow. 14. gall: wound.

Title. Pied: variegated. 1. dappled: spotted, mottled. 2. couple-colour: of two colors; brinded: streaked. 3. rose-moles: rose colored spots; stipple: spots. 4. Fresh- . . . -falls: probably an image from the appearance of a chestnut, fallen and partly split, revealing the rich red enclosed in the green. 5. pieced: divided; fold: animal enclosure; fallow: uncultivated land. 6. gear...trim: equipment. 7. counter: contrasting; original: unusual; spare: irregular. 8-9. freckled . . . dim: i.e., marked with the opposite qualities indicated. 10. He: God.

2. unleaving: shedding its leaves.

Áh! ás the heart grows older
It will come to such sights colder
By and by, nor spare a sigh
Though worlds of wanwood leafmeal lie;
And yet you will weep and know why.
Now no matter, child, the name:
Sórrow's springs áre the same.
Nor mouth had, no nor mind, expressed
What heart heard of, ghost guessed:
It ís the blight man was born for,
It is Margaret you mourn for.

SPELT FROM SIBYL'S LEAVES

Earnest, earthless, equal, attuneable, ˡvaulty, voluminous, . .
        stupendous
Evening strains to be tíme's vást, ˡwomb-of-all, home-of-all,
        hearse-of-all night.
Her fond yellow hornlight wound to the west, ˡher wild hollow
        hoarlight hung to the height
Waste; her earliest stars, earl-stars, ˡstárs principal, overbend us,
Fíre-féaturing heaven. For earth ˡher being has unbound, her
        dapple is at an end, as-
tray or aswarm, all throughther, in throngs; ˡself ín self steepèd
        and páshed—qúite
Disremembering, dísmémbering ˡáll now. Heart, you round
        me right

---

8. wanwood leafmeal: fallen leaves from barren trees. 13. ghost: spirit. 14. blight: destruction.

Title. Sibyl: prophetess; leaves: on which the Sibyl wrote her prophecies of the future; see *Æneid*, Book III. 3. fond: tender; hornlight: light of the crescent moon; wound: sunk; hoarlight: starlight. 3–4. height/Waste: empty high spaces. 5. dapple: variegated features. 6. throughther: through each other; pashed: beaten. 7. round: whisper to.

With: Óur évening is over us; óur night ᴵwhélms, whélms,
    ánd will end us.
Only the beak-leaved boughs dragonish ᴵdamask the tool-
    smooth bleak light; black,
Ever so black on it. Óur tale, O óur oracle! ᴵLét life, wáned,   10
    ah lét life wind
Off hér once skéined stained véined varíety ᴵupon, áll on twó
    spools: párt, pen, páck
Now her áll in twó flocks, twó folds—black, white; ᴵright,
    wrong; reckon but, reck but, mind
But thése two; wáre of a wórld where bút these ᴵtwó tell, each
    off the óther; of a rack
Where, selfwrung, selfstrung, sheathe-and shelterless, ᴵthóughts
    agaínst thoughts ín groans grínd.

GOD'S GRANDEUR

The world is charged with the grandeur of God.
    It will flame out, like shining from shook foil;
    It gathers to a greatness, like the ooze of oil
Crushed. Why do men then now not reck his rod?
Generations have trod, have trod, have trod;
    And all is seared with trade; bleared, smeared with toil;
    And wears man's smudge and shares man's smell: the soil
Is bare now, nor can foot feel, being shod.

And for all this, nature is never spent;
    There lives the dearest freshness deep down things;   10
And though the last lights off the black West went
    Oh, morning, at the brown brink eastward, springs—
Because the Holy Ghost over the bent
    World broods with warm breast and with ah! bright wings.

9. damask: throw into relief. 10. waned: declined. 11. skeined: coiled; part . . . pack: sort out. 12. reckon . . . mind: consider only. 13. But: only; ware: be aware; rack: instrument of torture. 14. sheathe-and shelterless: naked.

4. reck: pay attention to.

A. E. HOUSMAN (1859–1936)

1887

From Clee to heaven the beacon burns,
   The shires have seen it plain,
From north and south the sign returns
   And beacons burn again.

Look left, look right, the hills are bright,
   The dales are light between,
Because 'tis fifty years to-night
   That God has saved the Queen.

Now, when the flame they watch not towers
10   About the soil they trod,
Lads, we'll remember friends of ours
   Who shared the work with God.

To skies that knit their heartstrings right,
   To fields that bred them brave,
The saviours come not home to-night:
   Themselves they could not save.

It dawns in Asia, tombstones show
   And Shropshire names are read;
And the Nile spills his overflow
20   Beside the Severn's dead.

We pledge in peace by farm and town
   The Queen they served in war,
And fire the beacons up and down
   The land they perished for.

Title. 1887: Queen Victoria's Golden Jubilee. **1. Clee:** town in Shropshire. **9. they:** the dead **saviours** of line 15. **17. Asia** and **19. Nile:** areas where the British army had recently campaigned. **20. Severn:** the main river in Shropshire.

'God save the Queen' we living sing,
From height to height 'tis heard;
And with the rest your voices ring,
Lads of the Fifty-third.

Oh, God will save her, fear you not:
Be you the men you've been,   30
Get you the sons your fathers got,
And God will save the Queen.

LOVELIEST OF TREES

Loveliest of trees, the cherry now
Is hung with bloom along the bough,
And stands about the woodland ride
Wearing white for Eastertide.

Now, of my threescore years and ten,
Twenty will not come again,
And take from seventy springs a score,
It only leaves me fifty more.

And since to look at things in bloom
Fifty springs are little room,   10
About the woodlands I will go
To see the cherry hung with snow.

THE CARPENTER'S SON

'Here the hangman stops his cart:
Now the best of friends must part.
Fare you well, for ill fare I:
Live, lads, and I will die.

'Oh, at home had I but stayed
'Prenticed to my father's trade,
Had I stuck to plane and adze,
I had not been lost, my lads.

28. Fifty-third: name of a Shropshire regiment.

3. ride: a track for horseback riding.

'Then I might have built perhaps
10   Gallows-trees for other chaps,
Never dangled on my own,
Had I but left ill alone.

'Now, you see, they hang me high,
And the people passing by
Stop to shake their fists and curse;
So 'tis come from ill to worse.

'Here hang I, and right and left
Two poor fellows hang for theft:
All the same's the luck we prove,
20   Though the midmost hangs for love.

'Comrades all, that stand and gaze,
Walk henceforth in other ways;
See my neck and save your own:
Comrades all, leave ill alone.

'Make some day a decent end,
Shrewder fellows than your friend.
Fare you well, for ill fare I:
Live, lads, and I will die.'

'TERENCE, THIS IS STUPID STUFF'

'Terence, this is stupid stuff:
You eat your victuals fast enough;
There can't be much amiss, 'tis clear,
To see the rate you drink your beer.
But oh, good Lord, the verse you make,
It gives a chap the belly-ache.
The cow, the old cow, she is dead;
It sleeps well, the horned head:
We poor lads, 'tis our turn now
10   To hear such tunes as killed the cow.
Pretty friendship 'tis to rhyme
Your friends to death before their time
Moping melancholy mad:
Come, pipe a tune to dance to, lad.'

Title. Terence: originally the volume of poems called *The Shropshire Lad* was to be entitled *The Poems of Terence Hearsay.*

Why, if 'tis dancing you would be,
There's brisker pipes than poetry.
Say, for what were hop-yards meant,
Or why was Burton built on Trent?
Oh many a peer of England brews
Livelier liquor than the Muse,   20
And malt does more than Milton can
To justify God's ways to man.
Ale, man, ale's the stuff to drink
For fellows whom it hurts to think:
Look into the pewter pot
To see the world as the world's not.
And faith, 'tis pleasant till 'tis past:
The mischief is that 'twill not last.
Oh I have been to Ludlow fair
And left my necktie God knows where,   30
And carried half-way home, or near,
Pints and quarts of Ludlow beer:
Then the world seemed none so bad,
And I myself a sterling lad;
And down in lovely muck I've lain,
Happy till I woke again.
Then I saw the morning sky:
Heigho, the tale was all a lie;
The world, it was the old world yet,
I was I, my things were wet,   40
And nothing now remained to do
But begin the game anew.

Therefore, since the world has still
Much good, but much less good than ill,
And while the sun and moon endure
Luck's a chance, but trouble's sure,
I'd face it as a wise man would,
And train for ill and not for good.
'Tis true, the stuff I bring for sale
Is not so brisk a brew as ale: 50
Out of a stem that scored the hand
I wrung it in a weary land.
But take it: if the smack is sour,

18. **Burton:** Burton-on-Trent, famous brewery town. 21-22. **Milton . . . man:** this
was Milton's expressed aim in *Paradise Lost.* 29. **Ludlow:** a market town in Shropshire.
51. **stem:** stalk of a plant. 53. **smack:** taste.

The better for the embittered hour;
It should do good to heart and head
When your soul is in my soul's stead;
And I will friend you, if I may,
In the dark and cloudy day.
    There was a king reigned in the East:
60   There, when kings will sit to feast,
They get their fill before they think
With poisoned meat and poisoned drink.
He gathered all that springs to birth
From the many-venomed earth;
First a little, thence to more,
He sampled all her killing store;
And easy, smiling, seasoned sound,
Sate the king when healths went round.
They put arsenic in his meat
70   And stared aghast to watch him eat;
They poured strychnine in his cup
And shook to see him drink it up:
They shook, they stared as white's their shirt:
Them it was their poison hurt.
—I tell the tale that I heard told.
Mithridates, he died old.

EIGHT O'CLOCK

He stood, and heard the steeple
    Sprinkle the quarters on the morning town.
One, two, three, four, to market-place and people
    It tossed them down.

Strapped, noosed, nighing his hour,
    He stood and counted them and cursed his luck;
And then the clock collected in the tower
    Its strength, and struck.

68. Sate: sat. **76. Mithridates:** king who thus inured himself to poison.

EPITAPH ON AN ARMY OF MERCENARIES

These, in the day when heaven was falling,
    The hour when earth's foundations fled,
Followed their mercenary calling
    And took their wages and are dead.

Their shoulders held the sky suspended;
    They stood, and earth's foundations stay;
What God abandoned, these defended,
    And saved the sum of things for pay.

WILLIAM BUTLER YEATS (1865–1939)

THE ROSE OF THE WORLD

Who dreamed that beauty passes like a dream?
For these red lips, with all their mournful pride,
Mournful that no new wonder may betide,
Troy passed away in one high funeral gleam,
And Usna's children died.

We and the labouring world are passing by:
Amid men's souls, that waver and give place
Like the pale waters in their wintry race,
Under the passing stars, foam of the sky,
Lives on this lonely face.   10

Bow down, archangels, in your dim abode:
Before you were, or any hearts to beat,
Weary and kind one lingered by His seat;
He made the world to be a grassy road
Before her wandering feet.

5. **Usna:** in Irish mythology her three sons were treacherously killed by King Conchubar, because they had abducted Deirdre, a beautiful Irish princess, whom the king had planned to marry

THE MAGI

Now as at all times I can see in the mind's eye,
In their stiff, painted clothes, the pale unsatisfied ones
Appear and disappear in the blue depth of the sky
With all their ancient faces like rain-beaten stones,
And all their helms of silver hovering side by side,
And all their eyes still fixed, hoping to find once more,
Being by Calvary's turbulence unsatisfied,
The uncontrollable mystery on the bestial floor.

EASTER 1916

I have met them at close of day
Coming with vivid faces
From counter or desk among grey
Eighteenth-century houses.
I have passed with a nod of the head
Or polite meaningless words,
Or have lingered awhile and said
Polite meaningless words,
And thought before I had done
Of a mocking tale or a gibe
To please a companion
Around the fire at the club,
Being certain that they and I
But lived where motley is worn:
All changed, changed utterly:
A terrible beauty is born.

That woman's days were spent
In ignorant good-will,
Her nights in argument

Title. Magi: the three wise men who followed the star to the cradle of the infant Christ. 7. Calvary's turbulence: the disturbance associated with the crucifixion, which took place on the mount of Calvary.

Title. At Eastertime, 1916, the Irish staged an insurrection against the British, although the latter had already promised them Home Rule (see line 68). The revolt was quickly put down and certain ringleaders were shot. 14. motley: clowns' clothing. 17. That woman: Constance Markievicz, who received the death sentence in 1916, which was subsequently commuted to life imprisonment, which was terminated after the amnesty in 1917.

Until her voice grew shrill.   20
What voice more sweet that hers
When, young and beautiful,
She rode to harriers?
This man had kept a school
And rode our wingèd horse;
This other his helper and friend
Was coming into his force;
He might have won fame in the end,
So sensitive his nature seemed,
So daring and sweet his thought.   30
This other man I had dreamed
A drunken, vainglorious lout.
He had done most bitter wrong
To some who are near my heart,
Yet I number him in the song;
He, too, has resigned his part
In the casual comedy;
He, too, has been changed in his turn,
Transformed utterly:
A terrible beauty is born.   40

Hearts with one purpose alone
Through summer and winter seem
Enchanted to a stone
To trouble the living stream.
The horse that comes from the road,
The rider, the birds that range
From cloud to tumbling cloud,
Minute by minute they change;
A shadow of cloud on the stream
Changes minute by minute;   50
A horse-hoof slides on the brim,
And a horse plashes within it;
The long-legged moor-hens dive,
And hens to moor-cocks call;

23. **harriers:** hounds. 24. **This man:** Padraic Pearse, schoolteacher, leader of the assault in the Dublin Post Office; executed 1916. 25. **rode . . . horse:** was a poet (reference to Pegasus, the wingèd horse that symbolized poetic inspiration). 26. **This other:** Thomas MacDonagh, writer: executed 1916. 31. **This other:** John MacBride, soldier, separated husband of Yeats' beloved Maud Gonne: executed 1916. 34. **some:** Maud Gonne and her ward, Iseult.

Minute by minute they live:
The stone's in the midst of all.

Too long a sacrifice
Can make a stone of the heart.
O when may it suffice?
60   That is Heaven's part, our part
To murmur name upon name,
As a mother names her child
When sleep at last has come
On limbs that had run wild.
What is it but nightfall?
No, no, not night but death;
Was it needless death after all?
For England may keep faith
For all that is done and said.
70   We know their dream; enough
To know they dreamed and are dead;
And what if excess of love
Bewildered them till they died?
I write it out in a verse—
MacDonagh and MacBride
And Connolly and Pearse
Now and in time to be,
Wherever green is worn,
Are changed, changed utterly:
80   A terrible beauty is born.

THE SECOND COMING

Turning and turning in the widening gyre
The falcon cannot hear the falconer;
Things fall apart; the centre cannot hold;
Mere anarchy is loosed upon the world,

68. **England . . . faith:** Parliament had passed the Irish Home Rule bill before the 1914–18 war; whether they would keep faith and implement it after the war was a matter of opinion. 76. **Connolly:** James Connolly, commander-in-chief of the Easter Rising; executed 1916.

Title. Literally refers to the second coming of Christ, Matthew xxiv.29-44. The poem was written in 1919, in the aftermath of World War I, during times of civil strife in Ireland. 1. **gyre:** spiral. Yeats thought of history as winding itself off the base of a rotating cone at the end of its two-thousand-year cycle.

The blood-dimmed tide is loosed, and everywhere
The ceremony of innocence is drowned;
The best lack all conviction, while the worst
Are full of passionate intensity.

Surely some revelation is at hand;
Surely the Second Coming is at hand.   10
The Second Coming! Hardly are those words out
When a vast image out of *Spiritus Mundi*
Troubles my sight: somewhere in sands of the desert
A shape with lion body and the head of a man,
A gaze blank and pitiless as the sun,
Is moving its slow thighs, while all about it
Reel shadows of the indignant desert birds.
The darkness drops again; but now I know
That twenty centuries of stony sleep
Were vexed to nightmare by a rocking cradle,   20
And what rough beast, its hour come round at last,
Slouches towards Bethlehem to be born?

THE LEADERS OF THE CROWD

They must to keep their certainty accuse
All that are different of a base intent;
Pull down established honour; hawk for news
Whatever their loose fantasy invent
And murmur it with bated breath, as though
The abounding gutter had been Helicoi
Or calumny a song. How can they know
Truth flourishes where the student's lamp has shone,
And there alone, that have no solitude?
So the crowd come they care not what may come.   10
They have loud music, hope every day renewed
And heartier loves; that lamp is from the tomb.

12. Spiritus Mundi: spirit of the world. Yeats thought of it as a fund of communal images; it is similar to the concept of the collective unconscious, which the psychologist Jung considered to be a reservoir of memories common to all men.

6. Helicon: the mountain home of the nine Muses, who are the inspirers of artistic creation.

LEDA AND THE SWAN

A sudden blow: the great wings beating still
Above the staggering girl, her thighs caressed
By the dark webs, her nape caught in his bill,
He holds her helpless breast upon his breast.

How can those terrified vague fingers push
The feathered glory from her loosening thighs?
And how can body, laid in that white rush,
But feel the strange heart beating where it lies?

A shudder in the loins engenders there
10   The broken wall, the burning roof and tower
And Agamemnon dead.
                              Being so caught up,
So mastered by the brute blood of the air,
Did she put on his knowledge with his power
Before the indifferent beak could let her drop?

SAILING TO BYZANTIUM

I

That is no country for old men. The young
In one another's arms, birds in the trees
—Those dying generations—at their song,
The salmon-falls, the mackerel-crowded seas,
Fish, flesh, or fowl, commend all summer long
Whatever is begotten, born, and dies.
Caught in that sensual music all neglect
Monuments of unageing intellect.

Note. The union of Leda and Zeus (in the shape of a swan) produced the beautiful Helen, whose abduction by the Trojan Paris led to the Greeks' sack of Troy. The leader of the Greeks, King Agamemnon, was murdered by his wife Clytemnestra on his triumphant return to Mycenae.

Title. Byzantium: seat of the Roman Empire after the Fall of Rome. In *A Vision*, Yeats comments: "I think that in early Byzantium, maybe never before or since in recorded history, religious, aesthetic and practical life were one, that architect and artificers—though not, it may be, poets, for language had been the instrument of controversy and must have grown abstract—spoke to the multitude and the few alike."
1. That: Ireland.

II

An aged man is but a paltry thing,
A tattered coat upon a stick, unless   10
Soul clap its hands and sing, and louder sing
For every tatter in its mortal dress,
Nor is there singing school but studying
Monuments of its own magnificence;
And therefore I have sailed the seas and come
To the holy city of Byzantium.

III

O sages standing in God's holy fire
As in the gold mosaic of a wall,
Come from the holy fire, perne in a gyre,
And be the singing-masters of my soul.   20
Consume my heart away; sick with desire
And fastened to a dying animal
It knows not what it is; and gather me
Into the artifice of eternity.

IV

Once out of nature I shall never take
My bodily form from any natural thing,
But such a form as Grecian goldsmiths make
Of hammered gold and gold enamelling
To keep a drowsy Emperor awake;
Or set upon a golden bough to sing   30
To lords and ladies of Byzantium
Of what is past, or passing, or to come.

AMONG SCHOOL CHILDREN

I

I walk through the long schoolroom questioning;
A kind old nun in a white hood replies;
The children learn to cipher and to sing,
To study reading-books and history,

---

19. **perne in a gyre:** come spiralling down.

To cut and sew, be neat in everything
In the best modern way—the children's eyes
In momentary wonder stare upon
A sixty-year-old smiling public man.

II

I dream of a Ledaean body, bent
Above a sinking fire, a tale that she
Told of a harsh reproof, or trivial event
That changed some childish day to tragedy—
Told, and it seemed that our two natures blent
Into a sphere from youthful sympathy,
Or else, to alter Plato's parable,
Into the yolk and white of the one shell.

III

And thinking of that fit of grief or rage
I look upon one child or t'other there
And wonder if she stood so at that age—
For even daughters of the swan can share
Something of every paddler's heritage—
And had that colour upon cheek or hair,
And thereupon my heart is driven wild:
She stands before me as a living child.

IV

Her present image floats into the mind—
Did Quattrocento finger fashion it
Hollow of cheek as though it drank the wind
And took a mess of shadows for its meat?
And I though never of Ledaean kind
Had pretty plumage once—enough of that,
Better to smile on all that smile, and show
There is a comfortable kind of old scarecrow.

8. public man: Yeats, by the time he wrote this poem, was a Senator of the Irish Free State. **9. Ledaean:** pertaining to Leda, mother of Helen by Zeus in the form of a swan; cf. **daughters of the swan,** line 20. **15. Plato's parable:** In the *Symposium*, the legend is told that humans were originally spherical in form, bearing both male and female features. The instinct of love is attributed to male and female seeking to regain their original unity. **26. Quattrocento finger:** fifteenth-century Italian artist.

V

What youthful mother, a shape upon her lap
Honey of generation had betrayed,
And that must sleep, shriek, struggle to escape
As recollection or the drug decide,
Would think her son, did she but see that shape
With sixty or more winters on its head,
A compensation for the pang of his birth,
Or the uncertainty of his setting forth?   40

VI

Plato thought nature but a spume that plays
Upon a ghostly paradigm of things;
Solider Aristotle played the taws
Upon the bottom of a king of kings;
World-famous golden-thighed Pythagoras
Fingered upon a fiddle-stick or strings
What a star sang and careless Muses heard:
Old clothes upon old sticks to scare a bird.

VII

Both nuns and mothers worship images,
But those the candles light are not as those   50
That animate a mother's reveries,
But keep a marble or a bronze repose.
And yet they too break hearts—O Presences
That passion, piety or affection knows,
And that all heavenly glory symbolise—
O self-born mockers of man's enterprise;

VIII

Labour is blossoming or dancing where
The body is not bruised to pleasure soul,
Nor beauty born out of its own despair,
Nor blear-eyed wisdom out of midnight oil.   60

34. **Honey of generation:** Yeats uses the phrase to designate the drug that destroys the recollection of pre-natal freedom; also, the sexual act that has **betrayed** the soul of the child into mortality. 42. **ghostly . . . things:** Plato's concept that the natural world is but a pale reflection of an Ideal world that cannot be known by means of the senses. 43–44. **Solider Aristotle . . . king of kings:** Aristotle believed in the reality of the natural world. He played the taws, i.e., flogged, his pupil, Alexander the Great. 45–47. **World-famous . . . heard:** reference to the reputedly golden-hipped Pythagoras's belief that mathematics and music were related (harmony) and that the planets in their orbits gave off musical tones (music of the spheres), inaudible to earthly ears. 47. **Muses:** the goddesses who were traditionally thought to inspire the arts.

O chestnut-tree, great-rooted blossomer,
Are you the leaf, the blossom or the bole?
O body swayed to music, O brightening glance,
How can we know the dancer from the dance?

AFTER LONG SILENCE

Speech after long silence; it is right,
All other lovers being estranged or dead,
Unfriendly lamplight hid under its shade,
The curtains drawn upon unfriendly night,
That we descant and yet again descant
Upon the supreme theme of Art and Song:
Bodily decrepitude is wisdom; young
We loved each other and were ignorant.

EDWIN ARLINGTON ROBINSON (1869–1935)

REUBEN BRIGHT

Because he was a butcher and thereby
Did earn an honest living (and did right),
I would not have you think that Reuben Bright
Was any more a brute than you or I;
For when they told him that his wife must die,
He stared at them, and shook with grief and fright,
And cried like a great baby half that night,
And made the women cry to see him cry.

And after she was dead, and he had paid
10   The singers and the sexton and the rest,
He packed a lot of things that she had made
Most mournfully away in an old chest
Of hers, and put some chopped-up cedar boughs
In with them, and tore down the slaughter-house.

RICHARD CORY

Whenever Richard Cory went down town,
We people on the pavement looked at him:
He was a gentleman from sole to crown,
Clean favored, and imperially slim.

And he was always quietly arrayed,
And he was always human when he talked;
But still he fluttered pulses when he said,
"Good-morning," and he glittered when he walked.

And he was rich—yes, richer than a king—
And admirably schooled in every grace: 10
In fine, we thought that he was everything
To make us wish that we were in his place.

So on we worked, and waited for the light,
And went without the meat, and cursed the bread;
And Richard Cory, one calm summer night,
Went home and put a bullet through his head.

FOR A DEAD LADY

No more with overflowing light
Shall fill the eyes that now are faded,
Nor shall another's fringe with night
Their woman-hidden world as they did.
No more shall quiver down the days
The flowing wonder of her ways,
Whereof no language may requite
The shifting and the many-shaded.

The grace, divine, definitive,
Clings only as a faint forestalling;   10
The laugh that love could not forgive
Is hushed, and answers to no calling;
The forehead and the little ears
Have gone where Saturn keeps the years;
The breast where roses could not live
Has done with rising and with falling.

14. Saturn: Roman deity.

The beauty, shattered by the laws
That have creation in their keeping,
No longer trembles at applause,
20   Or over children that are sleeping;
And we who delve in beauty's lore
Know all that we have known before
Of what inexorable cause
Makes Time so vicious in his reaping.

MR. FLOOD'S PARTY

Old Eben Flood, climbing alone one night
Over the hill between the town below
And the forsaken upland hermitage
That held as much as he should ever know
On earth again of home, paused warily.
The road was his with not a native near;
And Eben, having leisure, said aloud,
For no man else in Tilbury Town to hear:

"Well, Mr. Flood, we have the harvest moon
10   Again, and we may not have many more;
The bird is on the wing, the poet says,
And you and I have said it here before.
Drink to the bird." He raised up to the light
The jug that he had gone so far to fill,
And answered huskily: "Well, Mr. Flood,
Since you propose it, I believe I will."

Alone, as if enduring to the end
A valiant armor of scarred hopes outworn,
He stood there in the middle of the road
20   Like Roland's ghost winding a silent horn.
Below him, in the town among the trees,
Where friends of other days had honored him,
A phantom salutation of the dead
Rang thinly till old Eben's eyes were dim.

21. delve: dig. 23. inexorable: relentless.

20. Roland: legendary hero who, when ambushed in the rear guard of the returning
French army in 778, declined to blow the horn and summon help until it was too late.

Then, as a mother lays her sleeping child
Down tenderly, fearing it may awake,
He set the jug down slowly at his feet
With trembling care, knowing that most things break;
And only when assured that on firm earth
It stood, as the uncertain lives of men   30
Assuredly did not, he paced away,
And with his hand extended paused again:

"Well, Mr. Flood, we have not met like this
In a long time; and many a change has come
To both of us, I fear, since last it was
We had a drop together. Welcome home!"
Convivially returning with himself,
Again he raised the jug up to the light;
And with an acquiescent quaver said:
"Well, Mr. Flood, if you insist, I might.   40

"Only a very little, Mr. Flood—
For auld lang syne. No more, sir; that will do."
So, for the time, apparently it did,
And Eben evidently thought so too;
For soon amid the silver loneliness
Of night he lifted up his voice and sang,
Secure, with only two moons listening,
Until the whole harmonious landscape rang—

"For auld lang syne." The weary throat gave out,
The last word wavered; and the song being done,   50
He raised again the jug regretfully
And shook his head, and was again alone.
There was not much that was ahead of him,
And there was nothing in the town below—
Where strangers would have shut the many doors
That many friends had opened long ago.

37. convivially: sociably. 39. acquiescent: compliant. quaver: tremble. 42. auld lang syne: old times

ROBERT FROST (1874–1963)

MENDING WALL

Something there is that doesn't love a wall,
That sends the frozen-ground-swell under it,
And spills the upper boulders in the sun;
And makes gaps even two can pass abreast.
The work of hunters is another thing:
I have come after them and made repair
Where they have left not one stone on a stone,
But they would have the rabbit out of hiding,
To please the yelping dogs. The gaps I mean,
10   No one has seen them made or heard them made,
But at spring mending-time we find them there.
I let my neighbor know beyond the hill;
And on a day we meet to walk the line
And set the wall between us once again.
We keep the wall between us as we go.
To each the boulders that have fallen to each.
And some are loaves and some so nearly balls
We have to use a spell to make them balance:
'Stay where you are until our backs are turned!'
20   We wear our fingers rough with handling them.
Oh, just another kind of outdoor game,
One on a side. It comes to little more:
There where it is we do not need the wall:
He is all pine and I am apple orchard.
My apple trees will never get across
And eat the cones under his pines, I tell him.
He only says, 'Good fences make good neighbors.'
Spring is the mischief in me, and I wonder
If I could put a notion in his head:
30   'Why do they make good neighbors? Isn't it
Where there are cows? But here there are no cows.
Before I built a wall I'd ask to know
What I was walling in or walling out,

And to whom I was like to give offense.
Something there is that doesn't love a wall,
That wants it down.' I could say 'Elves' to him,
But it's not elves exactly, and I'd rather
He said it for himself. I see him there
Bringing a stone grasped firmly by the top
In each hand, like an old-stone savage armed.   40
He moves in darkness as it seems to me,
Not of woods only and the shade of trees.
He will not go behind his father's saying,
And he likes having thought of it so well
He says again, 'Good fences make good neighbors.'

AFTER APPLE-PICKING

My long two-pointed ladder's sticking through a tree
Toward heaven still,
And there's a barrel that I didn't fill
Beside it, and there may be two or three
Apples I didn't pick upon some bough.
But I am done with apple-picking now.
Essence of winter sleep is on the night,
The scent of apples: I am drowsing off.
I cannot rub the strangeness from my sight
I got from looking through a pane of glass   10
I skimmed this morning from the drinking trough
And held against the world of hoary grass.
It melted, and I let it fall and break.
But I was well
Upon my way to sleep before it fell,
And I could tell
What form my dreaming was about to take.
Magnified apples appear and disappear,
Stem end and blossom end,
And every fleck of russet showing clear.   20
My instep arch not only keeps the ache,
It keeps the pressure of a ladder-round.
I feel the ladder sway as the boughs bend.
And I keep hearing from the cellar bin
The rumbling sound
Of load on load of apples coming in.

For I have had too much
Of apple-picking: I am overtired
Of the great harvest I myself desired.
There were ten thousand thousand fruit to touch,
Cherish in hand, lift down, and not let fall.
For all
That struck the earth,
No matter if not bruised or spiked with stubble,
Went surely to the cider-apple heap
As of no worth.
One can see what will trouble
This sleep of mine, whatever sleep it is.
Were he not gone,
The woodchuck could say whether it's like his
Long sleep, as I describe its coming on,
Or just some human sleep.

STOPPING BY WOODS ON A SNOWY EVENING

private
+ public
ones going to see him.

Whose woods these are I think I know.
His house is in the village though;
He will not see me stopping here
To watch his woods fill up with snow.

solitary
hint of
danger.

My little horse must think it queer
To stop without a farmhouse near
Between the woods and frozen lake
The darkest evening of the year.

He gives his harness bells a shake
To ask if there is some mistake.
The only other sound's the sweep
Of easy wind and downy flake.

woods are a place of dying.

The woods are lovely, dark and deep,
But I have promises to keep,
And miles to go before I sleep,
And miles to go before I sleep.

privacy - is a form of death; its wonderful.

ONCE BY THE PACIFIC

The shattered water made a misty din.
Great waves looked over others coming in,
And thought of doing something to the shore
That water never did to land before.
The clouds were low and hairy in the skies,
Like locks blown forward in the gleam of eyes.
You could not tell, and yet it looked as if
The shore was lucky in being backed by cliff,
The cliff in being backed by continent;
It looked as if a night of dark intent   10
Was coming, and not only a night, an age.
Someone had better be prepared for rage.
There would be more than ocean-water broken
Before God's last *Put out the Light* was spoken.

DESERT PLACES

Snow falling and night falling fast, oh, fast
In a field I looked into going past,
And the ground almost covered smooth in snow,
But a few weeds and stubble showing last.

The woods around it have it—it is theirs.
All animals are smothered in their lairs.
I am too absent-spirited to count;
The loneliness includes me unawares.

And lonely as it is that loneliness
Will be more lonely ere it will be less—   10
A blanker whiteness of benighted snow
With no expression, nothing to express.

They cannot scare me with their empty spaces
Between stars—on stars where no human race is.
I have it in me so much nearer home
To scare myself with my own desert places.

14. Put out the Light: from Othello's speech before killing Desdemona.

[Handwritten annotations: "He just passed a field snow covered ground with snow"; "and this night appears to be ... lonely to him. except he feels he's not apart of the beauty giving him a lonely peace feeling"; "The snow gives him an empty feeling"; "inferior complex"; "last time he desired needs snow to feel lonely ... cause"; "even without snow he feels lonely."]

DESIGN

I found a dimpled spider, fat and white,
On a white heal-all, holding up a moth
Like a white piece of rigid satin cloth—
Assorted characters of death and blight
Mixed ready to begin the morning right,
Like the ingredients of a witches' broth—
A snow-drop spider, a flower like a froth,
And dead wings carried like a paper kite.

What had that flower to do with being white,
The wayside blue and innocent heal-all?
What brought the kindred spider to that height,
Then steered the white moth thither in the night?
What but design of darkness to appall?—
If design govern in a thing so small.

COME IN

As I came to the edge of the woods,
Thrush music—hark!
Now if it was dusk outside,
Inside it was dark.

Too dark in the woods for a bird
By sleight of wing
To better its perch for the night,
Though it still could sing.

The last of the light of the sun
That had died in the west
Still lived for one song more
In a thrush's breast.

Far in the pillared dark
Thrush music went—
Almost like a call to come in
To the dark and lament.

2. heal-all: species of flower. 4. blight: destruction.

But no, I was out for stars:
I would not come in.
I meant not even if asked,
And I hadn't been.   20

WALLACE STEVENS (1879–1955)

PETER QUINCE AT THE CLAVIER

I

Just as my fingers on these keys
Make music, so the selfsame sounds
On my spirit make a music, too.

Music is feeling, then, not sound;
And thus it is that what I feel,
Here in this room, desiring you,

Thinking of your blue-shadowed silk,
Is music. It is like the strain
Waked in the elders by Susanna.

Of a green evening, clear and warm,   10
She bathed in her still garden, while
The red-eyed elders watching, felt

Title. Stevens borrows the name of the rustic director of the Pyramus and Thisbe interlude in *A Midsummer Night's Dream.* 9. Susanna: a figure in the Apocrypha whom two elders (leaders of the Hebrew community) attempted to seduce while she was bathing in her garden. When she repulsed them they charged her with adultery, but she was cleared of the charge by Daniel. The elders were executed (note the reference to death in line 63).

The basses of their beings throb
In witching chords, and their thin blood
Pulse pizzicati of Hosanna.

II

In the green water, clear and warm,
Susanna lay.
She searched
The touch of springs,
And found
Concealed imaginings.
She sighed,
For so much melody.

Upon the bank, she stood
In the cool
Of spent emotions.
She felt, among the leaves,
The dew
Of old devotions.

She walked upon the grass,
Still quavering.
The winds were like her maids,
On timid feet,
Fetching her woven scarves,
Yet wavering.

A breath upon her hand
Muted the night.
She turned—
A cymbal crashed,
And roaring horns.

III

Soon, with a noise like tambourines,
Came her attendant Byzantines.

They wondered why Susanna cried
Against the elders by her side;

15. **Hosanna:** exclamation of praise.

And as they whispered, the refrain
Was like a willow swept by rain.

Anon, their lamps' uplifted flame
Revealed Susanna and her shame.

And then, the simpering Byzantines
Fled, with a noise like tambourines.   50

IV

Beauty is momentary in the mind—
The fitful tracing of a portal;
But in the flesh it is immortal.

The body dies; the body's beauty lives.
So evenings die, in their green going,
A wave, interminably flowing.
So gardens die, their meek breath scenting
The cowl of winter, done repenting.
So maidens die, to the auroral
Celebration of a maiden's choral.   60
Susanna's music touched the bawdy strings
Of those white elders; but, escaping,
Left only Death's ironic scraping.
Now, in its immortality, it plays
On the clear viol of her memory,
And makes a constant sacrament of praise.

SUNDAY MORNING

I

Complacencies of the peignoir, and late
Coffee and oranges in a sunny chair,
And the green freedom of a cockatoo
Upon a rug mingle to dissipate
The holy hush of ancient sacrifice.
She dreams a little, and she feels the dark
Encroachment of that old catastrophe,
As a calm darkens among water-lights.
The pungent oranges and bright, green wings

---

59. auroral: of or like the dawn.

10   Seem things in some procession of the dead,
Winding across wide water, without sound.
The day is like wide water, without sound,
Stilled for the passing of her dreaming feet
Over the seas, to silent Palestine,
Dominion of the blood and sepulchre.

II

Why should she give her bounty to the dead?
What is divinity if it can come
Only in silent shadows and in dreams?
Shall she not find in comforts of the sun,
20   In pungent fruit and bright, green wings, or else
In any balm or beauty of the earth,
Things to be cherished like the thought of heaven?
Divinity must live within herself:
Passions of rain, or moods in falling snow;
Grievings in loneliness, or unsubdued
Elations when the forest blooms; gusty
Emotions on wet roads on autumn nights;
All pleasures and all pains, remembering
The bough of summer and the winter branch.
30   These are the measures destined for her soul.

III

Jove in the clouds had his inhuman birth.
No mother suckled him, no sweet land gave
Large-mannered motions to his mythy mind.
He moved among us, as a muttering king,
Magnificent, would move among his hinds,
Until our blood, commingling, virginal,
With heaven, brought such requital to desire
The very hinds discerned it, in a star.
Shall our blood fail? Or shall it come to be
40   The blood of paradise? And shall the earth
Seem all of paradise that we shall know?
The sky will be much friendlier then than now,
A part of labor and a part of pain,
And next in glory to enduring love,
Not this dividing and indifferent blue.

31. **Jove:** Jupiter, the chief god in the Roman pantheon, or system of gods. **35. hinds:** servants. **38. star:** i.e., star of Bethlehem.

IV

She says, "I am content when wakened birds,
Before they fly, test the reality
Of misty fields, by their sweet questionings;
But when the birds are gone, and their warm fields
Return no more, where, then, is paradise?"   50
There is not any haunt of prophecy,
Nor any old chimera of the grave,
Neither the golden underground, nor isle
Melodious, where spirits gat them home,
Nor visionary south, nor cloudy palm
Remote on heaven's hill, that has endured
As April's green endures; or will endure
Like her remembrance of awakened birds,
Or her desire for June and evening, tipped
By the consummation of the swallow's wings.   60

V

She says, "But in contentment I still feel
The need of some imperishable bliss."
Death is the mother of beauty; hence from her,
Alone, shall come fulfilment to our dreams
And our desires. Although she strews the leaves
Of sure obliteration on our paths,
The path sick sorrow took, the many paths
Where triumph rang its brassy phrase, or love
Whispered a little out of tenderness,
She makes the willow shiver in the sun   70
For maidens who were wont to sit and gaze
Upon the grass, relinquished to their feet.
She causes boys to pile new plums and pears
On disregarded plate. The maidens taste
And stray impassioned in the littering leaves.

VI

Is there no change of death in paradise?
Does ripe fruit never fall? Or do the boughs
Hang always heavy in that perfect sky,
Unchanging, yet so like our perishing earth,
With rivers like our own that seek for seas   80

52. **chimera**: fanciful invention. 54. **gat**: got.

They never find, the same receding shores
That never touch with inarticulate pang?
Why set the pear upon those river-banks
Or spice the shores with odors of the plum?
Alas, that they should wear our colors there,
The silken weavings of our afternoons,
And pick the strings of our insipid lutes!
Death is the mother of beauty, mystical,
Within whose burning bosom we devise
90   Our earthly mothers waiting, sleeplessly.

VII

Supple and turbulent, a ring of men
Shall chant in orgy on a summer morn
Their boisterous devotion to the sun,
Not as a god, but as a god might be,
Naked among them, like a savage source.
Their chant shall be a chant of paradise,
Out of their blood, returning to the sky;
And in their chant shall enter, voice by voice,
The windy lake wherein their lord delights,
100   The trees, like serafin, and echoing hills,
That choir among themselves long afterward.
They shall know well the heavenly fellowship
Of men that perish and of summer morn.
And whence they came and whither they shall go
The dew upon their feet shall manifest.

VIII

She hears, upon that water without sound,
A voice that cries, "The tomb in Palestine
Is not the porch of spirits lingering.
It is the grave of Jesus, where he lay."
110   We live in an old chaos of the sun,
Or old dependency of day and night,
Or island, solitude, unsponsored, free,
Of that wide water, inescapable.
Deer walk upon our mountains, and the quail
Whistle about us their spontaneous cries;

89. devise: imaginatively create. 100. serafin: seraphim, angels of the highest of the nine orders.

Sweet berries ripen in the wilderness;
And, in the isolation of the sky,
At evening, casual flocks of pigeons make
Ambiguous undulations as they sink,
Downward to darkness, on extended wings.   120

ANECDOTE OF THE JAR

I placed a jar in Tennessee,
And round it was, upon a hill.
It made the slovenly wilderness
Surround that hill.

The wilderness rose up to it,
And sprawled around, no longer wild.
The jar was round upon the ground
And tall and of a port in air.

It took dominion everywhere.
The jar was gray and bare.   10
It did not give of bird or bush,
Like nothing else in Tennessee.

BANTAMS IN PINE-WOODS

Chieftain Iffucan of Azcan in caftan
Of tan with henna hackles, halt!

Damned universal cock, as if the sun
Was blackamoor to bear your blazing tail.

Fat! Fat! Fat! Fat! I am the personal.
Your world is you. I am my world.

You ten-foot poet among inchlings. Fat!
Begone! An inchling bristles in these pines,

Bristles, and points their Appalachian tangs,
And fears not portly Azcan nor his hoos.   10

1. **caftan:** robe. 9. **tangs:** prongs

THE EMPEROR OF ICE-CREAM

Call the roller of big cigars,
The muscular one, and bid him whip
In kitchen cups concupiscent curds.
Let the wenches dawdle in such dress
As they are used to wear, and let the boys
Bring flowers in last month's newspapers.
Let be be finale of seem.
The only emperor is the emperor of ice-cream.

Take from the dresser of deal,
Lacking the three glass knobs, that sheet
On which she embroidered fantails once
And spread it so as to cover her face.
If her horny feet protrude, they come
To show how cold she is, and dumb.
Let the lamp affix its beam.
The only emperor is the emperor of ice-cream.

WILLIAM CARLOS WILLIAMS (1883–1963)

ARRIVAL

And yet one arrives somehow,
finds himself loosening the hooks of
her dress
in a strange bedroom—
feels the autumn
dropping its silk and linen leaves
about her ankles.
The tawdry veined body emerges
twisted upon itself
like a winter wind . . .!

9. deal: cheap wood.

POEM

As the cat
climbed over
the top of

the jamcloset
first the right
forefoot

carefully
then the hind
stepped down

into the pit of   10
the empty
flowerpot

THE RED WHEELBARROW

so much depends
upon

a red wheel
barrow

glazed with rain
water

beside the white
chickens.

THE DANCE

In Breughel's great picture, The Kermess,
the dancers go round, they go round and
around, the squeal and the blare and the
tweedle of bagpipes, a bugle and fiddles
tipping their bellies (round as the thick-
sided glasses whose wash they impound)
their hips and their bellies off balance

---

1. Breughel: Pieter Breughel (c. 1520–1569), Flemish painter, distinguished espe-
cially for scenes from peasant life full of vitality; The Kermess: annual fair in Belgium.

to turn them. Kicking and rolling about
the Fair Grounds, swinging their butts, those
10   shanks must be sound to bear up under such
rollicking measures, prance as they dance
in Breughel's great picture, The Kermess.

TO A DOG INJURED IN THE STREET

It is myself,
            not the poor beast lying there
                        yelping with pain
that brings me to myself with a start—
            as at the explosion
                        of a bomb, a bomb that has laid
all the world waste.
            I can do nothing
                        but sing about it
and so I am assuaged
            from my pain.

A drowsy numbness drowns my sense
            as if of hemlock
                        I had drunk. I think
of the poetry
            of René Char
                        and all he must have seen
and suffered
            that has brought him
                        to speak only of
sedgy rivers,
            of daffodils and tulips
                        whose roots they water,
even to the freeflowing river
            that laves the rootlets
                        of those sweet scented flowers
10   that people the
            milky

                        way

4. **assuaged**: relieved. 5. **hemlock**: poisonous drug (see Keats, "Ode to a Nightin-
gale," line 2). 6. **René Char**: French poet, born 1907. 8. **sedgy**: bordered by marsh
plants. 9. **laves**: washes.

I remember Norma
            our English setter of my childhood
                        her silky ears
and expressive eyes.
            She had a litter
                        of pups one night
in our pantry and I kicked
            one of them
                        thinking, in my alarm,
that they
            were biting her breasts
                        to destroy her.

I remember also
            a dead rabbit
                        lying harmlessly
on the outspread palm
            of a hunter's hand.
                        As I stood by
watching
            he took a hunting knife
                        and with a laugh
thrust it
            up into the animal's private parts.
                        I almost fainted.

Why should I think of that now?
            The cries of a dying dog
                        are to be blotted out
as best I can.
            René Char   20
                        you are a poet who believes
in the power of beauty
            to right all wrongs.
                        I believe it also.
With invention and courage
            we shall surpass
                        the pitiful dumb beasts,
let all men believe it,
            as you have taught me also
                        to believe it.

D. H. LAWRENCE (1885–1930)

COROT

The trees rise taller and taller, lifted
On a subtle rush of cool grey flame
That issuing out of the east has sifted
    The spirit from each leaf's frame.

For the trailing, leisurely rapture of life
Drifts dimly forward, easily hidden
By bright leaves uttered aloud; and strife
    Of shapes by a hard wind ridden.

The grey, plasm-limpid, pellucid advance
10   Of the luminous purpose of Life shines out
Where lofty trees athwart-stream chance
    To shake flakes of its shadow about.

The subtle, steady rush of the whole
Grey foam-mist of advancing Time
As it silently sweeps to its somewhere, its goal,
    Is seen in the gossamer's rime.

Is heard in the windless whisper of leaves,
In the silent labours of men in the field,
In the downward-dropping of flimsy sheaves
20   Of cloud the rain-skies yield.

In the tapping haste of a fallen leaf,
In the flapping of red-roof smoke, and the small
Footstepping tap of men beneath
    Dim trees so huge and tall.

For what can all sharp-rimmed substance but catch
In a backward ripple, the wave-length, reveal

9. **plasm-limpid:** clear and transparent as plasm, a clear quartz; **pellucid:** clear, transparent. 11. **athwart-stream:** opposing. 16. **gossamer:** cobweb; **rime:** hoarfrost.

For a moment the mighty direction, snatch
    A spark beneath the wheel!

Since Life sweeps whirling, dim and vast,
Creating the channelled vein of man
And leaf for its passage; a shadow cast
And gone before we can scan.

Ah listen, for silence is not lonely!
Imitate the magnificent trees
That speak no word of their rapture, but only
    Breathe largely the luminous breeze.

PIANO

Softly, in the dusk, a woman is singing to me;
Taking me back down the vista of years, till I see
A child sitting under the piano, in the boom of the tingling strings
And pressing the small, poised feet of a mother who smiles as she sings.

In spite of myself, the insidious mastery of song
Betrays me back, till the heart of me weeps to belong
To the old Sunday evenings at home, with winter outside
And hymns in the cosy parlour, the tinkling piano our guide.

So now it is vain for the singer to burst into clamour
With the great black piano appassionato. The glamour
Of childish days is upon me, my manhood is cast
Down in the flood of remembrance, I weep like a child for the past.

SNAKE

A snake came to my water-trough
On a hot, hot day, and I in pyjamas for the heat,
To drink there.

In the deep, strange-scented shade of the great dark carob-tree
I came down the steps with my pitcher
And must wait, must stand and wait, for there he was at the trough before me.

2. vista: view down a long corridor. 5. insidious: treacherous, sly. 10. appassionato: passionately.

He reached down from a fissure in the earth-wall in the gloom
And trailed his yellow-brown slackness soft-bellied down, over the edge
    of the stone trough
And rested his throat upon the stone bottom,
10 And where the water had dripped from the tap, in a small clearness,
He sipped with his straight mouth,
Softly drank through his straight gums, into his slack long body,
Silently.

Someone was before me at my water-trough,
And I, like a second comer, waiting.

He lifted his head from his drinking, as cattle do,
And looked at me vaguely, as drinking cattle do,
And flickered his two-forked tongue from his lips, and mused a moment,
And stooped and drank a little more,
20 Being earth-brown, earth-golden from the burning bowels of the earth
On the day of Sicilian July, with Etna smoking.
The voice of my education said to me:
He must be killed,
For in Sicily the black, black snakes are innocent, the gold are venomous.

And voices in me said, If you were a man
You would take a stick and break him now, and finish him off.

But must I confess how I liked him,
How glad I was he had come like a guest in quiet, to drink at my water-trough
And depart peaceful, pacified, and thankless,
30 Into the burning bowels of this earth?

Was it cowardice, that I dared not kill him?
Was it perversity, that I longed to talk to him?
Was it humility, to feel so honoured?
I felt so honoured.

And yet those voices:
If you were not afraid, you would kill him!

And truly I was afraid, I was most afraid,
But even so, honoured still more
That he should seek my hospitality
40 From out the dark door of the secret earth.

    21. **Etna:** volcano in Sicily.

He drank enough
And lifted his head, dreamily, as one who has drunken,
And flickered his tongue like a forked night on the air, so black;
Seeming to lick his lips,
And looked around like a god, unseeing, into the air,
And slowly turned his head,
And slowly, very slowly, as if thrice adream,
Proceeded to draw his slow length curving round
And climb again the broken bank of my wall-face.

And as he put his head into that dreadful hole,   50
And as he slowly drew up, snake-easing his shoulders, and entered farther,
A sort of horror, a sort of protest against his withdrawing into
        that horrid black hole,
Deliberately going into the blackness, and slowly drawing himself after,
Overcame me now his back was turned.

I looked round, I put down my pitcher,
I picked up a clumsy log
And threw it at the water-trough with a clatter.

I think it did not hit him,
But suddenly that part of him that was left behind convulsed
        in undignified haste,
Writhed like lightning, and was gone   60
Into the black hole, the earth-lipped fissure in the wall-front,
At which, in the intense still noon, I stared with fascination.

And immediately I regretted it.
I thought how paltry, how vulgar, what a mean act!
I despised myself and the voices of my accursed human education.

And I thought of the albatross,
And I wished he would come back, my snake.

For he seemed to me again like a king,
Like a king in exile, uncrowned in the underworld,
Now due to be crowned again.   70

And so, I missed my chance with one of the lords
Of life.
And I have something to expiate;
A pettiness.

73. expiate: to atone or make amends for.

EZRA POUND (1885–   )

A VIRGINAL

No, no! Go from me. I have left her lately.
I will not spoil my sheath with lesser brightness,
For my surrounding air hath a new lightness;
Slight are her arms, yet they have bound me straitly
And left me cloaked as with a gauze of æther;
As with sweet leaves; as with subtle clearness.
Oh, I have picked up magic in her nearness
To sheathe me half in half the things that sheathe her.
No, no! Go from me. I have still the flavour,
10   Soft as spring wind that's come from birchen bowers.
Green come the shoots, aye April in the branches,
As winter's wound with her sleight hand she staunches,
Hath of the trees a likeness of the savour:
As white their bark, so white this lady's hours.

IN A STATION OF THE METRO

The apparition of these faces in the crowd;
Petals on a wet, black bough.

PORTRAIT D'UNE FEMME

Your mind and you are our Sargasso Sea,
London has swept about you this score years
And bright ships left you this or that in fee:
Ideas, old gossip, oddments of all things,
Strange spars of knowledge and dimmed wares of price.

Title. Virginal: small harpsichord.

Title. Metro: underground railway in Paris.

Title. Portrait of a lady. 1. Sargasso Sea: the sea northeast of the West Indies: a
region of calms and mixing of ocean currents. 2. score: twenty. 3. in fee: as payment.

Great minds have sought you—lacking someone else.
You have been second always. Tragical?
No. You preferred it to the usual thing:
One dull man, dulling and uxorious,
One average mind—with one thought less, each year.   10
Oh, you are patient, I have seen you sit
Hours, where something might have floated up.
And now you pay one. Yes, you richly pay.
You are a person of some interest, one comes to you
And takes strange gain away:
Trophies fished up; some curious suggestion;
Fact that leads nowhere; and a tale or two,
Pregnant with mandrakes, or with something else
That might prove useful and yet never proves,
That never fits a corner or shows use,   20
Or finds its hour upon the loom of days:
The tarnished, gaudy, wonderful old work;
Idols and ambergris and rare inlays,
These are your riches, your great store; and yet
For all this sea-hoard of deciduous things,
Strange woods half sodden, and new brighter stuff:
In the slow float of different light and deep,
No! there is nothing! In the whole and all,
Nothing that's quite your own.
            Yet this is you.   30

THE RETURN

See, they return; ah, see the tentative
Movements, and the slow feet,
The trouble in the pace and the uncertain
Wavering!

See, they return, one, and by one,
With fear, as half-awakened;
As if the snow should hesitate
And murmur in the wind,

9. uxorious: submissive to one's wife. 18. Pregnant with mandrakes: full of wild stories, mandrakes being forked roots which were supposed to shriek when pulled out of the ground. 23. ambergris: substance used for making perfume, derived from whales. 25. deciduous: ephemeral.

and half turn back;
These were the "Wing'd-with-Awe,"
Inviolable,

Gods of the wingèd shoe!
With them the silver hounds,
        sniffing the trace of air!

Haie! Haie!
    These were the swift to harry;
These the keen-scented;
These were the souls of blood.

Slow on the leash,
        pallid the leash-men!

ROBINSON JEFFERS (1887–1962)

HURT HAWKS

I

The broken pillar of the wing jags from the clotted shoulder,
The wing trails like a banner in defeat,
No more to use the sky forever but live with famine
And pain a few days: cat nor coyote
Will shorten the week of waiting for death, there is game without talons.
He stands under the oak-bush and waits
The lame feet of salvation; at night he remembers freedom
And flies in a dream, the dawns ruin it.
He is strong and pain is worse to the strong, incapacity is worse.
The curs of the day come and torment him
At distance, no one but death the redeemer will humble that head,
The intrepid readiness, the terrible eyes.
The wild God of the world is sometimes merciful to those
That ask mercy, not often to the arrogant.
You do not know him, you communal people, or you have forgotten him;
Intemperate and savage, the hawk remembers him;
Beautiful and wild, the hawks, and men that are dying, remember him.

5. talons: claws. 12. intrepid: fearless.

II

I'd sooner, except the penalties, kill a man than a hawk; but the great redtail
Had nothing left but unable misery
From the bone too shattered for mending, the wing that trailed under his
    talons when he moved.   20
We had fed him six weeks, I gave him freedom,
He wandered over the foreland hill and returned in the evening,
    asking for death,
Not like a beggar, still eyed with the old
Implacable arrogance. I gave him the lead gift in the twilight. What
    fell was relaxed,
Owl-downy, soft feminine feathers; but what
Soared: the fierce rush: the night-herons by the flooded river
    cried fear at its rising
Before it was quite unsheathed from reality.

MARIANNE MOORE (1887–)

POETRY

I, too, dislike it: there are things that are important beyond
    all this fiddle.
    Reading it, however, with a perfect contempt for it, one
        discovers in
    it after all, a place for the genuine.
        Hands that can grasp, eyes
        that can dilate, hair that can rise
            if it must, these things are important not because a

high-sounding interpretation can be put upon them but
        because they are
    useful. When they become so derivative as to become
        unintelligible,
    the same thing may be said for all of us, that we
        do not admire what   10
        we cannot understand: the bat
            holding on upside down or in quest of something to

18. redtail: species of hawk.

eat, elephants pushing, a wild horse taking a roll, a tireless
          wolf under
a tree, the immovable critic twitching his skin like a
          horse that feels a flea, the base-
ball fan, the statistician—
          nor is it valid
               to discriminate against 'business documents and

school-books'; all these phenomena are important. One
          must make a distinction
however: when dragged into prominence by half poets,
          the result is not poetry,
20   nor till the poets among us can be
          'literalists of
          the imagination'—above
               insolence and triviality and can present

for inspection, 'imaginary gardens with real toads in them',
          shall we have
it. In the meantime, if you demand on the one hand,
the raw material of poetry in
          all its rawness and
          that which is on the other hand
               genuine, then you are interested in poetry.

IN DISTRUST OF MERITS

Strengthened to live, strengthened to die for
          medals and positioned victories?
They're fighting, fighting, fighting the blind
          man who thinks he sees,—
who cannot see that the enslaver is

17, 18. business documents and school-books: Miss Moore's note—"*Diary of
Tolstoy* (Dutton), p. 84. 'Where the boundary between prose and poetry lies, I shall
never be able to understand. The question is raised in manuals of style, yet the answer
to it lies beyond me. Poetry is verse: prose is not verse. Or else poetry is everything with
the exception of business documents and school books.' " 21, 22. Miss Moore's note—
" 'Literalists of the imagination.' Yeats: *Ideas of Good and Evil* (A. H. Bullen), p.
182. 'The limitation of his view was from the very intensity of his vision; he was a too
literal realist of imagination, as others are of nature; and because he believed that the figures
seen by the mind's eye, when exalted by inspiration, were "eternal existences," symbols
of divine essences, he hated every grace of style that might obscure their lineaments.' "

    2. positioned victories: of World War II.

enslaved; the hater, harmed. O shining O
  firm star, O tumultuous
    ocean lashed till small things go
  as they will, the mountainous
    wave makes us who look, know   10

depth. Lost at sea before they fought! O
  star of David, star of Bethlehem,
O black imperial lion
  of the Lord—emblem
of a risen world—be joined at last, be
joined. There is hate's crown beneath which all is
    death; there's love's without which none
      is king; the blessed deeds bless
    the halo. As contagion
      of sickness makes sickness,   20

contagion of trust can make trust. They're
  fighting in deserts and caves, one by
one, in battalions and squadrons;
  they're fighting that I
may yet recover from the disease, My
Self; some have it lightly; some will die. 'Man
    wolf to man' and we devour
      ourselves. The enemy could not
    have made a greater breach in our
      defences. One pilot-   30

ing a blind man can escape him, but
  Job disheartened by false comfort knew
that nothing can be so defeating
  as a blind man who
can see. O alive who are dead, who are
proud not to see, O small dust of the earth
    that walks so arrogantly,
      trust begets power and faith is
    an affectionate thing. We
      vow, we make this promise   40

to the fighting—it's a promise—'We'll
  never hate black, white, red, yellow, Jew,

11-14. O . . . Lord: symbols of Judaism, Christianity, and Ethiopia. 32. Job: unsin-
ning, he was afflicted by God as a trial of his faith; his friends "comforted" him by at-
tributing his sufferings to his transgressions. See The Book of Job.

Gentile, Untouchable.' We are
    not competent to
make our vows. With set jaw they are fighting,
fighting, fighting,—some we love whom we know,
    some we love but know not—that
        hearts may feel and not be numb.
    It cures me; or am I what
50   I can't believe in? Some

in snow, some on crags, some in quicksands,
    little by little, much by much, they
are fighting fighting fighting that where
    there was death there may
be life. 'When a man is prey to anger,
he is moved by outside things; when he holds
    his ground in patience patience
        patience, that is action or
    beauty', the soldier's defence
60   and hardest armour for

the fight. The world's an orphans' home. Shall
    we never have peace without sorrow?
without pleas of the dying for
    help that won't come? O
quiet form upon the dust, I cannot
look and yet I must. If these great patient
    dyings—all these agonies
        and woundbearings and bloodshed—
    can teach us how to live, these
70   dyings were not wasted.

Hate-hardened heart, O heart of iron,
    iron is iron till it is rust.
There never was a war that was
    not inward; I must
fight till I have conquered in myself what
causes war, but I would not believe it.
    I inwardly did nothing.
        O Iscariotlike crime!
    Beauty is everlasting
80   and dust is for a time.

---

43. Untouchable: a member of the lowest caste in India, whose touch is defilement
to Hindus. 78. Iscariotlike: an allusion to Judas Iscariot, the disciple who betrayed Christ.

SAINT NICHOLAS,

might I, if you can find it, be given
a chameleon with tail
that curls like a watch spring; and vertical
on the body—including the face—pale
    tiger-stripes, about seven;
        (the melanin in the skin
        having been shaded from the sun by thin
            bars; the spinal dome
                beaded along the ridge
            as if it were platinum).   10

    If you can find no striped chameleon,
might I have a dress or suit—
I guess you have heard of it—of *qiviut?*
and to wear with it, a taslon shirt, the drip-dry fruit
    of research second to none;
        sewn, I hope, by Excello;
        as for buttons to keep down the collar-points, no.
            The shirt could be white—
                and be "worn before six,"
            either in daylight or at night.   20

    But don't give me, if I can't have the dress,
a trip to Greenland, or grim
trip to the moon. The moon should come here. Let him
make the trip down, spread on my dark floor some dim
    marvel, and if a success
        that I stoop to pick up and wear,
        I could ask nothing more. A thing yet more rare,
            though, and different,
                would be this: Hans von Marées'
            St. Hubert, kneeling with head bent,   30

---

6. melanin: dark skin pigment. 13. *qiviut:* the under wool of the arctic ox. 29. Hans
von Marées: German painter of the Romantic school, 1837–1887. 30. St. Hubert: patron
saint of hunting. Having been fond of hunting, he devoted himself to religion after a
stag appeared before him, a crucifix between its horns, threatening him with damnation if
he did not repent.

form erect—in velvet, tense with restraint—

hand hanging down: the horse, free.

Not the original, of course. Give me

a postcard of the scene—huntsman and divinity—

hunt-mad Hubert startled into a saint

by a stag with a Figure entined.

But why tell you what you must have divined?

Saint Nicholas, O Santa Claus,

would it not be the most

40   prized gift that ever was!

T. S. ELIOT (1888–1965)

THE LOVE SONG OF J. ALFRED PRUFROCK

S'io credesse che mia risposta fosse
A persona che mai tornasse al mondo,
Questa fiamma staria senza più scosse.
Ma perciocche giammai di questo fondo
Non torno vivo alcun, s'i'odo il vero,
Senza tema d'infamia ti rispondo.

Let us go then, you and I,
When the evening is spread out against the sky
Like a patient etherised upon a table;
Let us go, through certain half-deserted streets,
The muttering retreats
Of restless nights in one-night cheap hotels
And sawdust restaurants with oyster-shells:
Streets that follow like a tedious argument
Of insidious intent
10   To lead you to an overwhelming question . . .
Oh, do not ask, "What is it?"
Let us go and make our visit.

Epigraph. From Dante's *Inferno*, XXVII, 61-66; literally translated: "If I believed my reply were to a person who could return to the world, this flame would stand without wavering any longer. But because no one ever returned alive from this depth, if I hear the truth, I reply to you without fear of infamy." These are the words of Guido da Montefeltro in the eighth circle of Hell, where the spirits are in the form of flames and speak through the wavering of their flames, replying to Dante, who, Guido believed, would also remain in Hell as one of the damned.

In the room the women come and go
Talking of Michelangelo.

— *cat.*

The yellow fog that rubs its back upon the window-panes,
The yellow smoke that rubs its muzzle on the window-panes
Licked its tongue into the corners of the evening,
Lingered upon the pools that stand in drains,
Let fall upon its back the soot that falls from chimneys,
Slipped by the terrace, made a sudden leap,   20
And seeing that it was a soft October night,
Curled once about the house, and fell asleep.

And indeed there will be time
For the yellow smoke that slides along the street,
Rubbing its back upon the window-panes;
There will be time, there will be time
To prepare a face to meet the faces that you meet;   *life is trivial*
There will be time to murder and create,   → *he imagines*
And time for all the works and days of hands   *his question is*   30
That lift and drop a question on your plate;   *so great.*
Time for you and time for me,
And time yet for a hunderd indecisions,
And for a hundred visions and revisions,
Before the taking of a toast and tea.

In the room the women come and go
Talking of Michelangelo.

And indeed there will be time
To wonder, "Do I dare?" and, "Do I dare?"
Time to turn back and descend the stair,
With a bald spot in the middle of my hair—   40
[They will say: "How his hair is growing thin!"]
My morning coat, my collar mounting firmly to the chin,
My necktie rich and modest, but asserted by a simple pin—
[They will say: "But how his arms and legs are thin!]
Do I dare   → *so big.*
Disturb the universe?
In a minute there is time
For decisions and revisions which a minute will reverse.

29. works and days: allusion to *Works and Days* by Hesiod, the ancient Greek
poet. It is one of the earliest didactic poems, offering precepts about many details of the
practical life.

For I have known them all already, known them all:—
50   Have known the evenings, mornings, afternoons,
I have measured out my life with coffee spoons;
I know the voices dying with a dying fall
Beneath the music from a farther room.
      So how should I presume?

And I have known the eyes already, known them all—
The eyes that fix you in a formulated phrase,
And when I am formulated, sprawling on a pin,
When I am pinned and wriggling on the wall,
Then how should I begin
60   To spit out all the butt-ends of my days and ways?
      And how should I presume?

And I have known the arms already, known them all—
Arms that are braceleted and white and bare
[But in the lamplight, downed with light brown hair!]
Is it perfume from a dress
That makes me so digress?
Arms that lie along a table, or wrap about a shawl.
      And should I then presume?
      And how should I begin?

                    .   .   .   .   .

70   Shall I say, I have gone at dusk through narrow streets
And watched the smoke that rises from the pipes
Of lonely men in shirt-sleeves, leaning out of windows?

I should have been a pair of ragged claws
Scuttling across the floors of silent seas.

                    .   .   .   .   .

And the afternoon, the evening, sleeps so peacefully!
Smoothed by long fingers,
Asleep . . . tired . . . or it malingers,
Stretched on the floor, here beside you and me.
Should I, after tea and cakes and ices,
80   Have the strength to force the moment to its crisis?
But though I have wept and fasted, wept and prayed,

82-83. **head . . . prophet:** allusion to the head of John the Baptist, brought in to
Herod upon a platter at the request of Salome, Matthew xiv.1-11.

Though I have seen my head [grown slightly bald] brought in upon
    a platter,
I am no prophet—and here's no great matter;
I have seen the moment of my greatness flicker,
And I have seen the eternal Footman hold my coat, and snicker,
And in short, I was afraid.

And would it have been worth it, after all,
After the cups, the marmalade, the tea,
Among the porcelain, among some talk of you and me,
Would it have been worth while,   90
To have bitten off the matter with a smile,
To have squeezed the universe into a ball
To roll it toward some overwhelming question,
To say: "I am Lazarus, come from the dead,
Come back to tell you all, I shall tell you all"—
If one, settling a pillow by her head,
    Should say: "That is not what I meant at all.
    That is not it, at all."

And would it have been worth it, after all,
Would it have been worth while,   100
After the sunsets and the dooryards and the sprinkled streets,
After the novels, after the teacups, after the skirts that trail along the
    floor—
And this, and so much more?—
It is impossible to say just what I mean!
But as if a magic lantern threw the nerves in patterns on a screen:
Would it have been worth while
If one, settling a pillow or throwing off a shawl,
And turning toward the window, should say:
    "That is not it at all,
    That is not what I meant, at all."   110

      . . . . .

No! I am not Prince Hamlet, nor was meant to be;
Am an attendant lord, one that will do
To swell a progress, start a scene or two,
Advise the prince; no doubt, an easy tool,

92-93. **squeezed . . . roll it:** allusion to Marvell's "To His Coy Mistress," lines
41-42. 94. **Lazarus:** raised from the dead by Christ, John xi.1-44. 105. **magic lantern:**
projector. 112-119. **attendant lord . . . Fool:** like Polonius in *Hamlet;* **progress:** state
procession; **sentence:** maximatic wisdom

Deferential, glad to be of use,
Politic, cautious, and meticulous;
Full of high sentence, but a bit obtuse;
At times, indeed, almost ridiculous—
Almost, at times, the Fool.

120   I grow old . . . I grow old
I shall wear the bottoms of my trousers rolled.

Shall I part my hair behind? Do I dare to eat a peach?
I shall wear white flannel trousers, and walk upon the beach.
I have heard the mermaids singing, each to each.

I do not think that they will sing to me.

escape with
dreams.

I have seen them riding seaward on the waves
Combing the white hair of the waves blown back
When the wind blows the water white and black.

We have lingered in the chambers of the sea
130   By sea-girls wreathed with seaweed red and brown
Till human voices wake us, and we drown.

SWEENEY AMONG THE NIGHTINGALES

ὤμοι, πέπληγμαι καιρίαυ πληγὴυ ἔσω.

Apeneck Sweeney spreads his knees
Letting his arms hang down to laugh,
The zebra stripes along his jaw
Swelling to maculate giraffe.

The circles of the stormy moon
Slide westward toward the River Plate,
Death and the Raven drift above
And Sweeney guards the hornèd gate.

Title. **Sweeney**: Eliot's personification, through several poems, of vulgar, sensual
man. **Epigraph**. Literally translated, "Oh! I have been stricken a mortal blow—within."
These are the words of Aeschylus's Agamemnon as he is stabbed. **4. maculate**: blotched.
6. River Plate: between Uruguay and Argentina. Elizabeth Drew, in *T. S. Eliot: The
Design of His Poetry*, notes that this is "the shallowest of rivers." **7. Raven**: Southern
constellation, *corvus;* the raven is also a bird of death, cf. the ballads "The Twa Corbies"
and "The Three Ravens." **8. hornèd gate**: the gate of sleep through which true dreams
come.

Gloomy Orion and the Dog
Are veiled; and hushed the shrunken seas;   10
The person in the Spanish cape
Tries to sit on Sweeney's knees

Slips and pulls the table cloth
Overturns a coffee-cup,
Reorganized upon the floor
She yawns and draws a stocking up;

The silent man in mocha brown
Sprawls at the window-sill and gapes;
The waiter brings in oranges
Bananas figs and hothouse grapes;   20

The silent vertebrate in brown
Contracts and concentrates, withdraws;
Rachel *née* Rabinovitch
Tears at the grapes with murderous paws;

She and the lady in the cape
Are suspect, thought to be in league;
Therefore the man with heavy eyes
Declines the gambit, shows fatigue,

Leaves the room and reappears
Outside the window, leaning in,   30
Branches of wistaria
Circumscribe a golden grin;

The host with someone indistinct
Converses at the door apart,
The nightingales are singing near
The Convent of the Sacred Heart,

And sang within the bloody wood
When Agamemnon cried aloud,
And let their liquid siftings fall
To stain the stiff dishonoured shroud.   40

9. **Orion and the Dog**: the northern constellation, including Sirius, the Dog-star.

JOURNEY OF THE MAGI

'A cold coming we had of it,
Just the worst time of the year
For a journey, and such a long journey:
The ways deep and the weather sharp,
The very dead of winter.'
And the camels galled, sore-footed, refractory,
Lying down in the melting snow.
There were times we regretted
The summer palaces on slopes, the terraces,
10   And the silken girls bringing sherbet.
Then the camel men cursing and grumbling
And running away, and wanting their liquor and women,
And the night-fires going out, and the lack of shelters,
And the cities hostile and the towns unfriendly
And the villages dirty and charging high prices:
A hard time we had of it.
At the end we preferred to travel all night,
Sleeping in snatches,
With the voices singing in our ears, saying
20   That this was all folly.

    Then at dawn we came down to a temperate valley,
Wet, below the snow line, smelling of vegetation;
With a running stream and a water-mill beating the darkness,
And three trees on the low sky,
And an old white horse galloped away in the meadow.
Then we came to a tavern with vine-leaves over the lintel,
Six hands at an open door dicing for pieces of silver,
And feet kicking the empty wine-skins.
But there was no information, and so we continued
30   And arrived at evening, not a moment too soon
Finding the place; it was (you may say) satisfactory.

    All this was a long time ago, I remember,
And I would do it again, but set down
This set down
This: were we led all that way for

Title. Magi: the three wise men who came to worship the infant Christ. 1-5. 'A
cold . . . winter': paraphrase of a passage in Lancelot Andrewes' Christmas Day sermon,
1622. 8. regretted: looked back nostalgically to. 10. sherbet: fruit drink.

Birth or Death? There was a Birth, certainly,
We had evidence and no doubt. I had seen birth and death,
But had thought they were different; this Birth was
Hard and bitter agony for us, like Death, our death.
We returned to our places, these Kingdoms,   40
But no longer at ease here, in the old dispensation,
With an alien people clutching their gods.
I should be glad of another death.

JOHN CROWE RANSOM (1888–   )

WINTER REMEMBERED

Two evils, monstrous either one apart,
Possessed me, and were long and loath at going:
A cry of Absence, Absence, in the heart,
And in the wood the furious winter blowing.

Think not, when fire was bright upon my bricks,
And past the tight boards hardly a wind could enter,
I glowed like them, the simple burning sticks,
Far from my cause, my proper heat and center.

Better to walk forth in the frozen air
And wash my wound in the snows; that would be healing;   10
Because my heart would throb less painful there,
Being caked with cold, and past the smart of feeling.

And where I walked, the murderous winter blast
Would have this body bowed, these eyeballs streaming,
And though I think this heart's blood froze not fast
It ran too small to spare one drop for dreaming.

Dear love, these fingers that had known your touch,
And tied our separate forces first together,
Were ten poor idiot fingers not worth much,
Ten frozen parsnips hanging in the weather.   20

41. **old dispensation:** the regime before the coming of Christ.

BELLS FOR JOHN WHITESIDE'S DAUGHTER

There was such speed in her little body,
And such lightness in her footfall,
It is no wonder her brown study
Astonishes us all.

Her wars were bruited in our high window.
We looked among orchard trees and beyond
Where she took arms against her shadow,
Or harried unto the pond

The lazy geese, like a snow cloud
Dripping their snow on the green grass,
Tricking and stopping, sleepy and proud,
Who cried in goose, Alas,

For the tireless heart within the little
Lady with rod that made them rise
From their noon apple-dreams and scuttle
Goose-fashion under the skies!

But now go the bells, and we are ready,
In one house we are sternly stopped
To say we are vexed at her brown study,
Lying so primly propped.

PIAZZA PIECE

—I am a gentleman in a dustcoat trying
To make you hear. Your ears are soft and small
And listen to an old man not at all,
They want the young men's whispering and sighing.
But see the roses on your trellis dying
And hear the spectral singing of the moon;
For I must have my lovely lady soon,
I am a gentleman in a dustcoat trying.

—I am a lady young in beauty waiting
Until my truelove comes, and then we kiss.

3. **brown study**: deep absorption. 5. **bruited**: reported. 11. **tricking**: maneuvering.

1. **dustcoat**: light overcoat. 5. **trellis**: a crisscross structure used as a screen or a support for vines. 6. **spectral**: ghostly.

But what grey man among the vines is this
Whose words are dry and faint as in a dream?
Back from my trellis, Sir, before I scream!
I am a lady young in beauty waiting.

ARCHIBALD MACLEISH (1892–   )

ARS POETICA

A poem should be palpable and mute
As a globed fruit,

Dumb
As old medallions to the thumb,

Silent as the sleeve-worn stone
Of casement ledges where the moss has grown—

A poem should be wordless
As the flight of birds.

A poem should be motionless in time
As the moon climbs,   10

Leaving, as the moon releases
Twig by twig the night-entangled trees,

Leaving, as the moon behind the winter leaves,
Memory by memory the mind—

A poem should be motionless in time
As the moon climbs.

A poem should be equal to:
Not true.

Title. The poetic art.

For all the history of grief
20   An empty doorway and a maple leaf.

For love
The leaning grasses and the two lights above the sea—

A poem should not mean
But be.

YOU, ANDREW MARVELL

And here face down beneath the sun
And here upon earth's noonward height
To feel the always coming on
The always rising of the night:

To feel creep up the curving east
The earthy chill of dusk and slow
Upon those under lands the vast
And ever climbing shadow grow

And strange at Ecbatan the trees
10   Take leaf by leaf the evening strange
The flooding dark about their knees
The mountains over Persia change

And now at Kermanshah the gate
Dark empty and the withered grass
And through the twilight now the late
Few travelers in the westward pass

And Baghdad darken and the bridge
Across the silent river gone
And through Arabia the edge
20   Of evening widen and steal on

And deepen on Palmyra's street
The wheel rut in the ruined stone
And Lebanon fade out and Crete
High through the clouds and overblown

Title. Andrew Marvell: seventeenth-century poet best known for his poem "To His Coy Mistress." See page 123. 1. here: the United States. 9. Ecbatan: ancient city in what is now Iran. 12. Persia: Iran. 13. Kermanshah: ancient city in what is now Iran. 17. Baghdad: capital of what is now Iraq. 21. Palmyra: ancient city in what is now Syria.

And over Sicily the air
Still flashing with the landward gulls
And loom and slowly disappear
The sails above the shadowy hulls

And Spain go under and the shore
Of Africa the gilded sand   30
And evening vanish and no more
The low pale light across that land

Nor now the long light on the sea:

And here face downward in the sun
To feel how swift how secretly
The shadow of the night comes on . . .

WILFRED OWEN (1893–1918)

STRANGE MEETING

It seemed that out of battle I escaped
Down some profound dull tunnel, long since scooped
Through granites which titanic wars had groined.
Yet also there encumbered sleepers groaned,
Too fast in thought or death to be bestirred.
Then, as I probed them, one sprang up, and stared
With piteous recognition in fixed eyes,
Lifting distressful hands as if to bless.
And by his smile, I knew that sullen hall,
By his dead smile I knew we stood in Hell.   10
With a thousand pains that vision's face was grained;
Yet no blood reached there from the upper ground,
And no guns thumped, or down the flues made moan.
"Strange friend," I said, "here is no cause to mourn."
"None," said the other, "save the undone years,
The hopelessness. Whatever hope is yours,
Was my life also; I went hunting wild
After the wildest beauty in the world,
Which lies not calm in eyes, or braided hair,

3. **granites:** hard, coarse-grained rocks; **titanic:** huge; **groined:** carved out.

20   But mocks the steady running of the hour,
        And if it grieves, grieves richlier than here.
        For by my glee might many men have laughed,
        And of my weeping something had been left,
        Which must die now. I mean the truth untold,
        The pity of war, the pity war distilled.
        Now men will go content with what we spoiled.
        Or, discontent, boil bloody, and be spilled.
        They will be swift with swiftness of the tigress,
        None will break ranks, though nations trek from progress.
        Courage was mine, and I had mystery,
30   Wisdom was mine, and I had mastery;
        To miss the march of this retreating world
        Into vain citadels that are not walled.
        Then, when much blood had clogged their chariot-wheels
        I would go up and wash them from sweet wells,
        Even with truths that lie too deep for taint.
        I would have poured my spirit without stint
        But not through wounds; not on the cess of war.
        Foreheads of men have bled where no wounds were.
40   I am the enemy you killed, my friend.
        I knew you in this dark; for so you frowned
        Yesterday through me as you jabbed and killed.
        I parried; but my hands were loath and cold.
        Let us sleep now. . . ."

DULCE ET DECORUM EST

        Bent double, like old beggars under sacks,
        Knock-kneed, coughing like hags, we cursed through sludge,
        Till on the haunting flares we turned our backs,
        And towards our distant rest began to trudge.
        Men marched asleep. Many had lost their boots,
        But limped on, blood-shod. All went lame, all blind;
        Drunk with fatigue; deaf even to the hoots
        Of gas-shells dropping softly behind.

        Gas! GAS! Quick, boys!—An ecstasy of fumbling,
10   Fitting the clumsy helmets just in time,

---

33. citadels: fortresses. 37. stint: limit. 38. cess: sewage. 43. parried: warded off;
loath: reluctant.

Title. It is sweet and fitting. 2. sludge: water-soaked mud.

But someone still was yelling out and stumbling
And floundering like a man in fire or lime.—
Dim through the misty panes and thick green light,
As under a green sea, I saw him drowning.

In all my dreams before my helpless sight
He plunges at me, guttering, choking, drowning.

If in some smothering dreams, you too could pace
Behind the wagon that we flung him in,
And watch the white eyes writhing in his face,
His hanging face, like a devil's sick of sin;   20
If you could hear, at every jolt, the blood
Come gargling from the froth-corrupted lungs,
Bitter as the cud
Of vile, incurable sores on innocent tongues,—
My friend, you would not tell with such high zest
To children ardent for some desperate glory,
The old Lie: Dulce et decorum est
Pro patria mori.

ANTHEM FOR DOOMED YOUTH

What passing-bells for these who die as cattle?
    Only the monstrous anger of the guns.
    Only the stuttering rifles' rapid rattle
Can patter out their hasty orisons.
No mockeries now for them; no prayers nor bells,
    Nor any voice of mourning save the choirs,—
The shrill, demented choirs of wailing shells;
    And bugles calling for them from sad shires.

What candles may be held to speed them all?
    Not in the hands of boys, but in their eyes   10
Shall shine the holy glimmers of good-byes.
    The pallor of girls' brows shall be their pall;
Their flowers the tenderness of patient minds,
And each slow dusk a drawing-down of blinds.

13. panes: the eye pieces of a gas mask. 16. guttering: melting. 23. cud: chewed-over food. 27–28: Dulce et decorum est pro patria mori: It is sweet and fitting to die for the fatherland.

4. orisons: prayers. 8. shires: counties in England. 12. pallor: whiteness; pall: covering over a coffin

E. E. CUMMINGS (1894–1962)

IN JUST-

in Just-
spring   when the world is mud-
luscious the little
lame balloonman

whistles   far   and wee

and eddieandbill come
running from marbles and
piracies and it's
spring

10   when the world is puddle-wonderful

the queer
old balloonman whistles
far   and   wee
and bettyandisbel come dancing

from hop-scotch and jump-rope and

it's
spring
and
        the

20   goat-footed

balloonMan   whistles
far
and
wee

A MAN WHO HAD FALLEN AMONG THIEVES

a man who had fallen among thieves
lay by the roadside on his back
dressed in fifteenthrate ideas
wearing a round jeer for a hat

fate per a somewhat more than less
emancipated evening
had in return for consciousness
endowed him with a changeless grin

whereon a dozen staunch and leal
citizens did graze at pause   10
then fired by hypercivic zeal
sought newer pastures or because

swaddled with a frozen brook
of pinkest vomit out of eyes
which noticed nobody he looked
as if he did not care to rise

one hand did nothing on the vest
its wideflung friend clenched weakly dirt
while the mute trouserfly confessed
a button solemnly inert.   20

Brushing from whom the stiffened puke
i put him all into my arms
and staggered banged with terror through
a million billion trillion stars

PITY THIS BUSY MONSTER,MANUNKIND

pity this busy monster,manunkind,

not.   Progress is a comfortable disease:
your victim(death and life safely beyond)

Title. Reference to the story of the Good Samaritan, Luke x.30-37. **5. per:** by means
of. **9. leal:** loyal.

plays with the bigness of his littleness
—electrons deify one razorblade
into a mountainrange;lenses extend

unwish through curving wherewhen till unwish
returns on its unself.
                    A world of made
10   is not a world of born—pity poor flesh

and trees,poor stars and stones,but never this
fine specimen of hypermagical

ultraomnipotence. We doctors know

a hopeless case if—listen:there's a hell
of a good universe next door;let's go

R-P-O-P-H-E-S-S-A-G-R

                              r-p-o-p-h-e-s-s-a-g-r
                    who
a)s w(e loo)k
upnowgath
          PPEGORHRASS
                              eringint(o-
aThe):l
        eA
          !p:
10   S   a
                    (r
rIvInG   .gRrEaPsPhOs)
                                        to
rea(be)rran(com)gi(e)ngly
,grasshopper;

ANYONE LIVED IN A PRETTY HOW TOWN

anyone lived in a pretty how town
(with up so floating many bells down)
spring summer autumn winter
he sang his didn't he danced his did

Women and men(both little and small)
cared for anyone not at all
they sowed their isn't they reaped their same
sun moon stars rain

children guessed(but only a few
and down they forgot as up they grew   10
autumn winter spring summer)
that noone loved him more by more

when by now and tree by leaf
she laughed his joy she cried his grief
bird by snow and stir by still
anyone's any was all to her

someones married their everyones
laughed their cryings and did their dance
(sleep wake hope and then)they
said their nevers they slept their dream   20

stars rain sun moon
(and only the snow can begin to explain
how children are apt to forget to remember
with up so floating many bells down)

one day anyone died i guess
(and noone stooped to kiss his face)
busy folk buried them side by side
little by little and was by was

all by all and deep by deep
and more by more they dream their sleep   30
noone and anyone earth by april
wish by spirit and if by yes.

Women and men(both dong and ding)
summer autumn winter spring
reaped their sowing and went their came
sun moon stars rain

I SING OF OLAF

i sing of Olaf glad and big
whose warmest heart recoiled at war:
a conscientious object-or

his wellbbelovéd colonel(trig
westpointer most succinctly bred)
took erring Olaf soon in hand;
but—though an host of overjoyed
noncoms(first knocking on the head
him)do through icy waters roll
10   that helplessness which others stroke
with brushes recently employed
anent this muddy toiletbowl,
while kindred intellects evoke
allegiance per blunt instruments—
Olaf(being to all intents
a corpse and wanting any rag
upon what God unto him gave)
responds, without getting annoyed
"I will not kiss your f.ing flag"

20   straightway the silver bird looked grave
(departing hurriedly to shave)

but—though all kinds of officers
(a yearning nation's blueeyed pride)
their passive prey did kick and curse
until for wear their clarion
voices and boots were much the worse,
and egged the firstclassprivates on
his rectum wickedly to tease
by means of skilfully applied
30   bayonets roasted hot with heat—
Olaf(upon what were once knees)
does almost ceaselessly repeat
"there is some s. I will not eat"

our president,being of which
assertions duly notified
threw the yellowsonofabitch
into a dungeon,where he died

4, **trig**: stylishly trim. 12. anent: concerning.

> Christ(of His mercy infinite)
> i pray to see;and Olaf,too
>
> preponderatingly because   **40**
> unless statistics lie he was
> more brave than me:more blond than you.

ALLEN TATE (1899–   )

ODE TO THE CONFEDERATE DEAD

Row after row with strict impunity
The headstones yield their names to the element,
The wind whirrs without recollection;
In the riven troughs the splayed leaves
Pile up, of nature the casual sacrament
To the seasonal eternity of death;
Then driven by the fierce scrutiny
Of heaven to their election in the vast breath,
They sough the rumor of mortality.

Autumn is desolation in the plot   **10**
Of a thousand acres where these memories grow
From the inexhaustible bodies that are not
Dead, but feed the grass row after rich row.
Think of the autumns that have come and gone!—
Ambitious November with the humors of the year,
With a particular zeal for every slab,
Staining the uncomfortable angels that rot
On the slabs, a wing chipped here, an arm there:
The brute curiosity of an angel's stare
Turns you, like them, to stone,   **20**
Transforms the heaving air
Till plunged to a heavier world below
You shift your sea-space blindly
Heaving, turning like the blind crab.

40. **preponderatingly:** most significantly.

1. **impunity:** freedom from penalty or harm. 4. **riven:** torn. 9. **sough:** sigh.

Dazed by the wind, only the wind
The leaves flying, plunge

You know who have waited by the wall
The twilight certainty of an animal,
Those midnight restitutions of the blood
30   You know—the immitigable pines, the smoky frieze
Of the sky, the sudden call: you know the rage,
The cold pool left by the mounting flood,
Of muted Zeno and Parmenides.
You who have waited for the angry resolution
Of those desires that should be yours tomorrow,
You know the unimportant shrift of death
And praise the vision
And praise the arrogant circumstance
Of those who fall
40   Rank upon rank, hurried beyond decision—
Here by the sagging gate, stopped by the wall.

Seeing, seeing only the leaves
Flying, plunge and expire

Turn your eyes to the immoderate past,
Turn to the inscrutable infantry rising
Demons out of the earth—they will not last.
Stonewall, Stonewall, and the sunken fields of hemp,
Shiloh, Antietam, Malvern Hill, Bull Run.
Lost in that orient of the thick and fast
50   You will curse the setting sun.

Cursing only the leaves crying
Like an old man in a storm

You hear the shout, the crazy hemlocks point
With troubled fingers to the silence which
Smothers you, a mummy, in time.

29. restitutions: restorations. 30. immitigable: what cannot be made milder or less severe; frieze: ornamented border. 33. Zeno, Parmenides: Greek philosophers who flourished in the fifth century B.C. Both believed in the unreality of motion or change. 36. Shrift: dismissal. 48. Shiloh, Antietam, Malvern Hill, Bull Run: sites of Civil War battles in 1861 and 1862

The hound bitch
Toothless and dying, in a musty cellar
Hears the wind only.

Now that the salt of their blood
Stiffens the saltier oblivion of the sea,   60
Seals the malignant purity of the flood,
What shall we who count our days and bow
Our heads with a commemorial woe
In the ribboned coats of grim felicity,
What shall we say of the bones, unclean,
Whose verdurous anonymity will grow?
The ragged arms, the ragged heads and eyes
Lost in these acres of the insane green?
The gray lean spiders come, they come and go;
In a tangle of willows without light   70
The singular screech-owl's tight
Invisible lyric seeds the mind
With the furious murmur of their chivalry.

We shall say only the leaves
Flying, plunge and expire

We shall say only the leaves whispering
In the improbable mist of nightfall
That flies on multiple wing:
Night is the beginning and the end
And in between the ends of distraction   80
Waits mute speculation, the patient curse
That stones the eyes, or like the jaguar leaps
For his own image in a jungle pool, his victim.

What shall we say who have knowledge
Carried to the heart? Shall we take the act
To the grave? Shall we, more hopeful, set up the grave
In the house? The ravenous grave?

Leave now
The shut gate and the decomposing wall:
The gentle serpent, green in the mulberry bush,   90
Riots with his tongue through the hush—
Sentinel of the grave who counts us all!

60. oblivion: forgetfulness. 63. commemorial: honoring the memory of. 66. ver-
durous: covered with green plants. 87. ravenous: very hungry.

THE SUBWAY

Dark accurate plunger down the successive knell
Of arch on arch, where ogives burst a red
Reverberance of hail upon the dead
Thunder like an exploding crucible!
Harshly articulate, musical steel shell
Of angry worship, hurled religiously
Upon your business of humility
Into the iron forestries of hell:

Till broken in the shift of quieter
100   Dense altitudes tangential of your steel,
I am become geometries, and glut
Expansions like a blind astronomer
Dazed, while the worldless heavens bulge and reel
In the cold revery of an idiot.

LANGSTON HUGHES (1902–1967)

JAZZONIA

Oh, silver tree!
Oh, shining rivers of the soul.

In a Harlem cabaret
Six long-headed jazzers play.
A dancing girl whose eyes are bold
Lifts high a dress of silken gold.

Oh, singing tree!
Oh, shining rivers of the soul!

Were Eve's eyes
10   In the first garden
Just a bit too bold?

1. **knell:** tolling of a bell. 2. **ogives:** Gothic arches. 10. **tangential:** digressive, breaking away from the line.

Was Cleopatra gorgeous
In a gown of gold?

Oh, shining tree!
Oh, silver rivers of the soul!

In a whirling cabaret
Six long-headed jazzers play.

COUNTEE CULLEN (1903–1946)

HERITAGE

(FOR HAROLD JACKMAN)

What is Africa to me:
Copper sun or scarlet sea,
Jungle star or jungle track,
Strong bronzed men, or regal black
Women from whose loins I sprang
When the birds of Eden sang?
One three centuries removed
From the scenes his fathers loved,
Spicy grove, cinnamon tree,
What is Africa to me?   10

So I lie, who all day long
Want no sound except the song
Sung by wild barbaric birds
Goading massive jungle herds,
Juggernauts of flesh that pass
Trampling tall defiant grass
Where young forest lovers lie,

---

12. **Cleopatra:** queen of Egypt during the first century B.C., renowned for her beauty.

Title. heritage: that which comes to one by reason of birth. 15. **Juggernauts:** large, overpowering, destructive objects.

Plighting troth beneath the sky.
So I lie, who always hear,
20   Though I cram against my ear
Both my thumbs, and keep them there,
Great drums throbbing through the air.
So I lie, whose fount of pride,
Dear distress, and joy allied,
Is my somber flesh and skin,
With the dark blood dammed within
Like great pulsing tides of wine
That, I fear, must burst the fine
Channels of the chafing net
30   Where they surge and foam and fret.

Africa? A book one thumbs
Listlessly, till slumber comes.
Unremembered are her bats
Circling through the night, her cats
Crouching in the river reeds,
Stalking gentle flesh that feeds
By the river bank; no more
Does the bugle-throated roar
Cry that monarch claws have leapt
40   From the scabbards where they slept.
Silver snakes that once a year
Doff the lovely coats you wear,
Seek no covert in your fear
Lest a mortal eye should see;
What's your nakedness to me?
Here no leprous flowers rear
Fierce corollas in the air;
Here no bodies sleek and wet,
Dripping mingled rain and sweat,
50   Tread the savage measures of
Jungle boys and girls in love.
What is last year's snow to me,
Last year's anything? The tree
Budding yearly must forget
How its past arose or set—

18. **Plighting troth:** making vows. 42. **doff:** take off (as clothes). 43. **covert:** thicket. 46. **leprous:** grotesque. 47. **corollas:** sets of petals.

Bough and blossom, flower, fruit,
Even what shy bird with mute
Wonder at her travail there,
Meekly labored in its hair.
One three centuries removed   60
From the scenes his fathers loved,
Spicy grove, cinnamon tree,
What is Africa to me?

So I lie, who find no peace
Night or day, no slight release
From the unremittant beat
Made by cruel padded feet
Walking through my body's street.
Up and down they go, and back,
Treading out a jungle track.   70
So I lie, who never quite
Safely sleep from rain at night—
I can never rest at all
When the rain begins to fall;
Like a soul gone mad with pain
I must match its weird refrain;
Ever must I twist and squirm,
Writhing like a baited worm,
While its primal measures drip
Through my body, crying, "Strip!   80
Doff this new exuberance.
Come and dance the Lover's Dance!"
In an old remembered way
Rain works on me night and day.

Quaint, outlandish heathen gods
Black men fashion out of rods,
Clay, and brittle bits of stone,
In a likeness like their own,
My conversion came high-priced;
I belong to Jesus Christ,   90
Preacher of humility;
Heathen gods are naught to me.

58. travail: labor.

Father, Son, and Holy Ghost,
So I make an idle boast;
Jesus of the twice-turned cheek,
Lamb of God, although I speak
With my mouth thus, in my heart
Do I play a double part.
Ever at Thy glowing altar
100   Must my heart grow sick and falter,
Wishing He I served were black,
Thinking then it would not lack
Precedent of pain to guide it,
Let who would or might deride it;
Surely then this flesh would know
Yours had borne a kindred woe.
Lord, I fashion dark gods, too,
Daring even to give You
Dark despairing features where,
110   Crowned with dark rebellious hair,
Patience wavers just so much as
Mortal grief compels, while touches
Quick and hot, of anger, rise
To smitten cheek and weary eyes.
Lord, forgive me if my need
Sometimes shapes a human creed.

All day long and all night through,
One thing only must I do:
Quench my pride and cool my blood,
120   *Lest I perish in the flood.*
Lest a hidden ember set
Timber that I thought was wet
Burning like the dryest flax,
Melting like the merest wax,
Lest the grave restore its dead.
Not yet has my heart or head
In the least way realized
They and I are civilized.

---

104. **deride:** ridicule. 123. **flax:** crop from which linseed oil is derived.

YET DO I MARVEL

I doubt not God is good, well-meaning, kind,
And did He stoop to quibble could tell why
The little buried mole continues blind,
Why flesh that mirrors Him must some day die,
Make plain the reason tortured Tantalus
Is baited by the fickle fruit, declare
If merely brute caprice dooms Sisyphus
To struggle up a never-ending stair.
Inscrutable His ways are, and immune
To catechism by a mind too strewn   10
With petty cares to slightly understand
What awful brain compels His awful hand.
Yet do I marvel at this curious thing:
To make a poet black, and bid him sing!

EARLE BIRNEY (1904–   )

THE BEAR ON THE DELHI ROAD

Unreal, tall as a myth
by the road the Himalayan bear
is beating the brilliant air
with his crooked arms.
About him two men, bare,
spindly as locusts, leap.
One pulls on a ring
in the great soft nose; his mate
flicks, flicks with a stick
up at the rolling eyes.   10

5. **Tantalus:** mythological king in hell suffering hunger and thirst, tantalized by water that receded when he tried to drink and by fruit that was out of his reach. 6. **baited:** tormented. 7. **caprice:** action or idea arising from whim or impulse; **Sisyphus:** mythological king in hell doomed forever to roll uphill a boulder which repeatedly rolls down again. 10. **catechism:** questioning.

Title. Delhi: city in India. 2. **Himalayan bear:** the bear had been captured in the Himalayan mountains between India and Tibet.

They have not led him here,
down from the fabulous hills
to this bald, alien plain
and the clamorous world, to kill
but simply to teach him to dance.
They are peaceful both, these spare
men of Kashmir, and the bear
alive is their living too.
If far on the Delhi way
around him galvanic they dance
it is merely to wear, wear
from his shaggy body the tranced
wish forever to stay
only an ambling bear
four-footed in berries.

It is no more joyous for them
in this hot dust to prance
out of reach of the praying claws
sharpened to paw for ants
in the shadows of deodars.
It is not easy to free
myth from reality
or rear this fellow up
to lurch, lurch with them
in the tranced dancing of men.

IRAPUATO

For reasons any
        brigadier
                could tell
this is a favourite nook for
                   massacre
Toltex by Mixtex Mixtex by Aztex
Aztex by Spanishtex Spanishtex by
Mexitex by Mexitex by Mexitex by Texaco

So any farmer can see how the strawberries
are the biggest and reddest
in the whole damn continent

17. Kashmir: state of Northern India. 20. galvanic: electrically. 22. tranced: hypnotized. 30. deodars: cedars.

6-8. The capitalized words are deliberate distortions of names such as Aztec and Toltec, referring to various groups which supplanted each other in the early history of Mexico. Texaco is Texaco.

but why
     when arranged under
               the market flies

do they look like small clotting hearts?

RICHARD EBERHART (1904–   )

NEW HAMPSHIRE, FEBRUARY

Nature had made them hide in crevices,
Two wasps so cold they looked like bark.
Why I do not know, but I took them
And I put them
In a metal pan, both day and dark.

Like God touching his finger to Adam
I felt, and thought of Michaelangelo,
For whenever I breathed on them,
The slightest breath,
They leaped, and preened as if to go.   10

My breath controlled them always quite.
More sensitive than electric sparks
They came into life
Or they withdrew to ice,
While I watched, suspending remarks.

Then one in a blind career got out,
And fell to the kitchen floor.   I
Crushed him with my cold ski boot,
By accident.   The other
Had not the wit to try or die.   20

And so the other is still my pet.
The moral of this is plain.
But I will shirk it.
You will not like it.   And
God does not live to explain.

6-7. **Like . . . Michaelangelo:** reference to Michaelangelo's painting of the creation of man on the ceiling of the Sistine Chapel in the Vatican.

AM I MY NEIGHBOR'S KEEPER?

The poetry of tragedy is never dead.
If it were not so I would not dream
On principles so deep they have no ending,
Nor on the ambiguity of what things ever seem.

The truth is his and shaped in veils of error,
Rich, unanswerable, the profound caught in plain air.
Centuries after tragedy sought out Socrates
Its inexplicable essence visits us in our lair,

Say here, on a remote New Hampshire farm.
10   The taciturn farmer disappeared in pre-dawn.
He had beaten his handyman, but no great harm.
Light spoke vengeance and bloodstains on the lawn.
His trussed corpse later under the dam
Gives to this day no answer, says I am.

C. DAY LEWIS (1904–   )

REST FROM LOVING

Rest from loving and be living.
Fallen is fallen past retrieving
The unique flyer dawn's dove
Arrowing down feathered with fire.

Cease denying, begin knowing.
Comes peace this way here comes renewing
With dower of bird and bud knocks
Loud on winter wall on death's door.

Title. Allusion to "Am I my brother's keeper?"—the reply of Cain to God when He asked the whereabouts of Abel, whom Cain had killed. Genesis iv.9. **5. his:** reference deliberately unspecific. Possibly the murderer. **7. Socrates:** whose doctrine, recorded by Plato, was that reality lay in Ideas (inexplicable essence of line 8). He was condemned to death by the city-state of Athens for misleading youth and forced to drink the lethal bitter hemlock.

7. dower: endowment.

Here's no meaning but of morning.
Naught soon of night but stars remaining,   10
Sink lower, fade, as dark womb
Recedes creation will step clear.

NEARING AGAIN THE LEGENDARY ISLE

Nearing again the legendary isle
Where sirens sang and mariners were skinned,
We wonder now what was there to beguile
That such stout fellows left their bones behind.

Those chorus-girls are surely past their prime,
Voices grow shrill and paint is wearing thin,
Lips that sealed up the sense from gnawing time
Now beg the favour with a graveyard grin.

We have no flesh to spare and they can't bite,
Hunger and sweat have stripped us to the bone;   10
A skeleton crew we toil upon the tide
And mock the theme-song meant to lure us on:

No need to stop the ears, avert the eyes
From purple rhetoric of evening skies.

WHEN THEY HAVE LOST

When they have lost the little that they looked for,
The poor allotment of ease, custom, fame:
When the consuming star their fathers worked for
Has guttered into death, a fatuous flame:
When love's a cripple, faith a bed-time story,
Hope eats her heart out and peace walks on knives,
And suffering men cry an end to this sorry
World of whose children want alone still thrives:
Then shall the mounting stages of oppression
Like mazed and makeshift scaffolding torn down   10
Reveal his unexampled, best creation—
The shape of man's necessity full-grown.
Built from their bone, I see a power-house stand
To warm men's hearts again and light the land.

4. **guttered**: melted rapidly. 10. **mazed**: labyrinthine.

FLORENCE: WORKS OF ART

Florence, father of Michelangelo,
Dante, da Vinci, Fra Angelico,
Cellini, Botticelli, Brunelleschi.
Giotto, Donatello, Masaccio!—

We shall not see their like, or yours, again.
Painters depart, and patrons. You remain,
Your bridges blown, your glory catalogued,
A norm for scholars and for gentlemen.

Reverend city, sober, unperplexed,
10   Turning your page to genius annexed
I breathe the mint and myrrh of Tuscan hills,
The tart aroma of some classic text.

Shields and medallions; overshadowing eaves
Like studious brows; the light that interleaves
Your past with amber: all's definitive, all
in changeless chiaroscuro one conceives.

I sometimes think the heart is ne'er so dead
As where some vanished era overspread
The soil with titan foliage, scattering down
20   Eternal rubies when its bloom was shed.

Where rode Lorenzo, panoplied and plumed,
Where Savonarola burned, and Ruskin fumed,
The lady artist sets her easel up,
The tourist with mild wonder is consumed.

Yet still the Arno navigably flows,
And saunterers past the Ponte Vecchio's

Title. Florence: city on the river Arno; capital of the province of Tuscany in Italy.
1-4: Michelangelo . . . Masaccio: Italian sculptors, painters, and a poet (Dante) of the
14th and 15th centuries. 8. norm: standard. 11. myrrh: gum from certain trees used as
incense, perfume, etc. 16. chiaroscuro: effects of light and shade. 19. titan: huge. 21. Lo-
renzo: "the magnificent" (1449–1492), member of the ruling family of Florence, the
Medici. 22. Savonarola: Girolamo (1425–1498), Italian Dominican monk; political and
religious reformer; burned as a heretic. Ruskin: John (1819–1900), English art critic
and author, disliked Renaissance art. 25. Arno: river flowing through Florence. 26. Ponte
Vecchio: famous old bridge over the Arno with shops on it.

Jewel shops cast a shadow: here is still
A taste for life, a market for the rose.

Ah no, it's not the Florentines who fade
Before the statued loggia, the arcade,   30
The cliffs of floral stone. They live enough
In a pure tongue and a congenial trade.

Should the past overawe them? It's not theirs,
More than a mansion is the caretaker's.
A church by Giotto does as well as any
Other for this day's rendezvous or prayers.

What if along the pot-holed boulevards
Slogans are scrawled, not cantos? if postcards
Stand in for masterpieces, and ice cream
Says more to them than edifying façades?   40

The past is all-encroaching; and unless
They lopped its tentacles, stemmed its excess
To clear the air for some domestic seed,
They'd soon be strangled by a wilderness.

It's not the Florentine who pales beside
That vast, rank efflorescence. The pop-eyed
Tourist it is who rushes on his doom,
Armed with good taste, a Leica and a guide.

The primitive forest, the renaissance range
So massive are, surely they will estrange   50
Him from himself, or send him yelping home
To plastic novelties, to art's small change.

Plodding the galleries, we ask how can
That century of the Uncommon Man,
Sovereign here in paint, bronze, marble, suit
The new narcissism of the Also-Ran.

30–31. statued loggia . . . floral stone: recognizable features of the city of Florence.
35. Giotto: (di Bondone) (1266?–1337), Florentine painter, architect, and sculptor.
40. edifying: uplifting. 46. efflorescence: blooming forth. 48. Leica: camera. 49. renais-
sance: the renewal of life in arts and letters during the 14th and 15th centuries in Italy.
55. sovereign: supreme. 56. narcissim: self-love. Subtitle. Singing Children: modeled
in the singing gallery Della Robbia made for the cathedral of Florence. Luca Della Rob-
bia: (1400?–1482), Florentine sculptor and ceramist.

As many men, so many attitudes
Before the artifact. One writhes: one broods:
One preens the ego and one curls the lip:
60   One turns to stone, one to adjacent nudes.

Each man must seek his own. What do I seek?
Not the sole rights required by snob and freak,
The scholar's or the moralist's reward
Not even a connoisseur's eye for technique;

But that on me some long-dead master may
Dart the live, intimate, unblinding ray
Which means one more spring of the selfhood tapped,
One tribute more to love wrung from my clay.

And if I miss that radiance where it flies,
70   Something is gained in the mere exercise
Of strenuous submission, the attempt
To lose and find oneself through others' eyes.

Singing Children: Luca Della Robbia

(T. H.)

I see you, angels with choirboy faces,
     Trilling it from the museum wall
As once, decani or cantoris,
     You sang in a carved oak stall,
Nor deemed any final bar to such time-honoured carollings
     E'er could befall.

I too gave tongue in my piping youth-days,
80   Yea, took like a bird to crochet and clef,
Antheming out with a will the Old Hundredth,
     Salem, or Bunnett in F.,

---

75. decani: pertaining to the epistle or liturgical south side of a church. cantoris: pertaining to the gospel or liturgical north side of a church. 80. crotchet: a quarter note; clef: musical symbol, indicating treble or bass. 81. Old Hundredth: a well-known metrical psalm tune. 82. Salem: an Episcopal hymn tune. Bunnett in F: The Magnificat and Nunc Dimittis in F, by Edward Bunnett (1835–1923), a popular piece of church music. 83. Primal Sapience: fundamental or original wisdom.

Unreckoning even as you if the Primal Sapience
    Be deaf, stone-deaf.

Many a matins cheerfully droned I
    To the harmonium's clacking wheeze,
Fidgeted much through prayer and sermon
    While errant bumblebees
Drummed on the ivied window, veering my thoughts to
    Alfresco glees.   90

But voices break—aye, and more than voices;
    The heart for hymn tune and haytime goes.
Dear Duomo choristers, chirping for ever
    In jaunty, angelic pose,
Would I had sung my last ere joy-throbs dwindled
    Or wan faith froze!

Judith and Holofernes: Donatello

(W. B. Y.)

... Next, a rich widow woman comes to mind
Who, when her folk were starving, dined and wined
Alone with Holofernes, until he
Grew rabid for her flesh. And presently,   100
Matching deceit with bitterer deceit,
She had struck off that tipsy captain's head
Upon the still untousled bed,
And borne it homeward in a bag of meat.

Old Donatello thought it out in bronze—
The wrists trailing, numb as it were from bonds;
The fuddled trunk lugged upright by a loop
Of hair; the falcon-falchion poised to stoop.

---

85. **matins:** morning church service. 90. **Alfresco:** in the open air; **glees:** unaccompanied songs. 93. **Duomo:** cathedral in Florence. **Subtitle. Judith and Holofernes:** Donatello. **Judith:** heroine of the Old Testament apocryphal book of Judith. **Holofernes:** a general of Nebuchadnezzar's slain by Judith. **Donatello:** 1386–1466, Italian sculptor. **Judith and Holofernes:** bronze statue in Florence. 100. **rabid:** mad. 108. **falchion:** a broad-bladed slightly curved medieval sword,

Tyrant, and tyrant's man, maybe:
110   Nevertheless, the sculptural face presents
A victim's irony, the mild innocence
Of passionate men whom passion has set free.

And she, the people's saviour, the patriot?
She towers, mouth brooding, eyes averted, not
In womanly compunction but her need
To chew and savour a vindictive deed;
Or so I construe it. One thing's sure—
Let a man get what issue he has earned,
Where death beds or love tussles are concerned
120   Woman's the single-minded connoisseur.

A political woman is an atrocious thing.
Come what may, she will have her fling
In flesh and blood. Her heady draughts cajole
A man only to cheat him, body or soul.
Judith took great Holofernes in.
For all the silver lamps that went before,
He made but a remnant on a knacker's floor:
She lives, the brazen kind of heroine.

Annunciation: Leonardo

(R. F.)

There was never a morning quite so tremendous again.
130   The birth, you think? I'm not for setting great store
By birth. Births aren't beginnings. And anyway
She only wanted to sleep off the pain
Which had made her a beast among beasts on the cow-house floor.

Shepherds and magnates tiptoeing through the hay
(You get all kinds at an inn, she drowsily thought),

111. irony: contradiction. 115. compunction: sense of guilt or remorse. 116. vindictive: revengeful. 117. construe: interpret. 118. issue: outcome. 123. cajole: wheedle. 127. knacker: buyer of animals or carcasses for food, fertilizer, etc. Subtitle. Annunciation: Leonardo: painting. Leonardo da Vinci: 1452–1519, Italian painter, sculptor, architect, musician, engineer, mathematician, and scientist. Annunciation: announcement by Gabriel to Mary that she was to bear Jesus. 134. magnates: big business people. Subtitle. Perseus Rescuing Andromeda: painting. Piero di Cosimo: (1462–1521), Florentine painter. Andromeda, whose mother had overpraised her beauty, was chained to a rock as a sacrifice to a sea monster in order to placate Poseidon. She was rescued by Perseus who killed the monster.

Even the babe—they were part of a snowdrift trance,
Almost unreal. He was to prove a good son
In his way, though his way was beyond her. Whatever he sought
When he left home and led his friends such a dance,
He did not forget her as other boys might have done.   140

Her morning of mornings was when one flew to bring
Some news that changed her cottage into a queen's
Palace; the table she worked at shone like gold,
And in the orchard it is suddenly spring,
All bird and blossom and fresh-painted green.
What was it the grand visitor foretold
Which made earth heaven for a village Mary?
He was saying something about a Saviour Prince,
But she only heard him say, "You will bear a child,"
And that was why the spring came. Angels carry   150
Such tidings often enough, but never since
To one who in such blissful ignorance smiled.

Perseus Rescuing Andromeda: Piero di Cosimo

(W. H. A.)

It is all there. The victim broods,
Her friends take up the attitudes
        Right for disaster;
The winsome rescuer draws his sword,
While from the svelte, impassive fjord
Breaches terrific, dense and bored
        The usual monster.

When gilt-edged hopes are selling short,   160
Virtue's devalued, and the swart
        Avenger rises,
We know there'll always be those two
Strolling away without a clue,
Discussing earnestly the view
        Or fat-stock prices.

To either hand the crisis throws
Its human quirks and gestures. Those

156. winsome: cheerful. 157. svelte: lithe, suave. 158. breaches: breaks surface.
160. gilt-edged: secure (of stocks and bonds); selling short: selling cheap to cut losses.
161. swart: black.

Are not essential.
170   Look rather at the oafish Dread,
The Cloud-man come to strike it dead,
Armed with a sword and gorgon's head—
Magic's credentials.

White on the rocks, Andromeda.
Mother had presumed too far.
The deep lost patience.
The nightmare ground its teeth. The saviour
Went in. A winning hit. All over.
Parents and friends stood round to offer
180   Congratulations.

But when the vast delusions break
Upon you from the central lake,
You'll be less lucky.
I'd not advise you to believe
There's a slick op. to end your grief
Or any nick-of-time reprieve.
For you, unlikely.

Boy with Dolphin: Verrocchio

(D. T.)

At the crack of spring on the tail of the cold,
When foam whipped over the apple tree aisles
190   And the grape skin sea swelled and the weltering capes were bold,
I went to school with a glee of dolphins
Bowling their hoops round the brine tongued isles
And singing their scales were tipped by a sun always revolving.

Oh truant I was and trident and first
Lord of fishes, bearleading all tritons
In the swim of my blood before the foam brewed bubble burst.

---

172. gorgon: monster with snakes for hair, one glance at which turned the beholder to stone. One of the gorgons, Medusa, was killed by Perseus. 185. slick op.: gimmick. Subtitle. Boy with Dolphin (*Putto with a Fish*): small bronze on a fountain in Florence. Verrocchio: Andrea del (1435–1488), Florentine sculptor and goldsmith. 191. glee: group. 194. trident: three-pronged; the spear associated with Neptune, God of the Sea. 195. tritons: sea gods, half man and half fish; snails.

And as I was nursling to mermaids, my sun.
Cooed through their nestling grottoes a cadence
Of thrummed and choral reefs for the whale sounded gulfs to hum.

Those were the gambolling days I led   200
Leviathan a dance in my sea urchin glee
Till the lurching waves shoaled out with a school of wishes. My head
Was shells and ringing, my shoulders broke
Into a spray of wings. But the sea
Ran dry between two bars of foam, and the fine folk

In the temple of fins were flailed away
And the weed fell flat and the mermilk curdled,
And buoyant no more to bliss are the miles where alone I play
My running games that the waves once aisled,
With a doll of a lithe dead dolphin saddled,   210
And cold as the back of spring is my tale of the applefroth isles.

STANLEY KUNITZ (1905–   )

FATHER AND SON

Now in the suburbs and the falling light
I followed him, and now down sandy road
Whiter than bone-dust, through the sweet
Curdle of fields, where the plums
Dropped with their load of ripeness, one by one.
Mile after mile I followed, with skimming feet,
After the secret master of my blood,
Him, steeped in the odor of ponds, whose indomitable love
Kept me in chains. Strode years; stretched into bird;
Raced through the sleeping country where I was young,   10
The silence unrolling before me as I came,
The night nailed like an orange to my brow.

---

200. gambolling: frolicking. 201. Leviathan: the whale.

How should I tell him my fable and the fears,
How bridge the chasm in a casual tone,
Saying, "The house, the stucco one you built,
We lost. Sister married and went from home,
And nothing comes back, it's strange, from where she goes.
I lived on a hill that had too many rooms:
Light we could make, but not enough of warmth,
And when the light failed, I climbed under the hill.
The papers are delivered every day;
I am alone and never shed a tear."

At the water's edge, where the smothering ferns lifted
Their arms, "Father!" I cried, "Return! You know
The way. I'll wipe the mudstains from your clothes;
No trace, I promise, will remain. Instruct
Your son, whirling between two wars,
In the Gemara of your gentleness,
For I would be a child to those who mourn
And brother to the foundlings of the field
And friend of innocence and all bright eyes.
O teach me how to work and keep me kind."

Among the turtles and the lilies he turned to me
The white ignorant hollow of his face.

END OF SUMMER

An agitation of the air,
A perturbation of the light
Admonished me the unloved year
Would turn on its hinge that night.

I stood in the disenchanted field
Amid the stubble and the stones,
Amazed, while a small worm lisped to me
The song of my marrow-bones.

28. **Gemara:** the commentary on the text of the Jewish civil and religious law (the Talmud).

2. **perturbation:** disturbance.

Blue poured into summer blue,
A hawk broke from his cloudless tower,   10
The roof of the silo blazed, and I knew
That part of my life was over.

Already the iron door of the north
Clangs open: birds, leaves, snows
Order their populations forth,
And a cruel wind blows.

W. H. AUDEN (1907–   )

LULLABY

Lay your sleeping head, my love,
Human on my faithless arm;
Time and fevers burn away
Individual beauty from
Thoughtful children, and the grave
Proves the child ephemeral:
But in my arms till break of day
Let the living creature lie,
Mortal, guilty, but to me
The entirely beautiful.   10

Soul and body have no bounds:
To lovers as they lie upon
Her tolerant enchanted slope
In their ordinary swoon,
Grave the vision Venus sends
Of supernatural sympathy,
Universal love and hope;
While an abstract insight wakes
Among the glaciers and the rocks
The hermit's sensual ecstasy.   20

Certainty, fidelity
On the stroke of midnight pass

11. silo: tower containing fodder for cattle.

Like vibrations of a bell,
And fashionable madmen raise
Their pedantic boring cry:
Every farthing of the cost,
All the dreaded cards foretell,
Shall be paid, but from this night
Not a whisper, not a thought,
30   Not a kiss nor look be lost.

Beauty, midnight, vision dies:
Let the winds of dawn that blow
Softly round your dreaming head
Such a day of sweetness show
Eye and knocking heart may bless,
Find the mortal world enough;
Noons of dryness see you fed
By the involuntary powers,
Nights of insult let you pass
40   Watched by every human love.

ONE EVENING

As I walked out one evening
    Walking down Bristol Street,
The crowds upon the pavement
    Were fields of harvest wheat.

And down by the brimming river
    I heard a lover sing
Under an arch of the railway:
    "Love has no ending.

I'll love you, dear, I'll love you
10   Till China and Africa meet,
And the river jumps over the mountain
    And the salmon sing in the street.

I'll love you till the ocean
    Is folded and hung up to dry,
And the seven stars go squawking
    Like geese about the sky.

15. **seven stars:** the Pleiades.

    The year shall run like rabbits,
        For in my arms I hold
    The Flower of the Ages,
        And the first love of the world."   20

    But all the clocks in the city
        Began to whirr and chime:
    "O let not Time deceive you,
        You cannot conquer Time.

    In the burrows of the Nightmare
        Where Justice naked is,
    Time watches from the shadow
        And coughs when you would kiss.

    In headaches and in worry
        Vaguely life leaks away,   30
    And Time will have his fancy
        Tomorrow or today.

    Into many a green valley
        Drifts the appalling snow;
    Time breaks the threaded dances
        And the diver's brilliant bow.

    O plunge your hands in water,
        Plunge them in up to the wrist;
    Stare, stare in the basin
        And wonder what you've missed.   40

    The glacier knocks in the cupboard,
        The desert sighs in the bed,
    And the crack in the tea-cup opens
        A lane to the land of the dead.

    Where the beggars raffle the banknotes
        And the Giant is enchanting to Jack,
    And the Lily-white Boy is a Roarer,
        And Jill goes down on her back.

47. Roarer: Roaring Boy, the Elizabethan equivalent of the Teddy Boy.

50
O look, look in the mirror,
    O look in your distress;
Life remains a blessing
    Although you cannot bless.

O stand, stand at the window
    As the tears scald and start;
You shall love your crooked neighbor
    With your crooked heart."

It was late, late in the evening,
    The lovers they were gone;
The clocks had ceased their chiming,
60
    And the deep river ran on.

MUSÉE DES BEAUX ARTS

About suffering they were never wrong,
The Old Masters: how well they understood
Its human position; how it takes place
While someone else is eating or opening a window or just
        walking dully along;
How, when the aged are reverently, passionately waiting
For the miraculous birth, there always must be
Children who did not specially want it to happen, skating
On a pond at the edge of the wood:
They never forgot
10
That even the dreadful martyrdom must run its course
Anyhow in a corner, some untidy spot
Where the dogs go on with their doggy life and the
        torturer's horse
Scratches its innocent behind on a tree.

In Brueghel's *Icarus,* for instance: how everything turns away
Quite leisurely from the disaster; the ploughman may
Have heard the splash, the forsaken cry,

14. **Brueghel's Icarus:** "The Fall of Icarus" by Pieter Brueghel the Elder (sixteenth century) shows the drowning of Icarus, son of Daedalus: father and son were escaping from imprisonment with home-made wings; ignoring his father's warning, Icarus flew too near the sun, which melted the waxen wings, causing him to fall into the sea and be drowned.

But for him it was not an important failure; the sun shone
As it had to on the white legs disappearing into the green
Water; and the expensive delicate ship that must have seen
Something amazing, a boy falling out of the sky,   20
Had somewhere to get to and sailed calmly on.

HAMMERFEST

For over forty years I'd paid it atlas homage,
    The northernmost township on earth, producing
The best deep-frozen fish sticks you can buy: for three days,
    I pottered round, a monolingual pilgrim,
And drank the beer of the world's most northern brewery.
    Though miles beyond the Moral Circle, I saw
No orgies, no great worms, nor dreamed of any during
    Three sunny nights: louts, though—German this time—
Had left their usual mark. How much reverence could I,
    Can anyone past fifty, afford to lose?   10

Was it as worldly as it looked? I might have thought so
    But for my ears: something odd was happening
Soundwise. A word, a laugh, a footstep, a truck's outcry,
    Each utterance rang singular, staccato,
To be cut off before it could be contradicted
    Or confused by others: a listening terrain
Seized on them all and never gave one back in echo,
    As if to land as desolate, as far up,
Whatever noise our species cared to make still mattered.
    Here was a place we had yet to disappoint.   20

The only communities it had to judge us by
    Were cenobite, mosses and lichen, sworn to
Station and reticence: its rocks knew almost nothing,
    Nothing about the glum Reptilian Empire
Or the epic journey of the Horse, had heard no tales
    Of that preglacial Actium when the huge

Title. Name of a town in Norway. 4. monolingual: speaking only one language.
6. Moral Circle: "A jocular term, used by southern Norwegians for the Arctic Circle"—
Auden's note. 8. German this time: "in 1945 the retreating *Wehrmacht* burnt down every
single house"—Auden's note. 22. cenobite: living a monastic life. 26. Actium: famous
battle, 31 B.C.

Archaic shrubs went down before the scented flowers,
        And earth was won for color. For all it knew,
    Religion had begun with the Salvation Army,
30   Warfare with motorized resentful conscripts.

    Ground so bare might take a century to realize
        How we behave to regions or to beings
    Who have anything we're after: to have disgusted
        Millions of acres of good-natured topsoil
    Is an achievement of a sort, to fail to notice
        How garden plants and farmyard beasts look at us,
    Or refuse to look, to picture all of them as dear
        Faithful old retainers, another, but why
    Bring that up now? My intrusion had not profaned it:
40   If innocence is holy, it was holy.

LOUIS MACNEICE (1907–1963)

BAGPIPE MUSIC

It's no go the merrygoround, it's no go the rickshaw,
All we want is a limousine and a ticket for the peepshow.
Their knickers are made of crêpe-de-chine, their shoes are made of python,
Their halls are lined with tiger rugs and their walls with heads of bison.

John MacDonald found a corpse, put it under the sofa,
Waited till it came to life and hit it with a poker,
Sold its eyes for souvenirs, sold its blood for whisky,
Kept its bones for dumb-bells to use when he was fifty.

It's no go the Yogi-Man, it's no go Blavatsky,
10 All we want is a bank balance and a bit of skirt in a taxi.

1. rickshaw: small oriental carriage pulled by a man. 3. knickers: women's under-pants; crêpe-de-chine: thin silk crepe. 9. Yogi-man: one who practices yoga, intense concentration achieved by physical discipline; Blavatsky: Madame Blavatsky, 1831–1891, Russian theosophist who founded the Theosophical Society in New York, 1875. Her puta-tive psychic powers gained her a large following, including W. B. Yeats.

Annie MacDougall went to milk, caught her foot in the heather,
Woke to hear a dance record playing of Old Vienna.
It's no go your maidenheads, it's no go your culture,
All we want is a Dunlop tyre and the devil mend the puncture.

The Laird o' Phelps spent Hogmanay declaring he was sober,
Counted his feet to prove the fact and found he had one foot over.
Mrs. Carmichael had her fifth, looked at the job with repulsion,
Said to the midwife "Take it away; I'm through with overproduction."

It's no go the gossip column, it's no go the ceilidh,
All we want is a mother's help and a sugar-stick for the baby.   20

Willie Murray cut his thumb, couldn't count the damage,
Took the hide of an Ayrshire cow and used it for a bandage.
His brother caught three hundred cran when the seas were lavish,
Threw the bleeders back in the sea and went upon the parish.

It's no go the Herring Board, it's no go the Bible,
All we want is a packet of fags when our hands are idle.

It's no go the picture palace, it's no go the stadium,
It's no go the country cot with a pot of pink geraniums,
It's no go the Government grants, it's no go the elections,
Sit on your arse for fifty years and hang your hat on a pension.   30

It's no go my honey love, it's no go my poppet;
Work your hands from day to day, the winds will blow the profit.
The glass is falling hour by hour, the glass will fall for ever,
But if you break the bloody glass you won't hold up the weather.

THE SUNLIGHT ON THE GARDEN

The sunlight on the garden
Hardens and grows cold,
We cannot cage the minute
Within its nets of gold,
When all is told
We cannot beg for pardon.

15. Laird: Lord; **Hogmanay:** New Year's Eve. **19. ceilidh:** traditional Gaelic dance. **23. cran:** 45 gallons of fresh herring. **31. poppet:** a term of endearment. **33. glass:** barometer.

Our freedom as free lances
Advances towards its end;
The earth compels, upon it
10   Sonnets and birds descend;
And soon, my friend,
We shall have no time for dances.

The sky was good for flying
Defying the church bells
And every evil iron
Siren and what it tells:
The earth compels,
We are dying, Egypt, dying

And not expecting pardon,
20   Hardened in heart anew,
But glad to have sat under
Thunder and rain with you,
And grateful too
For sunlight on the garden.

CUSHENDEN

Fuchsia and ragweed and the distant hills
Made as it were out of clouds and sea:
All night the bay is plashing and the moon
    Marks the break of the waves.

Limestone and basalt and a whitewashed house
With passages of great stone flags
And a walled garden with plums on the wall
    And a bird piping in the night.

Forgetfulness: brass lamps and copper jugs
10   And home-made bread and the smell of turf or flax
And the air a glove and the water lathering easy
    And convolvulus in the hedge.

7. free lances: individual, uncommitted agents.

Title. Cushenden: town in Northern Ireland. 5. basalt: kind of volcanic rock
10. flax: crop from which linseed oil is derived. 12. convolvulus: wild morning glory.

Only in the dark green room beside the fire
With the curtains drawn against the winds and waves
There is a little box with a well-bred voice:
    What a place to talk of War.

THEODORE ROETHKE (1908–1963)

WEED PULLER

Under the concrete benches,
Hacking at black hairy roots,—
Those lewd monkey-tails hanging from drainholes,—
Digging into the soft rubble underneath,
Webs and weeds,
Grubs and snails and sharp sticks,
Or yanking tough fern-shapes,
Coiled green and thick, like dripping smilax,
Tugging all day at perverse life:
The indignity of it!—   10
With everything blooming above me,
Lilies, pale-pink cyclamen, roses,
Whole fields lovely and inviolate,—
Me down in that fetor of weeds,
Crawling on all fours,
Alive, in a slippery grave.

IN A DARK TIME

In a dark time, the eye begins to see,
I meet my shadow in the deepening shade;
I hear my echo in the echoing wood—
A lord of nature weeping to a tree.
I live between the heron and the wren,
Beasts of the hill and serpents of the den.

What's madness but nobility of soul
At odds with circumstance? The day's on fire!

8. smilax: twining plant. **14. fetor:** bad smell.

I know the purity of pure despair,
10   My shadow pinned against a sweating wall.
That place among the rocks—is it a cave,
Or winding path? The edge is what I have.

A steady storm of correspondences!
A night flowing with birds, a ragged moon,
And in broad day the midnight come again!
A man goes far to find out what he is—
Death of the self in a long, tearless night,
All natural shapes blazing unnatural light.

Dark, dark, my light, and darker my desire.
20   My soul, like some heat-maddened summer fly,
Keeps buzzing at the sill. Which I is *I*?
A fallen man, I climb out of my fear.
The mind enters itself, and God the mind,
And one is One, free in the tearing wind.

ELEGY FOR JANE

I remember the neckcurls, limp and damp as tendrils;
And her quick look, a sidelong pickerel smile;
And how, once startled into talk, the light syllables leaped for her,
And she balanced in the delight of her thought,
A wren, happy, tail into the wind,
Her song trembling the twigs and small branches.
The shade sang with her;
The leaves, their whispers turned to kissing;
And the mould sang in the bleached valleys under the rose.

10   Oh, when she was sad, she cast herself down into such a pure depth,
Even a father could not find her:
Scraping her cheek against straw;
Stirring the clearest water.

My sparrow, you are not here,
Waiting like a fern, making a spiney shadow.
The sides of wet stones cannot console me,
Nor the moss, wound with the last light.

1. tendrils: threads of a climbing plant by which it clings to its support. 2. pickerel: variety of small fish.

If only I could nudge you from this sleep,
My maimed darling, my skittery pigeon.
Over this damp grave I speak the words of my love: 20
I, with no rights in this matter,
Neither father nor lover.

STEPHEN SPENDER (1909–   )

THE LANDSCAPE NEAR AN AERODROME

More beautiful and soft than any moth
With burring furred antennae feeling its huge path
Through dusk, the air liner with shut-off engines
Glides over suburbs and the sleeves set trailing tall
To point the wind. Gently, broadly, she falls,
Scarcely disturbing charted currents of air.

Lulled by descent, the travellers across sea
And across feminine land indulging its easy limbs
In miles of softness, now let their eyes trained by watching
Penetrate through dusk the outskirts of this town   10
Here where industry shows a fraying edge.
Here they may see what is being done.

Beyond the winking masthead light
And the landing ground, they observe the outposts
Of work: chimneys like lank black fingers
Or figures, frightening and mad: and squat buildings
With their strange air behind trees, like women's faces
Shattered by grief. Here where few houses
Moan with faint light behind their blinds,
They remark the unhomely sense of complaint, like a dog   20
Shut out, and shivering at the foreign moon.

In the last sweep of love, they pass over fields
Behind the aerodrome, where boys play all day
Hacking dead grass: whose cries, like wild birds,
Settle upon the nearest roofs
But soon are hid under the loud city.

4. sleeves: wind socks, cone-shaped cloth bags to indicate the direction of the wind.

Then, as they land, they hear the tolling bell
Reaching across the landscape of hysteria,
To where, louder than all those batteries
30   And charcoaled towers against that dying sky,
Religion stands, the Church blocking the sun.

NOT PALACES, AN ERA'S CROWN

Not palaces, an era's crown
Where the mind dwells, intrigues, rests;
Architectural gold-leaved flower
From people ordered like a single mind,
I build. This only what I tell:
It is too late for rare accumulation,
For family pride, for beauty's filtered dusts;
I say, stamping the words with emphasis,
Drink from here energy and only energy,
10   As from the electric charge of a battery,
To will this Time's change.
Eye, gazelle, delicate wanderer,
Drinker of horizon's fluid line;
Ear that suspends on a chord
The spirit drinking timelessness;
Touch, love, all senses;
Leave your gardens, your singing feasts,
Your dreams of suns circling before our sun,
Of heaven after our world.
20   Instead, watch images of flashing glass
That strike the outward sense, the polished will,
Flag of our purpose which the wind engraves.
No spirit seek here rest. But this: No one
Shall hunger: Man shall spend equally.
Our goal which we compel: Man shall be man.
        That programme of the antique Satan
Bristling with guns on the indented page,
With battleship towering from hilly waves:
For what? Drive of a ruining purpose
30   Destroying all but its age-long exploiters.
Our programme like this, but opposite,
Death to the killers, bringing light to life.

---

6. rare accumulation: the collecting of precious works of art, jewels, etc.

THE FUNERAL

Death is another milestone on their way.
With laughter on their lips and with winds blowing round them
They record simply
How this one excelled all others in making driving belts.

This is festivity, it is the time of statistics,
When they record what one unit contributed:
They are glad as they lay him back in the earth
And thank him for what he gave them.

They walk home remembering the straining red flags,
And with pennons of song still fluttering through their blood   10
They speak of the World State
With its towns like brain centres and its pulsing arteries.

They think how one life hums, revolves and toils,
One cog in a golden singing hive:
Like spark from fire, its task happily achieved,
It falls away quietly.

No more are they haunted by the individual grief
Nor the crocodile tears of European genius,
The decline of a culture
Mourned by scholars who dream of the ghosts of Greek boys.   20

CHARLES OLSON (1910–   )

A B C s (1)

The word forms
on the left: you must
stand in line. Speech
is as swift as synapse
but the acquisition of same

20. **Greek:** reference to the ancient Greek civilization. the source of modern European culture.

4. **synapse:** point of contact between two nerves.

is as long
as I am old

rat   on the first floor landing of the three-decker
       (grey)

10   black   eat a peck of storage batteries 'fore
                I die

       cabbage   my friend Cabbage, with whom to bake potatoes up
                  Fisher's Hill

       rust   in the bed of Beaver Brook—from the junk in it
               And the iris ("flags," we called 'em)
               And the turtle I was surprised by

               up to last night's dream, the long brown body pleased
               I kissed her buttock curve

               Interiors,
20   and their registration

               Words, form
               but the extension of
               content

               Style, est verbum

               The word
               is image, and the reverend reverse is
               Eliot

               Pound
               is verse

A B C s (2)

what we do not know of ourselves
of who they are who lie
coiled or unflown
in the marrow of the bone

     24. est verbum: is the word.

one sd:

> of rhythm is image
> of image is knowing
> of knowing there is
> a construct

or to find in a night who it is dwells in that wood where shapes hide
who is this woman or this man whose face we give a name to, whose shoulder
we bite, what landscape
figures ride small horses over, what bloody stumps
these dogs have, how they tear the golden cloak

And the boat,
how he swerves it to avoid the yelping rocks
where the tidal river rushes

ROBERT HAYDEN (1913–   )

MIDDLE PASSAGE

I.

Jesús, Estrella, Esperanza, Mercy:

> Sails flashing to the wind like weapons,
> sharks following the moans the fever and the dying;
> horror the corposant and compass rose.

Middle Passage:
> voyage through death
> > to life upon these shores.

5. sd: said.

Title. **Middle Passage:** the second of the three parts of an eighteenth-century slaving expedition: the first passage, from home port to Africa; the middle passage carrying slaves from Africa to the West Indies; the third, from the Indies to the home port. 1. *Jesus, Estrella, Esperanza, Mercy:* names of slaveships: *Estrella* (Spanish) star; *Esperanza* (Spanish) hope. 4. **corposant:** electric discharge seen sometimes at top of a mast.

"10 April 1800—
Blacks rebellious. Crew uneasy. Our linguist says
10   their moaning is a prayer for death,
ours and their own. Some try to starve themselves.
Lost three this morning leaped with crazy laughter
to the waiting sharks, sang as they went under."

Desire, Adventure, Tartar, Ann:

Standing to America, bringing home
black gold, black ivory, black seed.

Deep in the festering hold thy father lies,
of his bones New England pews are made,
those are altar lights that were his eyes.

20   Jesus Saviour Pilot Me
Over Life's Tempestuous Sea

We pray that Thou wilt grant, O Lord,
safe passage to our vessels bringing
heathen souls unto Thy chastening.

Jesus Saviour

"8 bells. I cannot sleep, for I am sick
with fear, but writing eases fear a little
since still my eyes can see these words take shape
upon the page & so I write, as one
30   would turn to exorcism. 4 days scudding,
but now the sea is calm again. Misfortune
follows in our wake like sharks (our grinning
tutelary gods). Which one of us
has killed an albatross? A plague among
our blacks—Ophthalmia: blindness—& we
have jettisoned the blind to no avail.
It spreads, the terrifying sickness spreads.
Its claws have scratched sight from the Capt.'s eyes

14. *Desire, Adventure, Tartar, Ann:* names of slaveships: *Desire:* first American
ship built specifically for slave trade. 30. exorcism: expulsion of evil spirit by rituals;
scudding: running before the wind. 33. tutelary: protecting. 35. ophthalmia: inflamma-
tion of the eye, frequently suffered by slaves. 36. jettisoned: thrown away.

& there is blindness in the fo'c'sle
& we must sail 3 weeks before we come   40
to port."

What port awaits us, Davy Jones'
or home? I've heard of slavers drifting, drifting,
playthings of wind and storm and chance, their crews
gone blind, the jungle hatred
crawling up on deck.

Thou Who Walked On Galilee

"Deponent further sayeth The Bella J
left the Guinea Coast
with cargo of five hundred blacks and odd   50
for the barracoons of Florida:

"That there was hardly room 'tween-decks for half
the sweltering cattle stowed spoon-fashion there;
that some went mad of thirst and tore their flesh
and sucked the blood:

"That Crew and Captain lusted with the comeliest
of the savage girls kept naked in the cabins;
that there was one they called The Guinea Rose
and they cast lots and fought to lie with her:

"That when the Bo's'n piped all hands, the flames   60
spreading from starboard already were beyond
control, the negroes howling and their chains
entangled with the flames:

"That the burning blacks could not be reached,
that the Crew abandoned ship,
leaving their shrieking negresses behind,
that the Captain perished drunken with the wenches:

"Further Deponent sayeth not."

Pilot Oh Pilot Me

39. fo'c'sle: forecastle: forward end of ship, quarters of the sailors. 48. Deponent: person giving testimony. 51. barracoons: temporary enclosures for the confinement of slaves. 60. Bo's'n: boatswain: petty officer in charge of the deck crew; piped all hands: called everybody on deck.

II.

70   Aye, lad, and I have seen those factories,
     Gambia, Rio Pongo, Calabar;
     have watched the artful mongos baiting traps
     of war wherein the victor and the vanquished

     Were caught as prizes for our barracoons.
     Have seen the nigger kings whose vanity
     and greed turned wild black hides of Fellatah,
     Mandingo, Ibo, Kru to gold for us.

     And there was one—King Anthracite we named him—
     fetish face beneath French parasols
80   of brass and orange velvet, impudent mouth
     whose cups were carven skulls of enemies:

     He'd honor us with drum and feast and conjo
     and palm-oil-glistening wenches deft in love,
     and for tin crowns that shone with paste,
     red calico and German-silver trinkets

     Would have the drums talk war and send
     his warriors to burn the sleeping villages
     and kill the sick and old and lead the young
     in coffles to our factories.

90   Twenty years a trader, twenty years,
     for there was wealth aplenty to be harvested
     from those black fields, and I'd be trading still
     but for the fevers melting down my bones.

III.

     Shuttles in the rocking loom of history,
     the dark ships move, the dark ships move,

70. factories: shore agencies in Africa where slaves were kept against the arrival of slave ships. 71. Gambia, Rio Pongo, Calabar: African rivers. 72. mongos: traders. 76–77. Fellatah, Mandingo, Ibo, Kru: names of tribes. 78. anthracite: a kind of coal. 79. fetish: embodiment or habitation of a spirit. 82. conjo: magic. 83. deft: skilled. 89. coffles: trains of men or beasts chained together. 94. (Author's note): Part 3 follows, in the main, the account of the *Amistad* mutiny given by Muriel Rukeyser in her biography of Willard Gibbs.

their bright ironical names
like jests of kindness on a murderer's mouth;
plough through thrashing glister toward
fata morgana's lucent melting shore,
weave toward New World littorals that are   100
mirage and myth and actual shore.

Voyage through death,
                    voyage whose chartings are unlove.

A charnel stench, effluvium of living death
spreads outward from the hold,
where the living and the dead, the horribly dying,
lie interlocked, lie foul with blood and excrement.

> *Deep in the festering hold thy father lies,*
> *the corpse of mercy rots with him,*
> *rats eat love's rotten gelid eyes.*   110

> *But, oh, the living look at you*
> *with human eyes whose suffering accuses you,*
> *whose hatred reaches through the swill of dark*
> *to strike you like a leper's claw.*

> *You cannot stare that hatred down*
> *or chain the fear that stalks the watches*
> *and breathes on you its fetid scorching breath;*
> *cannot kill the deep immortal human wish,*
> *the timeless will.*

> "But for the storm that flung up barriers   120
> of wind and wave, *The Amistad*, señores,
> would have reached the port of Príncipe in two,
> three days at most; but for the storm we should
> have been prepared for what befell.

---

99. fata morgana: mirage. 100. littorals: beaches. 103. chartings: coarse plottings. 104. charnel: corpse; effluvium: smell. 110. gelid: frozen. 121. *The Amistad* (Spanish for "Friendship"): slaveship bound for Cuba on which the slaves broke out of their chains, killed the captain and several others, and ordered their owners to navigate them back to Africa. These, however, sailed the ship to and fro until it was apprehended by a U.S. navy vessel, which brought it into New Haven, where the slaves were tried. After the case had been referred to the Supreme Court, the slaves were sent back to Africa and freed. 122. Príncipe: Portuguese island in the Gulf of Guinea.

Swift as the puma's leap it came. There was
that interval of moonless calm filled only
with the water's and the rigging's usual sounds,
then sudden movement, blows and snarling cries
and they had fallen on us with machete
130 and marlinspike. It was as though the very
air, the night itself were striking us.
Exhausted by the rigors of the storm,
we were no match for them. Our men went down
before the murderous Africans. Our loyal
Celestino ran from below with gun
and lantern and I saw, before the cane-
knife's wounding flash, Cinquez,
that surly brute who calls himself a prince,
directing, urging on the ghastly work.
140 He hacked the poor mulatto down, and then
he turned on me. The decks were slippery
when daylight finally came. It sickens me
to think of what I saw, of how these apes
threw overboard the butchered bodies of
our men, true Christians all, like so much jetsam.
Enough, enough. The rest is quickly told:
Cinquez was forced to spare the two of us
you see to steer the ship to Africa,
and we like phantoms doomed to rove the sea
150 voyaged east by day and west by night,
deceiving them, hoping for rescue,
prisoners on our own vessel, till
at length we drifted to the shores of this
your land, America, where we were freed
from our unspeakable misery. Now we
demand, good sirs, the extradition of
Cinquez and his accomplices to La
Havana. And it distresses us to know
there are so many here who seem inclined
160 to justify the mutiny of these blacks.
We find it paradoxical indeed
that you whose wealth, whose tree of liberty
are rooted in the labor of your slaves

---

130. marlinspike: pointed iron implement used in separating strands of rope.
137. Cinquez: leader of rebellious slaves.   **145. jetsam:** goods cast overboard to lighten
a vessel.   **147. us:** the two Cuban planters who owned the slaves.

should suffer the august John Quincy Adams
to speak with so much passion of the right
of chattel slaves to kill their lawful masters
and with his Roman rhetoric weave a hero's
garland for Cinquez. I tell you that
we are determined to return to Cuba
with our slaves and there see justice done. Cinquez— 170
or let us say 'the Prince'—Cinquez shall die."

The deep immortal human wish,
the timeless will:

Cinquez its deathless primaveral image,
life that transfigures many lives.

Voyage through death
                        to life upon these shores.

THOSE WINTER SUNDAYS

Sundays too my father got up early
and put his clothes on in the blueblack cold,
then with cracked hands that ached
from labor in the weekday weather made
banked fires blaze. No one ever thanked him.

I'd wake and hear the cold splintering, breaking.
When the rooms were warm, he'd call,
and slowly I would rise and dress,
fearing the chronic angers of that house,

Speaking indifferently to him,   10
who had driven out the cold
and polished my good shoes as well.
What did I know, what did I know
of love's austere and lonely offices?

164. John Quincy Adams: then ex-president; defended the slaves in the Supreme
Court. 166. chattel: movable article of property. 174. primaveral: new as spring.

9. chronic: long continuing.

FREDERICK DOUGLASS

When it is finally ours, this freedom, this liberty, this beautiful
and terrible thing, needful to man as air,
usable as earth; when it belongs at last to all,
when it is truly instinct, brain matter, diastole, systole,
reflex action; when it is finally won; when it is more
than the gaudy mumbo jumbo of politicians:
this man, this Douglass, this former slave, this Negro
beaten to his knees, exiled, visioning a world
where none is lonely, none hunted, alien,
10   this man, superb in love and logic, this man
shall be remembered. Oh, not with statues' rhetoric,
not with legends and poems and wreaths of bronze alone,
but with the lives grown out of his life, the lives
fleshing his dream of the beautiful, needful thing.

KARL SHAPIRO (1913–   )

AUTO WRECK

Its quick soft silver bell beating, beating,
And down the dark one ruby flare
Pulsing out red light like an artery,
The ambulance at top speed floating down
Past beacons and illuminated clocks
Wings in a heavy curve, dips down,
And brakes speed, entering the crowd.
The doors leap open, emptying light;
Stretchers are laid out, the mangled lifted
10   And stowed into the little hospital.
Then the bell, breaking the hush, tolls once,
And the ambulance with its terrible cargo
Rocking, slightly rocking, moves away,
As the doors, an afterthought, are closed.

Title. Frederick Douglass: 1817–1895. American ex-slave, abolitionist, and orator.
4. diastole and systole: the two parts of the heartbeat.

We are deranged, walking among the cops
Who sweep glass and are large and composed.
One is still making notes under the light.
One with a bucket douches ponds of blood
Into the street and gutter.
One hangs lanterns on the wrecks that cling,   20
Empty husks of locusts, to iron poles.

Our throats were tight as tourniquets,
Our feet were bound with splints, but now,
Like convalescents intimate and gauche,
We speak through sickly smiles and warn
With the stubborn saw of common sense,
The grim joke and the banal resolution.
The traffic moves around with care,
But we remain, touching a wound
That opens to our richest horror.   30
Already old, the question Who shall die?
Becomes unspoken Who is innocent?
For death in war is done by hands;
Suicide has cause and stillbirth, logic;
And cancer, simple as a flower, blooms.
But this invites the occult mind,
Cancels our physics with a sneer,
And spatters all we knew of denouement
Across the expedient and wicked stones.

CHRISTMAS EVE: AUSTRALIA

The wind blows hot. English and foreign birds
And insects different as their fish excite
The would-be calm. The usual flocks and herds
Parade in permanent quiet out of sight,
And there one crystal like a grain of light
Sticks in the crucible of day and cools.
A cloud burnt to a crisp at some great height
Sips at the dark condensing in deep pools.

I smoke and read my Bible and chew gum,
Thinking of Christ and Christmas of last year,   10

24. gauche: awkward. 26. saw: proverbial observation. 27. banal: trite. 36. occult mind: the mind that is interested in the mysterious. 38. denouement: resolution; here, at the end of a tragedy.

And what those quizzical soldiers standing near
Ask of the war and Christmases to come,
And sick of causes and the tremendous blame
Curse lightly and pronounce your serious name.

JOHN BERRYMAN (1914–   )

WINTER LANDSCAPE

The three men coming down the winter hill
In brown, with tall poles and a pack of hounds
At heel, through the arrangement of the trees,
Past the five figures at the burning straw,
Returning cold and silent to their town,

Returning to the drifted snow, the rink
Lively with children, to the older men,
The long companions they can never reach,
The blue light, men with ladders, by the church
10   The sledge and shadow in the twilit street,

Are not aware that in the sandy time
To come, the evil waste of history
Outstretched, they will be seen upon the brow
Of that same hill: when all their company
Will have been irrecoverably lost,

These men, this particular three in brown
Witnessed by birds will keep the scene and say
By their configuration with the trees,
The small bridge, the red houses and the fire,
20   What place, what time, what morning occasion

Sent them into the wood, a pack of hounds
At heel and the tall poles upon their shoulders,
Thence to return as now we see them and
Ankle-deep in snow down the winter hill
Descend, while three birds watch and the fourth flies.

WORLD'S FAIR

The crowd moves forward on the midway, back
And forward, men and women from every State
Insisting on their motion like a clock.
I stand by the roller-coaster, and wait.
An hour I have waited, fireworks on the lake
Tell me it's late, and yet it is not that
Which rattles at the bottom of my mind,
Slight, like a faint sound sleepy on the wind
To the traveller when he has lost his track.

Suddenly in torn images I trace   10
The inexhaustible ability of a man
Loved once, long lost, still to prevent my peace,
Still to suggest my dreams and starve horizon.
Childhood speaks to me in an austere face.
The Chast Mayd only to the thriving Swan
Looks back and back with lecherous intent,
Being the one nail known, an excrement;
Middleton's grave in a forgotten place.

That recognition fades now, and I stand
Exhausted, angry, beside the wooden rail   20
Where tireless couples mount still, hand in hand,
For the complex drug of catapult and fall
To blot out the life they cannot understand
And never will forgive. The wind is stale,
The crowd thins, and my friend has not yet come.
It is long past midnight, time to track for home
And my work and the instructor down my mind.

14. austere: stern and forbidding. 15. Chast Mayd: reference to *A Chaste Maid in Cheapside*, play by Thomas Middleton (1580–1627), line 18, performed at the Swan Theatre.

DYLAN THOMAS (1914–1953)

THE FORCE THAT THROUGH THE GREEN FUSE DRIVES THE FLOWER

The force that through the green fuse drives the flower
Drives my green age; that blasts the roots of trees
Is my destroyer.
And I am dumb to tell the crooked rose
My youth is bent by the same wintry fever.

The force that drives the water through the rocks
Drives my red blood; that dries the mouthing streams
Turns mine to wax.
And I am dumb to mouth unto my veins
10   How at the mountain spring the same mouth sucks.

The hand that whirls the water in the pool
Stirs the quicksand; that ropes the blowing wind
Hauls my shroud sail.
And I am dumb to tell the hanging man
How of my clay is made the hangman's lime.

The lips of time leech to the fountain head;
Love drips and gathers, but the fallen blood
Shall calm her sores.
And I am dumb to tell a weather's wind
20   How time has ticked a heaven round the stars.

And I am dumb to tell the lover's tomb
How at my sheet goes the same crooked worm.

Title. Fuse: tube or casing. 15. hangman's lime: the chemical in which the hanged
body is deposited.

THIS BREAD I BREAK

This bread I break was once the oat,
This wine upon a foreign tree
Plunged in its fruit;
Man in the day or wind at night
Laid the crops low, broke the grape's joy.

Once in this wine the summer blood
Knocked in the flesh that decked the vine,
Once in this bread
The oat was merry in the wind;
Man broke the sun, pulled the wind down.   10

This flesh you break, this blood you let
Make desolation in the vein,
Were oat and grape
Born of the sensual root and sap;
My wine you drink, my bread you snap.

A REFUSAL TO MOURN THE DEATH, BY FIRE, OF A CHILD IN LONDON

Never until the mankind making
Bird beast and flower
Fathering and all humbling darkness
Tells with silence the last light breaking
And the still hour
Is come of the sea tumbling in harness

And I must enter again the round
Zion of the water bead
And the synagogue of the ear of corn
Shall I let pray the shadow of a sound   10
Or sow my salt seed
In the least valley of sackcloth to mourn

The majesty and burning of the child's death.
I shall not murder
The mankind of her going with a grave truth

1-3. Read mankind . . . humbling as a single modifier of **darkness. 8. Zion:** the heavenly city.

Nor blaspheme down the stations of the breath
With any further
Elegy of innocence and youth.

Deep with the first dead lies London's daughter,
20   Robed in the long friends,
The grains beyond age, the dark veins of her mother,
Secret by the unmourning water
Of the riding Thames.
After the first death, there is no other.

FERN HILL

Now as I was young and easy under the apple boughs
About the lilting house and happy as the grass was green,
    The night above the dingle starry,
      Time let me hail and climb

    Golden in the heydays of his eyes,
And honoured among wagons I was prince of the apple towns
And once below a time I lordly had the trees and leaves
    Trail with daisies and barley
    Down the rivers of the windfall light.

10   And as I was green and carefree, famous among the barns
About the happy yard and singing as the farm was home,
    In the sun that is young once only,
      Time let me play and be
    Golden in the mercy of his means,
And green and golden I was huntsman and herdsman, the calves
Sang to my horn, the foxes on the hills barked clear and cold,
    And the sabbath rang slowly
    In the pebbles of the holy streams.

All the sun long it was running, it was lovely, the hay
20   Fields high as the house, the tunes from the chimneys, it was air
    And playing, lovely and watery
      And fire green as grass.
    And nightly under the simple stars

23. **Thames:** the river that runs through London.

3. **dingle:** small, deep, wooded valley. *25.* **nightjars:** nocturnal birds. **26. ricks:** haystacks.

As I rode to sleep the owls were bearing the farm away,
All the moon long I heard, blessed among stables, the nightjars
    Flying with the ricks, and the horses
      Flashing into the dark.

And then to awake, and the farm, like a wanderer white
With the dew, come back, the cock on his shoulder: it was all
    Shining, it was Adam and maiden,   30
      The sky gathered again
    And the sun grew round that very day.
So it must have been after the birth of the simple light
In the first, spinning place, the spellbound horses walking warm
    Out of the whinnying green stable
      On to the fields of praise.

And honoured among foxes and pheasants by the gay house
Under the new made clouds and happy as the heart was long,
    In the sun born over and over,
      I ran my heedless ways,   40
    My wishes raced through the house high hay
And nothing I cared, at my sky blue trades, that time allows
In all his tuneful turning so few and such morning songs
    Before the children green and golden
      Follow him out of grace,

Nothing I cared, in the lamb white days, that time would take me
Up to the swallow thronged loft by the shadow of my hand,
    In the moon that is always rising,
      Nor that riding to sleep
    I should hear him fly with the high fields   50
And wake to the farm forever fled from the childless land.
Oh as I was young and easy in the mercy of his means,
    Time held me green and dying
    Though I sang in my chains like the sea.

DO NOT GO GENTLE INTO THAT GOOD NIGHT

    Do not go gentle into that good night,
    Old age should burn and rave at close of day;
    Rage, rage against the dying of the light.

Though wise men at their end know dark is right,
Because their words had forked no lightning they
Do not go gentle into that good night.

Good men, the last wave by, crying how bright
Their frail deeds might have danced in a green bay,
Rage, rage against the dying of the light.

10   Wild men who caught and sang the sun in flight,
And learn, too late, they grieved it on its way,
Do not go gentle into that good night.

Grave men, near death, who see with blinding sight
Blind eyes could blaze like meteors and be gay,
Rage, rage against the dying of the light.

And you, my father, there on the sad height,
Curse, bless, me now with your fierce tears, I pray.
Do not go gentle into that good night.
Rage, rage against the dying of the light.

RANDALL JARRELL (1914–1965)

THE DEATH OF THE BALL TURRET GUNNER

From my mother's sleep I fell into the State,
And I hunched in its belly till my wet fur froze.
Six miles from earth, loosed from its dream of life,
I woke to black flak and the nightmare fighters.
When I died they washed me out of the turret with a hose.

Jarrell's note: A ball turret was a plexiglass sphere set into the belly of a B-17 or B-24, and inhabited by two .50 caliber machine-guns and one man, a short small man. When this gunner tracked with his machine-guns a fighter attacking his bomber from below, he revolved with the turret; hunched upside-down in his little sphere, he looked like the foetus in the womb. The fighters which attacked him were armed with cannon firing explosive shells. The hose was a steam hose.

4. flak: exploding antiaircraft shells

EIGHTH AIR FORCE

If, in an odd angle of the hutment,
A puppy laps the water from a can
Of flowers, and the drunk sergeant shaving
Whistles *O Paradiso!*—shall I say that man
Is not as men have said: a wolf to man?

The other murderers troop in yawning;
Three of them play Pitch, one sleeps, and one
Lies counting missions, lies there sweating
Till even his heart beats: One; One; One.
O murderers! . . . Still, this is how it's done: 10

This is a war. . . . But since these play, before they die,
Like puppies with their puppy; since, a man,
I did as these have done, but did not die—
I will content the people as I can
And give up these to them: Behold the man!

I have suffered, in a dream, because of him,
Many things; for this last saviour, man,
I have lied as I lie now. But what is lying?
Men wash their hands, in blood, as best they can:
I find no fault in this just man.   20

THE WOMAN AT THE WASHINGTON ZOO

The saris go by me from the embassies.

Cloth from the moon. Cloth from another planet.
They look back at the leopard like the leopard.

And I. . . .
          this print of mine, that has kept its color

Jarrell's note: "Eighth Air Force" is a poem about the air force which bombed the Continent from England. The man who lies counting missions has one to go before being sent home. The phrases from the Gospels compare such criminals and scapegoats as these with that earlier criminal and scapegoat about whom the Gospels were written.

1. hutment: a large army hut holding 15–20 men. 4. *O Paradiso:* words from an aria in the opera, *L'Africaine,* by Giacomo Meyerbeer. 14–20. phrases taken from Matthew xxvii.19 and 24, Luke xxiii.24, and John xix.5.

1. saris: long pieces of cloth, constituting the principal garments of Hindu women.

Alive through so many cleanings; this dull null
Navy I wear to work, and wear from work, and so
To my bed, so to my grave, with no
Complaints, no comment: neither from my chief,
10   The Deputy Chief Assistant, nor his chief—
Only I complain. . . . this serviceable
Body that no sunlight dyes, no hand suffuses
But, dome-shadowed, withering among columns,
Wavy beneath fountains—small, far-off, shining
In the eyes of animals, these being trapped
As I am trapped but not, themselves, the trap,
Aging, but without knowledge of their age,
Kept safe here, knowing not of death, for death—
Oh, bars of my own body, open, open!

20   The world goes by my cage and never sees me.
And there come not to me, as come to these,
The wild beasts, sparrows pecking the llamas' grain,
Pigeons settling on the bears' bread, buzzards
Tearing the meat the flies have clouded. . . .
                                        Vulture,
When you come for the white rat that the foxes left,
Take off the red helmet of your head, the black
Wings that have shadowed me, and step to me as man:
The wild brother at whose feet the white wolves fawn,
30   To whose hand of power the great lioness
Stalks, purring. . . .
                        You know what I was,
You see what I am: change me, change me!

THE ELEMENTARY SCENE

Looking back in my mind I can see
The white sun like a tin plate
Over the wooden turning of the weeds;
The street jerking—a wet swing—
To end by the wall the children sang.

The thin grass by the girls' door,
Trodden on, straggling, yellow and rotten,
And the gaunt field with its one tied cow—
The dead land waking sadly to my life—
10   Stir, and curl deeper in the eyes of time.

The rotting pumpkin under the stairs
Bundled with switches and the cold ashes
Still holds for me, in its unwavering eyes,
The stinking shapes of cranes and witches,
Their path slanting down the pumpkin's sky.

Its stars beckon through the frost like cottages
(Homes of the Bear, the Hunter—of that absent star,
The dark where the flushed child struggles into sleep)
Till, leaning a lifetime to the comforter,
I float above the small limbs like their dream: 20

I, I, the future that mends everything.

WILLIAM STAFFORD (1914–   )

WRITTEN ON THE STUB OF THE FIRST PAYCHECK

Gasoline makes game scarce.
In Elko, Nevada, I remember a stuffed wildcat
someone had shot on Bing Crosby's ranch.
I stood in the filling station
breathing fumes and reading the snarl of a map.

There were peaks to the left so high
they almost got away in the heat;
Reno and Las Vegas were ahead.
I had promise of the California job,
and three kids with me.   10

It takes a lot of miles to equal one wildcat
today. We moved into a housing tract.
Every dodging animal carries my hope in Nevada.
It has been a long day, Bing.
Wherever I go is your ranch.

17. the Bear, the Hunter: constellations.

Title. This is the sixth and last poem of a series called "The Move to California."

THE STAR IN THE HILLS

A star hit in the hills behind our house
up where the grass turns brown touching the sky.

Meteors have hit the world before, but this was near,
and since TV; few saw, but many felt the shock.
The state of California owns that land
(and out from shore three miles), and any stars
that come will be roped off and viewed on week days 8 to 5.

A guard who took the oath of loyalty and denied
any police record told me this:
10   "If you don't have a police record yet
you could take the oath and get a job
if California should be hit by another star."

"I'd promise to be loyal to California
and to guard any stars that hit it," I said,
"or any place three miles out from shore,
unless the star was bigger than the state—
in which case I'd be loyal to *it*."

But he said no exceptions were allowed,
and he leaned against the state-owned meteor
20   so calm and puffed a cork-tip cigarette
that I looked down and traced with my foot in the dust
and thought again and said, "Ok—any star."

TRAVELING THROUGH THE DARK

Traveling through the dark I found a deer
dead on the edge of the Wilson River road.
It is usually best to roll them into the canyon:
that road is narrow; to swerve might make more dead.

By glow of the tail-light I stumbled back of the car
and stood by the heap, a doe, a recent killing;
she had stiffened already, almost cold.
I dragged her off; she was large in the belly.

My fingers touching her side brought me the reason—
10   her side was warm; her fawn lay there waiting,

alive, still, never to be born.
Beside that mountain road I hesitated.

The car aimed ahead its lowered parking lights;
under the hood purred the steady engine.
I stood in the glare of the warm exhaust turning red;
around our group I could hear the wilderness listen.

I thought hard for us all—my only swerving—,
then pushed her over the edge into the river.

ROBERT LOWELL (1917–   )

THE HOLY INNOCENTS

Listen, the hay-bells tinkle as the cart
Wavers on rubber tires along the tar
And cindered ice below the burlap mill
And ale-wife run. The oxen drool and start
In wonder at the fenders of a car,
And blunder hugely up St. Peter's hill.
These are the undefiled by woman—their
Sorrow is not the sorrow of this world:
King Herod shrieking vengeance at the curled
Up knees of Jesus choking in the air,   10

A king of speechless clods and infants. Still
The world out-Herods Herod; and the year,
The nineteen-hundred forty-fifth of grace,
Lumbers with losses up the clinkered hill
Of our purgation; and the oxen near
The worn foundations of their resting-place,
The holy manger where their bed is corn
And holly torn for Christmas. If they die,
As Jesus, in the harness, who will mourn?
Lamb of the shepherds, Child, how still you lie.   20

Title. Refers to the festival of the Holy Innocents, December 28, celebrating the
slaughter of the children by Herod (line 9). See Matthew ii.16. **4. ale-wife run:** stream
in which this herring-like fish is found.

CHILDREN OF LIGHT

Our fathers wrung their bread from stocks and stones
And fenced their gardens with the Redman's bones;
Embarking from the Nether Land of Holland,
Pilgrims unhouseled by Geneva's night,
They planted here the Serpent's seeds of light;
And here the pivoting searchlights probe to shock
The riotous glass houses built on rock,
And candles gutter by an empty altar,
And light is where the landless blood of Cain
10 Is burning, burning the unburied grain.

AFTER THE SURPRISING CONVERSIONS

September twenty-second, Sir: today
I answer. In the latter part of May,
Hard on our Lord's Ascension, it began
To be more sensible. A gentleman
Of more than common understanding, strict
In morals, pious in behavior, kicked
Against our goad. A man of some renown,
An useful, honored person in the town,
He came of melancholy parents; prone
10 To secret spells, for years they kept alone—
His uncle, I believe, was killed of it:
Good people, but of too much or little wit.
I preached one Sabbath on a text from Kings;
He showed concernment for his soul. Some things
In his experience were hopeful. He

Title. Those supposed to have spiritual awareness; see the parable of the unjust steward, especially Luke xvi.8. 4. unhouseled: deprived of the sacraments of the Roman Catholic Church; Geneva's night: Calvinism. 5. Serpent: Devil. 9. Cain: the slayer of his brother, Abel; declared an exile by God. See Genesis iv.8-12.

Title. "The details of this poem are drawn mainly from two paragraphs near the end of the *Narrative of Surprising Conversions,* an expanded form of a letter originally written on May 30, 1735, to the Reverend Dr. Benjamin Colman of Boston by Jonathan Edwards (1703–58), the great Calvinist preacher and theologian. Edwards was at that time minister at Northampton, Massachusetts, which had been undergoing a religious revival." (James K. Robinson and Walter B. Rideout, *A College Book of Modern Verse* [White Plains, New York: Row, Peterson and Company, 1958], p. 499.) 3. Lord's Ascension: on Holy Thursday, forty days after Easter; it: the withdrawal of God's spirit; cf. lines 37 and 38. 4. sensible: apparent. 11. it: melancholy and/or aloneness.

Would sit and watch the wind knocking a tree
And praise this countryside our Lord has made.
Once when a poor man's heifer died, he laid
A shilling on the doorsill; though a thirst
For loving shook him like a snake, he durst   20
Not entertain much hope of his estate
In heaven. Once we saw him sitting late
Behind his attic window by a light
That guttered on his Bible; through that night
He meditated terror, and he seemed
Beyond advice or reason, for he dreamed
That he was called to trumpet Judgment Day
To Concord. In the latter part of May
He cut his throat. And though the coroner
Judged him delirious, soon a noisome stir   30
Palsied our village. At Jehovah's nod
Satan seemed more let loose amongst us: God
Abandoned us to Satan, and he pressed
Us hard, until we thought we could not rest
Till we had done with life. Content was gone.
All the good work was quashed. We were undone.
The breath of God had carried out a planned
And sensible withdrawal from this land;
The multitude, once unconcerned with doubt,
Once neither callous, curious nor devout,   40
Jumped at broad noon, as though some peddler groaned
At it in its familiar twang: "My friend,
Cut your own throat. Cut your own throat. Now! Now!"
September twenty-second, Sir, the bough
Cracks with the unpicked apples, and at dawn
The small-mouth bass breaks water, gorged with spawn.

SKUNK HOUR

(FOR ELIZABETH BISHOP)

Nautilus Island's hermit
heiress still lives through winter in her Spartan cottage;
her sheep still graze above the sea.
Her son's a bishop. Her farmer

---

28. Concord: city in Massachusetts.

is first selectman in our village;
she's in her dotage.

Thirsting for
the hierarchic privacy
of Queen Victoria's century,
10   she buys up all
the eyesores facing her shore,
and lets them fall.

The season's ill—
we've lost our summer millionaire,
who seemed to leap from an L. L. Bean
catalogue. His nine-knot yawl
was auctioned off to lobstermen.
A red fox stain covers Blue Hill.

And now our fairy
20   decorator brightens his shop for fall;
his fishnet's filled with orange cork,
orange, his cobbler's bench and awl;
there is no money in his work,
he'd rather marry.

One dark night,
my Tudor Ford climbed the hill's skull;
I watched for love-cars. Lights turned down,
they lay together, hull to hull,
where the graveyard shelves on the town. . . .
30   My mind's not right.

A car radio bleats,
"Love, O careless Love. . . ." I hear
my ill-spirit sob in each blood cell,
as if my hand were at its throat. . . .
I myself am hell;
nobody's here—

only skunks, that search
in the moonlight for a bite to eat.
They march on their soles up Main Street:
40   white stripes, moonstruck eyes' red fire

5. selectman: an elected municipal officer in a New England town. **15. L. L. Bean:** long-established in Maine as makers and purveyors of sporting goods.

under the chalk-dry and spar spire
of the Trinitarian Church.

I stand on top
of our back steps and breathe the rich air—
a mother skunk with her column of kittens swills the garbage
     pail.
She jabs her wedge-head in a cup
of sour cream, drops her ostrich tail,
and will not scare.

FOR THE UNION DEAD

"RELINQUUNT OMNIA SERVARE REM PUBLICAM."

The old South Boston Aquarium stands
in a Sahara of snow now. Its broken windows are boarded.
The bronze weathervane cod has lost half its scales.
The airy tanks are dry.

Once my nose crawled like a snail on the glass;
my hand tingled
to burst the bubbles
drifting from the noses of the cowed, compliant fish.

My hand draws back. I often sigh still
for the dark downward and vegetating kingdom   10
of the fish and reptile. One morning last March,
I pressed against the new barbed and galvanized

fence on the Boston Common. Behind their cage,
yellow dinosaur steamshovels were grunting
as they cropped up tons of mush and grass
to gouge their underworld garage.

Parking spaces luxuriate like civic
sandpiles in the heart of Boston.
A girdle of orange, Puritan-pumpkin colored girders
braces the tingling Statehouse,   20

Epigraph. "They relinquish all to serve the state."

shaking over the excavations, as it faces Colonel Shaw
and his bell-cheeked Negro infantry
on St. Gaudens' shaking Civil War relief,
propped by a plank splint against the garage's earthquake.

Two months after marching through Boston,
half the regiment was dead;
at the dedication,
William James could almost hear the bronze Negroes breathe.

Their monument sticks like a fishbone
30   in the city's throat.
Its Colonel is as lean
as a compass-needle.

He has an angry wrenlike vigilance,
a greyhound's gentle tautness;
he seems to wince at pleasure,
and suffocate for privacy.

He is out of bounds now. He rejoices in man's lovely,
peculiar power to choose life and die—
when he leads his black soldiers to death,
40   he cannot bend his back.

On a thousand small town New England greens,
the old white churches hold their air
of sparse, sincere rebellion; frayed flags
quilt the graveyards of the Grand Army of the Republic.

The stone statues of the abstract Union Soldier
grow slimmer and younger each year—
wasp-waisted, they doze over muskets
and muse through their sideburns . . .

Shaw's father wanted no monument
50   except the ditch,
where his son's body was thrown
and lost with his "niggers."

21-22. **Colonel Shaw . . . infantry:** Col. Robert Shaw led the 54th Massachusetts Infantry, the first negro regiment. He and more than half his men were killed and their bodies thrown into a common, unmarked ditch, cf. lines 50-52. **23. St. Gaudens' . . . relief:** the monument to the dead infantry which bears the motto printed as epigraph to this poem. **28. William James:** the philosopher who gave the address at the unveiling of the monument.

The ditch is nearer.
There are no statues for the last war here;
on Boyleston Street, a commercial photograph
shows Hiroshima boiling

over a Mosler Safe, the "Rock of Ages"
that survived the blast. Space is nearer.
When I crouch to my television set,
the drained faces of Negro school-children rise like balloons.   60

Colonel Shaw
is riding on his bubble,
he waits
for the blessèd break.

The Aquarium is gone. Everywhere,
giant finned cars nose forward like fish;
a savage servility
slides by on grease.

LAWRENCE FERLINGHETTI (1919–   )

CHRIST CLIMBED DOWN

Christ climbed down
from His bare Tree
this year
and ran away to where
there were no rootless Christmas trees
hung with candycanes and breakable stars

Christ climbed down
from His bare Tree
this year
and ran away to where   10
there were no gilded Christmas trees
and no tinsel Christmas trees

54. last war: World War II.

and no tinfoil Christmas trees
and no pink plastic Christmas trees
and no gold Christmas trees
and no black Christmas trees
and no powderblue Christmas trees
hung with electric candles
and encircled by tin electric trains
20   and clever cornball relatives

Christ climbed down
from His bare Tree
this Year
and ran away to where
no intrepid Bible salesmen
covered the territory
in two-tone cadillacs
and where no Sears Roebuck creches
complete with plastic babe in manger
30   arrived by parcel post
the babe by special delivery
and where no televised Wise Men
praised the Lord Calvert Whiskey

Christ climbed down
from His bare Tree
this year
and ran away to where
no fat handshaking stranger
in a red flannel suit
40   and a fake white beard
went around passing himself off
as some sort of North Pole saint
crossing the desert to Bethlehem
Pennsylvania
in a Volkswagen sled
drawn by rollicking Adirondack reindeer
with German names
and bearing sacks of Humble Gifts
from Saks Fifth Avenue
50   for everybody's imagined Christ child

25. intrepid: bold. 28. creches: models of the nativity scene with figures, cattle, etc.
33. Lord Calvert: popular brand of whiskey.

Christ climbed down
from His bare Tree
this year
and ran away to where
no Bing Crosby carollers
groaned of a tight Christmas
and where no Radio City angels
iceskated wingless
thru a winter wonderland
into a jinglebell heaven   60
daily at 8:30
with Midnight Mass matinees

Christ climbed down
from His bare Tree
this year
and softly stole away into
some anonymous Mary's womb again
where in the darkest night
of everybody's anonymous soul   70
He awaits again
an unimaginable
and impossibly
Immaculate Reconception
the very craziest
of Second Comings

I HAVE NOT LAIN WITH BEAUTY

I have not lain with beauty all my life
   telling over to myself
               its most rife charms

I have not lain with beauty all my life
            and lied with it as well
   telling over to myself
        how beauty never dies
     but lies apart
        among the aborigines
             of art   10

3. **rife:** widespread.

and far above the battlefields
                              of love

          It is above all that
                         oh yes
          It sits upon the choicest of
                              Church seats
          up there where art directors meet
          to choose the things for immortality
                                   And they have lain with beauty
20   all their lives
                                   And they have fed on honeydew
              and drunk the wines of Paradise
                                   so that they know exactly how
                 a thing of beauty is a joy
                    forever and forever
                                and how it never never
                    quite can fade
                              into a money-losing nothingness

          Oh no I have not lain
30   on Beauty Rests like this
              afraid to rise at night
                         for fear that I might somehow miss
          some movement beauty might have made

          Yet I have slept with beauty
                                   in my own weird way
          and I have made a hungry scene or two
                                   with beauty in my bed
             and so spilled out another poem or two
             and so spilled out another poem or two
40   upon the Bosch-like world

     40. Bosch: Hieronymus (c. 1460–1516), Dutch painter whose canvases are noted
for devils and monstrous creatures.

RICHARD WILBUR (1921–　　　)

GRASSE: THE OLIVE TREES

FOR MARCELLE AND FERDINAND SPRINGER

Here luxury's the common lot. The light
Lies on the rain-pocked rocks like yellow wool
And around the rocks the soil is rusty bright
From too much wealth of water, so that the grass
Mashes under the foot, and all is full
Of heat and juice and a heavy jammed excess.

Whatever moves moves with the slow complete
Gestures of statuary. Flower smells
Are set in the golden day, and shelled in heat,
Pine and columnar cypress stand. The palm　　　　　　10
Sinks its combs in the sky. This whole South swells
To a soft rigor, a rich and crowded calm.

Only the olive contradicts. My eye,
Traveling slopes of rust and green, arrests
And rests from plenitude where olives lie
Like clouds of doubt against the earth's array.
Their faint disheveled foliage divests
The sunlight of its color and its sway.

Not that the olive spurns the sun; its leaves
Scatter and point to every part of the sky,　　　　　　20
Like famished fingers waving. Brilliance weaves
And sombers down among them, and among
The anxious silver branches, down to the dry
And twisted trunk, by rooted hunger wrung.

Even when seen from near, the olive shows
A hue of far away. Perhaps for this

Title. Grasse: city in southern France. 15. plenitude: fullness. 16. array: impressive display. 27. dove . . . back: reference to the dove that Noah had sent to see if the Flood had abated. See Genesis viii.11.

The dove brought olive back, a tree which grows
Unearthly pale, which ever dims and dries,
And whose great thirst, exceeding all excess,
30   Teaches the South it is not paradise.

YEAR'S END

Now winter downs the dying of the year,
And night is all a settlement of snow;
From the soft street the rooms of houses show
A gathered light, a shapen atmosphere,
Like frozen-over lakes whose ice is thin
And still allows some stirring down within.

I've known the wind by water banks to shake
The late leaves down, which frozen where they fell
And held in ice as dancers in a spell
10   Fluttered all winter long into a lake;
Graved on the dark in gestures of descent,
They seemed their own most perfect monument.

There was perfection in the death of ferns
Which laid their fragile cheeks against the stone
A million years. Great mammoths overthrown
Composedly have made their long sojourns,
Like palaces of patience, in the gray
And changeless lands of ice. And at Pompeii

The little dog lay curled and did not rise
20   But slept the deeper as the ashes rose
And found the people incomplete, and froze
The random hands, the loose unready eyes
Of men expecting yet another sun
To do the shapely thing they had not done.

These sudden ends of time must give us pause.
We fray into the future, rarely wrought
Save in the tapestries of afterthought.
More time, more time. Barrages of applause
Come muffled from a buried radio.
30   The New-year bells are wrangling with the snow.

18. **Pompeii:** Italian city destroyed by the eruption of Vesuvius in A.D. 79 but pre-
served fossilized by the ash.

LOVE CALLS US TO THE THINGS
OF THIS WORLD

The eyes open to a cry of pulleys,
And spirited from sleep, the astounded soul
Hangs for a moment bodiless and simple
As false dawn.
                    Outside the open window
The morning air is all awash with angels.

Some are in bed-sheets, some are in blouses,
Some are in smocks: but truly there they are.
Now they are rising together in calm swells
Of halcyon feeling, filling whatever they wear   10
With the deep joy of their impersonal breathing;

Now they are flying in place, conveying
The terrible speed of their omnipresence, moving
And staying like white water; and now of a sudden
They swoon down into so rapt a quiet
That nobody seems to be there.
                              The soul shrinks

From all that it is about to remember,
From the punctual rape of every blessèd day,
And cries,   20
          "Oh, let there be nothing on earth but laundry,
Nothing but rosy hands in the rising steam
And clear dances done in the sight of heaven."

Yet, as the sun acknowledges
With a warm look the world's hunks and colors,
The soul descends once more in bitter love
To accept the waking body, saying now
In a changed voice as the man yawns and rises,

      "Bring them down from their ruddy gallows;
Let there be clean linen for the backs of thieves;   30
Let lovers go fresh and sweet to be undone,
And the heaviest nuns walk in a pure floating
Of dark habits,
                keeping their difficult balance."

Title. Quotation from St. Augustine. 1. pulleys: apparatus for manipulating the
laundry line, especially from apartment-house windows. 10. halcyon: calm. 33. habits:
uniforms worn by members of religious orders.

PHILIP LARKIN (1922–   )

THE WHITSUN WEDDINGS

That Whitsun, I was late getting away:
   Not till about
One-twenty on the sunlit Saturday
Did my three-quarters-empty train pull out,
All windows down, all cushions hot, all sense
Of being in a hurry gone. We ran
Behind the backs of houses, crossed a street
Of blinding windscreens, smelt the fish-dock; thence
The river's level drifting breadth began,
10   Where sky and Lincolnshire and water meet.

All afternoon, through the tall heat that slept
   For miles inland,
A slow and stopping curve southwards we kept.
Wide farms went by, short-shadowed cattle, and
Canals with floatings of industrial froth;
A hothouse flashed uniquely: hedges dipped
And rose: and now and then a smell of grass
Displaced the reek of buttoned carriage-cloth
Until the next town, new and nondescript,
20   Approached with acres of dismantled cars.

At first, I didn't notice what a noise
   The weddings made
Each station that we stopped at: sun destroys
The interest of what's happening in the shade,
And down the long cool platforms whoops and skirls
I took for porters larking with the mails,
And went on reading. Once we started, though,
We passed them, grinning and pomaded, girls
In parodies of fashion, heels and veils,
30   All posed irresolutely, watching us go,

Title. Whitsun: English holiday weekend in May, marking the feast of Pentecost.
8. windscreens: windshields. 10. Lincolnshire: county in middle of England. 19. nondescript: lacking individual character. 26. larking: fooling around. 28. pomaded: with perfumed hair.

As if out on the end of an event
  Waving goodbye
To something that survived it. Struck, I leant
More promptly out next time, more curiously,
And saw it all again in different terms:
The fathers with broad belts under their suits
And seamy foreheads; mothers loud and fat;
An uncle shouting smut; and then the perms,
The nylon gloves and jewellery-substitutes,
The lemons, mauves, and olive-ochres that   40

Marked off the girls unreally from the rest.
  Yes, from cafés
And banquet-halls up yards, and bunting-dressed
Coach-party annexes, the wedding-days
Were coming to an end. All down the line
Fresh couples climbed aboard: the rest stood round;
The last confetti and advice were thrown,
And, as we moved, each face seemed to define
Just what it saw departing: children frowned
At something dull; fathers had never known   50

Success so huge and wholly farcical;
  The women shared
The secret like a happy funeral;
While girls, gripping their handbags tighter, stared
At a religious wounding. Free at last,
And loaded with the sum of all they saw,
We hurried towards London, shuffling gouts of steam.
Now fields were building-plots, and poplars cast
Long shadows over major roads, and for
Some fifty minutes, that in time would seem   60

Just long enough to settle hats and say
  I nearly died,
A dozen marriages got under way.
They watched the landscape, sitting side by side
—An Odeon went past, a cooling tower,
And someone running up to bowl—and none

---

40. mauves: purplish-rose shades; olive-ochres: dark yellow-green colors. 57. gouts:
spurts. 65. Odeon: movie theater. 66. bowl: in the game of cricket.

Thought of the others they would never meet
Or how their lives would all contain this hour.
I thought of London spread out in the sun,
70   Its postal districts packed like squares of wheat:

There we were aimed. And as we raced across
        Bright knots of rail
Past standing Pullmans, walls of blackened moss
Came close, and it was nearly done, this frail
Travelling coincidence; and what it held
Stood ready to be loosed with all the power
That being changed can give. We slowed again,
And as the tightened brakes took hold, there swelled
A sense of falling, like an arrow-shower
80   Sent out of sight, somewhere becoming rain.

FIRST SIGHT

Lambs that learn to walk in snow
When their bleating clouds the air
Meet a vast unwelcome, know
Nothing but a sunless glare.
Newly stumbling to and fro
All they find, outside the fold,
Is a wretched width of cold.

As they wait beside the ewe,
Her fleeces wetly caked, there lies
10   Hidden round them, waiting too,
Earth's immeasurable surprise.
They could not grasp it if they knew,
What so soon will wake and grow
Utterly unlike the snow.

JAMES DICKEY (1923–   )

IN THE MOUNTAIN TENT

I am hearing the shape of the rain
Take the shape of the tent and believe it,
Laying down all around where I lie
A profound, unspeakable law.
I obey, and am free-falling slowly

Through the thought-out leaves of the wood
Into the minds of animals.
I am there in the shining of water
Like dark, like light, out of Heaven.

I am there like the dead, or the beast   10
Itself, which thinks of a poem—
Green, plausible, living, and holy—
And cannot speak, but hears,
Called forth from the waiting of things,

A vast, proper, reinforced crying
With the sifted, harmonious pause,
The sustained intake of all breath
Before the first word of the Bible.

At midnight water dawns
Upon the held skulls of the foxes   20
And weasels and tousled hares
On the eastern side of the mountain.
Their light is the image I make

As I wait as if recently killed,
Receptive, fragile, half-smiling,
My brow watermarked with the mark
On the wing of a moth

And the tent taking shape on my body
Like ill-fitting, Heavenly clothes.
From holes in the ground comes my voice   30
In the God-silenced tongue of the beasts.
"I shall rise from the dead," I am saying.

BUCKDANCER'S CHOICE

So I would hear out those lungs,
The air split into nine levels,
Some gift of tongues of the whistler

In the invalid's bed: my mother,
Warbling all day to herself
The thousand variations of one song;

It is called Buckdancer's Choice.
For years, they have all been dying
Out, the classic buck-and-wing men

Of traveling minstrel shows;
With them also an old woman
Was dying of breathless angina,

Yet still found breath enough
To whistle up in my head
A sight like a one-man band,

Freed black, with cymbals at heel,
An ex-slave who thrivingly danced
To the ring of his own clashing light

Through the thousand variations of one song
All day to my mother's prone music,
The invalid's warbler's note,

While I crept close to the wall
Sock-footed, to hear the sounds alter,
Her tongue like a mockingbird's break

Through stratum after stratum of a tone
Proclaiming what choices there are
For the last dancers of their kind,

For ill women and for all slaves
Of death, and children enchanted at walls
With a brass-beating glow underfoot,

Not dancing but nearly risen
Through barnlike, theatrelike houses
On the wings of the buck and wing.

9. **buck-and-wing:** a fast tap dance. 12. **angina:** heart disease.

DENISE LEVERTOV (1923–   )

FIVE POEMS FROM MEXICO

i   The Weave

The cowdung-colored mud
baked and raised up in random
walls, bears the silken
lips and lashes of erotic
flowers towards a sky of
noble clouds. Accepted
sacramental excrement
supports the ecstatic half-sleep
of butterflies, the slow
opening and closing of brilliant   10
dusty wings. Bite down
on the bitter stem of your nectared
rose, you know
the dreamy stench of death and fling
magenta shawls delicately
about your brown shoulders laughing.

ii   Corazón

When in bushy hollows between
moonround and moonround of hill, white clouds
loiter arm-in-arm, out of curl,
and sheep in the ravines
vaguely congregate, the heart
of Mexico sits in the rain
not caring to seek shelter,
a blanket of geranium pink drawn up
over his silent mouth.

ii. Title. Corazón: heart.

iii   The Rose

(FOR B.L.)

In the green Alameda, near the fountains,
an old man, hands
clasped behind his shabby back
shuffles from rose to rose, stopping
to ponder and inhale, and I
follow him at a distance, discovering
the golden rose, color of bees' fur, odor of honey,
red rose, contralto, roses
of dawn-cloud-color, of snow-in-moonlight,
10   of colors only roses know,
but no rose
like the rose I saw in your garden.

iv   Canticle

Flies, acolytes
of the death-in-life temple
buzz their prayers

and from the altar
of excrement arises
an incense

of orange and purple
petals. Drink,
campesino,

10   stain with ferment
the blinding white that clothes
your dark body.

v   Sierra

Golden the high ridge of thy back, bull mountain,
and coffee-black thy full sides.
The sky decks thy horns with violet,

iii. 1. the . . . Alameda: boulevard in Mexico City. iv. 9. campesino: peasant.
v. 6. zopilotes: Mexican vultures.

with cascades of cloud. The brown hills
are thy cows.   Shadows
of zopilotes cross and slowly
cross again
thy flanks, lord of herds.

TWO VARIATIONS

i   Enquiry

You who go out on schedule
to kill, do you know
there are eyes that watch you,
eyes whose lids you burned off,
that see you eat your steak
and buy your girlflesh
and sell your PX goods
and sleep?
She is not old,
she whose eyes   **10**
know you.
She will outlast you.
She saw
her five young children
writhe and die;
in that hour
she began to watch you,
she whose eyes are open forever.

ii   The Seeing

Hands over my eyes I see
blood and the little bones;
or when a blanket covers
the sockets I see the
weave; at night the glare softens
but I have power now
to see there is only gray
on gray, the sleepers, the
altar. I see the living

20   and the dead; the dead are
        as if alive, the mouth of
        my youngest son pulls my
        breast, but there is no milk, he
        is a ghost; through his flesh
        I see the dying of those
        said to be alive, they
        eat rice and speak to me but
        I see dull death in them
        and while they speak I see
30   myself on my mat, body
        and eyes, eyes that see a
        hand in the unclouded sky,
        a human hand, release
        wet fire, the rain that gave
        my eyes their vigilance.

WHAT WERE THEY LIKE?

1) Did the people of Viet Nam
   use lanterns of stone?
2) Did they hold ceremonies
   to reverence the opening of buds?
3) Were they inclined to quiet laughter?
4) Did they use bone and ivory,
   jade and silver, for ornament?
5) Had they an epic poem?
6) Did they distinguish between speech and singing?

10   1) Sir, their light hearts turned to stone.
          It is not remembered whether in gardens
          stone lanterns illumined pleasant ways.
       2) Perhaps they gathered once to delight in blossom,
          but after the children were killed
          there were no more buds.
       3) Sir, laughter is bitter to the burned mouth.
       4) A dream ago, perhaps. Ornament is for joy.
          All the bones were charred.
       5) It is not remembered. Remember,
20   most were peasants; their life

was in rice and bamboo.
When peaceful clouds were reflected in the paddies
and the water buffalo stepped surely along terraces,
maybe fathers told their sons old tales.
When bombs smashed those mirrors
there was time only to scream.
6) There is an echo yet
of their speech which was like a song.
It was reported their singing resembled
the flight of moths in moonlight.   30
Who can say? It is silent now.

LOUIS SIMPSON (1923–   )

TO THE WESTERN WORLD

A siren sang, and Europe turned away
From the high castle and the shepherd's crook.
Three caravels went sailing to Cathay
On the strange ocean, and the captains shook
Their banners out across the Mexique Bay.

And in our early days we did the same.
Remembering our fathers in their wreck
We crossed the sea from Palos where they came
And saw, enormous to the little deck,
A shore in silence waiting for a name.   10

The treasures of Cathay were never found.
In this America, this wilderness
Where the axe echoes with a lonely sound,
The generations labor to possess
And grave by grave we civilize the ground.

22. paddies: rice fields (under water).

1. siren: alluring singing female. 3. caravels: small sailing ships; Cathay: China.
8. Palos: town in Cuba.

WALT WHITMAN AT BEAR MOUNTAIN

Neither on horseback nor seated,
But like himself, squarely on two feet,
The poet of death and lilacs
Loafs by the footpath. Even the bronze looks alive
Where it is folded like cloth. And he seems friendly.

"Where is the Mississippi panorama
And the girl who played the piano?
Where are you, Walt?
The Open Road goes to the used-car lot.

10   "Where is the nation you promised?
These houses built of wood sustain
Colossal snows,
And the light above the street is sick to death.

"As for the people—see how they neglect you!
Only a poet pauses to read the inscription."

"I am here," he answered.
"It seems you have found me out.
Yet, did I not warn you that it was Myself
I advertised? Were my words not sufficiently plain?

20   "I gave no prescriptions,
And those who have taken my moods for prophecies
Mistake the matter."
Then, vastly amused—"Why do you reproach me?
I freely confess I am wholly disreputable.
Yet I am happy, because you have found me out."

A crocodile in wrinkled metal loafing . . .

Then all the realtors,
Pickpockets, salesmen, and the actors performing
Official scenarios,

    Title. Walt Whitman: American poet, 1819–1892 (see pages 296–304). **Bear Mountain:** name of the State Park in New York where Whitman's statue stands. **9. The Open Road:** reference to Whitman's poem "Song of the Open Road." **18. Myself:** reference to Whitman's poem "Song of Myself."

Turned a deaf ear, for they had contracted   30
American dreams.

But the man who keeps a store on a lonely road,
And the housewife who knows she's dumb,
And the earth, are relieved.

All that grave weight of America
Cancelled! Like Greece and Rome.
The future in ruins!
The castles, the prisons, the cathedrals
Unbuilding, and roses
Blossoming from the stones that are not there. . . .   40

The clouds are lifting from the high Sierras,
The Bay mists clearing.
And the angel in the gate, the flowering plum,
Dances like Italy, imagining red.

ROBERT BLY (1926–   )

COUNTING SMALL-BONED BODIES

Let's count the bodies over again.

If we could only make the bodies smaller,
The size of skulls,
We could make a whole plain white with skulls in the moonlight!

If we could only make the bodies smaller,
Maybe we could get
A whole year's kill in front of us on a desk!

If we could only make the bodies smaller,
We could fit
A body into a finger-ring, for a keepsake forever.   10

41. **Sierras:** California mountains. 42. **Bay:** San Francisco Bay.

DRIVING THROUGH MINNESOTA
DURING THE HANOI BOMBINGS

We drive between lakes just turning green;
Late June. The white turkeys have been moved
To new grass.
How long the seconds are in great pain!
Terror just before death,
Shoulders torn, shot
From helicopters, the boy
Tortured with the telephone generator,
"I felt sorry for him,
And blew his head off with a shotgun."
These instants become crystals,
Particles
The grass cannot dissolve. Our own gaiety
Will end up
In Asia, and in your cup you will look down
And see
Black Starfighters.
We were the ones we intended to bomb!
Therefore we will have
To go far away
To atone
For the sufferings of the stringy-chested
And the small rice-fed ones, quivering
In the helicopter like wild animals,
Shot in the chest, taken back to be questioned.

ALLEN GINSBERG (1926–   )

A SUPERMARKET IN CALIFORNIA

What thoughts I have of you tonight, Walt Whitman, for I walked down the sidestreets under the trees with a headache self-conscious looking at the full moon.

1. **Walt Whitman:** American poet, 1819–1892 (see pages 296–304).

In my hungry fatigue, and shopping for images, I went into the neon fruit supermarket, dreaming of your enumerations!

What peaches and what penumbras! Whole families shopping at night! Aisles full of husbands! Wives in the avocados, babies in the tomatoes!—and you, Garcia Lorca, what were you doing down by the watermelons?

I saw you, Walt Whitman, childless, lonely old grubber, poking among the meats in the refrigerator and eyeing the grocery boys.

I heard you asking questions of each: Who killed the pork chops? What price bananas? Are you my Angel?

I wandered in and out of the brilliant stacks of cans following you, and followed in my imagination by the store detective.

We strode down the open corridors together in our solitary fancy tasting artichokes, possessing every frozen delicacy, and never passing the cashier.

Where are we going, Walt Whitman? The doors close in an hour. Which way does your beard point tonight?

(I touch your book and dream of our odyssey in the supermarket and feel absurd.)

Will we walk all night through solitary streets? The trees add shade to 10 shade, lights out in the houses, we'll both be lonely.

Will we stroll dreaming of the lost America of love past blue automobiles in driveways, home to our silent cottage?

Ah, dear father, graybeard, lonely old courage-teacher, what America did you have when Charon quit poling his ferry and you got out on a smoking bank and stood watching the boat disappear on the black waters of Lethe?

TO AUNT ROSE

Aunt Rose—now—might I see you
with your thin face and buck tooth smile and pain
        of rheumatism—and a long black heavy shoe
           for your bony left leg
limping down the long hall in Newark on the running carpet
        past the black grand piano
        in the day room
          where the parties were

2. enumerations: lists. 3. penumbras: half-shadows; Garcia Lorca: Spanish poet, 1899–1936, killed by Fascists in Civil War. 9. odyssey: long wandering journey. 12. Charon: character in Greek mythology who ferried souls of the dead over the river into the underworld; Lethe: the rivre of the underworld that, when crossed, induced forgetfulness.

and I sang Spanish loyalist songs
10   in a high squeaky voice
                        (hysterical) the committee listening
                while you limped around the room
                        collected the money—
        Aunt Honey, Uncle Sam, a stranger with a cloth arm
                in his pocket
                        and huge young bald head
                                of Abraham Lincoln Brigade

—your long sad face
                your tears of sexual frustration
20   (what smothered sobs and bony hips
                                under the pillows of Osborne Terrace)
        —the time I stood on the toilet seat naked
                and you powdered my thighs with Calomine
                        against the poison ivy—my tender
                                and shamed first black curled hairs
        what were you thinking in secret heart then
                knowing me a man already—
        and I an ignorant girl of family silence on the thin pedestal
                        of my legs in the bathroom—Museum of Newark.
30   Aunt Rose
        Hitler is dead, Hitler is in Eternity; Hitler is with
                Tamburlane and Emily Brontë

        Though I see you walking still, a ghost on Osborne Terrace
                down the long dark hall to the front door
                limping a little with a pinched smile
                        in what must have been a silken
                                flower dress
                welcoming my father, the Poet, on his visit to Newark
                        —see you arriving in the living room
40   dancing on your crippled leg
                                and clapping hands his book
                                        had been accepted by Liveright

---

9. Spanish loyalist songs: songs of the government side in the Spanish Civil War,
1936–1939. 17. Abraham Lincoln Brigade: brigade of American volunteers assisting
the government forces in the Spanish Civil War. 32. Tamburlane: historical and fabulous
Mongol conqueror of the 14th century; Emily Bronte: 19th-century English novelist.
42. Liveright: American publishing house; published *Everlasting Minute,* 1937.

Hitler is dead and Liveright's gone out of business
The Attic of the Past and *Everlasting Minute* are out of print
        Uncle Harry sold his last silk stocking
     Claire quit interpretive dancing school
        Buba sits a wrinkled monument in Old
            Ladies Home blinking at new babies

last time I saw you was the hospital
       pale skull protruding under ashen skin   50
         blue veined unconscious girl
           in an oxygen tent
     the war in Spain has ended long ago
      Aunt Rose

FIRST PARTY AT KEN KESEY'S
WITH HELL'S ANGELS

Cool black night thru the redwoods
cars parked outside in shade
behind the gate, stars dim above
the ravine, a fire burning by the side
porch and a few tired souls hunched over
in black leather jackets. In the huge
wooden house, a yellow chandelier
at 3AM the blast of loudspeakers
hi-fi Rolling Stones Ray Charles Beatles
Jumping Joe Jackson and twenty youths   10
dancing to the vibration thru the floor,
a little weed in the bathroom, girls in scarlet
tights, one muscular smooth skinned man
sweating dancing for hours, beer cans
bent littering the yard, a hanged man
sculpture dangling from a high creek branch,
children sleeping softly in bedroom bunks,
And 4 police cars parked outside the painted
gate, red lights revolving in the leaves.

44. *The Attic of the Past* and *Everlasting Minute:* volumes of poetry by Louis Ginsberg (1896–   ), Allen's father. **47. Buba:** grandmother.

10. **Jumping Joe Jackson:** basketball player. **12. weed:** marijuana.

W. D. SNODGRASS (1926–   )

APRIL INVENTORY

The green catalpa tree has turned
All white; the cherry blooms once more.
In one whole year I haven't learned
A blessed thing they pay you for.
The blossoms snow down in my hair;
The trees and I will soon be bare.

The trees have more than I to spare.
The sleek, expensive girls I teach,
Younger and pinker every year,
Bloom gradually out of reach.
The pear tree lets its petals drop
Like dandruff on a tabletop.

The girls have grown so young by now
I have to nudge myself to stare.
This year they smile and mind me how
My teeth are falling with my hair.
In thirty years I may not get
Younger, shrewder, or out of debt.

The tenth time, just a year ago,
I made myself a little list
Of all the things I'd ought to know,
Then told my parents, analyst,
And everyone who's trusted me
I'd be substantial, presently.

I haven't read one book about
A book or memorized one plot.
Or found a mind I did not doubt.
I learned one date. And then forgot.
And one by one the solid scholars
Get the degrees, the jobs, the dollars.

And smile above their starchy collars.
I taught my classes Whitehead's notions;
One lovely girl, a song of Mahler's.
Lacking a source-book or promotions,
I showed one child the colors of
A luna moth and how to love.

I taught myself to name my name,
To bark back, loosen love and crying;
To ease my woman so she came,
To ease an old man who was dying.   40
I have not learned how often I
Can win, can love, but choose to die.

I have not learned there is a lie
Love shall be blonder, slimmer, younger;
That my equivocating eye
Loves only by my body's hunger;
That I have forces, true to feel,
Or that the lovely world is real.

While scholars speak authority
And wear their ulcers on their sleeves,   50
My eyes in spectacles shall see
These trees procure and spend their leaves.
There is a value underneath
The gold and silver in my teeth.

Though trees turn bare and girls turn wives,
We shall afford our costly seasons;
There is a gentleness survives
That will outspeak and has its reasons.
There is a loveliness exists,
Preserves us, not for specialists.   60

32. Whitehead: Alfred North (1861–1947), English philosopher, collaborated with Bertrand Russell (his ex-student) in *Principia Mathematica,* a distinguished work in logic. 33. Mahler: Gustav (1860–1911), Austrian composer. 45. equivocating: deceiving.

MANET:
THE EXECUTION OF THE EMPEROR MAXIMILIAN

"Aim well, muchachos; aim right
here," he pointed to his heart.
With face turned upward, he
waited, grave but calm.

These dapper soldiers, seen shooting the Emperor
    Just now, stand with heels in, toes out, like ballet girls
But not so tense. Chiefly, we're forced to be aware
    How splendid their spats and long white saber-holsters
Gleam. They should deduce this is some crucial affair
10   In view of their natty uniforms and dress gear,
Yet one of them has turned up late, naturally,
    For this, which should be the true peak of his career.
He stands aside, cocking his rifle, carefully.
    Still, politics may not mean much to him. Perhaps,
Since he looks less like a penguin or some old gaudy
    Dressform, since he sports a white band on a red cap,
Who knows?—he may be an officer who'll give the body
    The *coup de grâce*. All the grace, themselves, they could conceive,
The men peer down their long sight lines like some long shot
20   At billiards—some shot men might hope they could achieve
Yet they would scarcely be disgraced if they should not.

Miramón and Mejía fell at once.
A second volley was required for
Maximilian who had wished to be
shot in the body so that his
mother might see his face.

Scumbly, vague, the half-formed heads of these peasants stare
    Up over the background, which is a flat rock wall.
Some yawn, some sprawl on their elbows, and some rest their
30   Heads on their crossed arms. They peer down like men gone dull
With heat and flies watching some tenth-rate matadors

Title. Manet: Edouard, French painter (1833–1883); Emperor Maximilian: 1832–
1867; Emperor of Mexico 1864–1867; executed (see also last 6 lines of the poem). 1.
muchachos: lads. 5. dapper: smart. 8. saber: cavalry sword. 18. *coup de grâce:* final
shot or blow given to dying man or animal. 22. Miguel Miramón and Thomas Mejía:
Mexican generals, executed with Emperor. 27. scumbly: with softened outlines. 31. mata-
dors: bullfighters.

Practice, or angels bored with all these martyrs. True,
One waves and does look like he's yelling. yet of course
    That might mean triumph, outrage, or mere shock. Who
Will ever know? Maybe he thinks he knows someone
    Or just wants it known he's here. Caught by the drums
And dress gear, they don't even know the names; they wait
    For marvels, for a sign. Surely someone must come
Declare significance, solve how these things relate
    To freedom, to their life's course, to eternity.   **40**
Random and dusty, their clustering faces are
    Crumbled like rocks in the wall, from which they could be
An outgrowth—cool, distant, irrelevant as stars.

                    The mutilated body was given full
                    funereal honors by the Hapsburgs,
                    whose general downfall it prefigured.
                    On the place of execution, moreover,
                    was erected a small chapel to further
                    his remembrance on earth and his
                    forgiveness in heaven.   **50**

Still, for Maximilian, all perspective lines
    End in this flat rock wall. Some may find, in the distance,
An inkling of quiet streams, or pine-shadowed lanes;
    Just the same, we're cut off from all true hope of vistas
As men down a mine-shaft. The peasants, too, detached,
    Held back of this blank wall from their Emperor's passion;
And the soldiers, though close, we know their aim goes past
    Their victims, each fixed in his own plane of existence,
His own style—though they die, each in his own style and fashion.
    And if their Emperor holds his appointed place,   **60**
He's bleached out like some child's two-penny crucifixion;
    Stands in an impartial iconoclastic light
That will not hint where you might best direct your sight—
    At the unspotlighted center, just this blank space
That rifles cross; elsewhere, a baffling contradiction
    Of shadows as if each man smuggled strange forces
Into Mexico, and moved from his own light sources. . . .

---

45. Hapsburgs: German ruling family, of which Maximilian was a member. 46.
prefigured: anticipated. 53. inkling: hint. 54. vistas: views down corridors, natural or
other. 62. iconoclastic: destructive of conventional beliefs and attitudes.

                                        When the fraudulent French plebiscite
                                        failed to convince Maximilian he had
70   been elected by the peons, Napoleon
                                        threatened to offer the crown to
                                        some other candidate.

. . . Yet for Maximilian, who hoped he could unite
    The Old World and the New under one ordinance—
Unfortunately his own—bind the Divine Right
    Of Hapsburgs with half-chewed liberal sentiments,
Link the True Church to the freely divisive mind,
    Shape a fixed aim from all his own diversities,
Who in his wardrobe joined all the races of mankind;
80   For Maximilian, whose wife Carlotta endured
A lifetime mad with loss (or with some love disease
    He'd brought her from Brazil) confined to a convent
Where, though losing her worst fears, she always referred
    To him as Emperor of all the Firmament;
The Emperor who dreamed that one day he might stand
    At the top of some broad magnificent staircase
Vouchsafing from that height of infinite command
    One smile of infinite condescension and grace
On the human beings gathered around its base. . . .

90   It was as if some ne'er-do-well had
                                        found at last his true vocation; as
                                        martyr and sacrificial victim, he
                                        has seldom been surpassed.

. . . Still, for Maximilian . . . still, for the man who stands
    In the midst of his own life—or, to be exact,
Off to one side of his dying—he holds together
    Just these two who chose death with him; he holds their hands.
And they're almost obscured by the smoke. Then, in fact,
    Which IS the man? No doubt he should stand at the center,
100   Yet who gets shot in a frock coat and sombrero?
    In that man's bland face we see nothing, not that firm
Nobility which we demand, and *do* discern
    In this stranger by the wall, or can find elsewhere

-----

68. plebiscite: the vote of a whole electorate in a state (the plebiscite that endorsed Maximilian was spurious). 70. Napoleon: III, instrumental in Maximilian's installation in Mexico. 74. ordinance: rule.

Only in this bearded soldier of whom we know
  Nothing. Who knows? Perhaps it's this one, standing there
Spread-legged, whose clenched free hand flaps up like a doll's,
  Whose face twists upward in effort or possibly
Pain, as his chest's opened out by the rifleballs,
  His brain unties, atoms start hurtling out, blind, free,
And he, whoever he was, is all finished being.   110

> Born, July 6, 1832; brother of
> Franz Josef I, Emperor of Austria.
> 1854, naval administrator; 1857,
> viceroy to the Lombardo-Venetian
> kingdom; 1864, Emperor of Mexico.
> Died, 1867.

AN ARCHAIC TORSO OF APOLLO

We will not ever know his legendary head
Wherein the eyes, like apples, ripened. Yet
His torso glows like a candelabra
In which his vision, merely turned down low,

Still holds and gleams. If this were not so, the curve
Of the breast could not so blind you, nor this smile
Pass lightly through the soft turn of the loins
Into that center where procreation flared.

If this were not so, this stone would stand defaced, maimed,
Under the transparent cascade of the shoulder,   10
Not glimmering that way, like a wild beast's pelt,

Nor breaking out of all its contours
Like a star; for there is no place here
That does not see you. You must change your life.

Note. This poem is a translation of a sonnet by the German poet Rainer Maria
Rilke (1875–1926).

W. S. Merwin (1927–   )

LEMUEL'S BLESSING

> *Let Lemuel bless with the wolf, which*
> *is a dog without a master, but the Lord*
> *hears his cries and feeds him in the*
> *desert.*
>
> CHRISTOPHER SMART
> *Jubilate Agno*

You that know the way,
Spirit,
I bless your ears which are like cypruses on a mountain
With their roots in wisdom. Let me approach.
I bless your paws and their twenty nails which tell their own prayer
And are like dice in command of their own combinations.
Let me not be lost.
I bless your eyes for which I know no comparison.
Run with me like the horizon, for without you
10 I am nothing but a dog lost and hungry,
Ill-natured, untrustworthy, useless.

My bones together bless you like an orchestra of flutes.
Divert the weapons of the settlements and lead their dogs a dance.
Where a dog is shameless and wears servility
In his tail like a banner,
Let me wear the opprobrium of possessed and possessors
As a thick tail properly used
To warm my worst and my best parts. My tail and my laugh bless you.
20 Lead me past the error at the fork of hesitation.
Deliver me

From the ruth of the lair, which clings to me in the morning,
Painful when I move, like a trap;
Even debris has its favorite positions but they are not yours;

16. opprobrium: reproach. 21. ruth: compassion.

From the ruth of kindness, with its licked hands;
I have sniffed baited fingers and followed
Toward necessities which were not my own: it would make me
An habitué of back steps, faithful custodian of fat sheep;

From the ruth of prepared comforts, with its
Habitual dishes sporting my name and its collars and leashes of vanity;

From the ruth of approval, with its nets, kennels, and taxidermists;   30
It would use my guts for its own rackets and instruments, to play its own
    games and music;
Teach me to recognize its platforms, which are constructed like scaffolds;

From the ruth of known paths, which would use my feet, tail, and ears as curios,
My head as a nest for tame ants,
My fate as a warning.

I have hidden at wrong times for wrong reasons.
I have been brought to bay. More than once.
Another time, if I need it,
Create a little wind like a cold finger between my shoulders, then
Let my nails pour out a torrent of aces like grain from a threshing machine;   40
Let fatigue, weather, habitation, the old bones, finally,
Be nothing to me,
Let all lights but yours be nothing to me.
Let the memory of tongues not unnerve me so that I stumble or quake.

But lead me at times beside the still waters;
There when I crouch to drink let me catch a glimpse of your image
Before it is obscured with my own.

Preserve my eyes, which are irreplaceable.
Preserve my heart, veins, bones,
Against the slow death building in them like hornets until the place
    is entirely theirs.   50
Preserve my tongue and I will bless you again and again.

Let my ignorance and my failings
Remain far behind me like tracks made in a wet season,
At the end of which I have vanished,

---

27. **habitué**: frequenter. 30. **taxidermists**: those who stuff skins of dead animals.
33. **curios**: rare or curious art objects.

So that those who track me for their own twisted ends
May be rewarded only with ignorance and failings.
But let me leave my cry stretched out behind me like a road
On which I have followed you.
And sustain me for my time in the desert
60 On what is essential to me.

THE ASIANS DYING

When the forests have been destroyed their darkness remains
The ash the great walker follows the possessors
Forever
Nothing they will come to is real
Nor for long
Over the watercourses
Like ducks in the time of the ducks
The ghosts of the villages trail in the sky
Making a new twilight

10   Rain falls into the open eyes of the dead
Again again with its pointless sound
When the moon finds them they are the color of everything

The nights disappear like bruises but nothing is healed
The dead go away like bruises
The blood vanishes into the poisoned farmlands
Pain the horizon
Remains
Overhead the seasons rock
They are paper bells
20   Calling to nothing living

The possessors move everywhere under Death their star
Like columns of smoke they advance into the shadows
Like thin flames with no light
They with no past
And fire their only future

FLY

I have been cruel to a fat pigeon
Because he would not fly
All he wanted was to live like a friendly old man

He had let himself become a wreck filthy and confiding
Wild for his food beating the cat off the garbage
Ignoring his mate perpetually snotty at the beak
Smelling waddling having to be
Carried up the ladder at night content

Fly I said throwing him into the air
But he would drop and run back expecting to be fed   10
I said it again and again throwing him up
As he got worse
He let himself be picked up every time
Until I found him in the dovecote dead
Of the needless efforts

So that is what I am

Pondering his eye that could not
Conceive that I was a creature to run from

I who have always believed too much in words

ANNE SEXTON (1928–   )

YOUNG

A thousand doors ago
when I was a lonely kid
in a big house with four
garages and it was summer
as long as I could remember,
I lay on the lawn at night,
clover wrinkling under me,
the wise stars bedding over me,
my mother's window a funnel
of yellow heat running out,   10
my father's window, half shut,
an eye where sleepers pass,
and the boards of the house
were smooth and white as wax

and probably a million leaves
sailed on their strange stalks
as the crickets ticked together
and I, in my brand new body,
which was not a woman's yet,
20   told the stars my questions
and thought God could really see
the heat and the painted light,
elbows, knees, dreams, goodnight.

THOM GUNN (1929–   )

ON THE MOVE

"Man, you gotta Go."

The blue jay scuffling in the bushes follows
Some hidden purpose, and the gust of birds
That spurts across the field, the wheeling swallows,
Have nested in the trees and undergrowth.
Seeking their instinct, or their poise, or both,
One moves with an uncertain violence
Under the dust thrown by a baffled sense
Or the dull thunder of approximate words.

On motorcycles, up the road, they come:
10   Small, black, as flies hanging in heat, the Boys,
Until the distance throws them forth, their hum
Bulges to thunder held by calf and thigh.
In goggles, donned impersonality,
In gleaming jackets trophied with the dust,
They strap in doubt—by hiding it, robust—
And almost hear a meaning in their noise.

Exact conclusion of their hardiness
Has no shape yet, but from known whereabouts
They ride, direction where the tires press.

They scare a flight of birds across the field: 20
Much that is natural, to the will must yield.
Men manufacture both machine and soul,
And use what they imperfectly control
To dare a future from the taken routes.

It is a part solution, after all.
One is not necessarily discord
On earth; or damned because, half animal,
One lacks direct instinct, because one wakes
Afloat on movement that divides and breaks.
One joins the movement in a valueless world,   30
Choosing it, till, both hurler and the hurled,
One moves as well, always toward, toward.

A minute holds them, who have come to go:
The self-defined, astride the created will
They burst away; the towns they travel through
Are home for neither bird nor holiness,
For birds and saints complete their purposes.
At worst, one is in motion; and at best,
Reaching no absolute, in which to rest,
One is always nearer by not keeping still.   40

TO YVOR WINTERS, 1955

I leave you in your garden.
                              In the yard
Behind it, run the airedales you have reared
With boxer's vigilance and poet's rigour:
Dog-generations you have trained the vigour
That few can breed to train and fewer still
Control with the deliberate human will.
And in the house there rest, piled shelf on shelf,
The accumulations that compose the self—
Poem and history: for if we use   10
Words to maintain the actions that we choose,
Our words, with slow defining influence,
Stay to mark out our chosen lineaments.

Title. **Yvor Winters:** distinguished professor and critic of literature, 1900–1968.

Continual temptation waits on each
To renounce his empire over thought and speech,
Till he submit his passive faculties
To evening, come where no resistance is;
The unmotivated sadness of the air
Filling the human with his own despair.
20   Where now lies power to hold the evening back?
Implicit in the grey is total black:
Denial of the discriminating brain
Brings the neurotic vision, and the vein
Of necromancy. All as relative
For mind as for the sense, we have to live
In a half-world, not ours nor history's,
And learn the false from half-true premisses.

But sitting in the dusk—though shapes combine,
Vague mass replacing edge and flickering line,
30   You keep both Rule and Energy in view,
Much power in each, most in the balanced two:
Ferocity existing in the fence
Built by an exercised intelligence.
Though night is always close, complete negation
Ready to drop on wisdom and emotion,
Night from the air or the carnivorous breath,
Still it is right to know the force of death,
And, as you do, persistent, tough in will,
Raise from the excellent the better still.

TED HUGHES (1930–   )

THE JAGUAR

The apes yawn and adore their fleas in the sun.
The parrots shriek as if they were on fire, or strut
Like cheap tarts to attract the stroller with the nut.
Fatigued with indolence, tiger and lion

---

24. necromancy: black magic. 27. premisses: general bases for deductions.

3. tarts: loose women. 4. indolence: laziness.

Lie still as the sun. The boa-constrictor's coil
Is a fossil. Cage after cage seems empty, or
Stinks of sleepers from the breathing straw.
It might be painted on a nursery wall.

But who runs like the rest past these arrives
At a cage where the crowd stands, stares, mesmerized,   10
As a child at a dream, at a jaguar hurrying enraged
Through prison darkness after the drills of his eyes

On a short fierce fuse. Not in boredom—
The eye satisfied to be blind in fire,
By the bang of blood in the brain deaf the ear—
He spins from the bars, but there's no cage to him

More than to the visionary his cell:
His stride is wildernesses of freedom:
The world rolls under the long thrust of his heel.
Over the cage floor the horizons come.   20

GARY SNYDER (1930–   )

RIPRAP

Lay down these words
Before your mind like rocks.
          placed solid, by hands
In choice of place, set
Before the body of the mind
          in space and time:
Solidity of bark, leaf, or wall
          riprap of things:
Cobble of milky way,
          straying planets,   10

10. mesmerized: fascinated.

Title (Snyder's note). **Riprap**: a cobble of stone laid on steep slick rock to make a trail for horses in the mountains.

These poems, people,
        lost ponies with
Dragging saddles—
        and rocky sure-foot trails.
The worlds like an endless
        four-dimensional
Game of *Go*.
        ants and pebbles
In the thin loam, each rock a word
20   a creek-washed stone
Granite: ingrained
        with torment of fire and weight
Crystal and sediment linked hot
        all change, in thoughts,
As well as things.

SYLVIA PLATH (1932–1963)

BLUE MOLES

1

They're out of the dark's ragbag, these two
Moles dead in the pebbled rut,
Shapeless as flung gloves, a few feet apart—
Blue suede a dog or fox has chewed.

One, by himself, seemed pitiable enough,
Little victim unearthed by some large creature
From his orbit under the elm root.
The second carcase makes a duel of the affair:
Blind twins bitten by bad nature.

10   The sky's far dome is sane and clear.
Leaves, undoing their yellow caves
Between the road and the lake water,
Bare no sinister spaces. Already

7. **orbit:** circle of existence.

The moles look neutral as the stones.
Their corkscrew noses, their white hands
Uplifted, stiffen in a family pose.
Difficult to imagine how fury struck—
Dissolved now, smoke of an old war.

2

Nightly the battle-shouts start up
In the ear of the veteran, and again   20
I enter the soft pelt of the mole.
Light's death to them: they shrivel in it.
They move through their mute rooms while I sleep,
Palming the earth aside, grubbers
After the fat children of root and rock.
By day, only the topsoil heaves.
Down there one is alone.

Outsize hands prepare a path,
They go before: opening the veins,
Delving for the appendages   30
Of beetles, sweetbreads, shards—to be eaten
Over and over. And still the heaven
Of final surfeit is just as far
From the door as ever. What happens between us
Happens in darkness, vanishes
Easy and often as each breath.

ELM

FOR RUTH FAINLIGHT

I know the bottom, she says. I know it with my great tap root:
It is what you fear.
I do not fear it: I have been there.

26. topsoil heaves: reference to the mounds on the surface which betray presence of moles under the earth. 30. appendages: bits and pieces. 31. sweetbreads: the glands, either pancreas or thymus, when used as food; shards: the thin, hard wing cover of a beetle. 33. surfeit: excess.

Is it the sea you hear in me,
Its dissatisfactions?
Or the voice of nothing, that was your madness?

Love is a shadow.
How you lie and cry after it.
Listen: these are its hooves: it has gone off, like a horse.

10   All night I shall gallop thus, impetuously,
Till your head is a stone, your pillow a little turf,
Echoing, echoing.

Or shall I bring you the sound of poisons?
This is rain now, this big hush.
And this is the fruit of it: tin-white, like arsenic.

I have suffered the atrocity of sunsets.
Scorched to the root
My red filaments burn and stand, a hand of wires.

Now I break up in pieces that fly about like clubs.
20   A wind of such violence
Will tolerate no bystanding: I must shriek.

The moon, also, is merciless: she would drag me
Cruelly, being barren.
Her radiance scathes me. Or perhaps I have caught her.

I let her go. I let her go
Diminished and flat, as after radical surgery.
How your bad dreams possess and endow me.

I am inhabited by a cry.
Nightly it flaps out
30   Looking, with its hooks, for something to love.

I am terrified by this dark thing
That sleeps in me;
All day I feel its soft, feathery turnings, its malignity.

Clouds pass and disperse.
Are those the faces of love, those pale irretrievables?
Is it for such I agitate my heart?

I am incapable of more knowledge.
What is this, this face
So murderous in its strangle of branches?—

Its snaky acids kiss.   40
It petrifies the will. These are the isolate, slow faults
That kill, that kill, that kill.

DADDY

You do not do, you do not do
Any more, black shoe
In which I have lived like a foot
For thirty years, poor and white,
Barely daring to breathe or Achoo.

Daddy, I have had to kill you.
You died before I had time——
Marble-heavy, a bag full of God,
Ghastly statue with one grey toe
Big as a Frisco seal   10

And a head in the freakish Atlantic
Where it pours bean green over blue
In the waters off beautiful Nauset.
I used to pray to recover you.
Ach, du.

In the German tongue, in the Polish town
Scraped flat by the roller
Of wars, wars, wars.
But the name of the town is common.
My Polack friend   20

Says there are a dozen or two.
So I never could tell where you
Put your foot, your root,
I never could talk to you.
The tongue stuck in my jaw.

It stuck in a barb wire snare.
Ich, ich, ich, ich,

13. Nauset: original (Indian) name for Eastham, Cape Cod. 15. Ach, du: ah, you.
27. ich: I.

I could hardly speak.
I thought every German was you.
30   And the language obscene

An engine, an engine
Chuffing me off like a Jew.
A Jew to Dachau, Auschwitz, Belsen.
I began to talk like a Jew.
I think I may well be a Jew.

The snows of the Tyrol, the clear beer of Vienna
Are not very pure or true.
With my gypsy ancestress and my weird luck
And my Taroc pack and my Taroc pack
40   I may be a bit of a Jew.

I have always been scared of *you,*
With your Luftwaffe, your gobbledygoo.
And your neat moustache
And your Aryan eye, bright blue.
Panzer-man, panzer-man, O You——

Not God but a swastika
So black no sky could squeak through.
Every woman adores a Fascist,
The boot in the face, the brute
50   Brute heart of a brute like you.

You stand at the blackboard, daddy,
In the picture I have of you,
A cleft in your chin instead of your foot
But no less a devil for that, no not
Any less the black man who

Bit my pretty red heart in two.
I was ten when they buried you.
At twenty I tried to die

33. **Dachau, Auschwitz, Belsen:** camps in Germany where Jews were exterminated during World War II. 36. **Tyrol:** a part of western Austria. 39. **Taroc:** playing cards used in foretelling future events. 42. **Luftwaffe:** the German air force during World War II. 44. **Aryan:** Caucasian. 45. **panzer:** armored. 46. **swastika:** cross with bent arms, used as a Nazi party emblem. 48. **fascist:** one who believes in government by force.

And get back, back, back to you.
I thought even the bones would do.   60

But they pulled me out of the sack,
And they stuck me together with glue.
And then I knew what to do.
I made a model of you,
A man in black with a Meinkampf look

And a love of the rack and the screw.
And I said I do, I do.
So daddy, I'm finally through.
The black telephone's off at the root,
The voices just can't worm through.   70

If I've killed one man, I've killed two——
The vampire who said he was you
And drank my blood for a year,
Seven years, if you want to know.
Daddy, you can lie back now.

There's a stake in your fat black heart
And the villagers never liked you.
They are dancing and stamping on you.
They always *knew* it was you.
Daddy, daddy, you bastard, I'm through.   80

LeRoi Jones (1934–   )

PREFACE TO A TWENTY VOLUME SUICIDE NOTE
(FOR KELLIE JONES, BORN 16 MAY 1959)

Lately, I've become accustomed to the way
The ground opens up and envelops me
Each time I go out to walk the dog.
Or the broad-edged silly music the wind
Makes when I run for a bus . . .

65. **Meinkampf:** book by Hitler (1924) setting forth his plans for German domination.

Things have come to that.

And now, each night I count the stars,
And each night I get the same number.
And when they will not come to be counted,
I count the holes they leave.

Nobody sings anymore.

And then last night, I tiptoed up
To my daughter's room and heard her
Talking to someone, and when I opened
The door, there was no one there . . .
Only she on her knees, peeking into

Her own clasped hands.

NOTES FOR A SPEECH

African blues
does not know me. Their steps, in sands
of their own
land. A country
in black & white, newspapers
blown down pavements
of the world. Does
not feel
what I am.
          Strength
in the dream, an oblique
suckling of nerve, the wind
throws up sand, eyes
are something locked in
hate, of hate, of hate, to
walk abroad, they conduct
their deaths apart
from my own. Those
heads, I call
my "people."
          (And who are they. People. To concern
myself, ugly man. Who
you, to concern

the white flat stomachs
of maidens, inside houses
dying. Black. Peeled moon
light on my fingers
move under
her clothes. Where
is her husband. Black   30
words throw up sand
to eyes, fingers of
their private dead. Whose
soul, eyes, in sand. My color
is not theirs. Lighter, white man
talk. They shy away. My own
dead souls, my, so called
people. Africa
is a foreign place. You are
as any other sad man here   40
american.)

DON L. LEE (1942–   )

IN THE INTEREST OF BLACK SALVATION

Whom can I confess to?
The Catholics have some cat
They call father,
                mine cutout a long time ago—
Like His did.
I tried confessing to my girl,
But she is not fast enough—except on hair styles,
                                        clothes
                                        face care and
                                        television.   10
If ABC, CBS, and NBC were to become educational stations
She would probably lose her cool,
                        and learn to read
Comic Books.
My neighbor, 36-19-35 volunteered to listen but

I couldn't talk—
Her numbers kept getting in the way,
Choking me.
To a Buddhist friend I went,
20 Listened, he didn't—
Advise, he did,
            "pray, pray, pray and keep one eye open."
I didn't pray—kept both eyes open.

Visited three comrades at Fort Hood,
There are no Cassandra cries here,
No one would hear you anyway. They didn't.
Three tried to speak, "don't want to make war."
                                            why???
30 When you could do countless other things like
Make life, this would be—
Useless too . . .

When I was 17,
I didn't have time to dream,
Dreams didn't exist—
Prayers did, as dreams.
I am now 17 & 8,
I still don't dream.
Father forgive us for we know what we do.
Jesus saves,
40   Jesus saves,
                        Jesus saves—S & H Green Stamps.

BUT HE WAS COOL
OR: HE EVEN STOPPED FOR GREEN LIGHTS

super-cool
ultrablack
a tan/purple
had a beautiful shade.

he had a double-natural
that wd put the sisters to shame.

24. **Fort Hood:** Fort in Texas. 25. **Cassandra cries:** prophecies of doom, fated never to be believed.

his dashikis were tailor made
& his beads were imported sea shells
    (from some blk/country i never heard of)
he was triple-hip.   10

his tikis were hand carved
out of ivory
& came express from the motherland.
he would greet u in swahili
& say good-by in yoruba.
woooooooooooo-jim he bes so cool & ill tel li gent
        cool-cool is so cool he was un-cooled by
            other niggers' cool
        cool-cool ultracool was bop-cool/ice box
            cool so cool cold cool   20
        his wine didn't have to be cooled, him was
            air conditioned cool
        cool-cool/real cool made me cool—now
            ain't that cool
        cool-cool so cool him nick-named refrig-
            erator.

cool-cool so cool
he didn't know
after detroit, newark, chicago &c.,
we had to hip
        cool-cool/ super-cool/ real cool   30
    that
to be black
is
to be
very-hot.

7. dashikis: capelike shirts. 11. tikis: carved representations of ancestors, worn as pendants. 14. Swahili: language of East Africa. 15. Yoruba: the language of the West African coastal Negroes.

Appendix I

I. Wyatt's "they" ("They Flee From Me")

The editor of *Tottel's Miscellany* (1557), where Wyatt's poem was first printed, prefixed an elaborate title to it, 'The lover sheweth how he is forsaken of such as he sometime enjoyed.' It is not by any means certain, however, that Wyatt's poem is concerned with more than one mistress. The 'they' and 'them' of the first verse are at least partly metaphorical—deer perhaps, as in the sonnet. The vagueness is clearly intentional, and it throws the detailed picture of the second verse into greater relief. The third verse returns to the implications of the original metaphor. It appears that Wyatt and the lady are both of them alternately hunters and hunted. (i) When Wyatt was a potential source of *danger* the lady was *gentle* and *tame*, but with his new *gentleness* she has become *wild* and is *forsaking* him. (ii) Previously she had come *stalking* him and *caught* him, but now she has begun to *range*. And Wyatt's problem, since she is treating him *so kindly*, i.e. according to the law of kind, is what to do about it? In another poem he had written

it is of kind

That often change doth please a woman's mind.

His lady, he reflects, is only a wild thing after all, obeying her natural instinct to *continual change;* and to suggest that she may deserve a punishment is to invoke a moral law that would be beyond her comprehension. Wyatt is really more sorry for himself than irritated with this illogical inconsistent woman.

(from F. W. Bateson, English Poetry)

This poem, widely anthologized under the title given it in *Tottel's Miscellany* (1557), "The lover sheweth how he is forsaken of such as he sometime enjoyed," has been much admired but, I think, oversimplified and misunderstood. F. W. Bateson, in *English Poetry* (London, 1950), pp. 143-144, writes that it is by no means certain "that Wyatt's poem is concerned with more than one mistress. The 'they' and 'them' of the first verse are at least partly metaphorical—deer perhaps, as in the sonnet ['Whoso list to hunt']." He adds that, since woman's natural instinct is *continual change*, "to suggest that she may deserve a punishment is to invoke a moral law that would be beyond her comprehension. Wyatt is really more sorry for himself than irritated with this illogical inconsistent woman." But Bateson reads Wyatt himself as unnecessarily illogical and inconsistent when he equates the one of the second stanza with the many of the first.

The first stanza is wholly metaphorical. "They" are hardly mistresses or even deer, with naked foot stalking in his chamber, but the birds of an earlier season. The last line accurately describes birds hopping about to pick up bits of food, and "stalking" well describes the way birds walk. The latent content of the metaphor may include women, if not mistresses, but refers more immediately to courtiers, the hangers-on of princes' favorites, since the oldest meaning of putting oneself "in daunger" is to put oneself in the power or at the mercy of another.

(from S. F. Johnson, *Explicator*)

I should like to quarrel with S. F. Johnson's interpretation of Wyatt's *"They flee from me,"* (EXP., April, 1953, XI, 39). There is no point in calling a foot "naked" unless it is sometimes covered; it is not appropriate to the foot of a bird or of a deer; and though "stalking" in the modern sense may "well describe the way birds walk," in its primary sense, that current in Wyatt's time, it means walking warily, stealthily, noiselessly, as the lady naturally would when she sought the poet out in the chamber where he lay "broad waking." I do not perceive the logic of Mr. Johnson's statement that the latent content of the metaphor "refers more immediately to courtiers . . . *since* [my italics] the oldest meaning of putting oneself 'in daunger' is to put oneself in the power or at the mercy of another." The lady of whom the poet speaks may or may not have been a court lady, but in any case it is not difficult to see in what sense she put herself in danger.

"Thanked be fortune" takes up the "continual change" of the first stanza: it was thanks to fortune rather than to heaven that things were once better than they are now, for fortune is the deity who presides over this changeable lady. I assume like Mr. Bateson that the "they" of the opening line of the poem refers to one lady. It would be possible, I think, to find other examples of the use of "they" referring really to a single person: possibly to mark estrangement. (Shakespeare's *Sonnet* XCIV, *They that have power to hurt,* might be an example.) Much of the beauty of Wyatt's poem surely comes from the contrast between the veiled terms used in the first verse and the sharpness with which the lady is seen and heard in the second.

(E. E. Duncan-Jones, *Explicator*)

Bateson (*English Poetry*, London, 1950, pp. 143-47) was right in seeing metaphor in Wyatt's poem, "They Flee From Me," but (possibly because he had the bad luck to read this poem along with "Whoso list to hunt") he was wrong in believing that the metaphor is from hunting, an idea which led to the highly implausible suggestion that "they" are deer. It would seem to require a somewhat excessive suspension of disbelief to imagine even metaphorical deer in the bedroom of an Elizabethan gentleman. Johnson (*Exp*, April, 1953, XI, 39) is right in urging that "The first stanza is wholly metaphorical" and in his view that "they" are birds, but wrong in his notion that the metaphor, though it "may include women," "refers more immediately to courtiers."

The poem has nothing to do with either hunting or with politics, but is a love poem throughout, and the metaphor is directly relevant. The plain sense of the poem is well given in the old title, "The lover sheweth how he is forsaken of such as he sometime enjoyed." This theme is first stated metaphorically, then literally, with a concrete picture for each statement. Duncan-Jones (Exp., Nov., 1953, XII, 9) has well said, "Much of the beauty of Wyatt's poem surely comes from the contrast between the veiled terms used in the first verse and the sharpness with which the lady is seen and heard in the second." But what of the veiled terms, and in particular, who or what are "they"? Are they, as critics have variously suggested, women, a woman, deer, birds, or something else?

"They" are indeed birds, but not "the birds of an earlier season" (Johnson), or of any particular season. They are the doves of Venus, goddess of Love, and in describing how "gentill tame and meke" the birds once were, the poet is emphasizing the great favor he once enjoyed with Love's goddess, just as by his opening words, "They flee from me," he tells us that he is out of favor with Venus.

Duncan-Jones feels that "naked" is inappropriate for the foot of a bird. I should imagine the term suggested itself to Wyatt because of the pinkish or reddish color of pigeons' feet. (See, for instance, the colored pictures of the members of the family Columbidae in Witherby, Jourdain, Ticehurst, and Tucker, *Handbook of British Birds,* IV, London, 1947, Plate 102, facing p. 130 and Plate 103, facing p. 146. See, too, the almost spectacularly naked feet of the wood pigeon in E. F. Daglish, *Birds of the British Isles,* London, 1948, facing p. 23.) Also, of course, it fits the general sexy tone of the first two stanzas, and the naked feet of the birds can be felt as a metaphorical counterpart to the lady's falling gown.

Because of the ambiguity of the poem's opening "they," critics have speculated on the number of the poet's mistresses. If "they" means the doves of Venus, the word contributes nothing to this question—except possibly to remove it. The stanza in which Venus' doves appear is, in itself, quite consistent with the poet's possession of a harem. Taken with the rest of the poem, though, it pretty certainly, like stanza 2, is concerned only with the lady of long small arms and thin unstable gown. And indeed, I should say the two stanzas describe, metaphorically and literally, the same event, the visit of the lady to the poet's room.

(Frederick M Combellack, *Explicator*)

Let me begin my own demonstration by accepting Mr. Hainsworth's remark* that the poet's "gentilnes" is "The very quality, according to the love code, which ought to have *ensured* his mistress's favour." And let me take this on a further step by saying that the courtly code provides the elegantly framed mirror by means of which all the stripped, "natural" reflections of the poem are seen. The mirror, having served its rhetorical purpose of exhibiting the lady (and perhaps of

* J. D. Hainsworth, in *Essays in Criticism,* VII (Jan., 1957), 90-95.

exhibiting itself), can be abandoned by the poet's final "uncourtly" question con-
cerning the lady's deserts. But until the very end we see in the *frame* of the mirror
"gentilnes," constancy, secrecy, beauty, generous goodness, kind service, and the
bond which requires "leve." In the mirror itself, however, we see, on an ascending
scale, animality, sexuality, "new fangilnes."

Why the plural of "They flee from me"? One can of course take the plural
as literal, but this will finally raise more problems than it will solve. Since I want
to put my energy into following out another hypothesis, I won't pause to explore
what I consider a false path, but will proceed with my own argument. I, as other
interpreters, regard the *they* as a disguise. It is to be related in general, I think,
to the familiar disguises of convention, which protect the poet from himself, his
own unmediated feelings, and from exposure before others with power to hurt.
But I think we can be more specific. The disguise participates here in a sustained
dramatic tension between the impersonal and the personal, between the poet's own
raw, immediate feelings and the impersonal examination he is conducting and
resolving. (In another way the same conflict occurs between the formal imperson-
ality of the meter and the local movements that force the meter to convey the
personal and immediate.)

But there is another kind of disguise that the *they* can provide—a sort of
multiple mask afforded by the gentle lover observing the code of secrecy and
[discretion]. That is, I think, one possible effect of the *they*. And when the effect
changes, as it does, we are not required to begin again and cancel out our first
impression. For the first impression is right, as far as it goes, but must be swiftly
supplemented by a further impression which is instantaneously retroactive as well
as progressive. This is part of an unusual but not unprecedented demand on the
reader, as we shall be able to see when we examine the kinds of questions man-
aged by the poem's structure. But this is to get a little ahead of ourselves, for even
the second stanza is at first general and anonymous. *It* has been twenty times bet-
ter, but one special time. . . .

And then the *they* begins to move toward *she*, the particular, unmistakable
she whose identity is inseparably established in the intimate whisper: *"dere hert,
howe like you this?"* But the *she* who emerges from the one special scene of the
second stanza is, I think, the image back of the multiple images of the first
stanza—most immediately of the "naked fote stalking," the "gentill tame and
meke," the "daunger," the taking "bred at my hand." Then the "new fangilnes"
developed in the third stanza returns the *she* toward the *they*, and releases an
effect implicit in the poetic disguise. For the single image back of the multiple
images of the first stanza is the single image of infidelity, the mistress of multiple
desires and minds. We are forced to connect the furious images of animal activity,
the ranging and busily seeking, with their entirely human metamorphosis "Into a
straunge fasshion of forsaking." And it is the human quality of her goodness,
related as it is to the courtly code, which both gives him leave to go and her "to
use new fangilnes." So the *they* which begins as the polite disguise provided by
the lover s "gentilnes" and allegiance to the code, moves through the individual
she to the creature at the end of the poem; and unites that creature of multiple
activities with the *they* of the first stanza. She becomes a kind of *they*, and she
performs the metamorphosis herself assisted in the "turning" only by the poet's

"gentilnes" (again), and by his art, which commands inflections more subtle than those of grammar. As for the final question of what she has deserved, it may look forward but it also looks backward and answers itself: she deserves what she has become, and so deserves the poem.

(from Arnold Stein, "Wyatt's 'They Flee From Me,'" *Sewanee Review*)

Sir Thomas Wyatt's 'They fle from me' has been much explicated recently; the main result is that the poem is becoming more and more obscure. Explicators are even in utter disagreement as to whom the poet is writing about when using the pronouns 'they' in the first verse and 'she' in the second. A wide and wild variety of hypotheses have been put forward. On the literal level, 'they' are held to be deer, birds, or, more precisely, the doves of Venus; on the metaphorical plane we are offered the choice of courtiers and women; while 'she' is sometimes taken to be the poet's latest mistress and sometimes Fortune herself.

This affluence of interpretations and possible combinations makes it plain that the poem is characterised by a certain vagueness. 'Ambiguity' is of course the fashionable word, yet it might be well to avoid it. Its present-day connotations suggest a deliberate attempt on the part of the writer to impart several meanings at the same time, which is probably not so often the case as is usually assumed. Since so much scrutinising has failed to yield an irrefutable conceptual translation of the imagery, we may as well take it for granted that Wyatt himself did not think it essential to make identifiable the particular objects he must be supposed to have had in mind. At any rate, they are for ever beyond our grasp.

I would suggest that it does not matter greatly, because Wyatt's purpose lay in a different direction. We should keep in mind the aesthetic hierarchy of theme, motif and conceit. The visual and tactile images are conceits, which should not be perfectly congruent if the poem is not to appear as a mere allegory or geometrical proposition. At any rate, the images all point to one motif, woman's inconstancy, which itself is the central metaphor used as a vehicle for the main theme, the inconstancy of Fortune. This theme was described as early as 1816 and without undue fussiness by Nott:

Under the figure of a Lady offering to him unsolicited the tenderest marks of affection, he describes in a lively manner his early good fortune and success in life (. . .). Following the same figure he naturally refers his subsequent misfortunes to the constitutional levity, that strange fashion of forsaking, which is too common with the gentler sex.

With the cautious ambivalence of 'early good fortune', 'success in life' (not 'in love'), and 'misfortunes' (in the plural), Nott laudably refrained from committing himself to a definitely erotic interpretation. And indeed, as Mr. Hainsworth's treatment of the poem implies but does not state with sufficient emphasis, the main focus of interest is not located in the persons (male or female, courtiers or mistresses) who are now fleeing the poet, but in the mood of the deserted poet himself. Why, therefore, should Wyatt be under an obligation to specify who those deserters were? The ageing Don Juan growing out of favour with the fair sex, and the powerful nobleman fallen out of favour with his lord and therefore with his own flatterers, followers and sycophants, have at least one thing in common: they are both deserted, forlorn, isolated, frustrated. The central feeling of the poem is frustration, whatever its origin. And there is no valid reason why the poet should not resort to a variety of metaphors, the better to point out the contrast between the former adulation of those now fleeing from him and their present aloofness, weaving his metaphorical items with such intricate closeness that the zealous reader with a 'scientific' mind will find himself unable to make out whether he is talking about men or deer, birds or women.

(from Albert S. Gerard, "Wyatt's 'They Flee from Me,' " *Essays in Criticism*)

II. Keat's "Beauty is truth" ("Ode on a Grecian Urn")

The silence of the urn is stressed—it is a "bride of quietness"; it is a "foster-child of silence," but the urn is a "historian" too. Historians tell the truth, or are at least expected to tell the truth. What is a "Sylvan historian"? A historian who is like the forest rustic, a woodlander? Or, a historian who writes histories of the forest? Presumably, the urn is sylvan in both senses. . . . When we consider the way in which the urn utters its history, the fact that it must be sylvan in both senses is seen as inevitable. Perhaps too the fact that it is a rural historian, a rustic, a peasant historian, qualifies in our minds the dignity and the "truth" of the histories which it recites. Its histories, Keats has already conceded, may be characterized as "tales"—not formal history at all.

The sylvan historian certainly supplies no names and dates—"What men or gods are these?" the poet asks. What it does give is action—of men *or* gods, of godlike men or of superhuman (though not daemonic) gods—action, which is not the less intense for all that the urn is cool marble. . . .

The marble men and women lie outside time. The urn which they adorn will remain. The "Sylvan historian" will recite its history to other generations.

What will it say to them? Presumably, what it says to the poet now: that "formed experience," imaginative insight, embodies the basic and fundamental perception of man and nature. The urn is beautiful, and yet its beauty is based— what else is the poem concerned with?—on an imaginative perception of essentials. Such a vision is beautiful but it is also true. The sylvan historian presents us with beautiful histories, but they are true histories, and it is a good historian.

Moreover, the "truth" which the sylvan historian gives is the only kind of truth which we are likely to get on this earth, and, furthermore, it is the only kind that we *have* to have. The names, dates, and special circumstances, the wealth of data—these the sylvan historian quietly ignores. But we shall never get all the facts anyway—there is no end to the accumulation of facts. Moreover, mere accumulations of facts—a point our own generation is only beginning to realize—

are meaningless. The sylvan historian does better than that: it takes a few details and so orders them that we have not only beauty but insight into essential truth. Its "history," in short, is a history without footnotes. It has the validity of myth— not myth as a pretty but irrelevant make-belief, an idle fancy, but myth as a valid perception into reality.

(from Cleanth Brooks, The Well Wrought Urn)

If we glance at "Ode on a Grecian Urn," we shall see Keats trying to unify his pictorial effects by means of direct philosophical statement. "Do I wake or sleep?" at the end of the Nightingale ode asks the question: Which is reality, the symbolic nightingale or the common world? The famous Truth-Beauty synthesis at the end of the "Grecian Urn" contains the same question, but this time it is answered. As Mr. Kenneth Burke sees it, Truth is the practical scientific world and Beauty is the ideal world above change. The "frozen" figures on the urn, being both dead and alive, constitute a scene which is at once perceptible and fixed. "This transcendent scene," says Mr. Burke, "is the level at which the earthly laws of contradiction no longer prevail." The one and the many, the eternal and the passing, the sculpturesque and the dramatic, become synthesized in a higher truth. Much of the little that I know about this poem I have learned from Mr. Burke and Mr. Cleanth Brooks, who have studied it more closely than any other critics; and what I am about to say will sound ungrateful. I suspect that the dialectical solution is Mr. Burke's rather than Keats', and that Mr. Brooks' "irony" and "dramatic propriety" are likewise largely his own. Mr. Brooks rests his case for the Truth-Beauty paradox on an argument for its "dramatic propriety"; but this is just what I am not convinced of. I find myself agreeing with Mr. Middleton Murry (whom Mr. Brooks quotes), who admits that the statement is out of place "in the context of the poem itself." I would point to a particular feature, in the last six lines of stanza four, which I feel that neither Mr. Burke nor Mr. Brooks has taken into a certain important kind of consideration. Here Keats tells us that in the background of this world of eternal youth there is another, from which it came, and that this second world has thus been emptied and is indeed a dead world:

What little town by river or sea-shore
Or mountain-built with peaceful citadel,
Is emptied of this folk, this pious morn?
And, little town, thy streets for evermore
Will silent be; and not a soul to tell
Why thou art desolate, can e'er return.

Mr. Burke quite rightly sees in this passage the key to the symbolism of the entire poem. It is properly the "constatation" of the tensions of the imagery. What is the meaning of this perpetual youth on the urn? One of its meanings is that it is perpetually anti-youth and anti-life; it is in fact dead, and "can never return." Are we not faced again with the same paradox we had in the Nightingale ode, that the intensest life is achieved in death? Mr. Burke brings out with great skill the erotic equivalents of the life-death symbols; and for his analysis of the developing imagery throughout we owe him a great debt. Yet I feel that Mr. Burke's own dialectical skill leads him to consider the poem, when he is through with it, a philosophical discourse; but it is, if it is anything (and it is a great deal), what is ordinarily known as a work of art. Mr. Burke's elucidation of the Truth-Beauty proposition in the last stanza is the most convincing dialectically that I have seen; but Keats did not write Mr. Burke's elucidation; and I feel that the entire last stanza, except the phrase "Cold Pastoral" (which probably ought to be somewhere else in the poem) is an illicit commentary added by the poet to a "meaning" which was symbolically complete at the end of the preceding stanza, number four. Or perhaps it may be said that Keats did to some extent write Mr. Burke's elucidation; that is why I feel that the final stanza (though magnificently written) is redundant and out of form.

To the degree that I am guilty with Mr. Burke of a prepossession which may blind me to the whole value of this poem (as his seems to limit his perception of possible defects) I am not qualified to criticize it. Here, towards the end of this essay, I glance back at the confession, which I made earlier, of the distance and detachment of my warmest admiration for Keats. It is now time that I tried to state the reasons for this a little more summarily, in a brief comparison of the two fine odes that we have been considering.

Both odes are constructed pictorially in spatial blocks, for the eye to take in serially. Though to my mind this method is better suited to the subject of the Grecian Urn, which is itself a plastic object, than to the Nightingale ode, I take the latter, in spite of the blemishes of detail (only some of which we have looked at), to be the finer poem. If there is not so much in it as in the Grecian Urn for the lucidation of verbal complexity, there is nowhere the radical violation of its set limits that one finds in the last stanza of the Grecian Urn:

> *Thou shalt remain, in midst of other woes*
> *Than ours, a friend to man, to whom thou say'st,*
> *Beauty is truth, truth beauty,—that is all*
> *Ye know on earth, and all ye need to know.*

It is here that the poem gets out of form, that the break in "point of view" occurs; and if it is a return to Samuel Johnson's dislike of "Lycidas" (I don't think it is) to ask how an urn can say anything, I shall have to suffer the consequences of that view. It is Keats himself, of course, who says it; but "Keats" is here not implicit in the structure of the poem, as he is in "Ode to a Nightingale"; what he says is what the mathematicians call an extrapolation, an intrusion of matter from another field of discourse, so that, even if it be "true" philosophically, it is not a visible function of what the poem says. With the "dead" mountain citadel in mind, could we not phrase the message of the urn equally well as follows: Truth is *not* beauty, since even art itself cannot do more with death than preserve it, and the beauty frozen on the urn is also dead, since it cannot move. This "pessimism" may be found as easily in the poem as Keats' comforting paradox.

(from Allen Tate, *The Man of Letters in the Modern World*)

The urn, which is unalterably of the esthetic sphere, should not and could not speak to us in the commonsense language of men. What it says, then, is spoken from its special point of view; and within that sphere all that is beautiful is true, all that is true is beautiful, and only what is true and beautiful is real. So far we have not burst the bounds of orthodox neo-Platonism. But the last line and a half of the poem,

> that is all
> Ye know on earth, and all ye need to know.

—these lines pose a sizable problem. Are we to take them, in the first place, as the comment of the urn or of Keats? More cogent yet, to whom are they addressed? A textual confusion may throw a bit of light here. Keats's MS. and three transcripts of it place only a comma and dash in the penultimate line,

> Beauty is truth, truth beauty—that is all. . . .

But the magazine text of January, 1820 alters the comma to a period, and the text published in volume form (June, 1820) adds inverted commas around "Beauty is truth, truth beauty." Keats's tendency is thus to separate by increasingly high barriers the Urn's motto from the last line and a half of the poem. If this line and a half are not spoken on the same level as what precedes them, need they be supposed the words of the Urn at all? Perhaps, as the position of the closing quote suggests, we are to imagine Keats speaking them. But if we suppose them addressed (whether by the Urn or by Keats) to the human beings of stanza 5 and not to the eternally happy artifacts of stanza 3 they are obviously untrue, incongruous with Keats' philosophy elsewhere expressed, and inappropriate to the theme and structure of this very poem. If they are spoken by the Urn to men, but with a tacit limitation so that we are to sense them as ironically partial, that interpretation (persuasively championed by Mr. C. M. Bowra's *The Romantic Imagination*) is conceivable, though strained by the necessity of inventing the limitation. But perhaps the last words of the poem are not spoken *by* but *to* the Urn and the figures on it. The emphasis is then on the "ye's," which, if they cannot be directed to the singular Urn (Keats does not, within the limits of my observation, use "ye" as a singular form), may be directed to the figures on the Urn. The force of the passage is then vindictive; "It's enough for *you* to say, 'Truth and beauty are the same'—that's your function in the world. But we who are men know this and something else too." Whether or not the passage will bear this sense, the poem's closing remark is clearly intended in the esthetic sphere; it teases us into and out of thought, and in the very act of declaring our alienation from the sphere of the Urn, translates us into it.

(from Robert M. Adams, *"Trompe-l'oeil* in Shakespeare and Keats,"
Sewanee Review)

To return now to the concluding lines of the ode. Although the urn is able to reveal to man a oneness of beauty and truth, it is not able to inform him that this is the sum total of his knowledge on earth and that it is sufficient for his earthly existence ("all ye need to know"); for obviously he knows other things on earth, such as the fact that in the world beauty is not truth, and this should be even more valuable within the world than the knowledge that the two are one at heaven's bourne. But more important, the symbolic action of the drama at no point justifies the urn's limiting its message; nowhere has the urn acted out the fact that man knows no more on earth than this identity of beauty and truth, and that this knowledge is sufficient.

Now, it is significant that this is an ode *on* a Grecian urn. Had Keats meant *to*, he would have said so, as he did in the "Ode to a Nightingale." There the meaning of the poem arises out of the dramatic relations of the poet and the symbol; but *on* implies a commentary, and it is Keats who must make the commentary on the drama that he has been observing and experiencing within the urn. It is the poet, therefore, who speaks the words, "that is all / Ye know on earth, and all ye need to know," and he is addressing himself to man, the reader. Hence the shift of reference from "thou" (urn) to "ye" (man). I do not feel the objection frequently raised that if the last line and a half belong to the poet and are addressed to the reader, they are not dramatically prepared for. The poet has gradually been obtruding himself upon the reader's consciousness in the last two stanzas by withdrawing from his empathic experience and taking on identity. He has become distinctly present in the last stanza as a speaker addressing the urn, and proportionately the urn has shrunk from the center of dramatic interest; it is now but a short step for him to turn his address from urn to reader. Moreover, the reader has also been subtly introduced into the stanza, for the poet vividly marks his complete severance from the urn's essence by pluralizing himself ("tease us," "other woe / Than ours") and thus putting himself into a category wholly distinct from the urn; and by this act Keats has now involved the reader as a third member of the drama. Finally, when the reader has been filtered out of the plural "us" and "ours" by the reference to "man" (48), the poet may now address to him his final observations on the drama.

But the poet is no more justified than the urn would be in concluding that the sum of necessary earthly wisdom is the identity of beauty and truth. Certainly when he returned to the dimensional world in stanza four he found the two to be antithetical, not identical. Something of the difficulty Keats encountered in trying to orient his meaning is to be seen in the three versions of the final lines that have manuscript or textual authority. Keats' manuscript and the transcripts made by his friends read,

> *Beauty is truth, truth beauty,—that is all . . . .*

In the *Annals of the Fine Arts* for 1820, where the poem was first published, the line appears as

> *Beauty is Truth, Truth Beauty.—That is all. . . .*

And the 1820 volume of Keats' poems reads,

> *"Beauty is truth, truth beauty,"—that is all. . . .*

No one of these solves the problem, although each hints at the difficulty. Clearly each one strives to separate the aphorism from the following assertion by the poet; and at the same time each attempts to preserve a relation between the pronoun "that" and *something* that has gone before. Then, since we have seen that the antecedent of "that" cannot reasonably be the aphorism—since neither urn nor poet can be saying that all man knows and needs to know on earth is that beauty is truth—its antecedent must be the entire preceding sentence .

All that man knows on earth, and all he needs to know is that

> *When old age shall this generation waste,*
> *Thou [the urn] shalt remain, in midst of other woe*
> *Than ours, a friend to man, to whom thou say'st,*
> *Beauty is truth, truth beauty.*

Only this meaning can be consistent with the dramatic action of the poem, for it not only does not deny that in the world beauty is not truth, but also assimilates that fact into a greater verity. The sum of earthly wisdom is that in this world of pain and decay, where love cannot be forever warm and where even the highest pleasures necessarily leave a burning forehead and a parching tongue, art remains, immutable in its essence because that essence is captured in a "Cold Pastoral," a form which has not been created for the destiny of progressing to a heaven-altar, as warm and passionate man is. This art is forever available as "a friend to man," a power willing to admit man to its "sphery sessions."

(from Earl Wasserman, *The Finer Tone*)

The message of the Grecian Urn has, unhappily, more often teased critics out of thought than into it. This very brief study of a poem much discussed of late makes no pretensions to either originality or profundity; it seeks rather by careful study of the original texts to discover just how the famous apothegm of the urn fits into the poem. In doing so, we may discredit one or two older interpretations and show, at least, what the last two lines of the ode cannot mean. . . .

It is from the last stanza and particularly the last two lines that all our critical difficulties spring; there is no insuperable structural or verbal obstacle up to line 41. One troublesome question has been asked often enough but rarely answered with care: At the very end of the ode, who is saying what to whom? The first published version of the poem, in the *Annals of the Fine Arts,* early in 1820, read:

> Beauty is truth, truth beauty.—That is all
> Ye know on earth, and all ye need to know.

The second appearance of the lines in print, in the *Lamia* volume of 1820, bore slightly different punctuation:

> "Beauty is truth, truth beauty,"—that is all
> Ye know on earth, and all ye need to know.

These readings give rise to three possible interpretations: either both lines are spoken by the urn, but the extra-sententiousness of the first five words merits special pointing; or the first five words are spoken by the urn, the rest by the poet to the reader; or the first five words are spoken by the urn, the rest by the poet to the figures he has just described.

This last contention should die of natural incongruity. It is artistically as well as philosophically unthinkable that Keats would suddenly intrude himself in this way to tell the figures on the urn that they had grasped the one simple regimen of life and need know nothing else, that they were, indeed, probably better off in their pristine ignorance. Keats, to whom the world meant intensely, had no place in his philosophy for noble savages, even Greek ones.

The answer to the riddle of the proper reading, however, lies not in critical speculation but in textual analysis. The two original printings can claim no great authority. The *Annals* text was based on a copy 'begged' of Keats by Haydon, who was not noted for his trustworthiness. As for the *Lamia* version, it is well known that Keats was too ill to oversee the publication of his 1820 volume which was, partially at least, edited by John Taylor.

One must fall back on the manuscripts. Unfortunately no holograph is known to survive, but there are four transcripts, all unquestionably not far removed from the original, and all of them agree.

The transcript by George Keats (in the British Museum) reads:

> Beauty is truth,—Truth Beauty,—that is all
> Ye know on Earth, and all ye need to know.

Charles Wentworth Dilke (in his copy of *Endymion,* in the Keats Memorial House, Hampstead):

> Beauty is truth,—truth beauty,—that is all
> Ye know on earth, and all ye need to know.

Charles Armitage Brown (Harvard Keats Collection):

> Beauty is Truth,—Truth Beauty,—that is all
> Ye know on earth, and all ye need to know.

Richard Woodhouse (Harvard):

> Beauty is Truth,—Truth beauty,—That is all
> Ye know on earth, and all ye need to know.

All four transcripts, then, not only lack the full stop and inverted commas of the *Annals* and *Lamia* texts respectively, but they have an additional dash between the two phrases 'Beauty is truth' and 'truth beauty,' thus breaking up the concluding lines of the poem into three rather than two parts. A threefold division must negate completely the possibility of a dual statement which depends on some mechanical indication (a full stop or inverted commas) of the complete integrity of the initial five-word phrase. The transcripts obviously infer a single statement uttered by the urn without any interference on the part of the poet— a reading often proposed and accepted but not so often substantiated. What the message of the urn may mean is, of course, another matter.

(from Alvin Whitley, "The Message of the Grecian Urn,"
Keats-Shelley Memorial Bulletin)

III. Stevens' "Jar" ("Anecdote of the Jar")

. . . a wild and disorderly landscape is transformed into order by the presence of a symmetrical vase. . . . The jar acts in the imagination like one of the poles of the earth, the imaginary order of the lines of latitude and longitude projecting around the pole. The jar itself—simple and symmetrical, a product of the human consciousness and not of nature—is a very fitting symbol for man's dominion over nature. The appearance of the wilderness [is] deftly suggested; in contrast with it the jar is striking, but, after some familiarity with the poem, it is striking chiefly because it is so precisely an opposite to the wilderness.

(from Howard Baker, "Wallace Stevens and Other Poets," *Southern Review*)

[Winters quotes part of the above comment of Howard Baker and an excerpt from another critic who takes the position that the poem exalts any handicraft over nature.]

The jar is the product of the human mind, as the critics remark, and it dominates the wilderness; but it does not give order to the wilderness—it is vulgar and sterile, and it transforms the wilderness into the semblance of a deserted picnic ground. Its sterility is indicated in the last three lines . . . . The poem would appear to be primarily an expression of the corrupting effect of the intellect upon natural beauty, and hence a purely romantic performance.

(from Yvor Winters, *On Modern Poets* [also in *The Anatomy of Nonsense*])

Is not Yvor Winters' interpretation of this poem forced (*The Anatomy of Nonsense*, pp. 93-95)? The theme is not, he asserts, a statement of the superiority of man-created art over disordered nature; rather it suggests the corruption of natural beauty by a product of the human intellect: in brief, the poet's attitude is romantic and primitivistic in the most naive sense.

Mr. Winters interprets the lines, "It [the jar] made the slovenly wilderness / Surround the hill," as an ellipsis (and prolepsis?): the wilderness has been made slovenly by the domination of the jar. This assumption seems an unwarranted wrenching of the meaning to conform to the special pleading. The emphasis in the poem is certainly upon the aesthetic qualities of the jar: its symmetry, round-ness. The hitherto "slovenly" wilderness "surrounds" the hill and even rises up to the jar and thus is no longer "wild." The last three lines do not suggest vul-garity or sterility (*ibid.*, p. 94); the decorous grayness and bareness of the jar is in implied contrast to the lush riot of vegetation. "Tall and of a port," the jar represents qualities of line and contour not created by Nature, which in contrast sprawls, is slovenly. No wonder the wilderness rises up to the jar as if it were tamed, chastened of its original wildness. The meaning of the last two lines thus becomes clear: the poet has experimentally proved (see line 1) to himself that even a jar (not a Grecian urn) may show the qualities of man's creation superior to Nature's. This assurance might prove a personal solace to a poet of Mr.

Stevens' refined taste and hedonistic temperament (see Henry Wells, *New Poets for Old*, New York, 1940, p. 287), however transitory it might be—it might even be a compensatory illusion for the perception of a lack of design or purposefulness in Nature.

Mr. Winters' interpretation is perhaps induced by his belief in the consistency of the poet's anti-intellectualism, and in part by the poet's admiration for the splendid (but indifferent) Nature in poems such as "The Snow Man" and "The Death of the Soldier." But the emphasis in this poem is upon the aesthetic qualities of the jar, only imperfectly to be identified with the purely intellectual. The jar is rather the creation of the imagination: there is no form like it in Nature, in Tennessee or elsewhere (see lines 11-12). One is reminded that the dominant theme of the *Harmonium* volume is the extolling of the imagination as the source of all creative art. It would not be wholly idle to speculate on the jar and Nature as symbolical of the contrast between art and the disorder of contemporary society in which art exists, or as a meditation upon the role of art in society; but the poem seems best regarded as an immediate and quasi-fanciful moment of poetic perception, and is not to be given the validity or stature of a major philosophical conclusion.

(J. P. Kirby, *Explicator*)

Out of the oscillations between over- and underreading come modulations of the dominant frequency, overtones of lagging or pronounced response which will put a class at cross-purposes with itself, the skeptics and overeager beavers wrestling for the monkey wrench they will throw into the instructor's lesson plan. Some of these problems were illustrated for me when a student in an advanced class in poetry analysis submitted a paper on Wallace Stevens' "Anecdote of the Jar." . . .

The poem, he wrote, was obviously a Republican treatment of the TVA. This particular jar is Norris Dam, "on a hill" in that it joins two hills. "The jar was round . . ." refers to the shape and symmetry of the dam. Its "dominion" is oppressive, unproductive, wasteful ("gray and bare"); it stops river traffic (being a "port"); and it does not give "of bird or bush." This summary does not do justice to the student's paper, for it was full of subtlety and persuasion. When the class assailed him, the author asked them to tell him why after all the jar was placed on a hill in Tennessee, of all states? And was not the TVA the most significant unnatural establishment there?

Continued discussion brought out some conclusions about symbolism and its uses: One must begin and stay with the immediate sensuous texture of a poem, seeing what ideas or attitudes inhere in the plain language-and-situation of the poem and resisting that impulse to search for a "hidden"—which is what the tyro usually understands by a "symbolic"—meaning. "Anecdote of the Jar" must first be read as a poem about a jar placed on a wild hill in Tennessee. That is what the poem says. Examining how the poem says it, we find riches of suggestion in the words that characterize the situation. The wilderness is slovenly; it sprawls; but around the jar it takes shape and is no longer wild. Since the wilderness itself is just as wild as it was, however, the phrase "no longer wild" must refer to the new composition of the scene, with the round jar in the center. The words that qualify the jar and its effects, however, do far more than acknowledge its function of bringing order (or composition); they render an ambiguous attitude of reserved mockery, amusement, and scorn. The jar, "gray and bare" and "of a port in air," is not beautiful or impressive in itself; it has the color and texture of Norris Dam, but not its dignity; "of a port" is not magnificent or beautiful. It is plump and smug; it is insensitive to the magnitude and vigor of the wilderness over which it takes its curious dominion. Yet there is delight in the definition of these ambiguities, for they are sharply drawn.

Having got thus far by scrutinizing what the poem literally says and suggests, the class raised again the question of symbols and symbolism. It was agreed in general that any so-called symbolic interpretation would have to grow directly out of the tones and connotations found in the close literal reading of the poem— a conclusion arrived at negatively, after considerable discussion during which various fantastic readings were rejected. This negative conclusion is an enormous gain, for it assumes a continuum of meaning from the literal to the "symbolic." It carries with it the assumption that symbolic meanings, at their end of the continuum, will yield to the same close reading that is first applied to the literal statement. (Where the concrete particular and the abstract universal are not continuous, we have allegory—of which more later.)

Assuming the continuum, then, the class offered two propositions: (1) the jar is a symbol of Order; (2) the jar is a symbol of the quality and effects of the machine age.* Now which is the more general or universal idea, and which is more tenable for this poem? At first glance it would appear that the jar-as-machine-age is less general than the jar-as-Order and that the former depends on the latter. But no; testing the universal by close examination of the concrete particulars of the literal words, we discovered that the idea of Order is here included and subordinated to the specific idea of the machine age which the jar seems most definitely to symbolize. It is not abstract Order here but the particular kind of order brought by the machine. Universal Order is majestic. Linked to the gray, bare, and portly (mason?) jar, it becomes ludicrous and also formidable. Order under its auspices is a version of divine Reason, if you like, but its glory is yoked to the gray and pompous intentions of commerce. It therefore appears here in a grotesque, evil, and frustrating guise. By this time we find that we are talking about literal meanings, tones and attitudes, and symbolic meanings all at the same time, that no one of these elements can be isolated from the others or understood without considering them. If the reading has been tested and accepted, the continuum has been established and a fundamental method for getting at symbolism has been achieved.

(from C. C. Walcutt, "Interpreting the Symbol," College English)

* This interpretation is, of course, highly debatable. Stevens' favorite theme is the order imposed by art or the aesthetic imagination. If the words characterizing the jar make it seem beautiful, it would properly be seen as a symbol of art or the imagination; if it is a symmetrical but colorless jar, it might be a symbol of Order; if it is symmetrical but ugly, it may be a symbol of the machine or of the unlovely aspects of man-made order. Much depends on one's reading of the puzzling phrase "of a port."

Appendix II

(Poems are listed chronologically by title or short title within individual categories. They may appear in more than one category.)

I. Genres

A. *Ballad*

See "Contents" under BALLADS

Keats, *La Belle Dame* (literary ballad)

For modifications of this genre:

Coleridge, *Ancient Mariner* (literary ballad, longer, with formal modifications)

Auden, *One Evening* (ballad stanza, but meditative rather than narrative)

B. *Dramatic Monologue*

Tennyson, *Ulysses*
         Tithonus

Browning, *Soliloquy*
         My Last Duchess
         The Bishop Orders His Tomb
         Toccata of Galuppi's
         A Grammarian's Funeral
         Andrea del Sarto
         Porphyria's Lover

Eliot, *Prufrock*

The following poems exhibit certain qualities of the dramatic monologue:

Donne, *The Flea*

Housman, *The Carpenter's Son*

Eliot, *Journey of the Magi*

Lowell, *After the Surprising Conversions*

C. *Elegy*

Anon., *The Wanderer*

Jonson, *On My First Son*
       Epitaph on Salomon Pavy

Milton, *Lycidas* (pastoral elegy)

Gray, *Elegy*

Whitman, *When Lilacs Last*

Arnold, *Thyrsis* (pastoral elegy)

For modern variants of this form:

Ransom, *Bells for John Whiteside's Daughter*

Roethke, *Elegy for Jane*
Thomas, *A Refusal to Mourn*

D. *Narrative*

See "Contents" under BALLADS
Chaucer, *The Friar's Tale*
Pope, *Rape of the Lock*
Coleridge, *Ancient Mariner*
Keats, *La Belle Dame*
     St. Agnes's Eve
Tennyson, *Morte d'Arthur*
Robinson, *Reuben Bright*
     Richard Cory
     Mr. Flood's Party

E. *Ode*

Marvell, *Horatian Ode*
Gray, *Ode on the Death of a Favorite Cat*
Collins, *Ode to Evening*
Wordsworth, *Intimations of Immortality*
Coleridge, *Dejection*
Shelley, *To the West Wind*
Keats, *To a Nightingale*
     On a Grecian Urn

F. *Satire*

1. On Human Nature:
   Donne, *Go and catch*
        The Indifferent
   Pope, *Rape of the Lock*
   Hardy, *"Ah, are you digging?"*
   Eliot, *Sweeney*
   Cummings, *pity this busy monster*
2. On Society and the Establishment:
   Pope, *Rape of the Lock*
   Housman, *1887*
   Stafford, *The Star in the Hills*
   MacNeice, *Bagpipe Music*
   Ferlinghetti, *Christ Climbed Down*
3. On Poets:
   Dryden, *Mac Flecknoe*
   Stevens, *Bantams in Pine-Woods*

G. *Sonnet*

See "Contents" under Spenser, Sidney, Drayton, Shakespeare, Donne, Milton, Wordsworth, Keats
Wyatt, *I find no peace* (translation from Petrarch)
     My galley chargèd (translation from Petrarch)

Shelley, *Ozymandias*
      England in 1819
Hopkins, *God's Grandeur*
Yeats, *Leda and the Swan*
Robinson, *Reuben Bright*
Frost, *Design*
Pound, *Virginal*
Tate, *The Subway*
Cullen, *Yet Do I Marvel*
Eberhart, *Am I My Neighbor's Keeper?*
Snodgrass, *An Archaic Torso of Apollo*
  For variations on the sonnet form:
    Meredith, *Modern Love* (a series of sixteen-line sonnets)
        Lucifer in Starlight
    Hopkins, *The Windhover*
        Pied Beauty (a "curtal" sonnet: octave and sestet each proportion-
        ately smaller)
        Spelt from Sibyl's Leaves ("the longest sonnet ever written"—
        G. M. H.)

II. Subjects

A. *Art and Poetry*

  1. The Nature or Quality of Poetry:
    Sidney, *Sonnet 1*
    Herbert, *Jordon I*
    Dryden, *Mac Flecknoe*
    Keats, *On First Looking*
    Stevens, *Bantams in Pine-Woods*
    Moore, *Poetry*
    MacLeish, *Ars Poetica*
    Olson, *ABCs*
  2. Art and Immortality:
    Shakespeare, *Shall I compare thee*
    Gray, *Elegy*
    Landor, *Past Ruined Ilion*
    Keats, *On a Grecian Urn*
    Browning, *The Bishop Orders His Tomb*
    Yeats, *Easter 1916*
        Sailing to Byzantium
  3. Pictures
    Williams, *The Dance*
    Lawrence, *Corot*
    Lewis, *Florence: Works of Art*
    Auden, *Musée des Beaux Arts*
    Berryman, *Winter Landscape*
    Snodgrass, *Manet: The Execution of the Emperor Maximilian*

B. Brotherhood

Chaucer, *The Friar's Tale*
Blake, *Poison Tree*
Browning, *Soliloquy*
Arnold, *To Marguerite*
Frost, *Mending Wall*
Moore, *In Distrust of Merits*
Cummings, *a man who had fallen*
Eberhart, *Am I My Neighbor's Keeper?*
Spender, *The Funeral*
Hayden, *Middle Passage*
Lowell, *Children of Light*
        For the Union Dead

C. *Childhood and Youth*

Vaughan, *The Retreat*
Blake, *Introduction to "Songs"*
        The Lamb
Wordsworth, *It is a beauteous evening*
                Intimations of Immortality
Hopkins, *Spring and Fall*
Yeats, *Among School Children*
Lawrence, *Piano*
Ransom, *Bells for John Whiteside's Daughter*
Cummings, *in Just-*
Kunitz, *Father and Son*
Jarrell, *The Elementary Scene*
Thomas, *Fern Hill*
Snodgrass, *April Inventory*
Plath, *Daddy*

D. *Confrontation of Two Orders: Political, Religious, Social*

Milton, *On the Late Massacre*
        Lycidas
Marvell, *Horatian Ode*
Blake, *And did those feet*
        Mock On
Byron, *The Destruction of Sennacherib*
Tennyson, *Morte d'Arthur*
Swinburne, *Hymn to Proserpine*
Meredith, *Lucifer in Starlight*
Yeats, *The Second Coming*
Eliot, *Journey of the Magi*
Stevens, *Sunday Morning*
Spender, *Not palaces*
        The Funeral
Ferlinghetti, *Christ Climbed Down*

E. *Death*

  1. In the Abstract
    Stevens, *Sunday Morning*
    Jeffers, *Hurt Hawks*
    Ransom, *Piazza Piece*

  2. Contemplation of One's Own Death:
    Raleigh, *The Passionate Man's Pilgrimage*
    Donne, *Valediction: of Weeping*
        Death be not proud
    Keats, *When I have fears*
    Tennyson, *Crossing the Bar*
    Dickinson, *I heard a Fly buzz*
        Because I could not stop
    Swinburne, *The Garden of Proserpine*
    Hardy, *Afterwards*
    Frost, *After Apple-Picking*
    Jones, *Preface to a Twenty Volume Suicide Note*

  3. Contemplation of Another's Death:
    See "Elegy" under GENRES, above
    Shakespeare, *Song from "Cymbeline"*
    Pope, *On Two Lovers*
    Wordsworth, *She dwelt among the untrodden ways*
        A slumber
    Landor, *Rose Aylmer*
    Tennyson, *Break, Break, Break*
        Morte d'Arthur
    Housman, *Epitaph on an Army of Mercenaries*
    Robinson, *Reuben Bright*
        Richard Cory
        For a Dead Lady
    Stevens, *The Emperor of Ice-Cream*
    Tate, *Ode to the Confederate Dead*
    Auden, *Musée des Beaux Arts*
    Roethke, *Elegy for Jane*
    Shapiro, *Auto Wreck*
    Thomas, *Do Not Go Gentle*
    Dickey, *Buckdancer's Choice*
    Merwin, *The Asians Dying*

F. *Devotion to Duty*

  Anon., *Sir Patrick Spens*
    Three Ravens
  Herbert, *The Collar*
  Milton, *When I consider*
  Marvell, *Horatian Ode*
  Tennyson, *The Lotos-Eaters* (dereliction of duty)
    Morte d'Arthur
  Frost, *Stopping by Woods*

G. *Love*

    1. Request for Love:
       See "Carpe Diem" under TIME, below
       Anon., *Western Wind*
       Wyatt, *Forget not yet*
       Sidney, *Because I breathe not love*
       Marlowe, *The Passionate Shepherd to His Love*
       Raleigh, *The Nymph's Reply*
       Donne, *The Flea*
       Burns, *Mary Morison*
       Shelley, *The Indian Serenade*
       Tennyson, *Now sleeps the crimson petal*
       Jarrell, *The Woman at the Washington Zoo*
    2. Character or Quality of Love:
       Wyatt, *I find no peace*
            My galley chargèd
       Spenser, *Like as a ship*
       Sidney, *With how sad steps, O Moon*
       Shakespeare, *Sonnet 116*
       Donne, *The Sun Rising*
            The Good-Morrow
            Valediction: Forbidding Mourning
            The Canonization
            The Ecstasy
            The Relic
            The Indifferent
       Waller, *On a Girdle*
       Lovelace, *To Lucasta*
       Burns, *A Red, Red Rose*
       Keats, *On a Grecian Urn*
            La Belle Dame
       Browning, *Meeting at Night*
            Parting at Morning
            Love among the Ruins
       Meredith, *Modern Love*
       Hardy, *In Time of "The Breaking of Nations"*
       Auden, *Lullaby*
       Hayden, *Those Winter Sundays*
    3. Rejected or Lost Love:
       Wyatt, *They flee from me*
            My lute, awake
       Drayton, *Since there's no help*
       Campion, *When thou must home*
       Habington, *To Roses in the Bosom*
       Hardy, *Neutral Tones*
       Pound, *Virginal*
       Eliot, *Prufrock*
       Ransom, *Winter Remembered*

4. Description of Women:
   Spenser, *Epithalamion*
   Shakespeare, *My mistress' eyes*
   Campion, *There is a garden*
   Herrick, *Delight in Disorder*
   Pound, *Virginal*
           Portrait d'une Femme

H. *Man and God*

1. Celebration of the Divine:
   Anon., *I sing of a Maiden*
           The Cherry-Tree Carol
   Campion, *Come, let us sound*
   Herbert, *The Flower*
   Blake, *The Tiger*
   Emerson, *Brahma*
   Hopkins, *The Windhover* (possibly)
           Pied Beauty
           God's Grandeur
   Shapiro, *Christmas Eve: Australia*
   Thomas, *This Bread I Break*

2. Body and Soul:
   Anon., *Ubi Sunt Qui Ante Nos Fuerunt*
   Sidney, *Leave me, O love*
   Shakespeare, *Poor soul*
   Donne, *Death, be not proud*
   Herbert, *Virtue*
   Marvell, *Drop of Dew*
           The Garden
   Vaughan, *The Retreat*
   Browning, *Toccata of Galuppi's*
   Cullen, *Heritage*
   Roethke, *In a Dark Time*
   Wilbur, *Love Calls Us*

3. Man's Sinfulness:
   Shakespeare, *Poor soul*
   Donne, *At the round earth's*
           If poisonous minerals
           Batter my heart
           Hymn to God the Father
   Herbert, *The Collar*
   Vaughan, *The World*
   Blake, *London*
           Poison Tree
   Hopkins, *Spring and Fall*
   Moore, *In Distrust of Merits*
   Jarrell, *Eighth Air Force*

Lowell, *The Holy Innocents*
        Children of Light
        After the Surprising Conversions

I. *Nature*

    1. Seasons:
    Anon., *Sumer is icumen in*
    Shakespeare, *Song from "Love's Labor's Lost"*
    Shelley, *To the West Wind*
    Keats, *To Autumn*
    Arnold, *The Scholar Gypsy*
            Thyrsis
    Hardy, *The Darkling Thrush*
    Housman, *Loveliest of Trees*
    Frost, *Stopping by Woods*
    Williams, *Arrival*
    Ransom, *Winter Remembered*
    Kunitz, *End of Summer*
    Wilbur, *Year's End*
    2. Nature and the Mystery of Existence:
    Marvell, *The Garden*
    Vaughan, *The Waterfall*
    Collins, *Ode to Evening*
    Blake, *The Lamb*
           The Tiger
    Wordsworth, *Tintern Abbey*
                Intimations of Immortality
    Dickinson, *A narrow Fellow*
               Further in Summer
    Hardy, *The Darkling Thrush*
           The Convergence of the Twain
    Frost, *Design*
    Eberhart, *New Hampshire*
    Roethke, *Weed Puller*
    Thomas, *The Force That through the Green Fuse*
    Dickey, *In the Mountain Tent*
    3. Man's Injury to Nature:
    Burns, *To a Mouse*
    Coleridge, *Ancient Mariner*
    Lawrence, *Snake*
    Birney, *The Bear*
    Auden, *Hammerfest*
    Stafford, *Written on the Stub*
              Traveling through the Dark
    Merwin, *Fly*

J. *Parody*
    Lewis, *Florence: Works of Art*

K. *The Platonic "Idea": the Ideal Pattern as Reality*

   Spenser, *Leave, lady, in your glass*
          Men call you fair
   Shakespeare, *From you have I been absent*
   Shelley, *Hymn to Intellectual Beauty*
   Yeats, *The Rose of the World*
   Eberhart, *Am I My Neighbor's Keeper?*
   Stevens, *The Emperor of Ice-Cream* (anti-Platonic)

L. *Questioning*

  1. Cosmic:
    Blake, *The Tiger*
    Hardy, *Hap*
        The Darkling Thrush
        New Year's Eve
    Frost, *Design*
    Cullen, *Yet Do I Marvel*
  2. Personal:
    Donne, *Hymn to God the Father*
    Herbert, *The Collar*
    Milton, *When I Consider*
    Eliot, *Prufrock*
  3. Human Darkness:
    Shelley, *Stanzas Written in Dejection*
    Coleridge, *Dejection*
    Frost, *Desert Places*
    Roethke, *In a Dark Time*
    Lowell, *Skunk Hour*
    Plath, *Blue Moles*
       Elm

M. *Time*

  1. Destruction by Time:
    Shakespeare, *When I have seen*
    Shelley, *Ozymandias*
    MacLeish, *You, Andrew Marvell*
    Thomas, *The Force That through the Green Fuse*
  2. Aging:
    Shakespeare, *That time of year*
    Tennyson, *Ulysses*
        Tithonus
    Browning, *Toccata of Galuppi's*
    Arnold, *Thyrsis*
    Hopkins, *Spring and Fall*
    Housman, *Loveliest of Trees*
    Yeats, *Sailing to Byzantium*
        Among School Children
        After Long Silence

Thomas, *Fern Hill*
Shodgrass, *April Inventory*
3. Carpe Diem:
Campion, *My sweetest Lesbia*
Jonson, *Song: To Celia*
Herrick, *Corrina's Going A-Maying*
          To the Virgins
Waller, *Go, lovely rose*
Marvell, *To His Coy Mistress*
Emerson, *Days* (not concerned with love)
MacNeice, *The Sunlight on the Garden*
4. Ubi Sunt:
Anon., *The Wanderer*
          Ubi Sunt Qui Ante Nos Fuerunt
Tennyson, *Tears, Idle Tears*
Browning, *Toccata of Galuppi's*
Arnold, *Thyrsis*

N. *War*

Milton, *On the Late Massacre*
Lovelace, *To Lucasta*
Marvell, *Horatian Ode*
Byron, *Destruction of Sennacherib*
Hardy, *Channel Firing*
Housman, *Epitaph on an Army of Mercenaries*
Moore, *In Distrust of Merits*
Owen, *Anthem for Doomed Youth*
          Dulce et Decorum Est
          Strange Meeting
Cummings, *I sing of Olaf*
Tate, *Ode to the Confederate Dead*
MacNeice, *The Sunlight on the Garden*
          Cushenden
Shapiro, *Christmas Eve*
Jarrell, *Death of the Ball Turret Gunner*
          Eighth Air Force
Lowell, *Children of Light*
          For the Union Dead
Levertov, *What Were They Like*
          Two Variations
Bly, *Counting Small-Boned Bodies*
     Driving through Minnesota during the Hanoi Bombings
Merwin, *The Asians Dying*

Glossary of Critical Terms

abstract terms: words that refer to ideas or concepts rather than to material objects. See **concrete terms.**

accent: the relative emphasis accorded a syllable by the metrical pattern of a poem; sometimes used synonymously with stress. See **meter** and **stress.**

Alexandrine: a line of iambic hexameter occurring regularly or sporadically in otherwise iambic pentameter verse. See **Spenserian stanza.**

allegory: an extension of metaphor into a narrative in which the details of events and persons have deeper meanings, representing for example psychological, political, or ethical ideas. See **personification.**

alliteration: the repeated use of a consonant, especially at the beginning of stressed words or syllables. Alliteration was the organizing principle of the Old English poetic line (see "The Wanderer"). See also **consonance** and **assonance.**

ambiguity: multiple meaning that, when deliberately used, may enhance the richness of a poetic line or phrase.

anapest: metrical foot in which two unstressed syllables precede one stressed syllable. Usually indicated ⌣ ⌣ —.

apostrophe: calling upon a person, place, or thing by name, often preceded by "O!"

assonance: repetition of identical vowel sounds.

ballad: a short narrative poem, often designed to be sung. It generally contains ellipses, producing a dramatic effect by focusing upon key events and the emotional reactions they trigger; usually in ballad stanza form. See also **folk ballad.**

ballad stanza: traditionally, a four-line stanza consisting of alternating four-stress and three-stress lines (most often iambic tetrameter and iambic trimeter), rhyming *abcb* or *abab.*

bathos: a sudden shift from an elevated subject matter or tone to a trivial one. Often used to good effect in satire.

blank verse: unrhymed iambic pentameter, in verse paragraphs rather than stanzas.

cacophony: harsh or ugly sounds. See **euphony.**

caesura: a major pause within a line of verse, created by sense. It may fall within a metrical foot.

canto: a major division of a long poem.

chiasmus: a crossing; an arrangement of words and/or phrases in such a way that parallel items form a cross, an AB-BA pattern, e.g.,

A   B

"A cry of Absence, Absence, IN THE HEART,

B   A

And IN THE WOOD *the furious winter blowing."*

John Crowe Ransom, "Winter Remembered"

closed couplet: couplet in which the second line is followed by a full pause or period and the sense is completed.

conceit: an ingeniously elaborated simile or metaphor; a hallmark of seventeenth-century metaphysical poetry.

concrete terms: words that refer to material objects rather than to ideas or concepts. See **abstract terms.**

connotation: the nuances of meaning in a word or image, as distinguished from denotation.

consonance: repetition of consonant sounds, but not exclusively those of initial syllables. See **alliteration** and **assonance.**

context: designates a total situation when one is speaking of a particular element in it; e.g., the context of a word might be a line or a stanza; the context of an image might be the whole dramatic situation.

conventions: forms or techniques appropriate to certain genres of poetry (e.g., pastoral or elegy) and accepted as customary in them. Also used to suggest general practices in verse, such as rhyme, meter, etc.

couplet: two successive rhyming lines of verse of the same meter. See **closed couplet; heroic couplet.**

dactyl: metrical foot in which a stressed syllable precedes two unstressed syllables. Usually indicated – ◡ ◡.

decasyllabic: a line of poetry containing ten syllables.

denotation: the meaning of a word, without overtones. See **connotation.**

diction: the choice of words, resulting in a certain level of language or tone.

didactic: intended to be instructive. Certain poems, especially satires, tend to be didactic.

dimeter: a poetic line consisting of two feet. See **foot, meter.**

dramatic: (in poetry) indicative by implication of action or movement.

dramatic irony: a species of irony in which something is said or done by a character who is unaware of the full significance that the audience recognizes. See **irony**

dramatic monologue: a poem that is given over entirely to the speech of a single person, who, in addressing an unspeaking audience, reveals thereby his character and indicates the dramatic situation or movements in which he is involved.

elegy: a subjective poem, usually meditating the death of a specific person or a group.

ellipsis: the deliberate omission of parts of the syntax of a sentence or of coherence links in a narrative.

end-stopped line: a line in which the sense concludes with the end and a pause follows. See **enjamb(e)ment.**

English sonnet: poem of fourteen iambic pentameter lines divided into three quatrains and a couplet, usually rhyming *abab cdcd efef gg.* See **sonnet.**

enjamb(e)ment: protraction of sense beyond the end of a line of poetry so that words closely related by syntax are separated by the line ending. See **end-stopped line.**

epic: long narrative poem in elevated style, dealing usually with the lofty deeds of heroes and their peoples.

epic simile: see **Homeric simile.**

epigram: a succinct expression or poem, usually witty and sharp.

epitaph: lines, usually brief, supposedly composed for a tombstone.

epithet: an adjective, often repeated, that characterizes instead of merely describing the noun it modifies.

euphony: harmonious or pleasant sounds. See **cacophony.**

eye rhyme: a pair of words in rhyming position whose endings are similarly spelled but whose sounds are different, e.g., *blow/cow.* See **rhyme.**

feminine ending: an extra unaccented syllable at the end of a line.

feminine rhyme: rhyme in which two similar-sounding accented syllables are followed by two similar-sounding unaccented syllables, e.g., *turning/ spurning.* See **rhyme.**

figures of speech: various non-literal, imaginative uses of language. See **hyperbole, metaphor, metonymy, personification, simile, synecdoche.**

folk ballad: a ballad that has an oral origin and has been orally transmitted.

foot: the basic metrical unit, consisting usually of one relatively stressed and one or two relatively unstressed syllables. See **meter, scan; anapest, dactyl, iamb, pyrrhus, spondee, trochee.**

form: the overall, external shape of a poem; e.g., **sonnet** form, **quatrain, terza rima.** But the term is frequently used as synonymous with **structure.**

formal: refers to the parts of a poem which are non-semantic (do not by themselves directly express meaning).

free verse: verse informed by no regular length of line, no regular rhyme scheme, and no metrical pattern. See **verse.**

genre: a literary type, generally assuming a certain form according to convention, e.g., Horatian ode, pastoral elegy.

half rhyme: imperfect rhyme in which the vowel sounds do not match each other, e.g., *mice/mace*. See slant rhyme.

heroic couplet: a closed couplet in iambic pentameter.

hexameter: a line consisting of six metrical feet. See foot, meter.

Homeric simile: a simile that extends the description of the analogy beyond the relevant point of likeness. See simile.

Horatian ode: an ode as originated by the Roman poet Horace, in regular stanzas and generally light in tone. See ode.

hyperbole: overstatement or exaggeration.

iamb: metrical foot in which a single unstressed syllable precedes a single stressed syllable. Usually indicated ˘ ¯. The most common metrical foot in English poetry.

image: an expression in words of a sense experience, most often visual, but not necessarily so confined. The term is often more narrowly used to designate figures of speech.

imagery: a collective term to designate images.

incremental repetition: repetition of words or phrases with slight changes; this advances the action of the poem at the same time that it intensifies the emotion; it is particularly evident in the ballad.

internal rhyme: rhyme in which the matching sounds are in the same line; e.g., "We were the first that ever burst. . . ." See rhyme.

invocation: an appeal (to the Muse or God) for assistance with the work, at the beginning of a long poem.

irony: a discrepancy between the immediate, apparent meaning of a word, phrase, or situation and its underlying meaning. It involves a double point of view. See dramatic irony.

irregular ode: see Pindaric ode.

Italian sonnet: a poem of fourteen iambic pentameter lines divided into an octave (first eight lines) and a sestet (last six lines), the octave always rhyming *abba, abba;* the sestet using three (sometimes two) new rhymes in any combination except that which yields a concluding couplet. See sonnet.

kenning: a descriptive substitution of one of its aspects for the noun itself. Found especially in Old English verse; e.g., "whale-road" meaning "sea." It is a form of metaphor or synecdoche.

literary ballad: an artistic imitation of the folk ballad; e.g., Keats's "La Belle Dame Sans Merci."

litotes: a form of understatement.

lyric: a subjective poem, originally designed to be sung. Now generally a short poem expressing personal thought and emotion. Usually opposed to narrative and dramatic poems, though these may contain lyrical passages.

masculine rhyme: rhyme in which the identical sounds are in the last syllables of the rhyming words; e.g., *abound/aground*. See rhyme.

melodramatic: (in poetry) indicative of actions and feelings neither properly motivated nor satisfactorily explained.

metaphor: figure of speech which implies an identity between two normally unrelated things.

metaphysical: a term for certain poets of the seventeenth century (especially Donne) who used philosophical and scientific terms in their imagery. Their poetry is also characterized by use of conceits and wit.

meter: the regular disposition of accented and unaccented syllables in a line of verse. The basic metrical unit is called a foot. See monometer, dimeter, trimeter, tetrameter, pentameter, hexameter; scan.

metonymy: figure of speech in which one thing is designated by the name of something associated with it; e.g., you are now reading *Greenfield and Weatherhead*, i.e., their book. See synecdoche.

Miltonic sonnet: a variety of the Italian sonnet that does not always observe the break in thought between the octave and the sestet. Used principally but not exclusively by John Milton.

mock-epic (mock-heroic): in poetry, a work that uses the conventional apparatus of the epic poem, with its grandeur of style, to deal with a trivial subject. See epic.

monometer: a line consisting of one metrical foot. See foot, meter.

moral: human, in respect to man's relation to man, himself, and the universe, rather than his anatomical and physiological properties.

motif: sometimes used to indicate a pattern of images, as for instance the "clothing motif in *King Lear*," but frequently used synonymously with theme.

myth: an ancient, fabulous story dealing with the exploits of gods or heroes; originating as from a communal mind, which produced stories of remarkable similarity from Greece, Rome, Ireland, and Scandinavia, for example. The term is also used nowadays for an extensive imaginary world, created by a particular author throughout his works, by which poetic truth is embodied in fictitious characters and events.

narrative: poetry that tells a story.

octave: an eight-line stanza; usually refers to the first part of an Italian sonnet.

ode: a lyric invocation or celebration, generally of elevated subject matter and style. May be in regular stanza form (see **Horatian ode**) or irregular or complex (see **irregular ode** and **Pindaric ode**).

onomatopoeia: words or groups of words in which the sounds imitate the sense; e.g., *swish; murmur of innumerable bees.*

ottava-rima: an eight-line stanza in iambic pentameter, rhyming *abababcc.*

overtones: nuances that arise from the interplay of various poetic elements.

oxymoron: a yoking-together of terms that are literally contradictory; e.g., *living death.*

paradox: a statement that is apparently contradictory, but at a deeper level is in fact not so. For examples, see Donne's "Holy Sonnet 14."

parallelism: achieved by placing in equivalent positions words of the same part of speech and phrases, clauses, and sentences of the same syntax.

parody: imitation of a style, usually mocking it.

pastoral poetry: a genre in which the poem makes its statement in the guise of rural life, involving shepherds and their activities; a notable example is the pastoral elegy, such as "Lycidas." Sometimes used to make political or religious satire.

pathetic fallacy: the practice of bestowing human characteristics upon natural objects; e.g., *the cruel sea.*

pentameter: a line consisting of five metrical feet. See **foot, meter.**

persona: the fictitious speaker or "I," who is to be distinguished from the poet himself.

personification: a form of metaphor in which human status is given to abstractions; e.g., *Fortune turns her wheel.*

Petrarchan sonnet: see **Italian sonnet.**

Pindaric ode: an ode, imitating the Greek poet Pindar, but less precise, in which the stanzas are of irregular form, but more regular than in the **irregular ode.** See **ode.**

poetic diction: a choice of words particularly appropriate to poetry. Sometimes more specifically refers to the conventional artificial language (e.g. "finny prey" for fish) of such poems as "The Rape of the Lock." The term is often used in a pejorative sense by modern poets and critics.

poetic truth: fidelity to a moral, philosophical and/or aesthetic order of things as opposed to the fidelity to fact of scientific truth.

prosody: the theory of versification.

pyrrhus: metrical foot consisting of two unstressed syllables only. Usually indicated ⌣ ⌣.

qualitative verse: verse in which the meter depends upon the stress of syllables, rather than their length. Almost all English poetry is thus composed.

quantitative verse: verse in which the meter depends upon the length of syllables rather than their stresses; in contrast with **qualitative verse.** Classical poetry was thus structured.

quatrain: stanza consisting of four lines with various patterns of rhyme.

refrain: words, sounds, or phrases regularly repeated throughout a poem.

rhyme: an identity between final vowel sounds without following consonants (e.g., *flea/agree*) or between final vowel and following consonant sounds in stressed syllables (e.g., *demand/band*). Usually the matching syllables are at the ends of lines, but see **internal rhyme.** See also the following kinds of rhyme: **eye, feminine, half, masculine, slant.**

rhyme royal: a stanza consisting of seven lines of iambic pentameter, rhyming *ababbcc,* named for King James I of Scotland, who wrote poems in this form.

rhythm: sequence of stressed and unstressed syllables in a passage as determined by the inter-relationship of sense and syntax.

run-on line: see **enjamb(e)ment.**

satire: a work that ridicules or rebukes human vice or folly.

scan: to indicate the accented and unaccented syllables and the metrical feet in a line of a poem. The act of so doing is called scansion.

sentimentality: the evocation of more emotion than the situation in the poem warrants.

sestet: six line stanza; usually refers to the second part of an **Italian sonnet.**

Shakespearian sonnet: see **English sonnet.**

simile: figure of speech which explicitly states a similarity between two normally unrelated things by means of the words *like, as,* and sometimes *than.*

slant rhyme: imperfect rhyme in which the vowel sounds are slightly different; e.g., *lives/leaves.* See **half rhyme.**

sonnet: a poem consisting of fourteen lines of iambic pentameter, with various rhyme schemes. See **English, Italian,** and **Miltonic sonnet.**

Spenserian stanza: stanza of nine lines, rhyming *ababbcbcc;* the first eight lines are in iambic pentameter, the ninth is an **Alexandrine.** The stanza was created by Edmund Spenser for *The Faerie Queene.*

spondee: metrical foot consisting of two stressed syllables only. Usually indicated — —.

sprung rhythm: a kind of meter invented by Gerard Manley Hopkins of which each foot contains one accented syllable at the beginning and a varying number of unaccented ones. It is similar in some respects to Old English alliterative verse.

stanza: a separate group of lines of which the pattern is repeated throughout the poem. The term is sometimes used loosely to designate any one section of a divided poem.

stress: the relative emphasis accorded a syllable by the sense of the passage; sometimes used synonymously with accent. See **accent** and **rhythm**.

structure: systems of internal relationships of parts in a poem. One may speak of a rhythmic structure, sound structure; thematic, imagistic structures, etc. A poem's structure is unique, whereas many poems may have a common **form**.

style: in discussions about poetic style the term generally refers to the total effect produced by the combination of all the elements of the poem—diction, rhythm, syntax, and even subject matter, whether used for an individual poem, a writer's collected works, or the typical literary output of an age.

symbol: something perceptible that stands for an abstract idea to which it is related (a) conventionally, as a flag is symbolic of a country; (b) naturally, as darkness may be symbolic of death; or (c) privately, as Yeats's *gyre* in "The Second Coming" is symbolic of the movement of history.

synecdoche: figure of speech in which one thing is designated by the name of one part of it; or a part designated by the name of the whole; e.g., *a sail* for a ship; or in "the United States won the Davis Cup," where *United States* designates only the tennis team. See **metonymy**.

synesthesia: the description of one kind of sensory impression in terms of another; e.g., *the red blare of a trumpet.*

syntax: the disposition of words in a sentence that reveals their grammatical relationship.

tension: an effect of richness set up by the countering pulls of abstract and concrete, of denotation and connotation, of form and substance, of rhythm and meter, or of other opposed elements in a poem.

tercet: stanza of three lines, usually iambic and usually employing a single rhyme sound. It is used in Browning's "A Toccata of Galuppi's."

terza rima: an Italian verse form, originally, made up of *tercets* that contain interlocking rhyme: *aba bcb cdc,* etc., Shelley's "Ode to the West Wind" is the most notable English example.

tetrameter: a line consisting of four metrical feet. See **foot, meter**.

theme: the major idea, or one of a number of ideas, conveyed by a work. See **motif**.

tone: the attitude of the poet or of the **persona** toward the subject of the poem and/or toward the reader.

trimeter: a line consisting of three metrical feet. See **foot, meter**.

trochee: metrical foot in which a single stressed syllable precedes a single unstressed syllable. Usually indicated — ᴗ .

understatement: a device by which the full emotional significance of a situation is played down.

verse: a species of writing with significant line lengths. Usually involves regular line length and patterns of sound and rhythm, but see **free verse.**

wit: intellectual acuteness, but with varying specific meanings over the centuries. In modern usage, it may be synonymous with humor, but need not be.

Index of Authors, First Lines, and Titles